ALEXANDER ZHOLKOVSKY

T E X T
counter
T E X T

REREADINGS IN
RUSSIAN LITERARY
HISTORY

STANFORD UNIVERSITY PRESS • Stanford, California • 1994

Stanford University Press
Stanford, California
© 1994 by the Board of Trustees of the
Leland Stanford Junior University

Printed in the United States of America

CIP data are at the end of the book

Stanford University Press publications are
distributed exclusively by Stanford University Press
within the United States, Canada, and Mexico; they
are distributed exclusively by Cambridge University
Press throughout the rest of the world.

10004 66462

0804723168

Preface

This book is a product of my gradual shift from hard-core generativism to a moderate version of poststructuralism. In evolving my new theoretical position, I have been influenced by a host of cultural, professional, and personal factors—in particular, by an ongoing dialogue with colleagues. I feel especially indebted to Boris Gasparov, M. L. Gasparov, Boris Groys, L. A. Mazel, Igor Mel'chuk, Gary Saul Morson, Daniel Rancour-Laferrière, Michael Riffaterre, Omry Ronen, Yury Shcheglov, A. D. Siniavsky, Igor Smirnov, and Kiril Taranovsky. I have also benefited greatly from the discussion, advice, and help of S. G. Bocharov, A. P. Chudakov, Paul Debreczeny, Caryl Emerson, Susanne Fusso, S. I. Gindin, Marcus Levitt, Irene Masing-Delic, Eric Naiman, Irina Paperno, J. Thomas Shaw, S. N. Zenkin, and many others. Various parts and versions of the manuscript were read by Helena Goscilo, Gordon Newby, Sarah Pratt, and Thomas Seifrid, whose input on all levels of its discourse—intellectual, compositional, stylistic, and editorial—has been invaluable. For painstaking bibliographical assistance I am grateful to Jean Huston and Rebecca Varga; for technical love and care, to Susan Kechekian and Alan Tuttle.

The conception and emergence of the book in its present form are due to the kind initiative and encouragement of Helen Tartar and Gary Saul Morson. My work on the manuscript during the sabbatical year 1990–91 was generously supported by the Department of Slavic Languages and Literatures and the Humanities Division of the College of Letters Arts and Sciences, the University of Southern California (in particular, Dean Marshall Cohen); the American Council of Learned Societies; the National Humanities Center in North Carolina; and the Andrew W. Mellon Foundation. To these institutions I extend my sincere gratitude. I would also like to thank the organizers of those conferences and publications the participation in which first prompted me to develop the ideas now before the reader—among them, Boris Gasparov, Aage Hansen-Loeve and Tilmann Reuther, Robert Hughes, Andrei Kodjak, Lev Loseff, Priscilla Meyer and Susanne Fusso, Sidney Monas, Irina Paperno, Mark Popovsky, Daniel Rancour-Laferrière, M. V. Rozanova and A. D. Siniavsky, Dmitri Segal, and Willem Weststeijn.

I wish I knew how to do justice to the contribution of Olga Matich. Over the entire period of the book's germination and writing, she has acted in virtually all of the above capacities and played the difficult and thankless role of that most intimately close other voice without which authorial intent is left hanging in the void.

A few words may be in order concerning the organization of the text, especially regarding auxiliary information. Quotations longer than a few lines are set off from the text as extracts, in the text typeface but in a smaller size, full measure. A second type of extract treatment is reserved for my own asides, which include "paraphrases" (plot paraphrases, background discussions, or other material for the reader who is unfamiliar with the works being discussed) and "technical arguments" (which some readers may wish to skip entirely). These extracts are indented on the left and set in a typeface different from that of the rest of the text.

Bibliographical information is concentrated in the Works Cited, organized by author's name and publication date; where relevant, the date of the first writing or publication is supplied in brackets. In references to collected works, the date is followed, or where contextually redundant replaced, by volume numbers. Sometimes double references to the Russian and English editions are provided, separated by slashes.

I follow the Library of Congress system for transliteration of Russian words and names (omitting diacriticals), except where a different form has been accepted (as in Dostoevsky rather than Dostoevskii). Double quotes are used for citations, translations, and other quoted speech; single quotes for words as words and theoretical constructs; italics for short quotations from Russian (and other foreign languages) and occasionally for emphasis. In quoting, I resort whenever possible to existing translations (if no English version is referenced, the translations are mine), occasionally emending them and providing Russian originals or literal glosses. But on the whole I use Russian judiciously, especially in the main text. Exceptions had to be made in those chapters (5, 6, 8) where poems form the centerpiece of the analysis; there, Russian transliterations are provided, accompanied by English renderings as close to interlinears as intelligibility would bear.

Parts of the text have appeared previously in some form or other (in Russian or English, in the present or earlier versions). A version of Chapter 1 appeared in Susanne Fusso and Priscilla Meyer, eds., *Essays on Gogol: Logos and the Russian Word* (Northwestern University Press, 1992). Part of Chapter 3 appeared in the *Wiener Slawistischer Almanach* 22 (1989). A portion of Chapter 4 appeared in Russian in Boris Gasparov, Robert P. Hughes, and Irina Paperno, eds., *Cultural Mythologies of Russian Modernism: From the Golden Age to the Silver Age* (© 1992 The Regents of the University of California) and is used here with the permission of the University of California Press. Part of Chapter 5 was published in the *Slavic and East European Journal* 30, no. 3 (1986) and is reprinted with the permission of the American Association of Teachers of Slavic and Eastern European Languages. Part of Chapter 6 appeared in Daniel Rancour-Laferriere, ed., *Russian Literature and Psychoanalysis* (John Benjamins, 1989) and is used here courtesy of the publisher. Part of Chapter 9 was published in the *Slavic Review* 48, no. 1 (1989) and is reproduced with the permission of the *Review*. I am grateful for the permissions to reuse the material.

A. Zh.
1991

Contents

Text counter Text

Я получил блаженное наследство—
Чужих певцов блуждающие сны.
. . . .

И не одно сокровище, быть может,
Минуя внуков, к правнукам уйдет,
И снова скальд чужую песню сложит
И как свою ее произнесет.

I have received a blessed legacy—
The wandering dreams of alien bards.
. . . .

And, perhaps, more than one treasure will,
Bypassing grandsons, go to great grandsons,
And again a skald will compose another's song
And recite it as his own.

Mandelstam, "I Have Not Heard
the Tales of Ossian"

Я советую всем нарочно написать на бумаге Испания,
то и выйдет Китай.

I specifically advise everybody to take a piece of paper
and write "Spain" on it—it will come out "China."

Gogol, "Diary of a Madman"

Introduction: On Close Rereading

I f all reading is not necessarily rereading, criticism
for the most part is. On my first exposure to Harold
Bloom's theory of universal misprision bred by the anxiety of influence, I dismissed it as a bizarre projection of the mindset of faculty
vying for tenure. Such a response was of course overdetermined by a
"natural" privileging of literary art over literary scholarship and symbolic reflection over contextual impact. But I was soon able to read
the Bloomian schema itself as a cross between two influential narra-
tives: Freud's Oedipal myth and the Russian Formalist masterplot of
literary evolution, according to which a "secondary, or junior, branch"
achieves canonization by going over the heads of the "fathers" to the
"uncles" and "grandfathers." [1] I also gradually came to accept an essential kinship, where formalism and structuralism had taught me to
see unbridgeable gaps, between artistic (poetic, prosaic, fictional) and
nonartistic (ordinary, ideological, metapoetic, scientific) modes of discourse. And I learned to live with a relativistic plurality of readings,
first broached by Roland Barthes in a structuralist framework. [2] Incidentally, one corollary of such pluralism is that my later realizations
need not erase the initial deconstruction of sorts that I had performed
on Bloom's theoretical posture.

Be that as it may, Bloom has been successful—certainly under his own territorial definition. What terms does the book now before the reader propose for its fulfillment? Without waxing lyrical (and therefore speaking strictly in the third person), I would identify its tenor as a balancing act—in fact, a combination of several such acts. It is written about Russian literature for the English-speaking reader by somebody sandwiched between (or is it astraddle?) the two cultures. Moreover, inside each, he finds himself caught between opposites that he tries to reconcile. In his native Russian context, the major rift is between independence and engagement—that is, between cherished scholarly "objectivity" and various "right" causes, moral and political, some of which he may consciously or unwittingly espouse. In his American afterlife, he is torn between a structuralist past and the reigning poststructuralism, which he has tried to internalize, adaptation, after all, being the stuff émigrés are made on.[3]

Nor are these personal quandaries extraneous to the literary matters at hand. Roughly speaking, the book is about twentieth-century Russian literature rereading its classical era and pressing the past masters (and on occasion a master's own past, as in the chapter on Pasternak) into the service of more recent needs—avant-gardist, revolutionary, postrevolutionary, dissident, émigré. The twin projects of reaching back over a historical rupture and of adaptive (self-)hybridizing, so characteristic of the literary process, especially the Russian-Soviet one, are also germane to the problems faced by this writer, professionally as well as existentially. They may have given an additional urgency to his interest both in such critically sanctioned topics as intertextuality, rereading, cultural hybrids, collaborationist 'art of adaptation,' and so on, and in such high-and-low cultural phenomena as Gogol's and Zoshchenko's "bad writing" and Limonov's self-centered bodily and verbal acrobatics. Indeed, what the book strives for is a reconciliation, or at least a dynamic equilibrium, of various opposing forces. As a result, it ends up halfway between the conservative and radical poles of today's critical scene.

To begin with the book's title, the contraposition of 'text' to 'text' is a departure from relating 'texts' to purportedly nontextual, because properly dessicated, 'themes,' as practiced in my previous book (*Themes and Texts: Towards a Poetics of Expressiveness*, 1984). Yet the shift is not all that radical. To be sure, the privileged metatextual status of 'themes' has been effectively called into doubt by poststructuralism. Yet 'themes' have retained some of their usefulness: intertextual counterpoints often have to be formulated in thematic terms. In fact, one section in the 1984 book treated the use of a Pushkin subtext by Pasternak as a particular case of the general rhetorical strategy whereby any found material is pressed into the service of the author's (i.e., Pasternak's) themes. Finally, even my double stress on 'text,' while deemphasizing 'themes,' is also meant to reconfirm a rather traditional allegiance to comprehensive textual coverage and a refusal to settle for a mere identification of writers' ideological 'gestures.'

'Rereading' is consciously used in several senses at once. The book's principal thrust is to propose, as part of the ongoing cultural process, new interpretations of familiar texts. This study in rereading tends to take for granted an acquaintance with "*the* readings": the primary texts and their received—"standard"—secondary appreciation. In other words, the essays that follow both claim novelty and assume a degree of specialized knowledge, bringing out in the prefix *re* its challenging aspects. At the same time, 're-reading' (as distinct from the defiant *mis*-reading) is meant in the less startling sense of pleasurably revisiting a familiar text under different circumstances but with basically similar responses, sometimes reconfirmed in new ways. A measure of interpretive conservatism is also implied by the textbook connotations of "readings in" a subject. The rereadings are by no means offered as a new canon, yet they do presume to be detailed case studies in which innovation takes no precedence over thoroughness.

Such deliberate moderation stems in part from the inherent relativity of the very theories that have educated us as to the relativity of canons. A certain indeterminacy also haunts the identities of the 're-reader' and the 'reread,' which are defined in the context of this book by a somewhat untraditional combination of rereading perspectives. In different chapters, the focus may be on the way a writer deals with previous texts, on the way critical or theoretical texts are implicated in such processes and thus themselves become susceptible to reinterpretation, or on the way a writer can be reinterpreted in light of the current cultural climate rather than by comparison with a particular countertext.

All these cases share a common paradigm: the rereading of a text is undertaken from the point of view of another textual agency, which may vary from an actual text to a theoretical position or a generalized sensibility. Lurking behind this elusive textual agency is, of course, the scholar himself, who authors the rereading and should try to state as honestly as possible the perspective that underlies, and thereby problematizes, it.

As an illustration, take Victor Shklovsky's now textbook example of defamiliarization: the theater episode in *War and Peace* where the natural Natasha fails to follow the "wild and puzzling" conventions of the opera (Shklovsky 1965a [1917]). In addition to a remarkable conjunction of theoretical, critical, and prosaic discourses (the episode itself being a meta-interpretational one), Shklovsky's 1917 reading of Tolstoy's and his aristocratic yet folksy heroine's reading of the operatic text itself had an intertextual dimension. It was paralleled by a drastic revision, in the work of such contemporary authors as Mikhail Zoshchenko, of the rules of prose writing. Zoshchenko co-opted and canonized, albeit in an ambiguous manner, the cultural habits of his characters, "natural" to a fault, as instanced by his "lady aristocrat," whose reading of the institution of theater ignored the stage altogether, foregrounding the concession stand instead. This case features an entire rereading paradigm, complete with a classical author and two modern rereaders—a theorist-critic and a prosaist—and offers an opportunity to correlate and historicize all three discourses. By the same token, it calls into question any presumed vantage point, for example, Shklovsky's, as well as my own, suggesting that utmost self-critical caution be exercised in the art of rereading.

The tension between the extremes of reader conservatism and reinterpretive innovation is legitimate, often ideological, and hardly resolvable; rather, it calls for mediation. Literature thrives on rereading, and Russian literary history has been particularly rich in instances of ideological constructions imposed on literary texts, as in Belinsky's reading of Gogol. In time, they are overturned and replaced with new interpretations, as in the rereading of Pushkin by Pisarev or of Gogol by the Symbolists, then reactivated, only to be shelved again, depending on the prevalent discourse of the time and the critics' aesthetic preferences.

The promptings of the current situation are contradictory. Poststructuralist schools favor ideological and power-conscious constructions while advocating pluralist cohabitation of readings. Similarly, I may be engaged in a reinterpretive endeavor that is generationally and politically motivated (very roughly, dismantling the Soviet-era mentality) while at the same time revering the ideal of poetics for poetics' sake. The ensuing analyses try to combine probing with accuracy, ideological interest and perspectivism with structural completeness, integrative thematization with pluralistic reading.

A compromise is also pursued on the issue of 'intertext vs. structure.'

According to intertextualists, no text is an immanent, closed entity; all discourse occurs in dialogue with some other, which precedes it chronologically and/or ontologically.

Thus, the lyrical format of "Monument," so prestigious in Russian poetry until its subversion in Mayakovsky's *At the Top of My Voice*, has a long pedigree. It goes back through Pushkin to Derzhavin, Lomonosov, and by way of several European mediators (Shakespeare, Ronsard, Milton, Klopstock, among others; see Alekseev 1967: 97–99), all the way to Horace's *Carmina* (3: 30). Yet Horace, in turn, saw *his* highest achievement in having been the "first to transpose Aeolian song into Italian tunes," that is, in harking back to still further—Greek—predecessors.

The two principal versions of the anti-intrinsic argument maintain that all Judeo-Greco-Christian texts are (1) only notes in the margins of Plato and the Bible, thus *syntagms* of a vast single Text; (2) related, like Leibnizian monads, by common *paradigms*, thus mere variations on a single archetypal Text.

The syntagmatic (genetic) argument is on the whole more graphic, while the paradigmatic (typological) may seem more plausible on theoretical grounds. They are not irreconcilable.

For instance, Shklovsky (1972 [1919]) argued that affinities among texts from different traditions were due not to "wandering plots," i.e. borrowings, but rather to immanent laws of literary form. He thus supplied the paradigmatic theory, traditionally theme-oriented, with a component responsible for syntactic narrative structures.

Similarly, the typological 'laws' touted by the formalists had an important syntagmatic dimension, premised as they were on the defamiliarization of preceding textualities. Hence the formalists', especially Tynianov's (beginning with 1977a [1921]), consistent interest in the theory of parody and the practical study of literary innovation in historical context.

The Russian/Slavist intertextualist heirs to the formalist tradition[4] have preferred to elaborate on the genetic argument, looking for concrete 'subtexts': quotes, allusions, and so on. In this they differ consistently from Western scholars, who pursue 'intertexts' proper, interactions of generalized entities and forces: topoi, masterplots, and textual strategies. Thus, Michael Riffaterre (1978) conceives of poetic structure as an *expansion* and *conversion* of a given 'hypogram.'[5] The hypogram is envisioned as a stereotype (subtext, gnome, paradigm) that is present in the literary-cultural vocabulary and may or may not be instanced, as far as the analyzed text is concerned, by a specific verbal cliché. Thus, Riffaterre has the new text responding not so much to an actual previous text or writer but to a generalized discourse—to literature's *langue*, not only its *parole*.[6]

One Russian counterpart to this fusion of genetic and typological intertexts can be found in Mikhail Gasparov's studies on the 'semantic haloes' of verse meters. Proceeding from Kiril Taranovsky's pioneering discovery of a specific seme inscribed in a meter's signified by a particular poem, Gasparov redefined Taranovsky's framework.[7] He moved to a systematic analysis of all the texts written in a given meter, all its Russian and foreign sources, and all the stages of its evolution in order to list all the thematic overtones imprinted on the meter. In practical terms, this means that in choosing a meter, the poet enters into a dialogue not only with a concrete predecessor but also with 'the memory of the meter'—the entire paradigm of formal and thematic options that can be now appropriated, expanded, con- or subverted.

The term 'genre memory' was coined in the Russian context by Mikhail Bakhtin,[8] and despite his antiformalist stance, this concept, as well as that of dialogue, transcends the opposition between 'genetic' and 'paradigmatic.' A given genre (or a given dialogical situation) both unfolds in the actual history of literature and can be summed up as a structured set of possibilities. In this respect, the so-called formal entities, such as meters, are no different from more thematic ones, such as the historical novel, the "Monument" lyric, or the 'canine' story (as identified in Ziolkowski 1983).

Another analytical tool that straddles the boundary between syntagmatic and paradigmatic readings, as well as between closed structure and open-ended intertextuality, is the concept of 'thematic invariance.' Invariant motifs are a cross between Vladimir Propp's narrative 'functions,' established as common denominators of a class of similar texts, and the traditional as well as New Criticism's 'recurrent themes,' discovered by close reading as the text's rhetorical backbone.[9] Therefore, the invariants defining an author's poetic world form a *structure* that is both *intertextual* (within the limits of the oeuvre) and to a large extent *thematic*. By setting up a structural-intertextual-thematic correlative of the authorial persona, invariance transcends the programmatic impersonality of formalism's "literature without writers." Resurrected from complete diffusion in the Text, the Author again becomes the subject of biographical and psychoanalytic inquiry—tempered, to be sure, by the hard-won distinction between the real and implied author. Roman Jakobson's 1975 [1937] analysis of the 'statue' motif in Pushkin's poetry and life in light of its mythological underpinnings is an early example of structuralism going thematic, intertextual (indeed intercodal), and archetypal.

The chasm between structuralism and poststructuralist schools seems overrated. When Derrida, de Man, and their followers[10] expose the text's inherent self-subversiveness, they develop the structuralist and in fact New Critical concepts of opposition, mediation, and ambiguity. In unmasking the text's rhetoricity, its desire-driven tautological patterns of persuasion, they build on the concepts of semiotic codes, literary conventions, and expressive techniques devised by structural poetics. Arrogating critical supremacy over literature proper, they actually proceed with the structuralist's agenda of portraying writers' worlds as systems of signification; as part of the deal, they also inherit the experimental scientist's condescending attitude toward his guinea pigs. Even the questioning of criticism's discourse was prefigured by the structuralist preoccupation with metalanguage and the foundations of semiotics.

The move from modeling literature's and literary scholarship's arbitrary structures to denouncing them as ideologically suspect was both evolutionary and revolutionary. The accumulation of insights into the fundamental problems of discourse was accompanied by a startling rise in criticism's political temperature. Having discovered the omnipresence of textuality, poststructuralism seems to have unlearned the very pleasure of the text it had proverbialized (in Barthes 1974b [1973]). Taking its own metaphors of subversion too literally, it virtually ceased *liking* art—as if, once demystified, fictions no longer held any attraction. To be sure, this too had originated in the structuralist era, when it was chic to voice the fear that under the cold stare of Science, literature's Beauty would wither. Ironically, the forecast is coming true just as the idea of scientific cognition of literature falls into disrepute. The desire that animates much of today's critical practice suggests a hostile arrogance toward literature and a narcissist obsession with theory and the figure of the critic. The latest literary revolution has, as it were, brought about the canonization of the most secondary of genres, a virtual dictatorship of criticism, a.k.a. "secondary literature."

In the rereadings that follow, I try to garner the best of both worlds, avoiding their malignant extremes. A middle course is apt to draw fire from both sides. So far, I have been protecting my conservative flank, which faces the theater of intense theoretical hostilities. The other, "innovative," flank, facing Russian studies, may be no less vulnerable, as all rereading worthy of the name risks being. Here, however, the defense is less a matter of theory (once the general desirability of re-reading has been accepted) than of producing cogent new readings. As such, it is best left to specific chapters.

To put it bluntly, I still believe in literature's primary realities, texts and authors, finding them of more lasting interest than readers', crit-ics', or theorists' responses to them, including my own. Accordingly, in the spirit of Hemingway's matadors, I believe in "working close to the bull" and coming away with full-blooded (re)readings rather than mere illustrations of theoretical points. To qualify these anti-theoretical overstatements, I still believe in literature's very own layer of signification, defined by its structures—patterns, devices, motifs, invariants, clusters, masterplots. I consider these carriers of specific literary meanings much more deserving of our professional attention than various grand but hollow constructions placed on literature by critics whose aesthetic response is predominantly ideological. And I find sophomoric the idea that lists, diagrams, and other explicit for-mulations somehow circumscribe the text's freedom, monologizing and drying up the critical discourse.

Rereading's interest lies in its very pursuit of different—newer, truer, or otherwise provocative and rewarding—readings. Proceeding from the general semiotic assumption that special inquiry is needed to make texts yield their hidden meanings, rereading enacts the con-version scenario inscribed, according to Riffaterre, in the literary text itself. A typical strategy adopted in this book is to read one text with, so to speak, an unexpected but significant other text in hand, bring-ing their structures and invariants to bear on each other. Prominent among the countertexts thus engaged are not only historically related works but also the "eternally relevant" psychoanalytical and arche-typal paradigms.

Ideally, the process leads, in a sequence of conversions, to a deeper reading of the texts. The discovery procedure is both synchronic and diachronic, as it projects onto the studied text discourses from differ-ent times. The resulting interplay of meanings may produce an orderly hierarchy, a more or less harmonious chorus, or a set of incompatible alternatives. One major challenge, germane to the reconciliation of synchrony and diachrony, is learning to treat an author's evolution as a special case of self-rereading, a dialogue with oneself and the historical context.

Speaking of history, much of the rereading undertaken here centers on the great cultural divides of the turn of the century and the 1917 revolution. Shklovsky's discovery of defamiliarization is once again a pivotal concept and a historically relevant guide to the book's recurrent themes. Defamiliarization actually epitomizes rereading, revolutionary subversion of literary conventions, and the aesthetic legitimation of plebeian "bad writing."[11] Updated as Riffaterrian conversion, defamiliarization also underlies another major link between intertextuality and the Soviet cultural situation. Conversion breeds such literary hybrids as the Aesopian art of adapting traditional literary patterns and authors' idiosyncratic invariants to the dictates of political control and the dystopian revision of utopias (and other classical models) in light of postrevolutionary realities.

Helpful as they prove in providing clues to the book's problematic, these and other theoretical ideas are not above reexamination. The Formalists' kinship with the avant-garde and the discourse of the Revolution makes their poetics all the more historicizable and rereadable. A case in point is the revision of the Formalist treatment of story, discourse, and framing in Chapter 4.[12] Nor does Riffaterre's version of the Formalist/intertextual approach remain sacrosanct; its rigorously binary design (expansion—conversion) proves on occasion too confining and is then modified to accommodate multihypogram and multistage transformations (e.g., in Chapters 5, 9, 10).

I have outlined the book's major leitmotifs: structures, invariants, clusters; psychoanalytical and mythological archetypes; defamiliarization, conversion, hybrids, multiple readings; cultural and literary conventions, "bad" writing, Aesopian discourse, dystopias. These are accompanied by other research tools, which form the book's theoretical background: the notions of power politics of literary discourse (Bakhtin, Foucault) and the role of cultural institutions (Lotman, Ginzburg, and Uspenskii 1985, Todd 1986); the models of Socialist Realism as new classicism ([Siniavsky-]Tertz 1982 [1959]), ritualistic writing (Clark 1981), and avant-garde run amok (Groys 1988); the problematic of the body and carnival (Bakhtin 1968 [1965]); the Proustian superposition of the unique and the recurrent (Genette 1970, 1980); the iconization of ideological stances via narrative structures (e.g., of Olesha's 'envy' via a special 'invidious optic'; see Chapter 7); and others. All in all, the book can be said to aspire to an enlightened eclecticism with a structuralist and intertextualist base. The methods of various critical schools are enlisted in the same old search for strikingly new and yet compellingly plausible readings.

Two interrelated concerns guide this search: a theoretical exploration of intertextuality and a historical study of the Russian literary scene. They are additionally linked by the role played in the reinterpretive process by literary criticism.

The theoretical emphasis is on the types of intertextual contact. These are defined by

—the contact's level: among individual texts, entire oeuvres, or structural entities;

—the nature of the contact: typological affinity or direct influence;

—its dynamics: influence, dialogue, evolution;

—the resulting complexity of interpretation: single, double, multiple; and

—the pragmatic factors at play: literary, institutional, political, archetypal.

The book consists of ten comparative analyses grouped into five pairs that represent major types of intertextual rereading. Most analyses concentrate on a few short texts (stories, poems, chapters of longer works), which are discussed as representative of their authors' styles. Each essay forms something of a monographic whole that can be read independently of the rest.

Part I juxtaposes the sensibilities underlying entire poetic worlds. In its two chapters, the modernist and postmodernist writings of Mikhail Zoshchenko and Sasha Sokolov, respectively, are found to suggest new perspectives on their nineteenth-century "realist" counterparts. As a result, Gogol and Tolstoy emerge as inspirationally "bad" writers, unexpectedly relevant to recent and current problematics. Instrumental in these reinterpretations are various analytical models of "the Soviet phenomenon" as well as psychoanalytic and poststructuralist insights into the dynamics of social conventions, the power of writing, and writers' fragmented identities.

In Part II, intertextual linkage shifts to the level of more narrowly circumscribed thematic and structural constructs. One chapter recovers Tolstoy's "After the Ball" from its automatized textbook limbo by discerning in it a conversion, along the lines of his late thinking, of an archetypal plot. The analysis then focuses on the changing uses to which the same hypogram is put by three authors—prerevolutionary (Leo Tolstoy), postrevolutionary (Mikhail Zoshchenko), and post-Stalin (Eugenia Ginzburg)—uses that stem from their respective views of culture. The other essay examines the changes in the treatment, by a classic (Pushkin) and two modernists (Bunin and Nabokov), of narrative framing, and these changes too are found symptomatic of cultural shifts. In the process, a dialogue between two influential readings, of Pushkin by Mikhail Gershenzon (1919) and of Bunin by Lev Vygotsky (1971 [1925]), is established and put in historical perspective.

Part III is devoted to the derivation of a modern work from its textual prototype(s). Chapter 5 shows how a living poet (Brodsky) appropriates, under the guise of parody, a nineteenth-century masterpiece (by Pushkin) and the entire tradition of its rewriting to produce an epitome of his own poetics. Three sets of invariants (defining the two authorial oeuvres and the literary progeny of the original poem) are involved in this intercourse, which is shown to consist of several metamorphic transitions: from Pushkin's original—to progeny—to parody—to Brodsky's idiosyncrasies—to their ultimately Pushkinian base. The companion Chapter 6 features Brodsky's lesser-known and testily anticultural adversary, Eduard Limonov. The analysis of two of his texts, a lyric and a short story, establishes their deep archetypal roots but also reveals no less strong a link to subtexts (from Derzhavin, Pushkin, as well as Mandelstam, whom the author professes to ignore) than in Brodsky, the consummate intertextualist.

Part IV continues the close reading of subtexts with two studies of actual literary exchange and its role in literary evolution. Chapter 7 (re)constructs a tripartite dialogue between Bulgakov and Olesha (*Heart of a Dog—Envy—The Master and Margarita*) in the course of which a common motif cluster is gradually recast, as carnivalesque discourse comes to the fore. Chapter 8 analyzes a metaliterary poem typical of Pasternak's 1930s style whose motifs and diction exhibit an Aesopian compromise between the poet's invariants and the Soviet mythopoetics of the time. The adaptive dynamics takes shape in a dialogue with contemporaries (Briusov, Mayakovsky, Mandelstam), predecessors (Pushkin), and characteristic topoi of Russian poetry. Thus, in both chapters internal and external dialogues are found at the very roots of creativity and evolution.

In Part V, the readings proceed according to several different codes at once, yielding manifold but rather congruent spectrums of meaning. In Chapter 9, an episode from I. Ilf and E. Petrov's *The Golden Calf* (the story of the closet monarchist Khvorob'ev) is broken down into layers representing different kinds of literary discourse. Especially instructive is the mediation between the traditional genre of nightmare and the masterplot of dystopia that hinges on a subtext from Dostoevsky. Chapter 10, in turn, involves a mythological archetype, a classical subtext, a modernist one, and the author's invariants in the reading of a modern short story (Platonov's "Fro"), yielding a polyphonic score of meanings.

The book coheres in more ways than are suggested by the above methodological sketch. Although the subject matter spans two centuries of Russian literature—featuring poets, prosaists (with Pushkin and Limonov in both capacities), and nonfiction writers, from classics to modernists to living authors—the discussion clusters around several focal texts and issues. The chapter that presents Zoshchenko's ambiguous primitivism as an extreme case of Tolstoyan defamiliarization has a sequel in the next section, where this correlation illuminates the two writers' treatment of the 'body'; a similar corporeal problematic reappears in the chapter on Limonov. Another thread links the references to Dostoevsky as a forerunner of modern dystopian discourse (specifically to *The Village of Stepanchikovo*) in the context now of Gogol's quasi-totalitarian delusions, now of Ilf and Petrov's antitotalitarian dreamer. The dystopian theme and the attendant problems of adaptation are taken up in connection with Pasternak's self-harnessing to the Soviet juggernaut. In another thematic grouping, Pushkin's announced appearances in the chapters on Brodsky and on framing are supplemented by his subtextual habitation (especially as the creator of the "Prophet" hypogram) of other texts, notably, the Pasternak poem. Finally, a common topical interest (in the issue of cultural heritage) correlates the three recent texts (by E. Ginzburg, Brodsky, and Limonov), however different their attitudes toward that problem.

Despite the continuity of presentation, the book's genre remains halfway between a tight ("American") monograph and a looser ("European") collection of interrelated essays. An additional split, or polyphony, comes from the dual nature of writing in English about Russian literature. The book speaks, as it were, with a forked tongue as it addresses its mixed audience of Slavists and generalists. While the latter may be interested only in its position, rather conservative, on matters of theory, the former will probably see it primarily as a study in practical reinterpretation, rather unorthodox at times.

Rereading by definition claims novelty, and the recent upheavals in the Russian literary landscape are especially conducive to critical revaluation, consonant to an extent with the current deconstructive trends in the West. The rediscovery/canonization of entire strata of twentieth-century Russian literature (banned, émigré, dissident, or otherwise unofficial) has been accompanied by provocative reinterpretations of classics (e.g., of Pushkin and Gogol by Siniavsky-Tertz [1975a, 1975b] and Mayakovsky by Karabchievskii [1985]). Controversial as these are, they build on the scholarly tradition of tracing the changing fate of a writer's discourse in criticism and later writing.[13]

The exercises in rereading that follow have been undertaken in a spirit of political and aesthetic nonalignment, which in the Russian context may offend various sets of traditional values. The association of Zoshchenko with Tolstoy is completely new, as is the shadow of stylistic and ideological ambiguity it casts on both of them. More specifically, "After the Ball" has never been placed in such "odd" contexts as Zoshchenko's "Lady with Flowers" on one hand and folkloric wedding-tests imagery on the other. Somewhat risqué is also the treatment of *Selected Passages* (for some, a sacred text; for others, reactionary nonsense) as a "regular" Gogolian—grotesquely unreliable and megalomaniacal—*skaz* narrative. Conventional decorum is breached again in the chapter on Ilf and Petrov, who make strange bedfellows for Dostoevsky, Zamyatin, and Orwell, as for that matter does Limonov for Derzhavin, Mandelstam, and Brodsky. Indeed, the semiofficial 1930s satirists and the present-day enfant terrible of Russian letters and politics are hardly among the fashionable subjects of critical attention, largely because of their peculiar mix of dubious political credentials and wide popular appeal (and that despite the theoretical recognition of the intimate links between 'high' and 'low' in modern culture).

By the same token, my inquiry, objective to the point of cynical admiration, into the dynamics of Pasternak's early 1930s "collaborationism" may run afoul of the established perceptions of that poet as either obliviously above the fray or in righteous opposition to the regime. Similar ideological pieties will probably be offended by the profane dissection of Eugenia Ginzburg's account of her truly heroic experience in the Gulag, the promotion of Olesha to the top literary-and-dissident rank (usually reserved for the likes of Bulgakov), and the general stamp of aesthetic approval conferred on the 'art of adaptation' (Olesha's, Pasternak's, Ilf and Petrov's, Platonov's, Zoshchenko's, and others').

Potentially problematic also are some of my methodological positions. The rereading of Bunin's "Gentle Breathing" revises, with all due respect, the story's classical analysis by Vygotsky. The concepts of 'cluster' and 'progeny,' crucial to the intertextual placing of Brodsky's sonnet derived from a Pushkin subtext, differ significantly from the "standard" Taranovsky-Gasparov approach, based on homometrical corpuses. The prominence accorded the author's personality in the interpretation of *Selected Passages* is a departure from strictly textual analysis (admittedly excusable, though, in the case of Gogol, whom critics love to psychoanalyze). Finally, the idea of 'bad writing' may be seen by some as taken too far to promote "really bad" authors (i.e., depending on the critic, Chernyshevsky, Zoshchenko, Limonov) by lumping them together with the "greats" (Gogol, Tolstoy, Khlebnikov, Platonov).

But then, as has been said, rereadings can hardly be justified *in abstracto*—they are to stand or fall on their merits.

In case of doubt, reread.

PART I

Oeuvres and Intertexts

ONE

Rereading Gogol's Miswritten *Passages*

I f 'reading,' 'misreading,' 'inscribing,' and 'recon-textualizing' are among the master metaphors of current criticism, then Gogol, more than any other Russian classic, invites, indeed has invited, the exercise of these strategies. This in itself is a sufficient reason to start a book of rereadings with a chapter on Gogol. Effectively misread by his contemporary critics, above all Belinsky, who conferred on him the mantle of a civic "poet of reality," Gogol kept rereading and rewriting himself (Debreczeny 1966), underwent in the decades that followed his death several reception metamorphoses at the hands of various eminent readers, and later became the subject of a sustained reinterpretive effort that turned him into a modernist *avant la lettre*, justifying the programmatic title of the cumulative anthology *Gogol from the Twentieth Century* (Maguire 1974). A new round of Gogol reappraisals seems to be warranted by the current postmodern situation in general and its "sots-art" Russian version in particular, which aestheticizes all possible ideological discourses, including egregious totalitarianism.

In Russian prose fiction, the single most important new context for Gogolian writing is probably furnished by a leading émigré writer,

Sasha Sokolov, in *Palisandriia* (1985, 1989). Of Gogol's own texts, we will focus primarily on *Selected Passages from Correspondence with Friends* (hereafter abbreviated as *Selected Passages* or just *Passages*), his most "misprised" and "forgotten"[1] work, and accordingly the one most in need of and amenable to reinterpretation. But the point of the proposed study in rereading is not a revision of one individual text in light of another. It is rather an attempt to bring a cluster of current textual and critical strategies—concerned with antiutopian discourse, writing (*écriture*), polyphony, psychoanalysis, reader response, intertextuality, and literature as institution—to bear on Gogol's discourse in general, with *Selected Passages* as a challenging test case. I begin with the concept of *skaz*, introduced into Gogol criticism and literary theory by Eikhenbaum's historic essay (1974 [1919]) and problematized in interesting ways by *Selected Passages*.

Skaz, Gogol, and His Characters

The definition of *skaz* hinges on the distinction between the intellectually and stylistically unreliable narrator, on the one hand, and, on the other, the implied author, who towers above the narrator simply because we the readers cannot imagine an author ostensibly so stupid and inept. But what about *Selected Passages*, where just that is known to be the case? And how do we then deny Gogol the benefit of stupidity in his vintage *skaz* writing, whose striking similarity to *Selected Passages* has been noted by Gogol's contemporaries and many later critics, notably Gippius (1981 [1924]) and Tynianov (1977a [1921])?

In fact, some crucial aesthetic boundaries had been blurred already in such texts as "The Overcoat," where the absence of a consistent narrative perspective[2] foregrounds the act of writing itself rather than an identifiable, if flawed, narrator. *Selected Passages* constitutes a further confusion of author and character-narrator—and, in fact, Gogol himself admitted that in writing *Selected Passages* he had behaved like a Khlestakov.[3]

The affinity between Gogol and his characters is well known. Gogol, who was famous for impersonating the comic characters of his texts and of the scenes he improvised for his friends, saw his creative process as a satirical exorcism of the worst aspects of himself; he described the corresponding literary technique as "demotion from the rank of general to that of enlisted man."[4] Identifying secretly with his lowly *alter egos*, Gogol often endowed them with "authorial" status (e.g., Khlestakov, Chichikov, Nozdrev, Poprishchin, Akakii Akakievich, and Postmaster[5]) and ended up as a literary character himself. This began with anecdotes and continued with biographies—genres that treat the writer as character,[6] in Gogol's case, as a comic mask. A high point in fictionalizing Gogol qua Gogolian Character was reached in Ivan Bunin's short story "Mr. Mikhol'skii's Vest" (1934), which depicts Gogol as envious of an article of the narrator's clothing.[7]

Gogol qua Grotesque Author appeared even earlier—in Dostoevsky's *The Village of Stepanchikovo and Its Inhabitants* (Tynianov 1977a [1921]). Perhaps, there was poetic justice in this. After all, it was Gogol who started the game by placing Khlestakov on a friendly footing with Pushkin (in *The Inspector General*). Thus, Dostoevsky, in demoting the author from his privileged position above the characters (in the Bakhtinian sense), was only following in Gogol's narrative footsteps. Who else, then, should have inaugurated the carnival of professional and would-be writers in Dostoevsky's novels but Gogol—indeed, the Gogol of *Selected Passages*, in the guise of Foma Opiskin, the self-appointed "writer" of books and of the destinies of his entourage?

Foma's very name (the Russian version of Thomas) offers a vignette emblematic of the author-character oscillation. Dostoevsky probably had in mind the two Catholic Thomases, Aquinas and à Kempis. They were discovered by Gogol in the 1840s (Karlinsky 1976: 243), and apparently in *Selected Passages* he tried to emulate the latter's *Imitatio Christi* (Bogojavlensky 1981: 51ff.). To these two historical eminences Dostoevsky added the fictional Foma Grigor'evich, one of the "authors" of *Evenings on a Farm Near Dikanka*. In a typically Gogolian manner, Foma then became Foma Fomich (cf. Akakii Akakievich), with a pejorative-diminutive family name, Opiskin, structurally reminiscent of Bashmachkin. Also, semantically, *opiska*, "misspelling," evokes Akakii's profession (note the *oshibka*, "mistake," he almost made in copying while excited over his new overcoat) and more generally his status as a 'mis-person.' To complete the picture, among the numerous "poor clerks" in the pre-"Overcoat" literature, there was one Foma Fomich Openkin. He was a creation of Bulgarin (Gippius 1981: 129), the same Bulgarin who after the failure of "Hanz Küchelgarten" obtained for its author the position of collegiate registrar (which Gogol,

in the spirit of "Nevskii Avenue"'s Kovalev, was said to have sometimes passed off for that of collegiate assessor).[8]

Thus, Gogol started out both as an exalted but failed romantic poet
and as a "poor clerk" akin to the precursors of his characters. He
succeeded in promoting himself to the rank of author and in the process ambivalently elevated/degraded himself and his characters to the
status of a Khlestakov and Akakii. By authoring *Selected Passages* from
the position of such a character-writer, he practically set himself up for
the grotesque objectification that was to befall him in *Stepanchikovo*.[9]

Gogol's Identity, Writing, and Reception

The oscillations of Gogol's (self-)image stemmed from his problematic
sense of identity and its boundaries (as abundantly shown by Fanger).
Gogol himself insisted that he was a riddle. He identified completely
with his various roles (*GVS*: 45), could wear several facial expressions
in one day (and thus defy painterly portrayal [*GVS*: 290]), and change
toward an acquaintance overnight. He was pathologically unsure of
his performance (e.g., as lecturer) and slavishly adapted himself to the
tastes of his "superiors" (e.g., Pushkin). He partly reinvented his own
name, appropriating the semifictitious Gogol' and dropping Ianovskii
(Stillman 1966; Erlich 1969: 8), and when traveling signed it variously
as Gonol', Gogel', and so on (*GVS*: 137–38, 152).

Psychologically, this has been related to Gogol's identification with
his mother and desire to elude her control (*GVS*: 186) and his repressed homosexuality.[10] Some memoirs show him knitting, like the
embroidering governor in *Dead Souls*, and wearing women's clothes,
like Pliushkin (*GVS*: 112, 407). Gogol's fragile identity is most likely
at the root of his stylistic contrasts, his doubles, impostors, characters lacking selfhood, and of his two master themes: 'metamorphosis,'
which determined his evolution, and 'mistaken identity,' which permitted such different readings of his life and works. In particular,
Gogol's dual orientation toward the literary aristocrats and the lower-
brow public, mostly successful, was always fraught with a potential
for rift.

A major tension in Gogol's personality was between 'nonentity'
and 'grandeur.' Megalomaniacal in matters great and small, he prided
himself on his cultural mission and on his knack for buying cheap. He

tyrannized his friends, who were supposed to relieve him from menial trifles and expenses and otherwise "cherish" (*leleiat'*) him. He reprimanded them, exacted gratitude for living among them, and expected them to reread, copy, and circulate his letters. He imposed penances and died asking for a ladder to heaven. He also claimed for himself all possible roles. One contemporary saw him as a typical Ukrainian, *khokhol*, who wants to be everything—musician, painter, actor (*GVS*: 106)—and indeed he tried his hand at every literary genre—poetry, short story, novel-epic, drama, criticism, journalism, history, testimonial (Fanger 1979: 48). Siniavsky-Terts (1975b: 238) aptly compares him to Nozdrev, who claimed as his own, *moe*, even what lay beyond his boundaries. Gogol admired Senkovskii for being a one-man journal and lovingly ridiculed such a personality in the character of Khlestakov.

Gogol's writing has been described as an "orchestra of voices" (Vinogradov 1976: 191) and a ventriloquist's act (Fanger 1978: 77). A curious case of ventriloquism is provided by "After the Play": the fictional author eavesdrops and comments on the opinions of the viewers exiting from the hall, which of course have been preprompted by the real author, intent on prescribing his interpretation of the comedy. (In fact, Gogol would not let go of the play even then and wrote yet another rethematization: *Denouement of "The Inspector General"* [1846].)

This double authorial overkill is a telling manifestation of yet another facet of Gogol's megalomania: a desire for total control. Gogol could ill stand the presence of unfamiliar people, wrote out his lectures (or feigned sickness), and tried to monitor from Europe all the movements and exchanges of information related to him; for instance, the itineraries of acquaintances who could bring him messages or money (*GVS*: 202–3) as well as the circulation of his letters and the exchange of opinions about him, instructing his friends how to refute misrepresentations. He was notoriously secretive and inclined to manipulate people (*GVS*: 247), traveling under altered names and avoiding contacts with fellow travelers (he would go to such lengths as feigning sleep or pretending not to know them), and (like Petrushka) often slept fully dressed, armed, as it were, according to the always shrewd Annenkov (*GVS*: 260). In correspondence, he "falsified" his motives and personality (in Veresaev's formulation [1933: 5], quoted by Fanger [1979: 268]). He concealed his addresses, changed printers, misleading his associates (e.g., Shevyrev), and consorted with Belinsky's group clandestinely from the Slavophiles (*GVS*: 139, 302).

He also had a penchant for destroying his writings: he burned a juvenile novella, a romantic poem, a historical drama—after it put Zhukovsky to sleep (*GVS*: 229, 282)—and twice the second part of his "epic." Sure enough, after the failure of *Selected Passages* Gogol regretted not having burned it, as he is reported to have said to I. S. Turgenev and M. S. Shchepkin (*GVS*: 530). Gogol's annihilatory pyrotechnics can be viewed as a will to monopolize his literary rights, and his near-suicidal death, as a desperate gesture of control over his very life.

Most of Gogol's bids for power were always on the brink of collapse. They achieved control either by destroying their object or by the less dramatic strategy of withdrawal (evidenced by his celibacy, aloofness from mundane matters, avoidance of contacts, and self-imposed exile). In an ambivalent reversal of his manipulativeness, but not of his blissful unconcern for the boundaries of his self, Gogol deliberately surrendered many functions to others. Thus, he instructed his friends to pool their efforts, each in his own way, for his sake (*GVS*: 188) and in particular to take care of his mother, in a strategy that is reminiscent of Agaf'ia Tikhonovna's wishful collages of the features and virtues of her suitors, intended to fashion out of them one ideal husband (*Marriage*). Gogol delegated to Shevyrev all matters of money management, publication, and even the editing of his faulty style and grammar; to his correspondents, the drafting of his future texts, "asking, as it were, the readers to replace him in his authorial role, by sending him in an envelope the missing *Dead Souls*" (Siniavsky-Terts 1975b: 288);[11] and to censorship, the enforcement of artistic discipline (Fanger 1978: 71–75) in a gesture anticipatory of a provocative recent theory of censorship as a beneficial presence (Loseff 1984). Before burning *Dead Souls*, Gogol tried to leave the manuscript with A. P. Tolstoy and the decision what to do with it to the discretion of Filaret and others (*GVS*: 449, 509, 516).

Delegation of power naturally led to situations where others failed Gogol (as, for instance, when A. P. Tolstoy refused to keep the manuscript, effectively enabling Gogol to burn it, or when Aksakov decided not to pass on to Pogodin Gogol's offensive remarks about him)[12] and to delegation of guilt. Gogol blamed his friends for the advice to publish *Selected Passages*, Aksakov and Annenkov for the faults of the entire public,[13] and the "evil one" (*lukavyi*) for the burning of *Dead Souls*. Thus, the circumstances of this fatal burning are emblematic of both 'total control' and 'relinquished responsibility.'

The same interplay of grandeur, nonentity, and withdrawal determined Gogol's exclusive concentration on writing. He admitted that he did not know Russia,[14] or for that matter Ukraine (Debreczeny 1966: 6), and created out of nothing by sheer linguistic prowess because words (e.g., gleaned from the dictionary), he claimed, were all he required for his work. Gogol's worldly needs were minimal and his existence purely textual, so that there was nothing he could hide (!) from the public. An apotheosis of this rhetorical magic, *Selected Passages* is "purely literary" (Gippius 1981: 170), defined "by style alone" (Setchkarev 1965: 243) in a triumph of poetic control at the price of complete withdrawal from reality.

Failure of control and delegation of authority also marked Gogol's relationship with critics. In addition to reviews, he sought private information about responses to his work, especially negative ones, at first squirmed and rebutted (*GVS*: 293), but then adapted his self-image accordingly, letting his literary identity be redefined for him by others. For instance, in *Selected Passages*, he did become an ideologist, as Belinsky wanted him to, but, ironically, one of a persuasion prompted by the opposite camp (Siniavsky-Terts 1975b: 540).

Gogol's contradictory person, style, and reception cast a long historical shadow in the form of successive rereadings. Ever since, Russian literature has been busy working out Gogol's prophetic slips, with *Selected Passages* the grossest of all and the latest to be vindicated. The peripeties of Gogol's "tragedy of misdirection" by critics and its posthumous consequences for *Selected Passages* have been traced by Debreczeny (1966).

> In particular, he notes that Dostoevsky first "suffered for Belinsky's opinion" concerning *Selected Passages*,[15] then "was conditioned by Siberian brainwashing to love what he had hated, and eventually accepted Gogol's ideas, allying himself with Apollon Grigor'ev, the only critic who had wholeheartedly supported Gogol" (1966: 60).

Yet the same Dostoevsky also made double-edged fun of Gogol in *The Village of Stepanchikovo* (1861).

The "rehabilitation" of Gogol's oeuvre has proceeded along two main lines, those of form and content, and *Selected Passages* lies at the intersection of both.

Selected Passages and the Importance of Writing Badly

In *Selected Passages*, Gogol pushed his grandiloquent sermonizing to an extreme. Branded as reactionary by liberal critics (beginning with Belinsky's open "Letter," 1847) and downright silly by almost everyone, his message did find a sympathetic response (from Grigor'ev) and was later endorsed and developed by Dostoevsky, Tolstoy, Rozanov, and others.[16] Gogol's conversion prefigured those of Dostoevsky and Tolstoy, being the first attempt at legitimizing that very Russian blend of fictional and ideological discourse that informed—deformed, in the view of some—the narrative mode of such texts as *War and Peace* and *Doctor Zhivago*. The effect was not purely ideological but stylistic as well, liberating the direct, aesthetically imperfect voice of the author.[17] Thus, Gogol's notoriously miswritten book was his final and ironic defeat—final, because, as Bulgarin's *Northern Bee* correctly predicted, "after this volume nothing further could be expected of Gogol" (Debreczeny 1966: 53); ironic, because exclusive concentration on writing should have guaranteed a perfect text. But in a sense its "bad" writing was the best thing about it—according to Siniavsky-Terts, "a genius . . . is the one who dares write badly" (340).

From the start, Gogol produced "bad" texts, which he had to renounce and destroy.[18] Even in his most acclaimed prose critics were quick to point out provincialisms, dubious taste, and ungrammaticalities. His worst mistakes would be edited out, but most of his "irregular" writing remained intact, soon to be recognized as innovative and eventually canonized when Gogol was proclaimed a forerunner of modernism. His stylistic "failures" were appropriated by the comprehensive cultural revolution of the past hundred years.

"Miscontrolled" writing signaled the liberation of a previously repressed and disciplined "lower" voice. This was analogous to such manifestations of literary decontrol as the "works" of Koz'ma Prutkov, Dostoevsky's "hurriedly unpolished" manner, Leo Tolstoy's deliberately primitive "truth-searching" discourse (sometimes quite Akakii-like), Leskov's *skaz*, Rozanov's homely homilies, Khlebnikov's quasi-graphomaniac poetics, Zoshchenko's coy primitivism, down to Limonov's stark uncouthness, which prompted a traditionalist contemporary's (Naum Korzhavin's) provocative labeling *personazhi pishut*: "[Now it is the] characters [who do the] writing."

Korzhavin's formula invites comparison with Fanger's statement that "giving up the freedom of a creator, Gogol took on that of a fictitious character" (1979: 212) and Siniavsky-Terts's observations on the "deliberate unprepossesiveness and foolishness [*durakovatost*']" of *Selected Passages* (1975b: 84) and on the way *Dead Souls* had already reduced the author to the role of a "belated second-rate character" (p. 200; see also p. 286). A likely common source of these insights is found in Pasternak: "Mayakovsky . . . is a Dostoevsky character writing lyrical poems—one of his young rebels, the 'Raw Youth' or Hippolyte or Raskolnikov" (*Doctor Zhivago*, 6: 4; 1958: 149).

In a broader, philosophical sense, the effect of "characters writing" is akin to such modern cultural phenomena as Nietzschean relativization of values, Freudian triple-voicedness of the psyche, and Dostoevskian-Bakhtinian dialogism.[19]

Is *Selected Passages* dialogic, then? Certainly not in intent, although Gogol tries to pass off his own (real, edited, and fictional) letters for a "correspondence," i.e., an exchange of opinions. To be sure, according to Bakhtin, dialogism does not equal dramatic (in particular, epistolary) mode: the "other" voice is to be heard in the single speaker's allegedly onefold discourse. This does happen in *Selected Passages*, but the peremptory authorial voice dominates all others. Or does it? Thanks to bombast and inconsistencies, its persuasiveness unravels. The decontrol is, of course, involuntary—Gogol is not a Prutkov, but he comes so close to him that some contemporaries even believed *Selected Passages* to be "a deliberate Ukrainian prank by which Gogol intended to attract public attention" (Debreczeny 1966: 53). In other words, the book is "camp," in the sense given the word by Susan Sontag.

Although Sontag draws her examples of "camp" mostly from fin-de-siècle kitsch, which is very unlike *Selected Passages*, many of her formulations are surprisingly pertinent to Gogol's book:

Camp . . . emphasizes . . . style at the expense of content. . . . Camp which knows itself to be Camp . . . is . . . less satisfying. . . . Camp . . . reeks of self-love . . . , seriousness that fails. . . . The hallmark of Camp is . . . the proper mixture of the exaggerated, the fantastic, the passionate, the naive, . . . the outlandish . . . , the spirit of extravagance . . . , something *démesuré* in the quality of the ambition . . . on the part of one man to do what it takes a generation, a whole culture to accomplish. . . . Camp . . . cannot be taken . . . seriously because it is 'too much.' . . . A work can be close to Camp, but not make it, because it succeeds. . . . We are better able to enjoy a fantasy . . . when it is not our own. . . . Time liberates the work of art from moral relevance, delivering it over to Camp sensibility. . . . Camp is the glorification of 'character' . . . , the unity, the force of the person. . . . The peculiar relation between Camp and homosexuality has to be explained. . . . The discovery of the good taste of bad taste can be liberating. . . . The ultimate Camp statement: it's good because it's awful (1961: 278–92).

Gogol's guilelessly "pure" camp calls for an appropriately "campy," postmodern rereading.

A further twist to this virtual dialogism is given by the nature of the monologic voice. The authorial stance is Domostroi-like,[20] autocratic; Siniavsky-Terts, in discussing *Selected Passages*, draws parallels with Poprishchin's claims to the Spanish throne (1975b: 65–67) and with the "statist" spirit of the Petrine epoch (p. 646). Pretending, with pervasive megalomania, to the role of Russia's official savior,[21] Gogol resembles Prutkov in the latter's role of senior official and author of "A Project for Introducing Uniformity of Thought in Russia." The relationship between Poet and Czar/State is, of course, a master myth of Russian culture, but in Gogol's version it envisions a union rather than rebellious opposition, foreshadowing Khlebnikov's (and other avant-gardists') Poetic Chairmanship.

As I have argued elsewhere (Zholkovsky 1986f), Khlebnikov's poetic discourse involved three major strategies: (1) bold stylistic innovations and fast-paced shifts (*sdvigi*) on every textual level; (2) "bad," infantile, primitivist, quasi-amateurish writing; and (3) megalomaniacal claims to the role of the supreme savant of language and history and Chairman of the Globe (*Predsedatel' Zemnogo Shara*).

All three were integral aspects of a single poetic personality. In a nutshell, it took the naive, but very loud, "hamming" voice, autocratically certain of its world-historical grandeur, to juggle and hold together—naturalize—the disparate, fragmented, and kaleidoscopically shifting components of his discourse, which threatened to fall apart at every turn.

Thus, ironically, Khlebnikov "accomplished his revolutionary [artistic] tasks, destructive and liberating at the same time, by recourse, albeit parodic, to the authoritarian poetic tradition . . . in a combination strikingly reminiscent of the history of Russian Communism" (Zholkovsky 1986f: 585). Khlebnikov presents a "figure, which, fulfilling as it did the general European cultural command of the early twentieth century [roughly speaking, avant-gardist] remained, in fact, a typically Russian one, flesh of the flesh of the Russian literary tradition, featuring the age-old confrontation/identification of the Poet and Czar, or of 'literature and police' " (584), in the words of Nabokov. Both Khlebnikov and Gogol embody the "pro-state" variant of this monarchic-poetic paradigm—Khlebnikov in a characteristic avant-gardist grab for total aesthetic-political power, Gogol in a conservative, romantic, religiously paternalistic spirit. Both, and many others, are subsumed in Sokolov's tongue-in-cheek amalgam.

Indeed, the oxymoronic combination in *Selected Passages* of liberating bad writing with grandiose political pretensions can be compared to the later alliance between the avant-garde and totalitarianism. Lest these dystopian overtones sound hollow, we might recall that not unlike Stalin (the Best Friend of Dairymaids, among others), the author of *Selected Passages* insists on knowing every woman's "hobby," in order to better manipulate her, and the names and patronymics of all the important personages in town so that he could "be their friend . . . , to all, without exception" (125/311).[22] This prophetic anticipation of Big-Brotherly love for every subject has in fact materialized in a direct cultural lineage: it was on the author of *Selected Passages* that Dostoevsky modeled his Foma Fomich, an early version of the Grand Inquisitor, who in turn was a precursor of and a warning against dystopian rulers.[23]

Furthermore, since according to a recent view (Groys 1987a, 1988) Stalin and Stalinist culture were a runaway version of the Russian avant-garde, such postmodern refractions of the entire paradigm as Sasha Sokolov's *Palisandriia* should come as no surprise. The myth of Palisander Dahlberg—the great graphomaniac, savior of Russia, Kremlin ruler, and repository of all possible roles and attributes— is all the more relevant to the problem, since Palisander does mention Gogol on several occasions. Palisander's "romantically official-ese" writing bears distinct traces of Gogol's influence and overtly plays with specific Gogol intertexts, notably the dead souls scam (in a variation on both Gogol and Nikolai Fedorov, Palisander buys up the graves of eminent émigrés to transport back to Russia its glory; see Matich 1986a).

Here, finally, Gogol's camp is recycled into its highest possible counterpart. Sokolov's novel, too, is provocatively "reactionary" in its affectionate portrayal of the powers that be (Uncle Joseph, for one), held together by its lofty rhetoric alone, and obsessively metaliterary.

•

In an analysis of *Palisandriia* (Zholkovsky 1987c), I have shown that Soko-lov's "eclectic posture" of "mock remythologizing the Kremlin *and* Silver Age decadence *and* dissident and émigré sensibility" has "Palisander's physical polymorphism as its emblematic embodiment. . . . Creating a credible hy-brid of a Kremlin ruler (a Stalin), poet (a Blok), political exile (a Solzhenitsyn), and obsessed bisexual (an Edichka) called . . . [also] for a stylistic *tour de force*" that would combine turn-of-the-century 'rococo' aestheticism with a military-bureaucratic "throwback to eighteenth-century classicism."

Remarkably, Siniavsky-Terts discusses Gogol's *Selected Passages* and *Taras Bulba* as manifestations of the same 'heroic' spirit, outdated already by the time Gogol wrote (1975b: 244–47, 93–94). "It is, therefore, only natural that post-modernist 'revaluation' of Stalinism, for instance, in *sots-art*, should make use of the odic and epic archaics. Komar and Melamid's painting 'Comrade Stalin and the Muses' (1982) shows Stalin in his Generalissimo uniform, Socialist Realist style, attended by Classicist muses draped in semitransparent tunics. *Palisandriia* is written in the same stylistic key, but goes the painting one step further by fusing Stalin and the muses into one character: Palisander" (Zhol-kovsky 1987c: 380–81). (The classicist nature of Socialist Realism was, of course, established by Siniavsky-Terts's famous 1982 [1959] essay.)[24]

As for *Selected Passages*, the prominence in it of metaliterary themes is well known (Sobel 1981). Yet the author's preoccupation with writ-ing in Letter 21 ("What the Wife of a Provincial Governor Is"), the text we will be concentrating on, has so far escaped critical notice. This must be due to the fact that the letter ostensibly constitutes advice to the *gubernatorsha* on how to serve public good, not a treatise on *écriture*. The critics' failing thus dramatizes the discrepancy between the writer's purported message and the readers' virtual ability to see through it, offering yet another instance of decontrol and involun-tary *skaz*.

Grandeur, Information, and Media Manipulation

Letter 21 is a typical Gogol text. The speaker's persona appears as both self-aggrandizing and self-deprecating. On the one hand, he boasts of his predictions that have come true, his near omniscience and close ties to God; he poses as the ultimate arbiter who can put everything in order; and he demands unconditional obedience. On the other, he admits that he is completely uninformed about the town and Russia in general, that he is not a *vseznaika* (know-it-all) but just "a fool" (*glup, reshitel'no glup*) (134/319–20), and that if his opinion is unique, after all ("and if there is in me whatever small drop of reason, not possessed by all"), it is, in a characteristic high-low mediation, thanks to his familiarity with "abominations" (135/321).

The theme of grandeur is projected onto the bureaucratic hierarchy, reflecting Gogol's love-hate of rank and the addressee's premier position in town. At the top, second only to God, Gogol places himself, an ideal order-enforcing official, *chinovnik* (125); then comes the *gubernatorsha*, whose good example will trickle down through the ranks,[25] or else she can threaten the unhelpful priests with the bishop, the supreme government, and the emperor himself. Even spiritual re-education is metaphorized as law enforcement: the stupid sheep must be driven with the whip of shame and conscience.

So far, my analysis of Gogol's imperial ways has been quite Belinskian. However, prefiguring the spirit of our century, Letter 21 combines the routines of bureaucratic coercion with public-relations techniques. Gogol meticulously plans the manipulative use of balls, dinner invitations, fashions, legal procedures, public ostracism, rumors, sermons, and the influence of lady socialites on their husbands. These strategies are to target all social groups—bureaucracy, gentry, women, clergy, merchants, and lower-middle class (*meshchanstvo*)—with their respective systems of subordination.

All of this hinges on communication. Not unlike an American campaign manager, Gogol charts the flow of data, analyzes ratings, prepares media events, relies on image manipulation. In fact, the entire fourteen-page-long letter deals with nothing but various forms of information processing.

First, information has to be gathered, a task Gogol delegates to his correspondent.

> She must personally interview every important official (Gogol has a questionnaire of three standard questions ready); supplement the dossier with information gathered from others; talk with and learn "through and through" (*naskvoz'*) about "the entire female half of the town" (126/312), meet with every priest, polling them, as well as the chief of police, with whom a hearty talk is recommended, about every citizen of the middle and lower-middle class, and interviewing personally some of the latter.

The search for information ends with the scrutiny of all possible *merzosti* (abominations, disgusting things) (135/320–21).

Information must then be carefully filed, and Gogol repeatedly instructs his correspondent on the art of note taking.

Like a "diligent schoolgirl" (134/319) and "sensible official" and unlike a "passionately chaotic woman" (125/311), she must start a special notebook and record in it all conversations as accurately as possible, using the margin or separate pieces of paper for additional notes. This activity must be alotted regular hours, yet somehow every conversation must also be taken down right away ("Having found out, go straight [*otpravliaites'*] to your room and immediately put it all down on paper for me" [125/312]).

The contradiction between regular and immediate note taking is a typical inconsistency characterizing the flawed authorial voice of the *Passages*.

In fact, while replete with injunctions concerning orderliness, Gogol's own text is so repetitive and chaotic that toward the end he has to admit it, but of course blames it on the addressee: "Everything in [my letter] is haphazard, not in strict logical order, which, however, is your fault" (136/321). Reinterpreted as a stylistic pattern, Gogol's inconsistent voice exhibits a subtle use of *skaz* for maximum effect: the unreliable speaker gets away with making two opposite points.

To return to information processing,

gossip is to be recorded too, either "guilelessly, the way it was," or exactly "the way it was reported to you by trustworthy people" (126/313). All these data must be shared with other media personalities, for example, the bishop, but above all with Gogol himself, who will help put the chaotic information in good order.

Referring to the correspondent's previous letters, he keeps criticizing her for her failure to supply sufficient well-processed information—in a familiar gesture of delegated guilt.

However, mere streamlining of the information flow is not all. To influence events, information must be manipulated through a panoply of techniques:

—by raising one's own consciousness ("convince yourself that . . . [all your subjects] are your kinsmen and people close to your heart, and then everything will change before you") (123–24/310);

—by prayers (advised of the problems, Gogol will use his personal access to God, who will enlighten him: "[He] might send to my mind the gift of understanding [*vrazumlenie*], and my mind, made understanding by God, might be able to do something better than a mind which has not been made understanding by Him"—that is, than the less creative mind of the correspondent);

—by engineering facts and appearances that will be taken as role models and disseminated by fashion and other "aping" mechanisms—*obez'ianstvo*

(123/309; Gogol suggests wearing the same simple dress to parties, refusing to visit a bad official, publicly praising good behavior, and firing offenders);

— by interviewing strategies (the very course of the conversation will advise people of their problems and desirable cures);

— by influencing the perceptions of key communicators (the bishop, the wives) in order to enhance the persuasiveness of their acts (sermons, brainwashing of husbands);

— and, above all, by recourse to Gogol's own creative and prophetic gifts— in particular, his ability to divine the future (for him, "it is sufficient to observe the present more attentively, and the future will suddenly appear all by itself" [134/320]).[26]

Writing About Writing

The amount of attention Gogol devotes to writing and creativity and the supreme position he reserves for himself make suspect the declared purpose of this writerly pyramid—the improvement of life in the provincial city.

> The symbolic meaning of this city becomes clear in light of Gogol's retrospective comments, in his *Denouement of "The Inspector General,"* on the city portrayed in that play as the Inner City of Soul. Compare St. Augustine's City of God, the various utopian cities, the "soulful" double entendre in the title of *Dead Souls*, and the references to the *gubernatorsha*'s soul in the letter under analysis ("you yourself say that I have helped you in the affairs of your soul" [124/310]; "it will be impossible not to love you if your soul is known" [133/319]).

On the one hand, the manipulation of files and images sounds almost like a twentieth-century cross of Stalin's *ars apparatoria* with Nixon's wiretapping and Reagan's Great Communicatorship, which brings out Gogol's *mania grandiosa* and love of rank and control. But he emerges even more absorbed with *écriture*, his main claim to romantic grandeur. In a curious replay of "Diary of a Madman," the writer of *Selected Passages* pretends to the crown of the Poet/Czar of the City he has blessed with his attention.

Indeed, all this power play is purely literary and Gogolian. The fixation on the minutiae of text production (i.e., orderliness, regular hours, special notebooks and scraps of paper, etc.) is reminiscent of "The Overcoat"'s Akakii Akakievich, the writer, and *Dead Souls*'s Petrushka, the reader. The process of writing is likely to evoke strong emotions: "If, in the course of the descriptions you will be making for me . . . , our [Russian] regrettable aspects should strike you too hard and outrage your heart" (130/316). But in compensation it will yield a legitimite *plaisir du texte*: "pleasure, repose, spiritual relaxation [*razvlechen'e dukha*]" (132/318). Small wonder, since Gogol expects from his correspondent genuine acts of artistic creation.

> To impress on Gogol her situation, she must "sketch everything down to the last vivid detail, making it literally appear before [their] eyes, so that your town, as if alive, would constantly abide in [their] thoughts" (130/316).

Like a literary critic, Gogol insists that the images she creates be graphic and typical,[27] but allows also for caricature:

> I must have someone *live* [*zhiv'em*—italicized in the text] from among them, so that I may observe him from head to foot in all detail. . . . All this information will serve to paint an *exemplary picture* [*primernyi obraz*—italicized in the text] . . . of the middle-class person and merchant as they really should be; in a monster you will recognize the ideal of that which, as a caricature, has become a monster (131/317).

The literary talents Gogol expects from his correspondent and other women are quite extraordinary:

> If you only know how to speak to them in the language of their souls, . . . to sketch out for a woman a lofty career that the world expects of her today—her heavenly career to be the source which propels us to everything that is right, noble, and honest, to summon man to noble aspirations—[she] will suddenly blaze up . . . , push her husband to the honest fulfilment of his duty, and, tossing her rags aside, convert everyone to action (133/319).

These rhetorical talents are, of course, carbon copies of his own rare gift: "If you give me a full understanding of their [the town people's] character . . . , I will tell you in what way . . . it is possible to instigate them: there are secret strings in the Russian, unknown even to himself, which one needs but pluck for him to throb everywhere" (132–33/318).

In fact, it is Gogol's own, not the *gubernatorsha's*, activity that is the ultimate goal of all the information processing, and through a thin disguise we recognize Gogol's notorious pleas for material, indeed, for ready-made writer's sketches that would enable him to write about Russia: "For my sake, you must . . . begin an examination of your . . . town. . . . I need this" (125/311). She must refrain from any activity other than communicating with Gogol: "For the time being it is better not to hurry; do nothing, even if it seems to you that you can do something. . . . It is better meanwhile to observe closely . . . [and] transmit . . . to me; . . . without that I do not even understand how it is possible to give counsel" (126/312).

Only having accumulated complete knowledge would Gogol be able to articulate the magic word: "Then will I be able to tell you certain things, and you will see that much of what seemed impossible is possible. . . . Until that time I will say nothing, because I could make a mistake, and I would not want to do that. I would like to speak such words, as would strike the mark precisely" (127/313).

To this problem of his writing block Gogol, in an obvious echo of his failure to finish *Dead Souls*, returns again and again: "In the first place . . . , but . . . my words may be beside the point, it would be better not to pronounce them at all" (132/318). "I feel that I am beginning to speak of things which are perhaps not at all fitting to your town, . . . but the fault is yours, for you have not conveyed detailed information on anyone to me" (134/319). To overcome the block, toward the end of the letter he tries to work himself out of it by invoking his ability to prophesy the future through a scrutiny of the present. Then follows a sweeping dip into all the "abominations" (*merzosti*) of the present. Or, rather, the direction is both downward and upward, for the passage is a characteristic Gogolian excercise in masochistic yet lofty rhetoric, with the root *merz-* repeated thirteen times, five of them in the recurrent phrase *vsmatrivat'sia pobol'she vo vsiakie merzosti*, "to scrutinize as much as possible all kinds of abominations" (134/320)— an incantatory monotony worthy of Stalin.

Do not be troubled by abominations, serve every abomination up to me! I find nothing unusual in abomination: I have enough abomination of my own. So long as I was not myself sunk in abominations, each abomination troubled me . . . ; since then, I began to observe abomination more closely, my soul became more lucid. . . . And . . . I thank God for having honored me . . . with a knowledge of abomination. . . . And if I should succeed in helping . . . you, it is because I have observed my abominations more. And if I have finally acquired a love for people, . . . it is . . . for the same reason—that I have observed every kind of abomination more. So do not be intimidated by abomination and . . . disgusted by those people who seem . . . abominable (135/320–21).[28]

Cleansed from the "disgusting" depths, as well as by them, Gogol rises to spiritual clarity and concludes on what is meant as a hopeful note. This ending is emblematic of the entire enterprise of *Selected Passages*. Gogol still refrains from pronouncing the Last Judgment—in the same way as in *Dead Souls*, where he in fact ended by offering *Selected Passages* as a sort of interim report instead.

> Pending his attainment of omniscience and the magic Word, he commands his addressee to "reread the [present] letter five, six times. . . . The substance of my letter must remain totally within you; let my questions be your questions and my desire your desire, so that each word and letter may haunt you and torment you, so long as you have not fulfilled my petition exactly as I wish" (136/321).

One cannot fail to notice the sadistic streak that accompanies Gogol's exercise of his authorial power over his reader. But on the whole, the letter finally comes to formulate explicitly its metaliterary theme— writing writ large, *écriture* foregrounded, message perpetuated for message's self-referential sake.

Today, much of *Selected Passages*, including Letter 21, reads as hilariously funny. As in most of Gogol's texts, this results from the way the speaking voice subverts itself, allowing the reader to see around the speaker. That in *Selected Passages* the character-narrator who is preoccupied with writing but fails to control it is the author himself does not seem to spoil the reader's fun. To account for this response, only a subtle shift in the critical viewpoint is necessary—the one prompted by the figures of Koz'ma Prutkov and Palisander Dahlberg. All the miswritten book asks for is to be misread into place, and, I believe, the postmodern sensibility as well as Gogol's insistent pleas for help from readers suggest just that. Through the programmatic message of *Selected Passages*, so tearfully "visible to the world," we will then be able to bring into focus and appreciate the book's "invisible laughter."

TWO

Through Revolution's Looking Glass:
Tolstoy into Zoshchenko

At first glance, the juxtaposition of the two names may sound bizarre. In fact, Zoshchenko (1928: 8–11) was at pains to distance himself from the great forebear. Ridiculing the officially sanctioned order ("social command") for a "red Leo Tolstoy," something hopelessly dated from his point of view, "almost Karamzinian," Zoshchenko insisted on delivering literary production of a "bad," "petty," lowbrow, and "little respected" sort. But he also claimed that in this way he actually filled the bill as the only proletarian Leo Tolstoy possible—a parodic one.[1] The two could accordingly be yoked together by contrast, with Zoshchenko instantiating the formalist "canonization of a junior branch," but that would cast Tolstoy as a generic "senior," a role better fit by a figure like Turgenev, perhaps the most correct and uncontroversial among the nineteenth-century greats.[2] Yet there *is* a common feature that makes the juxtaposition of Zoshchenko with Tolstoy meaningful—defamiliarization.

Theater and Truth

The concept of defamiliarization was introduced by Shklovsky (1965a [1917]), whose master example was the episode of Natasha's perception of the opera.

> In the center of the stage sat some girls in red bodices and white shirts. One very fat girl in a white silk dress sat apart on a low bench, to the back of which a piece of green cardboard was glued. They all sang something. When they had finished their song the girl in white went up to the prompter's box. . . . [The] man with bare legs jumped very high and waved his feet about very rapidly. (He was Duport, who received sixty thousand rubles a year for this art). . . . After her life in the country, and in her present serious mood, all this seemed grotesque and amazing to Natasha. (Tolstoy 1966, 7, 9: 620–23)

Shklovsky was primarily interested in defamiliarization as an overall aesthetic strategy of creating "a special perception of the object . . . a 'vision' . . . instead of . . . 'recognition' " (1965a: 18–19), i.e. "a way of experiencing the artfulness of the object" (12). But he was also aware of its specifically Tolstoyan ideological potential, inherent in the refusal to take things for granted and the tendency to see them in an unpreconceived and therefore more perceptive way. Tolstoy later used similar techniques ("typical of [his] way of pricking the conscience," 13) in his attacks on the institutions of marriage ("The Kreutzer Sonata"), property ("Strider"), law and church (*Resurrection*), urban life, and others. In an anticipation of modern theories of discourse, Shklovsky stressed the heuristic power of art, claiming that such "perceptions had unsettled Tolstoy's faith" (18).

In fact, a closer look at the opera episode shows that it, too, is exploited for moralistic rather than purely aesthetic purposes. In the space of a short chapter, Tolstoy has Natasha make the transition from her "natural" failure to understand opera—first, to a reluctant acquiescence in the norms and ways of the world ("I suppose it has to be like this"; Tolstoy 1966: 620)[3] and then to their complete and joyous acceptance ("Natasha no longer thought this strange. She looked about with pleasure"; 624). Moreover, speaking in French, she agreed with Hélène that Duport was "delightful" (*admirable*, in French in the Russian text) in a sign of utter moral disorientation that foreshadows her stumbling into the snares of Anatole. Tolstoy's logic here is essentially the same as in the later and extremist "Kreutzer Sonata" (1889): "Why

is gambling forbidden while women in costumes which [are prosti-
tutelike and] evoke sensuality are not forbidden?" (chap. 9; see 1968b:
137). It is only a short step from speaking French and admiring opera
to moral fall.

What, then, is the target of this denunciatory rhetoric? According
to Lenin, Tolstoy's "tearing away of all masks" (see Tolstoy 1966: 1393)
and conventions[4] was undertaken in the name of the revolutionary
"genuine muzhik" ("And you know something? . . . You couldn't find
a genuine muzhik in literature until this Count came on the scene";
Gorky 1932: 51). In semiotic terms, this reads as a total rejection of
culture and symbolic systems.

> "For Tolstoy, desirable communication occurs when the sign matches exactly
> the 'thing,' or, ideally, when signs are altogether absent" (Pomorska 1982:
> 387). Tolstoy resented the more arbitrary signs—symbols and indexes—and
> partially accepted icons and ostensive signs, based respectively on similarity
> with and direct pointing to the signified object (ibid.: 385–88).

Conventions, much as they were reviled by Lenin and Tolstoy (and
Rousseau before them),[5] became a foundation of modern social science. The realization of the symbolic—and therefore inevitably conventional, that is, arbitrary—nature of language, art, and culture in
general started with the critique of the notion of the 'natural man' and
subsequently absorbed a variety of intellectual inputs: Nietzschean
relativization of cultural values, Saussurean concept of language as
a system, superstructure as a reflection of the base, and others. In
the twentieth century, the ongoing interrogation of the foundations of
culture coincided with the era of mass revolutionary movements and
relativistic revision of the entire philosophical and scientific picture of
the world.

In this historical context one is tempted to ask, When did Natasha
go to the opera? In the novel's fictional time, circa 1812, when the influence of the Enlightenment and Sentimentalism was still recent? Or
at the time of the writing, half a century later, in the period of social
ferment and questioning of traditional values, in particular of Pushkin's aristocratic aestheticism by such radical critics as Pisarev? Or
perhaps when the episode was at long last accorded a congenial reading (a "vision" rather than mere "recognition") in Shklovsky's 1917
article? In that case, Natasha's "grotesque" perception of the opera
can be said to have taken place in the revolutionary year 1917, that

is, soon after Lenin saw "The Living Corpse" (see note 4), not long
before he tried to close down the Bolshoi, and just at the time when
the theater was to be discovered by Mikhail Zoshchenko's characters,
who were "natural" to a fault.

In Zoshchenko's oeuvre, which has been aptly summarized as the
"encyclopedia of an 'un-culture'" (Shcheglov 1986b), theatergoing is
a recurrent theme.

> In fact, his famous "The Lady Aristocrat" (1963: 127–30) is about a theater
> outing: "There, in the theater, she unfurled her ideology to its full length" (127).
>
> In the no less famous "Bathhouse" (1963: 131–33) the theme would seem
> to be out of place but is brought up anyway, as a powerful negative metaphor:
> " 'This isn't the czarist regime, that you can go around bashing people with
> buckets. . . . This isn't a theater.' . . . 'We're not here to watch over the holes [in
> your tattered clothes]. This isn't a theater,' the attendant replied. . . . 'Citizens,
> I can't undress a third time. This isn't a theater. At least reimburse me for the
> soap.' They won't" (132–33).

In a word, theater connotes political reaction and tiresome, pro-
hibitively expensive conventions, among which is the dress code, enforced by the authorities on the poor natural man. Characteristically,
the leitmotif ("This isn't a theater") refers not to the theater per se, i.e.
the staged performance, but rather to the checkroom.

This is emblematic of the way theater is portrayed in the dozen or
so "theatrical stories" where the protagonist invariably displays what
Shcheglov describes as a shameful "inadequacy to cultural challenge"
(1986b: 61–63). The masterplot of these stories is as follows:

> Unwilling to pay, the spectators either fail to materialize or insist on having
> free passes; when they do buy tickets, they often try to get their money back.
>
> Financial problems begin at the box office, and more turmoil takes place at
> the crowded entrance to the hall, with doors being broken, clothes torn, and
> so on.
>
> Another hurdle is the checkroom, where the visitors must, but cannot—for
> lack of money or because of the shabby condition of their wardrobe—leave
> their coats.[6]
>
> Inside, their attention focuses on the toilet ("I wonder whether the water
> pipes work here," says the plumber protagonist of "The Lady Aristocrat" try-
> ing to make a conversation piece out of his professional interests) and the
> concession stand with its financial and gastronomic connotations.
>
> Even when seated, the characters keep being immersed in practical rather
> than aesthetic experiences:

—they mend their torn clothes, not noticing "what the picture is about";

—do athletic exercises to get warm, obstructing the view of others;

—"Go to Riga" (a street euphemism for vomiting);

—use theater as a way of staying on the wagon (while in fact they merely move their drinking to another night) or for dating "in the marriage sense."

Further obstacles to the proper reception of the performance can come from:

—the spectators, who misinterpret what they see (e.g., by assuming different performers to be the acts of one and the same quick-change artist and thus missing the actual content of the show);

—the stagehands, who are in the way of the production (e.g., a cocky electrician "refus[ing] to light your production" ["The Electrician," Zoshchenko 1961: 47–48]);

—the actors themselves (who rob a newcomer of his wallet "in the course of this here drama" ["The Actor," Zoshchenko 1961: 37–39]);

—or the narrator's focus, which just does not encompass the stage.

Only in three stories does information about the performance come across —in those narrated from the point of view of behind the stage. But it is precisely in these that "pure art" either sustains losses ("Theater for Oneself") or "reaches the masses in a somewhat strange form" ("An Incident in the Provinces"—with the quick-change artist), or succeeds only because stealing (always rampant in Zoshchenko's world) finds its way even onto the stage ("The Actor").

Despite obvious differences, this script resembles at some level Natasha's visit to the opera and can be seen as a parodic actualization, intentional or unintentional, of Tolstoy's ideas. Like the real lady-aristocrat, Countess Natasha Rostova, Zoshchenko's heroes arrive at the theater straight from the country, but unlike her—and Count Tolstoy himself—they *are* "genuine muzhiks." That is why their defamiliarization—shall we say, misprision?—of the theater is much more drastic. In Natasha's case, the unfamiliarity with the operatic conventions results in her registering indiscriminately the irrelevant aspects of the performance along with relevant ones—those that are skillfully ignored by the experienced, "cultured" spectator. But Zoshchenko's simpletons are foreign even to the rules of minimal decency that concern dress, hygiene, food, mutual respect, and public order. In a nutshell, if Natasha misses, on the stage, the performance for the props, Zoshchenko's characters miss the stage itself for the buffet and the coat check.

Some correspondences are striking. For instance, Tolstoy's sentence "They all sang something" is not only germane to the aesthetic deafness of Zoshchenko's heroes but literally recurs in his stories; for example, "Then one [woman] sang" (at a party, in the story "U pod"ezda" "At the Door"); "he sang something or other" (a drunk in "The Earthquake"). As for Tolstoy's aside about Duport's honoraria, it prefigures the endless financial reckonings around the box office in Zoshchenko's stories as well as his frequent narrative digressions about the reader's right to get his money's worth of storytelling. In fact, sometimes Tolstoy brings Natasha dangerously close to a Zoshchenko-like level of vulgar misunderstanding.

> During a reception at Hélène's, the famous French actress "Mademoiselle George looked sternly and gloomily at the audience and began reciting some French verses describing her guilty love for her son. In some places she raised her voice, in others she whispered . . . ; sometimes she paused and uttered hoarse sounds, rolling her eyes" (1966: 632). What's more, the naive mix-up of the actor with the role is here the responsibility of Tolstoy as narrator, rather than of Natasha, who, we are told, "looked at the fat actress, but neither saw nor heard nor understood anything" (632).

This device is a favorite with Zoshchenko's narrators.

> In quoting poetry, they will comically confuse the speaker with the poet himself and either "ignore the conventions of verse as some sort of noise that drowns out the message or take them literally. . . . Commenting on a poet's lines: 'I will build a new home / In her unknown heart,'[7] the narrator says: 'Sounds like the poet wants to move in with this lady'" (Shcheglov 1986b: 80).
>
> In the theatrical stories, since the content of the plays is largely ignored, there is not much room for this kind of confusion. The only example is "The Actor," where the "mistake" is committed not so much by the naive spectators or the amateur recruited on the spot from their midst (the narrator-protagonist playing the victim of robbery) but by seasoned actors who "lift his wallet for real"—in a comic variation on the 'mousetrap' motif, where the quoted play interacts with the offstage plot.

Property Versus Theft

In another major example cited by Shklovsky, "Strider: The Story of a Horse" (1856–85; see Tolstoy 1964: 377–418), Tolstoy defamiliarizes the institution of property. This time, the unconventional refusal to suspend disbelief is entrusted to so radically "natural" a creature as a horse.

I could not at all understand what they meant by speaking of *me* as being a man's property. . . . They like not so much to do or abstain from doing something, as to be able to apply conventional words to different objects. Such words, considered very important among them, are *my* and *mine*. . . . They have agreed that of any given thing only one person may use the word *mine*. . . . Many of those who called me their horse did not ride me, quite other people rode me; nor did they feed me—quite other people did that. . . . In this lies the essential difference between men and us. Therefore, . . . in the scale of living creatures we stand higher than man. (396–98)

The portrayal of humans through animal eyes often uses defamiliarizing means, but not necessarily to denunciatory ends, as the example of Chekhov's canine stories shows.

In "Kashtanka" (1887; see Chekhov 1959: 14–37), tears are perceived as "shining drops, such as one sees on the window pane when it rains" (30), and an elephant as "one fat, huge countenance with a tail instead of a nose and two long gnawed bones sticking out of his mouth" (32). Both images are very vivid but without an ideological ax to grind. Even the culmination scene, where the dog, recognizing her previous master, makes a spectacular exit from the circus arena, is surprisingly free of what could have been an effective defamiliarization of a crumbling convention.

In "Whitebrow" (1895; see Chekhov 1979: 128–32), Chekhov resorts to defamiliarization to portray drunkenness: "Sometimes he used to sing, and as he did so, staggered violently, and often fell down (the wolf thought the wind blew him over)" (129); the effect is again rather amusing than moralistic.[8]

On the whole, despite his focus on the breakdown of communication in the world of clichéd cultural postures (Shcheglov 1986a), Chekhov did not go in for the radical tearing off of masks or pin his hopes on the "natural" in man (see also note 12).

Not unlike Natasha's "resolution about the opera," Strider's "Communist Manifesto" of sorts also had an instructive postrevolutionary sequel. In Mikhail Bulgakov's *Heart of a Dog*, the dog-turned-man, Sharikov, commenting on the *Correspondence Between Engels and Kautsky*, has this suggestion: "Just take everything and divide it up" (89). The discussion between Sharikov and his Frankensteinian creator, Professor Preobrazhenskii, covers a wide ideological ground.

The Professor likes opera and professionalism in art: "I am an advocate of the division of labor. Let them sing at the Bolshoi, and I will operate. And there will be no ruin [*I nikakikh razrukh*]" (39). He commands handsome fees as a physician and most likely would have no quarrel with the price tag of Duport's leaps. He is annoyed by the amateur choruses of his Soviet neighbors and

Sharikov's balalaika playing, and one wonders how he would have reacted to Natasha's folk-song-and-dance act (of which Tolstoy makes such a big point).

For Sharikov's educational entertainment the Professor recommends if not opera then at least drama. Sharikov predictably prefers the circus. " 'Everyday the circus,' Philip Philipovich remarked benignly. . . . 'In your place, I would go to the theater for once.' —'I won't go to the theater,' Sharikov said peevishly. . . . 'Nothing but fooling around. . . . Talk, talk. . . . Counterrevolution, that's what it is' " (88). Thus Sharikov, too, associates theatrical conventions with reactionary values.

Discussing another convention, table manners, Sharikov echoes the Zoshchenko formula 'at the theater' = 'under czardom': " 'All those rules you keep to, always on parade. . . . Napkin here, tie there, and *pardon me*, and *please*, and *merci*—but for the real thing, it isn't there. Torturing your own selves, just like in Czarist times' " (87).

Bulgakov ridiculed the critique of the allegedly exploitative elitist culture waged by the populist-egalitarian ideologues on behalf of the "natural soil." He stacked his narrative deck accordingly: for the honest workaholic Strider, he substituted the lazy lout and drunkard Sharikov; for the parasitic libertine Prince Serpukhovskoi, the valuable specialist Doctor Preobrazhenskii. And as a programmatic solution of the conflict, he offered the counterrevolutionary second surgery, after which Sharik(ov) was to resume his proper place at his master's feet. (Sharikov's canine self is "a perfectly delightful dog" [102], akin to Kashtanka and Strider.)

Zoshchenko's position was more ambiguous. He also produced a "Strider" of sorts: "The Adventures of a Monkey" (1963: 316–24), famous for Zhdanov's vicious attack on it.

Zoshchenko . . . portrays Soviet people as idlers and monsters, primitive, stupid people . . . ; put[s] into the monkey's mouth a disgusting anti-Soviet sentence, in which he claims that life in the zoo is better than outside and that it is easier to breathe inside a cage than amongst Soviet people . . . ; [makes] the monkey the highest judge of our social life, and makes him preach a code of morals to the Soviet people. The monkey is portrayed as a . . . source of reason, which sets the standards of people's behavior. (Zhdanov 1978: 47–48)

Zhdanov's last item could as well be addressed to "Strider," since the major target of the story's barbs is the conventionality of property.

With his tail he couldn't go into a restaurant. . . . And besides, he had no money. No reduced rates. He didn't have any ration cards. . . . No, he wasn't going to stand in line. . . . He ran to the salesgirl right along the customers' heads. . . . He didn't ask how much a kilo of carrots cost. Just grabbed a whole bunch of carrots. . . .[9] And he ran along, chewing on his carrot, having breakfast. He didn't know what was going on. . . . The monkey grabbed Grandmother's piece of candy and crammed it into his mouth. Well, he was only a monkey. Not a human being. A human being, if he took something, wouldn't do it right under Grandmother's nose. But the monkey did it right in Grandmother's presence. (317–20)

Later on, the monkey himself becomes the object of litigation, which culminates in a sort of collective judgment of Solomon on the problem of ownership (323–24). To whom does the monkey belong? To the handicapped Gavrilych, who claims it as "my monkey, which I want to sell at the market tomorrow . . . my own monkey, which bit me on the finger"? To the driver who brought him to town in his car? Or to the little boy Alyosha, "who is holding him lovingly in his arms"? The public rules in favor of the latter. Thus, contrary to Zhdanov's accusations, Soviet society as portrayed by Zoshchenko realizes the "natural ideal" propounded by Marx ("Land belongs to those who till it") and Tolstoy (the horse should be called "mine" by those who feed, ride, and take care of him).

Moreover, in the epilogue, the monkey is reconciled with cultural conventions. "He doesn't run away anywhere. . . . He wipes his nose with a handkerchief. And doesn't take other people's candy," for Alyosha has "brought it up like a human being, and now he sets a good example for all children and even for some grownups" (p. 324). The outcome is no less idyllic than in Bulgakov and much more optimistic as to the acculturation of the "natural man."

But the difference does not end there. With whom does the author of "The Adventures of a Monkey" sympathize and identify? The sugary "conflictless" ending (this is, after all, a Soviet story for children from 1945) is preceded by rather ambiguous episodes. Zoshchenko is torn between simian "nature" and human "culture." In fact, the story varies the recurrent Zoshchenkovian quandary: barbarism and thievery are criticized from the perspective of an ideologically pure and nice "simple" character, whose simplicity, however, turns out to be part and parcel of the all-pervasive stealing. (There is a Russian proverb to the effect that "simplicity [i.e., stupidity] is worse than theft.") What makes this particular variation on the theme special is that in simian disguise, the "natural" character stands out more clearly from the context, while at the same time his anticultural behavior seems more excusable.

The theme of property's pernicious effects, shared with Tolstoy, underlies a large group of Zoshchenko's plots. Many of them are about the victims of greed: the newly rich who would rather swallow their gold than part with it; the émigrés who come to touch their expropriated possessions; and the rank-and-file Soviets who, as a result of hitting the lottery jackpot, go on a drinking binge, quarrel with their family, or otherwise show themselves unequal to the challenge of putting the unexpected treasure to sensible use.

In fact, the motif of 'failure to meet the challenge of culture' is crucial not only to the Tolstoy-Zoshchenko connection but to the problematic of the Russian Revolution as a whole. Tolstoy's rigorism and his dream of "going simple" (oproshchenie) were in accord with an influential trend of Russian liberal and populist thinking. One of the philosophers of the Russian spiritual renaissance, S. L. Frank, devoted his contribution in the 1909 Landmarks collection to a detailed analysis of what he termed the "nihilist ethic" of the Russian leftist intelligentsia. Frank (1977 [1909]) identified the pivotal contradiction of its mentality as deep-seated mistrust and fear of wealth in all its forms, coupled with the aspirations of leading the people from poverty to prosperity, that is, the maligned riches. By subsuming the various objects of hatred—financial, material, cultural, artistic, and spiritual—under one general heading, 'wealth,' Frank in effect pointed out the discursive, i.e., cultural, character of the problem (and thus, prophetically, of the future historical catastrophe). Zoshchenko's focus on the motif of 'cultural challenge' is one more demonstration of how attuned he was to the sensitive issues of his time.[10]

Irrespective of this wider intellectual context of the two writers' common anticapitalist moralism, Zoshchenko's similarities with Tolstoy (in particular with "The False Banknote" and such parables for children as "Equal Inheritance") are evident. Sometimes they are acknowledged openly. For instance, one of Zoshchenko's stories bears a pointedly Tolstoyan title "How Much Does One Need" (the hero rides the free merry-go-round until he literally loses consciousness).[11]

Incidentally, the original 1885 Tolstoy story is believed to have provoked Chekhov's polemical response in "Gooseberries" (1898; see Chekhov 1979: 185–94),[12] where the narrator, Ivan Ivanych, says: "They say man only needs six feet of earth. But it is a corpse, and not man, which needs these six feet. It is not six feet of earth, not a country-estate, that man needs, but the whole globe, the whole of nature, room to display his qualities and the individual character-istics of his free spirit" (188). This rejoinder agrees well with Chekhov's general stance, which was pro-culture and against "going simple." It also highlights in Tolstoy's ethical rigorism an embryonic form of withdrawal from 'culture's challenge.'

Leaving aside for the moment the many obvious differences be-tween Tolstoy and Zoshchenko, let us concentrate on their profound affinities in one more sphere—aesthetics.

"Good" Ideas—"Bad" Writing

The common interest in addressing adolescent or otherwise "simple" readers was an outgrowth of the programmatic search for a way of writing "accessible to the poor," i.e., to the people at large, and Tolstoy's direct influence on Zoshchenko in this respect is not ex-cluded.[13] Each in his way, but both in the general civic spirit of Russian literature, gradually moved away from conventional artistic forms and toward openly ideological writing. Tolstoy, who from the start had been obsessively searching for the meaning of life, underwent a reli-gious conversion and ended up renouncing his earlier masterpieces, thus following in a sense in the footsteps of Gogol (to whose *Selected Passages* he "gave . . . high marks" [Shklovsky 1978: 86]).

Zoshchenko traveled a similar route. From the tongue-in-cheek spoof of naive Soviet preaching in his comic stories of the 1920s and early 1930s, he moved to a more earnest—monologic and authorita-tive—discourse in his Socialist-Realist tales of the 1930s, on the one hand, and in his semifictional search for his inner self and its physi-cal and spiritual salvation in *Youth Regained* (1933) and *Before Sunrise* (1943), on the other.[14] It so happened that the latter led to its author's fall from official grace—in an ironic replay of Tolstoy's excommunica-tion from the church (and also of Gogol's ideological chastisement by Belinsky).

A transitional stage in this process was *The Sky-Blue Book* (1935), where Zoshchenko used his earlier parodic style to produce an ideo-logically correct but entertaining primer in the history of mankind.

Striving as he did at this time to live the master myth of the Russian Poet turned Citizen, Zoshchenko, however, wanted to be seen not as a purveyor of entertainment but as a Master Teacher. "The preacher in his book [*Before Sunrise*] took the upper hand over the artist,—a familiar fate of typically Russian talents beginning with Gogol and Tolstoy, who renounced the charms of art in the name of serving the people directly. . . . Zoshchenko belonged to this breed of writers" (Chukovskii 1981: 64).

Contemporaries testified to his grim seriousness; for instance, Ilf and Petrov have the following vignette in one of their stories: "He even takes offence, when they tell him that he again wrote something funny. One must now speak to him like this: 'Mikhail Mikhailovich, with your tragic talent, you are a real Grand Inquisitor'" ("Literaturnyi tramvai," 1961, 3: 175).

Already in his early period, Zoshchenko, or rather his literary mask, would often intersperse fictional narrative with mock-instructive disquisitions about art. They form a strange seriocomic sequel to Tolstoy's own pronouncements, in particular his critique of Shakespeare and Guy de Maupassant and his harshly doctrinaire dismissal of contemporary Western poetry in "What Is Art?"

Tolstoy's critical fervor seems to have had its roots in his pointed rejection elsewhere (e.g., in *War and Peace*) of all that smacked of "unnaturalness" and "amorality." The heuristic interrelation between ideology and style is especially relevant to the later writings of such authors as Gogol, Tolstoy, and Zoshchenko. It hinges on the problematic of boundaries between defamiliarization (*skaz*, unreliable narrative, etc.) and serious authorial philosophizing. A typical round of oscillations involves the writer's earlier purely aesthetic stage, a later ideological literalization of the technique, and as often as not, a posthumous aesthetic reinterpretation even of the most passionately ideological texts (like the one undertaken in Chapter 1).

In a remarkable twist, two decades after Tolstoy had denounced the decadent art of Baudelaire, Verlaine, and Mallarmé, Zoshchenko was to repeat the gesture. Switching from a juvenile imitation of the Russian progeny of the French symbolists (see Mikhail Zoshchenko and Vera Zoshchenko, 24–47), Zoshchenko came to a decisive break with the "high" aristocratic tradition. Soon after the Revolution he stated that the old intelligentsia-oriented literature was over, that it was meaningless to write for "readers who are not there" and "pile up verses about flowers," pretending that "nothing had happened in the country" (Zoshchenko 1940: 334–36). This primitivist anticultural stance, which can be seen as an extension of Tolstoy's, was not a mere product of adaptation to the new reality by a writer of gentry origin and high artistic sophistication. It ran deep in Zoshchenko's psyche, connected as it was with his search for primordial health and simplicity (an echo of the Tolstoyan return to the soil), and thus endured throughout his life and works, including the quite un-Soviet *Before Sunrise*.

This proximity of aesthetic views may account for the similarities between Zoshchenko's notoriously "poor language" and certain tendencies of Tolstoy's style. As noted by Shklovsky (in an article about Zoshchenko!—see 1976 [1928]: 409–10):

> "Tolstoy's language is not neutral," resulting from defamiliarization proper, "the alternation between French and Russian," and the calquelike "projecting of forms from one language into the sphere of the other for the reader." For example, " 'You are a scoundrel and a blackguard, and I don't know what deprives me from the pleasure of smashing your head with this!' said Pierre, expressing himself so artificially because he was talking French" (Tolstoy 1966: 656). Shklovsky points out that "the translation belongs to Tolstoy," who thus "resorts to *skaz* without motivation," i.e., rather than "forcing Pierre to speak clumsily in Russian," does so himself.[15]

Such studied linguistic incompetence is akin to defamiliarization. Exponents of the "natural" outlook (Natasha, Pierre, Strider, Tolstoy's fictional narrators, and his nonfictional preaching self) struggle with the multilayered shell of conventions, rules, and other manifestations of the hated *comme il faut*, trying to get through to the simple, fundamental, unconventional Truth. This results in "non-neutral," awkward, poor, but "true" discourse, groping for the real essence of things and not ashamed of its own aesthetic uncouthness.

This aspect of Tolstoy's style was noted and even parodied by his contemporaries.[16] The parodies, taking off on Tolstoy's openly didactic texts as well as the publicistic passages in such later works as *Resurrection*, help to bring out less jarring but essentially similar stylistic tendencies in other texts. For example: " ' "Obviously he knows something that I don't," I said to myself, thinking of the colonel. "If I knew what he knows, I would understand what I saw and it wouldn't torment me." But however much I thought, I couldn't understand what the colonel knew . . ." ' and so on and so forth." ("After the Ball"; see Richards 1981: 239–50, 249). The lack of verbal skills in the narrator-hero, who tells about his spiritual quest in a manner that at times resembles that of Gogol's Akakii, is supposed to certify the genuine and uncompromising nature of that quest, just as Natasha's perplexity at the opera is evidence of her moral integrity.

Tolstoy was evidently quite deliberate about writing "badly." "Gorky . . . said to Erdman about Tolstoy: 'You think his awkwardness came easy to him? He knew very well how to write. He would scratch out [peremaryval] nine times—and on the tenth it would come out really awkward" (L. Ginzburg 1989: 11–12).

Zoshchenko's narrator can be said to have adopted and further "simplified" this style (his sentences are even shorter, as in fact are Tolstoy's when he writes for peasant children). Among the manifold uses to which he put it, a major one was to mark a rupture with the self-assured diction of traditional "great literature," associated with the names of Bunin, Turgenev, Karamzin, and Tolstoy in his "monumental" role.[17] Less authoritative still is the speech of Zoshchenko's characters, for example, "Ia vykhozhu za Nikolaia, eta za togo, a eti tak" (i.e., literally, "I am marrying Nikolai, this one here [marries] that one, and these [will stay] like this [unmarried]"; "An Amusing Adventure" [1935], Zoshchenko 1963: 218–28). This below-zero-degree writing forms the linguistically "virgin" soil from which grows the discourse of the implied author—"the red Leo Tolstoy."

Cultural Roles

The parallels between the two writers are many, including some interesting biographical coincidences.

> Both Tolstoy and Zoshchenko were brave, battle-seasoned officers. Both were on the verge of dueling with a fellow writer (Tolstoy with I. Turgenev, Zoshchenko with V. Kaverin; see Kaverin 1981: 98–101). Both pondered and wrote about existential issues, connecting them with nutritional ones (cf. Tolstoy's vegetarianism and Zoshchenko's—terminal—anorexia, which is even more reminiscent of Gogol).

Rather than continuing with the list of biographical and literary similarities, let us try to pin down the underlying connection. In Tolstoy, the comparison brings out his fundamentalist anticulturalism, featuring him as a prophet of the coming revolution, spokesman of the radicalized peasantry, forerunner of ideological Scythianism and of the actual barbarity that was soon to break loose in the country.

Even terrorism was not totally alien to Tolstoy, which should not come as a surprise if one draws the conclusions implicit in his praise of "the cudgel of the people's war" as opposed to the rules (!) of fencing in *War and Peace* (1966: 1147).

According to Korolenko (1978: 244–46), Tolstoy "half-approved of the terrorist assassinations" in the early 1900s. "When they told him . . . about the latest attempt, . . . he made an impatient gesture and said with annoyance: 'And, I am sure, he missed again. . . . I can't help saying: this is reasonable. . . . The muzhik is fighting directly for what is more important for him.' . . . Tolstoy argued . . . as a maximalist. It is fair and moral that land should belong to the toilers, . . . and by what means—was for Tolstoy (a non-resister who even denied the right to physical self-defense!) irrelevant."

In his "Thou Shalt Not Kill" (1900), Tolstoy explained (if not approved outright) terrorist assassinations as a natural response to the much more cruel and unjust violence by the powers that be. The mistrust of due process, Western-style, is evidenced as early as in the ironic portrayal of Speransky and his reforms in *War and Peace* (and later on in a similar picture of the gentry elections in *Anna Karenina*).

But the earliest manifestation of this attitude was, of course, the refusal to come to terms with the rules of *comme il faut*, as reflected in the autobiographical trilogy. Of special interest here is the evolution of the image of ballroom gloves from *Childhood* (1852, chap. 21) and *Youth* (1857, chap. 31) to "After the Ball" (1903). In particular, the episode with the torn glove in *Childhood* has a parallel in the chapter "Was It Worth the Hanging" of Zoshchenko's *Before Sunrise*. There the protagonist, a prerevolutionary student, is "getting ready to go to a dance. . . . He didn't feel like washing his hands. He was in a hurry. He stuck his fingers in a box of face powder and whitened the dirt under his nails"—a curious blend of the Pushkin-Rousseau portrait of Grimm (see note 5) with Zoshchenko's postrevolutionary types who try to keep washing to a minimum, as, for instance, in "The Operation": the protagonist, coming in for eye surgery, says: "I have changed the shirt, that yes, but the rest I haven't really touched," as "the disease is, so to speak, an eye one, a top one," so that "the socks . . . are really uninteresting, not to say worse."

And in the aesthetic realm, Tolstoy can be seen as a precursor of the primitively didactic Socialist Realism.

Zoshchenko (along with Bulgakov, Babel, Platonov, and others), having entered literature after the Revolution, had to reap the bitter cultural fruits of the utopia come true. He proceeded to satirize the monstrous realizations of the ideals that go back to Tolstoy among others: the barbarity and primitivism thinly veiled by the well-meaning "sympathy for hurricane [i.e., revolutionary] ideas." Zoshchenko's theatergoers were a grotesque caricature of Natasha at the opera, while the writer's own literary persona offered a travesty of the Tolstoyan aesthetics of populist "natural simplicity." Ironically, such artistic posturing resulted in Zoshchenko's assuming the Tolstoyan role as critic of the established—Soviet—culture. This did not pass unnoticed, his tongue-in-cheek style notwithstanding, and like Tolstoy, Zoshchenko became a symbol of dissident martyrdom.

The above assessment of Tolstoy's role, almost indicting Tolstoy as a proto-Bolshevik, is, of course, a rhetorical oversimplification.[18] In the sphere of ideology, Tolstoy's position did not boil down to the "anticonventionality complex." His ethical maximalism was tempered by his Christian message of nonviolence, which so clearly opposed him to Bolshevism (making Lenin expose his "glaring contradictions," Tolstoy 1966: 1392). Even his rejection of the dominant culture, which in light of subsequent history proved destructive, was quite understandable, especially given the incurable parasitism of the prerevolutionary establishment.

In the literary sphere, Tolstoy was part of the complex process of art's democratization and relativization. Thematically, his anticultural stance was cognate to the general tendency to give the floor to the underdog: the "little man," serf, horse, dog, insect. In prose, this is evident in the work of Gogol, Turgenev (*A Sportsman's Sketches*, "Mumu"), Dostoevsky (see especially Raskol'nikov's identification with the victimized horse in his dream), Leskov (notably his folksy *skaz* narrators), Kuprin ("Emerald," a horse story), Chekhov (in addition to the two cited canine stories, see "Heartburn," where the little man's only interlocutor is his horse). In poetry, Nekrasov's peasant muse was followed by the canine and equine lyrics of Esenin and Mayakovsky and the prominence of entomological motifs in the works of Mandelstam and the Oberiu.[19]

A further move away from the traditional anthropocentrism led to the granting to inanimate nature and artifacts of equal artistic rights with man in the poetics of Pasternak (who inherited this principle from, among others, Tolstoy, in particular from his "Three Deaths"). Pasternak's was, so to speak, a benign version of the man-demoting tendency, whose other variant was the subordination of man to machine in the mythology of Futurism, Constructivism, and eventually Socialist Realism.

In the post-socialist-realist poetic of Aksyonov, a further step was taken: the cast iron of the production novel was both demythologized—demoted into pathetic wooden refuse ("the surplus tare of barrels" of the eponymous 1968 novella)—and mock-remythologized into something cozy, close to nature (wood) and the people, something not unlike the Pasternakian boat, whose row locks are confused with lovers' clavicles ("Oars at Rest").

This entire surrealist strand in Russian literature, like many others, goes back to Gogol. Gogol managed to combine in a very unsettling way a sympathy for the little man, oppressed by both his superiors and the absurd surrounding trifles, with an aesthetic promotion of those trifles. Ideologically he was, so to speak, "for" Akakii Akakievich and "against" the Important Personage and the overcoat, but stylistically he was "for" the overcoat, the shoe, the nose, and "against" the underdog.

Ideological reforms led to changes in the sphere of discourse: the demise of the authoritative authorial voice and the modernistic rise to power of the characters' incompetent and uncouth speech. This was especially pronounced in the "strange" prose of Gogol, Dostoevsky, Leskov, Rozanov, Remizov, Babel, Zoshchenko, and Platonov, and in the poetically "low road" taken by Koz'ma Prutkov, Blok (as the author of "The Twelve"), Khlebnikov, Mayakovsky, Pasternak (inasmuch as the pointed "ordinariness" of his diction was concerned), the early Zabolotskii and the Oberiu poets, and finally such contemporary figures as Limonov and Prigov. The Tolstoy-Zoshchenko connection formed an integral part of this stylistic revolution.

Similar processes went on in the other arts as well, notably in the theater, where the presence of conventions was noticed, questioned, and played with. This began with Stanislavsky in the name of greater realism, i.e. naturalistic verisimilitude, but soon gained momentum under the banner of modernist expressionism in the work of Meyerhold, Vakhtangov, and their Western counterparts such as Max Reinhard and Gordon Craig. The parallel with Tolstoy's insistence on naturalness and truth ushering in avant-gardist "bad writing" suggests itself, and a coincidental but telling detail provides an additional link: according to Stanislavsky's famous motto, the overhauled theater was to begin emblematically at the coat check, and that was where it ironically began and ended for Zoshchenko's heroes.

On a more serious note, Stanislavsky abolished the conventional frontal staging (where the actors faced the audience most of the time), introducing instead the concept of the "fourth wall." This transparent wall was to be imagined as coinciding with the boundary of the stage, and the characters could well turn their backs on it and the audience, as in "real life." In fact, however, the invisible zero-signifier fourth wall was a powerful new modernistic convention. It was very much in the minimalist spirit of the time that was to see a subversion of all temporal, spatial, and other theatrical oppositions (stage acting versus putting on of costumes and make-up, change of sets, intermission; actor versus role; sets versus vacant stage).

Thus Tolstoy's Natasha, like Lion Feuchtwanger's "wise fool," Jean-Jacques Rousseau,[20] proved to be an unwitting prophet of the revolution in the arts. And Zoshchenko's actor, robbed "for real" in the course of the play, became a comic forerunner of the speaker of Pasternak's "Hamlet," who combines quite explicitly the personalities of the actor, the role (Hamlet), the imitated model (Christ), and implicitly those of the fictional poet (Yurii Zhivago) and the actual author (Boris Pasternak).

Tolstoy's "anticultural" stance secured him a privileged position in this process by channeling his negative energy into the interrogation of the very foundations of signification and verbal art. It is at such fundamental levels that great artistic discoveries are possible, so that in a sense we owe the entire set of Tolstoyan literary techniques involving defamiliarization and incompetent discourse to the writer's utopian search for an ideally direct and honest expression of the Truth—the search that eventually led him to abandon *belles lettres*.

The paradox of ideological pathos bearing purely aesthetic fruits is neither spurious nor superficial. In fact, it is one of the general laws of the evolution of sign systems—for instance, languages—where full-meaning lexemes routinely become grammaticalized over long enough time spans. In Tolstoy's case, it is remarkable that his defamiliarizing strategies should have been done explicit justice by none other than a founder of the Formalist school, which concentrated on studying the literariness of literature, inaugurating a new round of art-for-art's-sake sensibility.

Yet the Formalist movement was flesh of the flesh of that same cultural upheaval that resulted from the advent on the historical scene of a new, "plebeian" generation of thinkers, scholars, and writers. For them, the obsolescence, and thus relativity, of traditional values and conventions was obvious, and it enabled them to notice the deconstructive tendencies in the authors of the past as well as in their own contemporaries. In fact, the entire Formalist view of the literary process was patterned on the dialectical model of class struggle, thus offering a curious amalgam of revolutionary drive with a zealous defense of art's autonomy. In a broader sense, the paradigm of new—plebeian—influx into the world of culture included also the Formalists' opponent Mikhail Bakhtin, whose valorization of "the alien word" has been read (Gasparov 1984b) as a strategy for mastering the traditional culture.

Zoshchenko was one of those who came to claim Tolstoy's negative legacy, its "minimalist" wealth and aesthetic of ugliness. Belonging to an advanced stage of the twentieth-century artistic revolution as well as to the post-October period of Russian history, his work represented an ambiguously conservative reaction to the social-cultural upheaval that had just taken place. This attitude determined his "alienness" to mainstream Soviet culture and sealed his fate. But as with Tolstoy, the matter was not that simple.

Zoshchenko's view of the new culture and that imaginary proletarian writer whom he "replaced" was not defined by irony pure and simple. Zoshchenko had gone through an early infatuation with Nietzscheanism and had been impressed by Blok's attempts at infusing high literature with elements of barbarity, but at the same time he was wary of such relativistic experimentation.

Zoshchenko's ambivalence vis-à-vis Blok was already evident in his early paper on "The Scythians" and "The Twelve," given at Chukovskii's workshop (in 1919). The paper was written, according to Chukovskii, from the point of view and in "the style of the [fictitious] vulgarian Vovka Chuchelov." Commenting on this episode, Chudakova (1979: 17–33) also quotes Zoshchenko's notes on various writers partial to the word-motif *narochno*, "deliberately, as make-believe, for fun"; for example, on Mayakovsky: "Is he a Futurist or is it make-believe [*narochno*]?" (21). This underscores Zoshchenko's keen interest in the problematic of disguising one's own identity, so central to art in general and to Zoshchenko's *skaz* in particular.

In a remarkable parallel, Shcheglov (1986b: 79–80) identifies the *narochno* gesture as a recurrent motif in Zoshchenko's prose; for instance: "The way he's walking! Just watch, folks, how he is deliberately [*narochno*] placing his feet!" (about the quick-change artist in the "Incident in the Provinces," discussed above). Shcheglov concludes that "the examples with '*narochno*' demonstrate that Zoshchenko's character, looking at art with the fresh eyes of a savage . . . , displays a sharpened sensitivity to any kind of artistic phenomena in surrounding life," as well as in art. Taking this observation a little further, we could say that the 'narochno' response is nothing but a special kind of defamiliarization, namely, enthusiastic instead of denunciatory.

Trying to thread his way between Soviet primitivism and the "highbrow" tradition, Zoshchenko cut a controversial and suspicious figure. His attempts (especially in the 1930s) to carve out a niche in the official Soviet literature were not purely opportunistic: there was in his voice a note of genuinely primitivist renunciation of the "cursed prerevolutionary past" in favor of new "simple values." But it was not the only or even dominant one. Even in his dyed-in-the-wool Soviet texts one could always discern an unorthodox playfulness that prevented his voice from merging harmoniously with the official chorus. The inseparable fusion of these two opposite attitudes in his literary mask (and even in his nonfiction and letters) is probably what makes his artistic contribution so valuable.

In historical reality, however, the cultural projects of the two writers were less fruitful than in the literary sphere. Both Tolstoy's "cavalry raid"[21] on the laws of culture and signification and Zoshchenko's ambivalent masquerading as a "red Tolstoy" were to suffer ironic defeats. It may be said that as Bulgakov's "perfectly delightful dog" turned into "such filthy scum that your hair stands on end to think of it" (Bulgakov 1968: 102–3), he started imposing his tastes on art. Then the "truth-seeking" incompetence of Tolstoyan discourse became ossified into Stalin's authoritative tautologies; Strider's theorizing found its reification in Commander Budennyi's criticism of Babel's *Red Cavalry* "from the level of the horse" (Gorky); and Zoshchenko's house super (*upravdom*)—the author of illiterate mock-Dostoevskian "Pushkin Speeches" (Zoshchenko 1963: 273–78, spoofing the official cult of Pushkin in the 1930s, especially in connection with his 1937 centennial)—appointed himself the arbiter of Soviet arts and took upon himself the reeducation of Zoshchenko, Akhmatova, Shostakovich, and others. In a word, the "proletarian writer who did not exist" was to emerge from Zoshchenko's parodistic test tube, gain control of the literary process, and start leaning on his creator.[22]

But the irony did not stop there. When the new art seemed to have actualized the primitive-didactic Tolstoyan precepts, it was to discover that it could not, and would not, dispose once and for all of formal conventions. The essential impossibility of transcending culture came to haunt the projects for its abolition as Socialist Realism was born from the ashes of previous schools resplendent with a neoclassicist ritualism (Siniavsky-Terts 1982 [1959]; Clark 1981). One of the more conservative and rigidly formalized of Soviet arts has been that of the Bolshoi Opera and Ballet, an ironically conservative symbol of Soviet "progressiveness." Another was the martial art of revolutionary (and therefore always just) war, where utmost cruelty is combined with the imperial pageantry of military parades in the style of Paul I, oppressive hierarchy of ranks, Prussian goose step, and, last but not least, the obligatory gloves, which had been repeatedly disparaged by Tolstoy.[23]

Two sets of conclusions are in order: metatheoretical and metacultural.

The Tolstoy-Zoshchenko connection instantiates intertextual relations between oeuvres rather than between specific motifs or texts. Hence a survey of Zoshchenkovian parallels to both Natasha and Strider as well as to Tolstoy's aesthetic views and stylistic preferences. The link between the two anticultural strategies, although not claimed here to have been a direct relay or a conscious response, *was* mediated by a critic, Shklovsky, whose own theoretical discovery of defamiliarization may have been influenced by the atmosphere of cultural upheaval at the time of his and Zoshchenko's work. The surrounding cultural context involved, at a closer or more distant range, such diverse figures as Rousseau, Pisarev, Lenin, M. Bulgakov, S. Frank, Stanislavsky, Meyerhold, Zhdanov. Also, Tolstoy's relevance to what can be called the "cacographic" strand in Russian literature, to *skaz*, polyphony, and other important aspects of the literary tradition, has been invoked.[24] Another such counterpart that should be mentioned is minimalism: the apophatic, as well as suprematist, aesthetic of 'nothingness' (see Bowlt 1988), which in a sense completed the round of cleaning the cultural slate begun by Tolstoy. Finally, if there is one general principle behind the entire picture, it is the ironic interplay of Tolstoy's very Russian, realistic, religious-ideological intentions with the rather universal aesthetic, modernist-formalist results they were to bring about.

With all due reservations, one would have to agree that Tolstoy-style anticultural fundamentalism has not been constructive, at least not in the Russian context so far. To paraphrase Lenin, Russia suffers not so much from culture as from its underdevelopment.[25] In this connection, Pushkin's view of the "senseless and ruthless Russian rebellion" (1983: 347) and his defense of the beauty of polished nails seem preferable to Tolstoy's worship of the "cudgel of the people's war" and denunciation of a war waged according to the rules of fencing, gloves, and other "fruits of enlightenment." Granted, in other times and places such a radical deconstruction of culture may prove more productive.

Art, by definition, is one of those "other" chronotopes. There (and only there, as seems to be the Russian way with innovation) the experiments of the two cultural abolitionists have been vindicated. As a result, from our safe distance we can now delight in the subtle interplay of the two mirrors: Tolstoy's, which reflected the oncoming revolution and was in turn to be refracted in Zoshchenko's, whose warpedness strove to reflect adequately the fun-house wonderland behind the October looking glass.

PART II

Structures and Variations

Before and After "After the Ball": Variations on the Theme of Courtship, Corpses, and Culture

Leo Tolstoy, 1903

Although Tolstoy's story derives its title from what happened "after the ball,"[1] it consists of two episodes. The first, "at the ball," is the longer one, but functionally it serves as a foil to the second ("From that one night, or rather that one morning onwards my whole life changed"). This bipartition was reflected in the draft title, "the story about a ball and through the gauntlet" (1928–58, 34: 552), and is crucial to the structure we will explore in this chapter.

BEFORE

At the ball, the narrator-protagonist, Ivan Vasil'evich, an average young aristocrat of the 1840s ("In our university at that time there were no philosophical circles and no theories, we were simply young"), dances and falls more and more in love with Varen'ka. The 'rules,

or laws,' of the ball are repeatedly stressed. The hero fails to 'legitimately' secure the mazurka with his beloved ("According to the rules
[*po zakonu*, lit. "the law"] . . . I didn't dance the mazurka with her"),
because a rival has beaten him to her while he was busy outfitting
himself with gloves. Another rule concerns the choice of partner by
guessing his or her emblem, or "quality" (*kachestvo*). Such appurtenances of ballroom etiquette as the girl's glove and fan become the
souvenir symbols of the heroes' highly 'cultural' love.

> The motif of 'gloves' appears already in Tolstoy's *Childhood* (1852), in chap-
> ter 21, "Before the Mazurka" (!), where the young Nikolen'ka lacks the ap-
> propriate kid gloves, is publicly shamed by his grandmother for the old torn
> glove he intends to wear dancing, but eventually befriends the charming
> Sonechka and is accepted by the ballroom company. In the subsequent chap-
> ters, "Mazurka" and "After the Mazurka" (!), the 'glove' theme continues, and
> there also appear the motifs of guessing the dancing partner's "quality," blind
> infatuation, and the heroine's being driven away in a carriage. Striking par-
> allels also abound in the unfinished story "A Christmas Eve" ("Sviatochnaia
> noch'," 1853, 3: 241–65; see Zhdanov 1971: 100): the young hero is at a ball
> and in love with a beauty, dances a mazurka with her as if in a dream, keeps
> a similar souvenir, and is initiated into adult company.

The 'glove' and its 'legalistic' connotations, are further reinforced
as Varen'ka's father prepares to dance with her: "He . . . took his
sword out of its sheath and handed it to an obliging young man. . . .
Then, pulling a suede glove onto his right hand, he said with a smile,
'Everything according to the rules [*po zakony*, lit. "law"].' "
    The cultural symbolism of the provincial ball goes even further and
higher up: from 'legal' to 'regal.' The hostess, the wife of the marshal
of the province, resembles the pictures of Empress Elizaveta Petrovna;
the girl's father is a Nicholas I look-alike. "He had . . . a white upswept
moustache à la Nicholas I . . . [and] the highly disciplined manner of
an old campaigner under Nicholas [*nikolaevskoi vypravki*]." His tallness
and military bearing are echoed by Varen'ka's "majestic" stature (the
epithet was several times omitted and restored in the drafts [Zhdanov
1971: 101]), and her "regal look[, which] . . . would have frightened
people away from her, had it not been for the tender . . . smile on her
lips and in her brilliant, captivating eyes."
    This "had it not been for" is very characteristic. The cultural at-
mosphere of the ball is pronouncedly 'benign.' Everybody admires
Varen'ka and her father, while the father and others smilingly ap-

prove of the heroes' mutual attraction. The 'imperial' hostess is emblematized by the bare shoulders (lit. "shoulders and bosom") of the fun-loving eighteenth-century czarina. The heroes mostly dance together, and even when dancing with others smile only at each other. Moreover, the 'rules' themselves are sometimes bent for their benefit ("She would come boldly forward across the whole length of the room straight to me, and I would jump up without waiting for an invitation") and sometimes downright violated: after dancing with his daughter, the colonel leads her up to the narrator and insists he should dance with her, although "I said I was not her partner."

The couple's love in the cultural lap of benevolent society expands to encompass the whole world. First, the protagonist's love and adoration of Varen'ka envelop the father, who is linked to her both by similarity in looks, especially the smile ("The same tender, merry smile as radiated from his daughter sparkled in his eyes and on his lips"), and by contiguity as they dance together ("I couldn't help uniting the two of them in a single overwhelming feeling of affection"). They are evidently one of those Tolstoy families sharing physical and psychological features; one of the draft titles was "Daughter and Father" (34: 550).[2] The good feeling spreads to include others, among them the protagonist's rival: "I loved the hostess with her . . . Elizabethan neckline, and her husband, and her guests, and her servants, and even Anisimov, the engineer, who was sulking because of me. . . . I embraced the whole world with my love. . . . Even though I seemed to be infinitely happy, my happiness continued to grow."[3]

This excess of love's quantity is, of course, a hubristic flaw of the protagonist. Another is the quality of his love—perfectly ideal and "unearthly": "I was not only cheerful and contented, I was happy, I was blissful, I was good, I was not myself, but some otherworldly being, ignorant of evil and capable only of good." His passion is pointedly incorporeal as he thinks away his own and his beloved's bodies:

"I waltzed with her over and over again and could not feel my body." "What do you mean? . . . When you put your arms around her waist I think you must have felt a lot, not only your own body, but hers too," said one of the guests. . . . "The more passionately I was in love, the less physical [*bestelesnee*, lit. "the more bodiless"] she became for me. Today you . . . undress the women you love, for me, though, . . . the object of my love was always clad in bronze [*bronzovye odezhdy*, lit. "bronze garments"]. Far from undressing, we strove, like the good son of Noah, to cover up their nakedness."[4]

The "bronze garments" not only symbolize the hero's 'platonism' but also reflect his willing and total acceptance of conventions, in a metaphoric epitome of all the kid and suede gloves, Varen'ka's satin shoes, the father's touchingly cheap calfskin boots, and so on (in fact, the association of man's identity with the cut of his boots already preoccupied the protagonist of *Youth* [chap. 31, "Comme il faut"]). The function of these and other items of clothing is precisely to "cover up the nudity," blinding man to the starkly naked unconventional Truth. An additional comment on this "cover-up" is inherent in the Noah metaphor, which invokes once again the Varen'ka-colonel affinity, stressing the fixation on the father figure and the institutions it represents.

AFTER

With all this hubris stacked against him, the hero is rightly "afraid . . . that something might spoil [his] happiness" (245). The mechanism of excess prevents him from sleep, drives him outdoors and to his beloved's house, and makes him witness the ugly gauntlet-running supervised by the colonel.[5] The scene, which makes the hero fall out of love and change spiritually (abandoning any socially meaningful career), forms a negative replica of the ballroom episode. (The photographic metaphor is all the more justified as the heroine's white dress and other 'white' motifs give way to black uniforms.) This too is a conventional social gathering, in fact a law-enforcing procedure (punishment of a deserter) that takes the form of a specially arranged sequence of movements to music—in a musical counterpoint deliberately played up by Tolstoy. Approaching Varen'ka's house, the hero heard "the sound of pipe and drum. My heart still sang, and now and again I could still hear the tune of the mazurka. But this was some other kind of music, cruel and harsh [*nekhoroshaia*, lit. "not good"]."

The similarity of the two episodes is enhanced by the presence of both the hero (with his first-person account) and the colonel. The narrative dwells upon the colonel's familiar appearance and the "suede-gloved hand" with which he now hits a weakling soldier on the face for failing to flog properly. Another plot rhyme links Varen'ka and the flogged Tatar, who are the centers of attention (of the narrator as well as all present) in the two scenes; and like Varen'ka, the Tatar is led up to the hero by the colonel as the danse macabre approaches.

The common features of the two scenes now display their ominous underside: the music is *nekhoroshaia*, "not good"; deviations from the 'law' are no longer tolerated but severely punished (both in the case of the deserter and in that of the weak flogger); the colonel's upright bearing and gloves now express arrogant cruelty; the smile is gone from his ruddy face; on seeing the hero, he "pretended he didn't know" him. The most striking reversal involves the motif of '(in)corporeality.' While the body of the beautiful Varen'ka remained covered and ignored, the Tatar's frightful body is half naked from the start ("something terrible coming towards me . . . a man stripped to the waist"). The "jerking body" rivets the narrator's attention, and an epiphany takes place—characteristically, despite the hero's reluctance to see and believe, and therefore in a defamiliarized manner: "Once the column had passed where I was standing I caught a glimpse . . . of the prisoner's back. It was something so motley, wet, red, and unreal, I could not believe it was the body of a man" (248). To make the reversal complete, the hero now gets to "feel" not only the other's body but his own as well, getting nauseous to the point of vomiting: "My heart had become so full with an almost physical anguish, that . . . it seemed as if my stomach were about to heave and purge itself of all the horror" (249).

Thus, exposure to crude reality laid bare undoes the disembodied, conventional, societal love, which fails to deliver on its promise to embrace the whole world, including its dark side. But the story is a soft sell: the narrator suspends general judgment about good and evil ("Well, do you think I decided there and then that what I had seen was evil? Not at all"), making only a personal choice and somewhat naively conceding that the colonel might know something that would justify the cruelty.[6]

The hero's spiritual conversion has distinctly Tolstoyan overtones, relevant to the problematic of the 'body.' The ball is given "on the last day of Shrovetide"; consequently, the flogging falls on the first day of Lent. This timing, geared to significant dates of the Christian and pre-Christian calendar, highlights the ritualistic aspects of the story— not unlike "A Christmas Eve," which explicitly plays with the genre of the Christmas tale. For Tolstoy, the Shrovetide ball connotes false merriment and denial of corporeality by an "unearthly" hero. The only 'sensuous' presence at the ball is the hostess, her "plump elderly [lit. "old"] white shoulders and bosom bare." Thus, the sexual aspect of societal rituals seems to be deemphasized here—not as in, say, "The Kreutzer Sonata." Accordingly, the revelation of 'carnal knowledge' through the body of the punished soldier that takes place in the time of Lent—i.e. of mortification of flesh and, more generally, of the passions of Christ—is distinctly uncarnivalesque (in the Bakhtinian sense) and piously Christian.

The flogged man kept uttering some words, which the hero made out only when the gauntlet party came closer: "Have mercy, brothers."[7] Also, a bystanding blacksmith said: "Oh, Lord," and it was for 'merciful hitting' that the colonel brutally attacked a soldier. (The "puny" soldier "patted" the victim [mazal], unlike the other "brothers [, who] had no mercy," but whether he did so deliberately remains unclear.) Thus, in a replay of Calvary, the colonel reconfirms his 'imperial' (Caesar's = Nicholas I's) stance, as opposed to the 'godliness' of the tortured Christ-like body and the compassion shown by the weakling soldier, the blacksmith, and the narrator. Moreover, since in this configuration the Tatar functions as Varen'ka's counterpart, the scene can be said to emblematize the replacement of societal love with love for a suffering Christ.

> In the drafts, Tolstoy tried to individualize the flogged man but ended up presenting him as a generic "man stripped to the waist" (Zhdanov 1971: 104–5), in accordance with the universality of the *ecce homo* theme. Tolstoy's emphasis on the 'natural (i.e., anticultural) nakedness' of the flogged body should not be taken at face value: although physically bared, semiotically it is clothed in cultural garb—that of the Christian myth. Like Pierre, Tolstoy (and his narrator in the story) seems doomed forever to rend the "bronze garments" of convention after convention only to take every subsequent painted *matreshka* doll for an absolute embodiment of 'naturalness.'

Such a finale is characteristic of late Tolstoy—man and writer whose conflict with official institutions involved a virtual rejection of marriage, including his own. The closure neatly reintegrates the narrator's naive idealism, platonism, body covering, unearthly kindness, and universal love (including love of his "enemy" Anisimov). This idealism, undermined as it were by the plot, lends psychological credibility to the protagonist's eventual conversion.[8] Tolstoy seems to imply that the unearthly kindness and love, misused and exploited by the pagan-pharisaical conventional 'culture-and-family,' do have a place in true Christianity.

Commentary: From a Reading to Variations

Standard interpretations of "After the Ball" (e.g., Trostnikov 1965, Zhdanov 1971) stress the Tolstoyan denunciation of the czarist establishment as based on hypocrisy and violence. The story is aligned with such publicistic texts as "Nicholas the Stick" and "For What?" Critics have shown how this political message is served by the rhetorical symmetry of the episodes *at* and *after* the ball, and by the father-daughter similarities. They have pointed out some of the negative elements already apparent in the ballroom scene (e.g., the "Elizabethan" hostess). The protagonist's romantic love for Varen'ka, however, has remained above suspicion, despite the fact that the denouement holds her responsible for her father's cruelty. For instance, Zhdanov, having noted how the word 'majestic' links Varen'ka to the colonel, fails to see in it an ominous foreshadowing and states that "Varen'ka's portrayal is one-dimensional, without shadows" (1971: 101). The contrast between the two episodes has been analyzed quite thoroughly from the formal point of view,[9] without, however, affecting the accepted thematization along the familiar political lines.

While including the traditional interpretation, my analysis strives to refine and enrich it by pinpointing additional expressive nuances. Where it differs and becomes a virtual rereading is in isolating the motifs of 'cultural conventions,' '(in)corporeality,' 'nakedness versus covering up,' and 'worldly love-and-marriage versus Christian love'; in tracing the plot rhymes and other narrative techniques used to elaborate these themes; and in drawing on Tolstoy's entire oeuvre to corroborate the relevance of the suggested new thematization. A further broadening of perspective, prompted by these new semes, would place this short story in the context of the age-old topos of 'love, death, and culture,' found at the very origins of the genre.

Over the centuries, the themes of 'love' and 'death' have been treated and evaluated in various ways, finding themselves on different sides of the 'nature/culture' opposition. The heroine of Petronius's "The Ephesus Widow" starts out 'hypercultural' in her sanctified loyalty to her deceased husband lying in state; she then desacralizes every convention by giving her own passionate body and even her husband's dead one in exchange for sex with a stranger (Shcheglov 1970). Medieval courtly love to the point of death was self-sacrificially platonic (i.e., programmatically cultural). Classicism sharply contraposed love to the civic (i.e., cultural) duty, and the conflict usually led to tragic death. "Natural" sentimentalist love in the graveyard challenged existing cultural conventions, while the romantics developed a clearly antisocial cult of love and death and Pushkin explored the manifold hybrids of the two (Zholkovsky 1984a: 159–78). Realism brought a sobering reappraisal of romantic stereotypes, but they died hard, lingering in the works of a Turgenev and even a Dostoevsky.

It took a late Tolstoy to demythologize 'cultured love' by opposing it, in a stark reversal of the romantic *argumentum ad mortuum*, to 'death's body.' To subvert the myth of 'love as culture's way of overcoming death,' Tolstoy switched the order of episodes: if "The Ephesus Widow" opens with a picture of death and ascetic mourning and proceeds to sexual ecstasy, "After the Ball" starts with love and ends with its refutation at the sight of a tortured body. This narrative formula (and the various structural and stylistic subtleties that flesh it out), along with the open-ended composition, Hemingwayesque *avant la lettre*, which culminates in the protagonist's emotional shock and ends with his "leaving town" (as in "The Killers"), seem to be Tolstoy's original contribution to the art of storytelling.

Tolstoy's stance is not "realistic" in some privileged sense, nor should the previous treatments of the theme be dismissed as mere "stereotypes." In what follows, I examine two later Russian texts based on the same hypogram—'love as culture's way of overcoming death'—and treat it in ways both similar to and different from "After the Ball." The intertextual links thus established are in all probability purely typological. It is therefore all the more interesting to see how, in the absence of direct influence, the openly anticultural posture of the nineteenth-century iconoclast was developed and then reversed during the Soviet period.

Mikhail Zoshchenko, 1929

In light of the discussion in Chapter 2, the possibility of finding a Zoshchenko variation on the paradigm of Tolstoy's story should not come as a surprise, and indeed one is provided by "Lady with Flowers." [10] Zoshchenko liked borrowing famous titles for his comic stories with a different—opposite or unrelated—content (see Chapter 2, note 11). He consistently subverted the values and conventions of high literature, arguing that one could not go on writing as if "nothing had happened in our country" (1940: 335). The title, topos, and some details of "Lady with Flowers" point to Karamzin's "Poor Liza" (a title also used by Zoshchenko), to *La dame aux camélias* (*Dama s kameliiami* in Russian) by A. Dumas fils, to Chekhov's "Lady with a Lapdog," to Turgenev's "A Quiet Spot (The Backwater),"[11] and, in a widening circle, to Lermontov's "Taman'," Tolstoy's *Anna Karenina*, Blok's beautiful ladies (in particular "The Unknown Lady"), Shakespeare's Ophelia, and many others.

In fact, the entire romantic love-and-death myth is targeted, as the narrator states bluntly that the story is about "how one day through an unfortunate accident it became definitely clear that all kinds of mysticism, idealisticism, various unearthly loves and so on and the like are just bull and nonsensism. And that in life, only a real materialist approach is valid and, unfortunately, nothing more."

Several common motifs make "After the Ball" a relevant point of reference for "Lady with Flowers." It is, so to speak, in the direction of Tolstoy's story (and beyond) that Zoshchenko reworks his "Poor Liza" hypogram, "reshaping" it according to the 'before-after' formula.

BEFORE

"Lady with Flowers" tells, with many a good-naturedly cynical "philosophical" digression, the story of an old-time intelligentsia couple living out in deliberate isolation from the Soviet environment the dream of ideal romantic love. They rent a dacha in Otradnoe,[12] where the wife is given to typically romantic pastimes: "In a word, here was this poetic person, capable of smelling the whole day long flowers and nasturtiums or sitting cozily on the bank and gazing into the distance, as if there is something definite there, like fruits or sausage."[13] Her husband, an engineer, lives only for the moments he spends with his wife. Leaving for his work in Leningrad, he blows her kisses from the steamboat; returning, he brings presents, embraces her, and talks about his love. The narrator finds all this "disgusting."

The husband complains about "crude reality," performs no social work, and is nostalgic for the idealistic values of the past:

He, in a word, liked the past bourgeois life with all kinds of little pillows, consommé, and so on. . . . I, says he, am a person of profound intellectuality, for me, says he, it is accessible to understand many mystical and abstract pictures of my childhood. . . . I, says he, was brought up on many beautiful things and bagatelles, I understand subtle love and do not see anything decent in crude embraces. . . . I, says he, . . . only take into consideration spiritual life and the needs of my heart.

The 'reactionary and idealistic' complex includes ignoring the physical aspect of life. The husband despises "crude embraces"; the wife walks "on thin intelligentsia legs," "does not ask for food," and never smiles: even when given presents, she will only "frown her little nose." As for her "habit of bathing," it is an idle and effete, rather than athletic, pastime, and the verb used by the narrator is pointedly *kupat'sia*, "bathe," rather than *plavat'*, "swim," which she is fatally no good at. Other characteristic appurtenances of the *ancien* way of life are, according to the naive 'proletarian' narrator, the useless, expensive, or simply foreign-name objects: "bagatelles," "consommé," "cute little peignoir," "smartly dressed" (cf. the glove motif in Tolstoy), and so on.

In a word, the couple represents the 'dead culture' of the past, and without fail, death is what happens next. The lady wanted to go bathing, "went out after the rain on her little French heels—and fell." "Of course, had she worked out . . . , in due time, she . . . would have swum up. But as it is, with her flowers and all, as soon as she took a dip—she went down all the way to the bottom, without resisting Nature." The narrator considers and dismisses the probability of suicide, but archetypally the woman is as suicidal as any mermaid-aux-camélias heroine, of which she is a caricature. The absence of a specific cause of death—unlike Ophelia or poor Liza, she is loved, not abandoned—mockingly underscores the point.

Her death shifts the focus to the hero, whose love now attains its graveyard apex: "I loved her with a completely unearthly love, and my only job now, says he, is to find her, to get in touch with her remains and to bury her in a decent little grave, and to keep visiting that little grave every Saturday in order to spiritually communicate with her and have otherworldly conversations." Zoshchenko spoofs the 'unearthly' topos (the word 'nezemnaia' is the same as in "After the Ball"), lumping together poor Liza's or Klara Milich's posthumous haunting of the hero, poetic (e.g., Pushkinian) conversations beyond the grave, river dragging (e.g., in Turgenev's "A Quiet Spot"), sentimentalist grave tending, planned here in advance. All this is told in the habitual Zoshchenkovian stylistic jumble, well-intentioned but pathetically semiliterate.

AFTER

The most important things happen in the presence of the dead body, which is at first looked for in vain. The engineer offers a reward, grieves on at the dacha, and a month later fishermen find the disfigured corpse. The hero hurries to the side of his beloved: "He went up to his former girlfriend and stopped near her." The description of the dead body as a living person "revives" it, setting it up for the ensuing desacralization. "The engineer . . . bent over . . . and here a complete grimace of disgust disfigured his intelligentsia lips. With the tip of his boot he turned over the face of the drowned lady" and left in revulsion, having paid the fishermen an extra five rubles "to somehow bury her by themselves at the local cemetery."

Confronted with the 'body' (the word 'telo' recurs several times), the hero reverses himself completely, renouncing his love and interest in the grave and beyond. Also, contrary to the generic expectations but in accordance with the narrator's posture of deflating all mysticism, the dead beloved fails to haunt the hero. In fact, it is now that he finally "betrays" her with another woman: "And recently they saw him—he was going down the street with some lady. He was leading her gentle like by her elbow and was insinuating something interesting to her."

This is, of course, a complete reversal of, say, "Poor Liza," where betrayal causes suicide, which in turn enables Liza to reclaim, from beyond the grave, Erast's loyalty. The 'haunting woman' syndrome in Russian literature began with Liza's sketchily outlined posthumous emotional impact on Erast. In Pushkin's *The Mermaid*, it took the form of physical aggression (attempts to drown the seducer, later spoofed in Lermontov's "Taman'"). Dostoevsky's Nastas'ia Filippovna succeeded in morally destroying all guilty and innocent males alike— already in this world (Matich 1987: 55). Finally, in Blok, the femme fatale attained the peak of domination over the male persona—literally to get the boot in the denouement of Zoshchenko's story.

Like Tolstoy, Zoshchenko plays up the hero's dread of the disfigured body, implying that 'unearthly spirituality' means a reluctance to face the down-to-earth facts of life. The shunning of the body was foreshadowed by the engineer's escapist ignoring of "crude reality" and "crude embraces," and "turning his personality (*lichnost'*) away from everything."

Remarkably, the plot's macabre transition from 'idealism' to 'materialism' is echoed by a parallel shift in the representation of the social environment. In the beginning, the hero's ' "wrong" spirituality' is contrasted with the down-to-earth and even crude but ' "correctly" idealistic' Soviet values (social work, workouts, writing articles, etc.). In the end, however, Soviet 'materialism,' which provides the supposedly positive contrast to the ugly denouement of the love story, is downright crass. The fishermen, in a variation of graveside humor, mistake the hero's departure for avoidance of payment: "And, hey, what about the money—the money he dangled like, and now, look, he is splitting, never mind that he is a former *intelligent* with a cap on and all!"

Zoshchenko's fishermen fill the role of 'epiphanic witnesses,' analogous to that of the God-fearing blacksmith in "After the Ball." Their talk of money is clearly not beyond culture; rather, it represents the new set of values. As for their being (of all trades) fishermen, but of a human body, not the soul, it may be correlated with the story's cynical tenor and contrasted with the Christian ending of "After the Ball." In a sense, the fishermen leave the hero looking less repugnant. Although he shows no compassion, at least he does betray some emotion: "He bowed his head and whispered to himself: 'Yes, that is her.' "

What is, then, the balance of Zoshchenko's message? Writing after the Revolution and from behind its looking glass, Zoshchenko takes Tolstoy's anticultural stance to an ambiguous extreme (see Chapter 2). His heroes belong to a culture that is suppressed and gone, not the dominant one, and the open debunking of the former is supplemented with a *skaz*-type subversion of the latter. No positive characters—except, as the saying goes, laughter itself—appear in the story, and the picture gets increasingly grimmer toward the end.

On a deeper level, Zoshchenko endows his heroes with his own traumas (the husband, who is "fortyish," is approximately the writer's age): preoccupation with childhood memories, fear of or attraction to water, problems with eating, anxiety about or overcompensatory interest in sex, femininity, and ostentatious clothing. The fear of excessive pretensions, possessions, and culture seems to have haunted Zoshchenko from his infancy. In his psycho-autobiography, *Before Sun-*

rise,[14] there is an episode where little Misha and his sisters flee from a storm. When his elder sister reproaches him for losing his bunch of flowers (!), he replies: "With such a storm, who needs bunches of flowers?" (Zoshchenko 1974: 111). These words are emblematic of the writer's bleak view of culture at the time of the Revolution and anticipate the philosophical pronouncements in "Lady with Flowers": "Let them see in how much unnecessary stuff they have wrapped themselves"; "in life, only a real materialist approach is valid and, unfortunately, nothing more."

Eugenia Ginzburg, 1977

Strictly speaking, our next variation on courtship-and-corpses belongs to a different literary genre: Ginzburg's "Paradise under the Microscope" is a chapter from the second part of her memoirs.[15] *Journey into the Whirlwind* (1967) and *Within the Whirlwind* (1981) tell the enthralling story of an idealistic Communist's survival in the Gulag, thanks to her exceptional vitality, spiritual integrity, and good luck. In a sense, the book is an uplifting idyll, portraying the triumph of the human spirit and culture over tremendous odds—a harmony of all positive elements against the backdrop of horror and suffering. The chapter in question, although purportedly nonfictional, exhibits so high a degree of literary organization that it can be analyzed as a short story in its own right, alongside those of Tolstoy and Zoshchenko.

BEFORE

The paradise placed under the microscope is a tolerable spot in the Gulag, the Taskan food-processing plant, where the narrator-heroine is a nurse and thus a member of a humane circle of the camp's medics. The circle is headed by Dr. Walter—German, Catholic, a "jolly saint," and Ginzburg's second-husband-to-be.

Death is an everyday experience here. The prisoners are "almost otherworldly figures," and the medics' job is "directed toward preventing deaths during working hours." Food is a matter of life and death:

The inhabitants of Taskan were unlike those of the real paradise up above in that their thoughts never strayed from their daily bread. . . . [Deaths were] concealed from the authorities . . . so that the deceased's bread ration [*paika*] would keep coming. [To claim it,] sometimes they even paraded the corpse at roll call, placing him in the back row, propping him up with their shoulders on either side, and replying for him to the question about his personal data.

And yet this life on the brink of death is governed by 'laws.' The doctors save the slave-laborers so they can die 'legitimately.' "People were *supposed* [*polozheno*—Ginzburg's italics] to die in infirmary beds. . . . If someone were to fall into a snowdrift, you could look for hours, you would have to raise alarm for an escaped prisoner, and you'd have to account for the occurrence." As for the dead man's ration, it can be bequeathed to a friend, and this unwritten rule is solemnly upheld and enforced by the prisoner community. "Such bequests were often made in my presence; I have even acted as a sort of notary. . . . These bequests were strictly observed. General condemnation and sometimes physical reprisal were meted out to those jackals who looked for a chance to steal a dying man's bread ration."

Along with such fundamentals of culture as 'laws,' the elitist circle also has access to spiritual nourishment in the form of 'books' (which the doctor obtains from the free citizens he treats) and 'intellectual dialogues.' The paramedic "Confucius lived up to his nickname by developing various arguments to prove the unprovable, for example, that joy and sorrow were . . . one and the same thing because both were transitory."

A redeeming role is also played by 'memory,' developed in the tragicomic episode with the Kazakh prisoner Baigildeev. He kept forgetting the name of *his* article of the penal code (i.e. the one according to which he had been convicted) and "was as pleased as a little child" when the roll-calling guard, nicknamed Beast (*Zver'*), supplied it ("ASMC," for "Anti-Soviet Military Conspiracy").

The narrator's and the doctor's trips into the woods for medicinal herbs (i.e., flowers!) produce a synthesis of their nascent love, humanistic culture, and union with nature: "The brief flowering of the taiga . . . awoke in us an almost forgotten delight [lit. "tenderness"] in the world around us, . . . in the elegant flowers of the willow herb, which resembled tall-stemmed purple goblets [!]. The doctor . . . named it in three languages: Russian, German, Latin."

The mention of Latin, which foreshadows the role that language will play in the plot, also connotes the doctor's extraordinary spiritual powers. The doctor becomes not only the heroine's husband but also her priestly guide, who converts her to Christianity. He mediates between this world and the other (this was ironically prefigured by the convicts' "otherworldliness"), gains the heroine's love by listening to her stories about her dead son, and teaches her how to care for others.

He was the only person to whom I could talk about Alyosha. He somehow steered our conversation so that there seemed to be no difference between those who had departed and we who were still on earth. . . . This helped to soften . . . the constant pain. Sometimes the doctor would . . . mention my suffering in connection with our . . . everyday concerns. "You must take the occasion to go and look after Sergei . . . in the second ward. . . . For Alyosha's sake."

It is, therefore, in a highly 'cultural' way that the relationship develops. "The doctor went about his courtship with old-fashioned courtesy and gentleness. He told me about his childhood.[16] He told me about his scientific hypotheses. He patiently endured the torrents of poetry that I launched at him. When it was no longer possible to be silent, his declaration of love was not in oral but in written form."

The arrival of the love letter forms a major plot event: it is motivated by the doctor's absence (a trip to a distant campsite) and takes place at the very moment when the heroine is treating her son's miraculously convalescing double, Sergei. And—ostensibly for conspiratorial reasons—the letter is in Latin. The heroine can barely understand Latin (she knows some French) but is moved anyway by the "high-flown, almost bombastic words: 'Amor mea, mea vita, mea spes.'" This perfect fusion of love and culture is all the more striking as it reshapes the famous Levin-Kitty declaration of love by initials, which was pointedly anticonventional and antisymbolic.[17]

At night she composes her answer—alas, in Russian, but in verse (germinating from the immaculate trochees of the doctor's Latin incantation) and in classical Roman terms:

How beautiful is the Capitol! What wonderful old stone! / A perfect day, a happy day, and now we are alone. / The bad is clean forgotten beneath the sky's blue rays, / You whisper, 'amor mea, mea vita, mea spes.' / Life is sweet, I ask you and ask again, my dove, / Only in Latin, always in Latin, speak to me of love.

This response echoes the doctor's use of a special, ultracultured language and connotes culture not only by its literariness, written as it is in verse, but also by its intertextual strategy. The heroine's poem is a reworking of a specific source: Akhmatova's "My heart beats calmly, steadily . . ." ("Serdtse b'etsia rovno, merno . . ."), a vintage specimen of stoical self-healing by recourse to memory and culture.[18]

But even borrowing from such a kindred 'cultural' spirit, Ginzburg has to make a significant change—for the idyllic. In Akhmatova, the declaration of freedom: "You are free, I am free" ("Ty svoboden, ia svobodna") means putting a good, stoical, and culturally acceptable face on broken love. In Ginzburg's paraphrase, the same words imply release from the camps. As for love, it remains unquestioned: love, culture, and the heroes are in league, not in conflict.

AFTER

At this high point the idyll is brutally shattered.

In the middle of the night the heroine is summoned to the hospital ward and ordered to save the life of a convict and identify the meat in his bowl. She feels like vomiting: the meat is human, the prisoner, a cannibal. He has murdered a fellow *zek* (to be sure, one earlier saved by Dr. Walter) and has been secretly cooking parts of his body—in a macabre counterpoint to the 'lawful' and friendly use of corpses (to get extra rations) in the beginning of the chapter.

The prisoner's name, Kulesh, which in Russian means "simple grub with meat," adds a probably unintended but powerful irony to the episode.

The author—and History—have upped the ante: in Tolstoy we had a tortured live body, in Zoshchenko a desecrated corpse, and now the epiphany takes the form of peering into a pot of human flesh. The disciplinary officer (*nachal'nik rezhima*) takes the grotesque even further. Cracking a black-humor joke that links the corpse with the heroine directly (if figuratively), he says to the murderer: "What are you goggling at the medic for? . . . She'd doubtless make more tender cutlets . . . , is that it?"

For protection from this horror, the narrative turns to 'culture.' The prisoner must be cured in order to be tried and executed—in a replay of the irony of camp medicine mentioned earlier in the chapter. But now the narrator-heroine finds herself identifying with the jailers, albeit reluctantly and ambivalently:

I felt so ill, physically and mentally, that I could hardly stand on my feet. Were we to save him so that he could be shot? . . . Why not let him die there and then? . . . I caught myself thinking that for the first time in all these years . . .

I was perhaps closer to the bosses than to a prisoner. . . . I had something in common with the disciplinary officer: we both felt the same revulsion toward the two-legged wolf who had overstepped the bounds of what is human.

The 'wolf' metaphor was foreshadowed by the "jackals" who would not honor ration bequests. Incidentally, it does not carry as absolute a conviction as the narrator assumes: Tolstoy, the author of "The Strider," and Pilnyak, the author of *Machines and Wolves*, might well take the side of the wolf against the humans and their conventions (cf. Chapters 2 and 7). Indeed, Ginzburg's stance differs remarkably from that of "After the Ball." There, the 'benign' aristocratic culture was successfully subverted by the body it victimized; in Ginzburg, the 'benign laws' of the Gulag community are unexpectedly upheld, while the dead body is laid at the door of an isolated criminal, not the cultural establishment.

Confronted with the 'body,' the heroine reacts very much like the protagonists of Tolstoy and Zoshchenko: "I looked into the pot and could hardly refrain from retching. The fibers of this meat were minute, unlike anything I was accustomed to seeing" (123–24). She is about to renounce her pro-culture stance when the reversal of the familiar paradigm takes place. Next morning, the doctor returns and addresses the heroine for the first time by the intimate second-person singular *ty* (see the Russian version, 1985: 106). This *TY*, capitalized and placed at the end of the chapter as its last word, is a clear allusion to *the* Russian arbiter of culture, love, and death—Pushkin[19]— and lends additional force to the doctor's concluding words. He assures her that one *can* face the facts: "Don't despair. True, man has a beast in him [cf. the nickname of the brutal guard, *Zver'*], but the beast cannot triumph over man in the end" (125). Love and culture join hands against the cadaverous antibody. In fact, the doctor, in true Enlightenment spirit, has from the start advocated sober scrutiny of reality, in words that gave the chapter its title: "I see that you need to take a closer look at our paradise—under the microscope."

The role of the 'epiphanic witness,' however, devolves to the disciplinary officer: the doctor gets to pronounce his verdict after him, in accordance with the narrative's strategy of rewriting crude reality in cultural terms. Writing is indeed crucial to Ginzburg's text, which belongs to the neoromantic/modernist tradition that casts the writer as protagonist. Hence the proliferation of cultural activities in the story: correspondence, verse writing, addressing a convict (the messenger and a suspected informer) in the style of A. Dumas pere ("Tell the duke there will be no answer. . . . Good night, viscount"), and other literary reminiscences, all of which lends this writing a romancelike or even fairy-tale-like aura.

Commentary: Back to Archetypes

The variations on the topos have come almost full circle. Tolstoy shook the foundations of officially sanctioned love, which is rooted in violence done to Nature's and Christ's body. Zoshchenko, writing amid cultural ruins, exaggerated Tolstoy's deadly (virtually avant-gardist) critique of old values and extended it, ambivalently, to the new without offering anything positive in their place. Shocked back into the cultural fold by the wildest avant-garde nightmares come true (in fact, according to Groys, 1988, Stalinism *was* a runaway version of the Russian avant-garde), Ginzburg sought to reclaim the traditional values of love *and* culture, reintegrating them with Nature, Christianity, and even official authority, in a kind of blueprint for post-Soviet Russia.

Characteristically, the harsher the reality confronted by the text, the more defensive the discourse chosen for its portrayal. Tolstoy probes the (half-)dead body with realistic seriousness; Zoshchenko takes refuge from the desecrated corpse in heartless deadpan; Ginzburg shields herself from cannibalism with the rose-colored glasses of an idyll. And, of course, such an ideal harmony is open to—almost sets itself up for—a new round of deconstruction and postmodernist mock remythologizing.[20]

Instead of seeking out the latest reverberations of this paradigm, let us try to follow the historical clock in the opposite direction. So far, the discussion has concentrated on the 'cultural' issues overtly thematized in the texts. However, as mentioned, the courtship-and-corpse motif boasts venerable literary lineage; the ever-intriguing question in such cases is naturally whether and in what way the time-hallowed hypogram, dormant underneath the text's surface structure, is relevant to its interpretation.[21] Often, hypogrammatic analysis is invited by the text itself, some of whose elements remain unaccounted for by the straightforward reading and thus offer clues to the covert archaic layers of meaning.

Indeed, the reading of "After the Ball" outlined above could be accepted as fairly exhaustive were it not for its overly simplistic black-and-white moralism. The story itself leaves a more ambiguous and disturbing impression, especially when perceived in a wider context. Does the story of "love that began to wane from that very day" (p. 250) reflect in any way the septuagenarian Tolstoy's views not only on corporal punishment and official culture but on love and marriage as well? How does the plot straddling Shrovetide and Lent correlate with Tolstoy's complicated religiosity? Can the perfect symmetry of courtship and punishment episodes be purely rhetorical? Love and violence do form a natural pair, but then why are they juxtaposed in so oblique a manner? If the soldier's tortured body replaces and lays bare for the hero that of his beloved, what are we to make of such an unexpected resolution of the story's erotic, as well as narrative, tension? And what subliminal interpretations would account for the reverse projection of the violence done to the Tatar onto the colonel's dancing with his daughter? Such loose ends strengthen the intuitive feeling that in any case, Tolstoy's short masterpiece about love and death must have rich archetypal underpinnings—unlike such fiction-alized denunciations of corporal punishment as Nikolai Leskov's "The Sentry" (1887)[22] or Tolstoy's own pamphlets against the same, and very much like his other late fiction.

An insight into the hidden workings of "After the Ball" is furnished by "A Christmas Eve" (see note 3).

> In that story, the protagonist's ballroom infatuation with a young countess is followed by a visit to a brothel, where he loses his virginity in the arms of a prostitute, the countess's double (3: 265). The plot is similar to that of "After the Ball," with the difference that the hero's initiation into worldly customs and carnal knowledge occurs on one and the same plane—amorous. The initiation theme is underscored by the hero's interest in "joining the adult society" and by the guidance he gets, both at the ball and in the brothel, from his elders, intent on "debauching" him.

The idea of 'initiation' is clearly germane to the problematic of "After the Ball," with its focus on learning "what they [the colonel and the powers that be in general] knew," on cultural stereotypes, the religious calendar, and the ritual of punishment. The atmosphere of fairy-tale irreality and participation in mysterious rites is reinforced by the motifs of 'sleepless night' and 'intoxication' (first with love and then with alcohol), as well as by the figure (prominent in Slavic folk-lore) of the 'blacksmith' who guides the hero through the unknown place. Taking the fairy-tale metaphor seriously, we could try to reread the story, so to speak, with Propp's *The Historical Roots of the Folktale* in hand.[23]

> In that 1946 book, Propp undertook a thematic interpretation of his earlier, "formalist" *Morphology of the Folktale* (1971 [1928]) by mapping its purely syntagmatic formulae onto the archaic structures reflected in myths and initiation and wedding rituals. Parallel work has been conducted in the West (by Claude Lévi-Strauss, Georges Dundes, Georges Dumezil, and others), while Propp's Soviet followers established the 'wedding' theme as the dominant of the fairy-tale paradigm (see Meletinsky 1958, 1970; Meletinsky et al. 1969; Levinton 1970a, 1970b, 1975a, 1975b; Baiburin and Levinton 1972). Propp was also an early practitioner of the mythological approach to literary texts, namely, to Sophocles' *Oedipus* cycle in light of Greek folklore (see Propp 1976; Edmunds 1985).

Let us then look for whatever "historical roots" may hide beneath the "morphology" of Tolstoy's story.

"After the Ball" as Folktale

THE HYPOGRAM

The colonel's similarity with the Emperor and Varen'ka's "regality" can be said to typify the initial fairy-tale situation of a king with an eligible princess to give away.[24] Her hand is claimed by an Ivan (Vasil'evich) to whom, before disappearing, she leaves her—so to speak, Firebird's—feather. He becomes restless and leaves home in search of the princess. Transportation to the faraway "thirtieth" kingdom is often achieved by flying—in particular, after metamorphosis into a bird (cf. in "After the Ball," the feather and the hero's perception of himself as "an unearthly being"). Sometimes the trip takes place during sleep; note the nighttime setting and the hero's altered state. In the otherworldly journey the hero is assisted by a helper(-donor)— for example, a forest creature called Copper Forehead (*Mednyi Lob*), which is halfway between the Firebird and the blacksmith, and in some tales simply by a blacksmith (!).

The faraway kingdom represents the other world and at the same time the territory of the bride's tribe. It is an open space with the king's palace in the middle—just like the colonel's quarters by the parade ground. The faraway kingdom is also associated with the sun (cf. the shining eyes of the father and daughter and the fact that the flogging takes place at daybreak). The hero's exploits are often performed to the magic sounds of flutes and drums (!).

The actions of the folktale hero are a reflection of wedding rituals. He must be tested by the king and his daughter, and one major type of princess tries to destroy the pretender to her hand.[25] What makes Varen'ka amazonlike is her similarity to her warrior father—her tallness, "bony physique," and "thin, pointed [lit. "sharp"] elbows"; in fact, her "frightening" regality sounds like a replica of the "frightening away" of suitors by the princess as described by Propp (1946: 284). Furthermore, the feather links Varen'ka to the Firebird, i.e. the bride-villain. The Russian word 'kostliavyi',' "bony," associates her with the hostile donor of Russian folktales, Baba-Yaga, Kostianaia Noga (lit. "Baba-Yaga, the Bony Leg"), and the "bronze garments" would fit the proverbial bellicose virgin (bogatyr'-devitsa) of Russian folklore. The 'bronze' element is also in accord with the presence of the blacksmith, a figure endowed by folklore with magic powers, in particular in the matrimonial sphere: he is asked "to forge the crown, the ring, the staff [bulava] for the wedding, and the wedding itself." The blacksmith also has such sacerdotal functions as forging the tongue and voice (Ivanov and Toporov 1974: 88–89).

To qualify for marriage, the hero was supposed to pass tests, and, being traditionally passive, he had them performed for him by magic helpers. Thus in "After the Ball," the blacksmith, the colonel, and the floggers leave the reluctant but enthralled observer-hero only with the emotional experiencing of the scene. Among prewedding tasks was that of becoming invisible—echoed in the story by the colonel's ostensible failure to "see" the hero. The folkloric hero was also asked to recognize the bride even in disguise, in animal shape or skin (especially in the tales about the lecherous father, of which more presently), a task related to the elimination of 'false brides' and to the custom of mummery. In "After the Ball," this is paralleled by the 'clothing' motifs (from gloves all the way to bronze garments) and the substitution of the Tatar for Varen'ka.

Wedding-night tests had the twofold function of ascertaining the hero's ability to tame the bride both sexually and socially.[26] The bride's attempts to strangle or otherwise harm the hero challenged his sexual power, symbolically reifying the fear of vagina dentata. To enforce defloration, the hero's helper flogged the princess with three kinds of switches or rods (*prut'ia*); note, in "After the Ball," the colonel's order to "bring fresh rods" (249). On the social level, the taming certified the hero's control over the princess and her kin-tribe and foreshadowed his eventual coronation (sometimes accompanied by the killing of the old king-father).

The motif of wedding-night violence is close to the folkloric motif of battle.[27] Sigurd, in his first encounter with his future bride, slashes her breast with a sword.

The swordstroke is a euphemism of possessing . . . , defloration . . . , a substitute of marriage. . . . In the forest . . . , Sigurd sees . . . a wall of shields (cf. the forest house with a fence in Russian folktales) and a fully armed warrior. Removing the warrior's helmet, he discovers that before him is a woman. "She was in armor, and the armor fitted her so tightly as if it had grown one with the body. And he slashed the armor open from the neck aperture all the way down" (Levinton 1975a: 84–85; he also mentions a similar Russian plot, Sviatogor's marriage).

In "After the Ball," this is literally or figuratively paralleled by the military formation, the bronze garments, and their slashing open in the flogging scene.[28] In fact, the treatment of the bride as described in the verbal part of Russian wedding rituals bears resemblance to certain maneuvers of the folkloric battle, for example, "tearing the adversary in half [*na-poly*] in *bylinas*. . . . Such tearing up is quite natural, especially in light of the well-known magic tale motif: the helper cuts the bride in half, cleans her insides of 'evil ones' [*ot 'gadov'*], then puts her together again and revives her" (Baiburin and Levinton 1972:73). Prewedding tests also included the branding of the hero by the bride and other ways of mixing the blood of the two partners.

As for the princess's relations with the king, they often imply incest. The lecherous father may try to marry his own daughter (Motif T411, according to Aarne-Thompson [Thompson 1977:499]) and/or act as the protagonist's testing adversary and the deflorator of the bride; these functions can also be filled by the bride's other totemic ancestors. The ancestor figure appears in folktales in the guise of magician, dragon, Koshchei, and so on; one who sexually possesses the princess and is routinely killed in the course of the tests. Of special relevance to "After the Ball" is the tale of "The Danced-out Shoes."

The maiden absents herself at night and . . . returns with her shoes danced to pieces. She is offered in marriage to the man who can solve the mystery of her conduct. She has succeeded in giving a narcotic to all those who have tried to follow her, but the hero refuses to drink and accompanies her on a magic underground journey. He . . . make[s] himself invisible, . . . is able to observe her when she dances with the supernatural being [and is able to claim the princess] (Aarne-Thompson Tale Type 306 [Thompson 1977: 34]).

In addition to the obvious parallels in "After the Ball," let us mention also Varen'ka's promise of a quadrille after supper "if they don't take me away," which in turn is reminiscent of *Childhood* (chaps. 20, 23), where the desirable Sonechka Valakhina is spectacularly unwrapped from and wrapped back into her furs as she arrives at and is taken away from the party.

Along with wedding motifs, prominent among the folktale's "historical roots" are initiation tests. In fact, as Propp, Meletinsky et al., and others have stressed, the two groups have much in common and often overlap in folktales and even more so in literature. The process of initiation into the tribe's sacred lore (cf. Ivan Vasil'evich's attempts to learn "what they knew") took place to the sounds of magical instruments (esp. flutes) and involved prohibition to sleep (cf. the hero's insomnia), poisoning, and temporary madness (cf. the hero's intoxication and nausea as he tries to make sense of the flogging). The initiates underwent temporary death (cf. the physical state of the victim and the hero's shock). One of the tools used for ritual killing was a "deadly shirt" (*rubashka na smert'*).[29] On returning to normal life, the initiates could forget their names and stop recognizing their parents (cf. Ivan Vasil'evich's dropping out of the entire official culture). Initiation was administered by the donor, the folktale counterpart of the tribe's elders and magicians; note in "After the Ball" the hero's passive fascination with the colonel both at the ball and on the parade ground, which is reminiscent of the hero's initiation by adults in "A Christmas Eve."

CONVERSION

Parallels with the folktale as a repository of archaic codes do not in themselves determine a definitive interpretation of the text. Much depends on the privileging of either wedding or initiation motifs and the way these fit into the story's structure and the recurrent patterns of Tolstoy's oeuvre.

Under the 'wedding' construction, "After the Ball" appears to ex-

press a subliminal, but intense, fear of the sensuous body, defloration, *vagina dentata*. Censure of sex, even in marriage, was characteristic of late Tolstoy. In the opinion of Pozdnyshev ("The Kreutzer
Sonata"), marriage is institutionalized debauchery, marriage proponents are pagan "priests [*zhretsy*] of science" and "sorcerers" (*volkhvy*).
Developing the pagan analogy, he says that with the social position
of women, "it is as if cannibals fattened their captives to be eaten and
at the same time declared that they were concerned about their prisoners' rights and freedom," wherefore continence and even virginity
are advisable (chap. 13, 1968b: 149).

According to late Tolstoy, conjugal and sexual love in general breeds
mutual hatred, violence, and eventually homicide. In "The Kreutzer
Sonata," the outcome is murder; in "The Devil" and *Anna Karenina*,
suicide; in "Father Sergius," self-mutilation (the hero hacks off his own
finger) symbolizing self-castration (dactylotomy was also a form of initiation and prewedding mixing of blood). The equation of carnal love
with murder controls the narrative of Vronskii and Anna's first tryst,
in which, incidentally, the "dead body" and "spiritual nakedness" are
prominent.

He felt what a murderer must feel when looking at the body he has deprived
of life . . . [i.e.] their love, the first period of their love. . . . The shame she
felt at her spiritual nakedness communicated itself to him. But in spite of the
murderer's horror of the body of his victim, the body must be cut in pieces
and hidden away, and he must make use of what he had obtained by murder.
Then as the murderer desperately [lit. "angrily"] throws himself on the body,
as though with passion, and drags it and hacks it, so Vronskii covered her
face and shoulders with kisses" (2: 11; 1968a: 135–36).

To be sure, in *Anna Karenina* the murder metaphor is deployed
against adultery, but as early as in "A Christmas Eve" any marriage
not based on pure love was denounced as debauchery and voluntary mutual deception. Small wonder, then, that in its hidden depths
"After the Ball" seems to read as a rejection of the violence underlying
all marriage, of which gauntlet running serves as an apt hyperbole.
Its pagan cruelty (recall Pozdnyshev's reference to cannibals) has its
ethnographic counterparts in ritual cannibalism and mutilation during
rites of passage.

The relevance of these archetypal motifs to Tolstoy's late fiction
is further confirmed by the "Posthumous Papers of the Elder Fedor
Kuzmich" (1905),[30] where the same cluster appears in explicit form.

Czar Alexander I leaves the throne to become a monk, motivated by his shocked reaction to a gauntlet-running, which he associates with his ambivalence toward married life and sex: "Still more terrible was it to be with . . . my wife. We were supposed to be spending a second honeymoon [!], but it was a hell in forms of respectability. . . . The murder of that beauty—the spiteful Nastasia . . . had aroused desire [lit. "lust"] in me, and I could not sleep all night. . . . The thought of the murdered, voluptuously beautiful Nastasia and of the soldier's body being lashed by rods, merged into one stimulating sensation" (Tolstoy 1935: 388–90).

Many details coincide with "After the Ball": first encounter with gauntlet-running on an early morning; sounds of drum and flute; punishment; desertion; the victim's back and "hopeless jerking"; the observer-protagonist's nausea; his readiness to "admit that my whole life . . . was bad, and . . . to abandon everything, go away, and disappear" (391). In fact, that is what he does, having passed through the state of quasi-death—by "pretend[ing] to be ill and dying" (394) and having replaced his own "corpse" with that of the soldier flogged to death. Later on, as an elder, he comes to the conclusion that "this approach to death, is the only reasonable wish a man can have . . . a release from passions and temptations of that spiritual element that dwells in every man" (408), and he also concludes that "chastity is better than marriage."

To return to "After the Ball," in the wedding-oriented scheme of things, the flogged Tatar stands in for the bride, while the colonel plays the role of the helper taming the bride cum hostile ancestor-deflorator (especially in view of the colonel's dancing with Varen'ka). All this additionally dramatizes the alienation of the protagonist from the "totemic culture" of Nicholas I's "tribe" he is expected to join. Incidentally, since the colonel administers the flogging not personally but through his soldiers, he too qualifies as a bridegroom.

The 'imperial incest' has interesting parallels in other Tolstoy texts.

In "Father Sergius," Nicholas I, like Varen'ka's father at the ball, continues smiling at the protagonist and conferring his approval on the marriage that his behavior (his affair with the bride) has effectively ruined.

In War and Peace, the Kuragins combine incest (implied, between Hélène and Anatole) with amoral politicking and careerism, while the old Count Rostov's connivance in the (abortive) seduction of Natasha by Anatole is presented in a benevolent light. Varen'ka can thus be seen as Natasha transposed, by an increasingly misogynous Tolstoy, into the Kuragin family.

On the other hand, should we opt for the "initiation" reading, the distribution of roles would be somewhat different. The flogged soldier would symbolically represent the protagonist himself; in some archaic rituals captive slaves were killed instead of initiates, a practice reflected in magic tales (Propp 1946: 79–80). The colonel would in turn act as the magician-ancestor supervising the initiation (in folktale terms, the magic tester-donor). Indeed, Ivan Vasil'evich is linked to the Tatar in several ways: emotionally, by the compassion he feels; plotwise, by the shared motif of shunning military service; and in the system of characters, by the intermediate figure of the soldier who "pats" the deserter and is then himself beaten. Empathizing with the flogged Tatar, the protagonist gradually passes, as it were, from the class of victimizers (i.e., the colonel and his daughter) to that of victims.

> A similar identification of the observer-protagonist with the victim is quite explicit in the "Posthumous Notes," where it is reified in the motif of corpse substitution. "That man was I: he was my double . . . well known . . . on account of his likeness to me. They used jokingly to call him Alexander II. . . . I ought myself to have been in the place of that wretched man. . . . I . . . saw him or myself—I could not tell which of us was I" (391–92).
>
> An additional tour de force is achieved by fusing this cluster of roles with the 'imperial' figure (colonel = Nicholas = Alexander): "I . . . had . . . often sanctioned that form of punishment. . . . I had evidently been recognized. . . . My . . . feeling was that I ought to approve of what was being done to this double of mine; or . . . at least acknowledge that it was the proper thing to do, but I could not" (390–91). The last words are an almost exact replica of Ivan Vasil'evich's pondering of "what the colonel knew."

Under either construction, wedding or initiation, the protagonist of "After the Ball" fails the test. As a bridegroom, he refuses to approve of the taming and enjoy its fruits by marrying the 'princess.' As an initiate warrior, he withdraws from the cruel rite of passage, does not learn "what they knew," and stays away from military service. Principled rejection of the establishment and its social institutions was characteristic of late Tolstoy and many of his characters: Father Sergius, Pozdnyshev, Prince Nekhliudov, Alexander I. Therefore, for the narrator-protagonist, flunking the rites of passage is far from being a defeat; in his own way, he triumphs over the colonel and his daughter.

How? Interesting light is shed on this problem by Father Sergius's reasons for entering the monastery:

He felt that God's call . . . transcended all other considerations. . . . By becoming a monk he showed contempt for all that seemed most important to others and had seemed so to him while he was in service, and he now ascended a height from which he could look down on those he had formerly envied (i.e., the circle of his former fiancée and the Emperor himself; chap. 1, 1968b: 307).

The protagonist of "After the Ball" is less vain, but Tolstoy does let him "lord it over" the princess and her father by endowing him with the power of narration. In fact, the hero's spiritual conversion is matched in the structure of the story by a literary 'conversion' (in the sense of Riffaterre 1978), of which the failure-turned-victory is a clear-cut case. Conversion, that is, a textually well-grounded reinterpretation of existing cultural hypograms, is crucial to literary dynamics and deserves attention here.

The radical rereading of the gauntlet scene is naturalized by drawing on five latent possibilities:

1. The Tolstoyan refusal to identify with cruelty and violence, in particular with the harsh disciplining of the "bride," is legitimized as a redefinition of the traditional passivity of the folkloric hero.

2. Folklore also offers partial precedents for what Tolstoy develops into a total renunciation of marriage: sometimes the folktale hero, after passing the tests, goes into hiding (but is later found and brought to the wedding). In epic texts, the marriage may effectively fail to materialize, which is accompanied by the loss of the acquired sacred knowledge. Potential subversion of marriage is also implicit in the motif of false brides, whose rejection is now applied to the heroine as well. The revision of the cruel custom may also be prompted by the view of the bridegroom as a "destroyer" (*pogubitel'*), voiced in the course of the wedding ritual by the bride.

3. Christian reinterpretation of wedding-ritual violence is a tendency evidenced by such Slavic customs as that of hitting with a branch (switch, rod), sometimes performed on the last Sunday of Lent. Hitting young girls, the boys uttered the same verbal formulae that "are . . . used during preparations for the first wedding night. . . . In some cases the [pagan meaning of the ritual] is lost under the influence of Christian perceptions" (N. I. Tolstoi 1982: 63, 67).

4. The element of 'torture' was shared by wedding tests and initiation rituals, of which the corporal punishment of children and soldiers is a surviving vestige. It was also an integral part of the custom of scapegoating and thus a pagan prototype of the martyrdom of Christ. Thus, rereading 'torture' in a Christian key by siding with the victim,

Tolstoy follows the well-known pattern of reforms of ritual codes, recurrent in the history of religion (e.g., the replacement of human sacrifices with animal ones, reflected in the story of Abraham and Isaac).

5. The 'Christian' labeling of the transformation relies on extant folkloric (i.e., pagan) motifs: for instance, the pivotal reference to "Lord" is entrusted to the blacksmith, whom folklore portrays as a dragon slayer and possessor of sacred and poetic powers.[31]

Thus, "After the Ball" can be seen as looking both forward to its Soviet-era refractions and back to a folkloric formulation (and subsequent literary reformulations) of the underlying topos. Against the background of this "genre memory," Tolstoy manages within the laconic limits of a short story to enact a symbolic transition from the paganism of official culture to his own version of Christianity. In the context of the Silver Age preoccupation with unconventional syntheses of various cultural models—in particular, pagan and Christian—Tolstoy's solution stands out as pointedly ascetic. As for this chapter's focus on themes and variations, the archaic substratum tapped (whether deliberately or unconsciously) by Tolstoy seems to have been successfully channeled into its new use: to root the overt message of the story in the deeper levels of literary structure by equating marriage with flogging and culture, with pagan cruelty. If there is any surplus ideological value accruing from this operation, it may consist in those misogynist, homosexual, and sadistic elements injected in the narrative, albeit subliminally and under repression, by the archaic hypogram and typical of Tolstoy's late life and works.

In "Lady with Flowers," both the story's declared theme and its less obvious personal authorial purport have interesting archetypal counterparts. The heroine is a kind of sleeping beauty,[32] or rather Eurydice, who has to be reclaimed from the netherworld. On the way there, her "prince" has to pay the Charon-like fishermen (their mistrust may be correlated with Orpheus's nonpayment). In fact, she is dead from the start (she does not eat or smile) and accordingly divided by water from her husband, who leaves for work by boat (cf. Zoshchenko's fear of water, as confessed in *Before Sunrise*). Having found her, instead of redeeming her with a kiss and taking her with him, he rejects her and blithely returns to the other shore alone, thus reversing the story's archaic hypogram. As in Tolstoy, this conversion serves to reinforce the story's explicit, if ambiguous, (anti)cultural message.

Ginzburg's memoirs read as adventures of a Cinderella in distress, who is lost in the forest, at the mercy of evil "stepmothers" (the female camp commandants in other chapters), but who eventually finds her Prince Charming, alias good sorcerer, to whom she is an apprentice. In her quest she is helped by (the spirit of) her fairy "godmother"— Akhmatova. More or less overt, these fairy-tale motifs lead us further down into the hidden archaic underpinnings of the plot.

The core motif of the pot of human flesh combines at least two such elements. On the one hand, it symbolically represents the dead body of the bridegroom (hence the doctor's absence) awaiting magical rebirth (hence his prompt return). Initiation and wedding rituals included various types of bloodletting, cutting, roasting, and dismemberment of young males (supposed to endow them with a magic knowledge of animal languages, among other things) and, on occasion, females, whence the possibility of the heroine-to-meat-loaves metamorphosis. The performance of these acts of mutilation could be entrusted to other agents (slaves, villains, ogres, animal helpers). In this connection, the wolf, with whom the cannibal convict is equated, can be seen as the totem of the hero or heroine, especially in light of the positive image of the "gray wolf" in Russian folklore.

On the other hand, by identifying correctly the meat in the pot, the heroine (unlike Tolstoy's and Zoshchenko's protagonists) does pass the test. Among initiation and prewedding tests for the bride were the tasting and cooking of food and handling of the oven; pots and other crockery were also prominent in wedding rituals and their literary reflections (Propp 1946; Freidenberg 1936).

The joint effect of the two motifs is, again, to provide a powerful subliminal accompaniment to the text's explicit agenda. But this time the task is pointedly affirmative: rehabilitation of marriage, culture, and society. Verging as it does on the idyllic, such a discourse can only profit from an infusion of some bad blood from archaic rituals.

To conclude: the three texts are linked by their overt agenda of problematizing 'love as culture's way of overcoming death.' They treat this common topos differently, in response to the different cultural-political situations. The texts' overt messages are supported and enriched by the archaic hypograms they tap, update, and convert, each in their own ways.

FOUR

A Study in Framing:
Pushkin, Bunin, Nabokov, and
Theories of Story and Discourse

From variations on a theme we now turn to a complementary case: different uses of a formal pattern. Just as in the preceding chapter the common denominator had extended from the thematic to the structural ('before-after'), the texts we will be examining now share not only a formal feature but elements of content as well, making comparison more graphic. The rereading of primary texts will again affect their critical echoes; in fact, the secondary prong of the argument will have to be even sharper than usual: while accepted thematizations tend to be impersonal, "universal," it takes a strong theoretician to articulate a response to structural patterns. The discussion will focus on the treatment of compositional framing in Ivan Bunin's 1916 short story "Gentle Breathing," as identified by Lev Vygotsky,[1] and will enter, in an attempt to revise this double, literary-and-critical classic, a field of strong reinterpretive forces.

Framing and Rereading Around 1917

The story's writing and its theoretical reception belong to a period of sweeping ideological and stylistic change, which was accompanied by a massive reformulation of the literary tradition and modes of theorizing, involving such critical schools as symbolist, Marxist, sociological, formalist, Freudian, and Bakhtinian. Structurally, framing is a narrative device directly engaged in rereading the *fabula*, or 'story' proper, in the terminology the Russian Formalists introduced to distinguish 'story' from 'discourse,' or *siuzhet*.[2] Distinguish to the point of opposing, because in the revolutionary spirit of the time they insisted on emphasizing the antagonistic struggle: extratextual, between literary trends, and intratextual, between components of the work, particularly between 'form' and 'material.'

Form was, of course, their favorite: a technique of purposeful reshaping of "reactionary" and inert matter. They visualized matter not necessarily as "raw" but rather as imprisoned in the worn-out shell of tradition, from which it had to be liberated by a new, "defamiliarizing" formal effort in a dialectical negation of negative old forms. Hence the theoretical myth of *siuzhet*'s creative and desirable dictatorship over *fabula*, a logical product of the activist, world-remaking mentality of the avant-garde. In a characteristic utopian gesture, the Formalist critics extolled framing as a means of destroying the story's given chronological order and thus releasing it from the clutches of empirical history into a new, timeless life. Also, the "noticing" and upgrading of various traditionally subordinate, peripheral, and "irrelevant" elements of the text, by writers and critics alike, led to a rearrangement of the narrative hierarchy in a move cognate with the parallel promotion of the cacographic "lower" voices discussed in Chapter 1. (The Formalist theory of literary evolution as canonization of the "junior branch" prefigures Deconstruction's attention to the marginal, with the difference that the latter is somehow supposed to become privileged without taking over the center.)

The approaches pursued by individual scholars were not uniform. In rejecting the "organicist" tradition (epitomized by Belinsky and Potebnia), some, like Victor Shklovsky, were extreme "destructionists," believing that mere 'negation' (today's 'subversion') was all that had to be, and was, accomplished by art. Others, for instance Sergei Eisenstein, took a more dialectical path. On the one hand, he stressed the conflict between 'content' and the techniques of its expression, preferring a contrapuntal, 'cheerful' portrayal of 'sadness' to the organic 'sorrowful sorrow' and 'joyful joy' (1949: 150–53). But he always insisted on controlling the production of specific meanings, which are inherent in the material/content and must be brought out by manipulative framing.

Eisenstein's analysis of the portrait of Ermolova by Valentin Serov (1905), a contemporary and, roughly speaking, painterly counterpart to Bunin, will illustrate Eisenstein's 'synthetic' approach.[3]

> Eisenstein begins by stating that the painting, despite its austerity (monotony of colors, static pose, scanty setting), successfully conveys the inspirational power of the actress. This is achieved by innovative compositional means as the lines of the background (floor, mirror, ceiling reflected in the mirror) cut up the picture into several "frames" (in the cinematographic sense): from a long shot of the standing figure to a midshot of the torso, to a bust portrait, to a close-up of the head. This gradual enlargement is accompanied by a parallel shifting of perspective from the downward view of the feet to the level view of the middle part of the body to the upward foreshortening of the top, with the additional effect of the head's projection against the ceiling, thanks to the complex mirroring. These (and some other devices) impress on the viewer the sense of literally 'looking up' at (and to) the actress, or, what amounts to the same thing, of her 'growing' on the viewer.
>
> Emphasizing the innovativeness of Serov's framing, Eisenstein claimed that it anticipated the use of frames in cubist painting and even in cinematic montage: "The means used here lie . . . already beyond the boundaries of that stage of painting to which the picture still belongs. . . . A great work of art *always* . . . contains as a *partial device* elements of what . . . will constitute the *principles* and *methods* of the new stage of that art's progress" (377).[4]

Where did Lev Vygotsky stand? In theory, he echoed Shklovsky's 'antithetic' view of form; accordingly, he spoke of the "destruction of content by form" (1971: 156) and made a point of contrasting Bunin's material ('vulgar life') with the meaning read into it by the framing devices ('lightness'). But by the same token, in his practical analysis he ascribed a quite definite content value to the essentially negative operations.[5]

In what follows I try to bridge the gap (unwittingly leapt over by Vygotsky) more or less along Eisensteinian lines. The identification of the metaphors that underlay Vygotsky's criticism is supposed to alert us to the misreadings they may have imposed on the author (Bunin), whose strategies may or may not have coincided with the critic's. On the whole, the proposed close rereading of "Gentle Breathing" claims, in a traditional way, to retrieve the story's "true" structure by revising an earlier interpretation and turning for evidence to the "text itself" as well as to intertextual parallels and counterexamples.

The thrust of Vygotsky's argument was that Bunin avoided writing up the short and insignificant—"turbid" (*mutnaia*)—love life of Olia Meshcherskaia as a romantic thriller.

> The third-person narrative begins by Olia's grave and outlines her adolescence as a provocatively vivacious schoolgirl who virtually drives a schoolmate to suicide. The principal reprimands Olia on her prematurely bold feminine ways only to be told that she has already been deflowered, and by none other than the principal's brother. A month later, Olia is shot dead by another lover, whom she had refused to marry and had provoked even more by showing her diary entry about the original seduction. The narrative then shifts to a spinsterly classmistress visiting Olia's grave, reminiscing about Olia's short-lived charms, and recalling Olia's fascination with the idea that she did have light breathing, an epitome of feminine beauty according to an old book she had read. This light breathing, concludes the narrator, has now dispersed itself in the wind blowing at the cemetery.

To set in relief the deliberate lack of suspense in Bunin's narrative, Vygotsky sketched an alternative, traditionally fabulaic treatment of the plot, against which the actual "Gentle Breathing" is to be read.

> If the story of [her] life were told to us in chronological sequence, suspense would be almost intolerable until the moment of her death. . . . The suspense of our interest, which each new episode . . . stresses and directs toward the next solution, would have filled this short story to excess. . . . We would learn how Olia seduced the officer, how she began a liaison with him, how she swore she loved him and talked about marriage, and how she began to make fun of him. We would witness the scene at the railway station, and with almost unbearable suspense would be there watching her during those last moments when the officer, her diary in his hands, steps onto the platform and shoots her. . . . It is the culmination. (P. 155)

To instantiate this kind of writing, one can turn to a real contemporary text. Alexander Kuprin's very popular and much anthologized "The Garnet Bracelet" (1911, see Proffer 1969: 403–46) can indeed be envisaged as a virtual negative inspiration for "Gentle Breathing."

> The story of the poor telegraphist Zheltkov's fatal love for the perfect—unattainable, beautiful, noble, rich, and happily married—Princess Vera is told by an impersonal omniscient narrator mainly in chronological order, with a

suspenseful deceleration toward the dramatic culmination. The action begins on the day of Vera's birthday. Zheltkov, who for years has bombarded Vera with letters of loving veneration, sends her a garnet bracelet, connoting love and violent death. Pressured by Vera's family to stop pursuing her, Zheltkov commits suicide, his last wish being that Vera listen to a Beethoven sonata, which she does after first visiting his body and depositing on its "cold, moist forehead a long, affectionate kiss." She imagines him speaking to her with love and forgiveness ("Hallowed be thy name!") and realizes that an exceptional love had passed her by. Bathed in tears, she feels reconciled with life and herself.

Thematically, Kuprin's story (not unlike Bunin's) is about overcoming death. Fabulaically, it stresses the modest insignificance of the hero and his class inferiority to the heroine, features reverent 'graveyard witnesses,' and uses nature (an autumnal landscape) to foreshadow death, and memory and art (music) to transcend it. Compositionally, it foregrounds a symbolic detail (the bracelet); includes several framed texts (other stories of love; Zheltkov's letters; the newspaper item about his death; the husband's cartoon spoofs of the telegraphist's love for Vera), thus deviating to an extent from temporal linearity and structural tightness; and presents some events as fulfillment of wishes and fears (Vera has a premonition of Zheltkov's suicide; he predicts her visiting his dead body; her friend Jennie empathetically chooses to play the right sonata).

Kuprin puts all this to remarkably traditional use. Death is transcended (contrary to Bunin's story) not by 'life as is' but by a 'great love,' whose modesty is only a romantic appearance concealing inner uniqueness. This love is overdramatized by its platonic nature, princely object, self-sacrificial ending, and tear-jerking social casting (romantic underdog victimized by high society). Of 'graveyard witnesses' there are, despite the absence of a literal graveyard, no fewer than two, both presented in dead seriousness: the pianist and the landlady (to whom Zheltkov is "like a son" and through whom he prearranges his posthumous communication with Vera and the final sanctification of the bracelet, to be hung on the image of the Holy Virgin). Art and cultural memory are represented by their most sublime icons (Christianity, Beethoven, Pushkin, and Napoleon; the dead protagonist's face is compared to the "death masks of two great martyrs, Pushkin and Napoleon").

Compositionally, the narrative lacks framing, beginning as it does with a lengthy landscape and ending with a lengthy musical recital (cum otherworldly voice-over). The many embedded stories openly function as parables for the main plot, and in the one case where the plot is duplicated by its framed stylization, the strategy is unabashedly romantic: the tragifarcical cartoons precede the melodramatic denouement, which thus has the earnest last word.

> This can be seen as a clumsy imitation of the use of pictures in "The Stationmaster" (see below). In fact, one of the cartoon vignettes is a clear allusion to Pushkin's "Domik v Kolomne": "Here, dressed as a countrywoman, he takes up the duties of dishwasher in our kitchen. But the excessive favor which Luka the cook bestows upon him puts him to flight."

As for the story's emblematic detail, it is a hackneyed valuable ("precious stone"), heavily overplayed throughout the plot but deprived of the closural role by a succession of other "strong finales." These include the parting posthumous kiss, the posthumous note about *Largo Appassionato*, the actual music playing, the chantlike refrain "Hallowed be thy name!", the concluding reflections, and the tears. One wonders whether Kuprin intended to imitate some of Beethoven's interminable endings.

It is difficult to separate the structural flaws of Kuprin's story from its general narrative overkill, which after all is the reverse side of the story's kitschy romanticism. Quantitatively, the overkill takes the form of excessive length, twin characters (Vera and her flirtatious sister; Vera's nice husband and his meaner brother-in-law Nikolai; the two 'graveyard witnesses'), and other redundancies and *longueurs*. Qualitatively, the author always plays it safe, trying to have it both ways.

> For instance, Vera both gets her 'great love' and remains faithful to her husband, and this is repeated in her sister, ostensibly a flirt but actually another faithful wife. Vera is both the cause of the hero's death and our perfectly good heroine. Similarly, her husband can afford to be a 'nice guy' while his brother-in-law plays 'bad cop' to his good one. And finally, the mix of the 'poor clerk,' the Bible, Beethoven, Pushkin, Napoleon, and the "beautiful people"—the Prince and the Princess—lacks any common denominator other than a general romantic blur.

On the whole, Kuprin's narrative remains, despite all its frames and redundancies, basically unframed, fabulaic, and suspenseful, while its counterpart in Bunin is, as we will see, trim in the very way it creates the impression of anticlimactic looseness. In "Gentle Breathing," according to Vygotsky, Bunin systematically disrupts chronology and undercuts suspense to perform a miraculous purification of life's "turbid waters." This reading, however, leaves many questions unanswered. Was Olia's fabulaic 'life as is' all that meaningless? Can purely disruptive strategies be responsible for the effect of 'lightness and clarity'? Is that effect the most accurate thematization of the story? In particular, should not the spatial, contiguous (and thus atemporal) aspect of 'framing' find its place in the picture? What is the historical context of Bunin's narrative innovations?

The adversative relation between story and discourse is an age-old device, in Russian literature going back at least as far as Pushkin. In fact, a Pushkin narrative underwent spectacular critical rereading at a date halfway between Bunin's writing and Vygotsky's reading of "Gentle Breathing." It took Russian literary criticism some ninety years and a modernist focus on framing to notice in "The Stationmaster" (1831) the writing on the wall of the station: as pointed out by Mikhail Gershenzon (1919), the funny German pictures illustrating the parable of the prodigal son form an ironic counterpoint to the heroine's actual success story. The facts of Dunia's life belie the sentimental fictions of the prodigal-son cartoons as well as the more transparent Karamzinian subtext, "Poor Liza."[6] Pushkin's techniques laid the foundations for later play with frames, in particular by Bunin, whose strategies were, however, clearly different, a difference that underscores the problem of identifying precisely which framing devices are responsible for which specific effects.

"The Stationmaster": Bracketing Reality

Pushkin's narrative abounds in framing patterns.

> First of all, there is the hierarchy of narrating sources: Pushkin (author), A. P. (publisher), I. P. Belkin (collector-editor), A. G. N. (primary first-person character-narrator), Samson Vyrin (protagonist-narrator), Van'ka (minor character-narrator), plus the many extra- and intratextual voices: Viazemskii, Radishchev, Dmitriev, Karamzin; the doctor, the cabdriver.
>
> Then there are the pictorial frames: literal—the prodigal-son pictures—and figurative—the three "stills," or tableaux, that stop the action. These include the kiss given by Dunia to the primary narrator in the hallway of the station and summed up in retrospect by a verse quotation; the stylized genre painting

of Dunia and Minsky glimpsed by Vyrin through the doorframe; and Dunia's prostrate pose on her father's grave, as seen and reported by the boy Van'ka.

In each case, frames, stylization, and their subsequent ironization by further framing overshadow the "reality" they bracket. They serve not so much to set off the story as to distance it from the reader. Moreover, since much about the heroine's actions remains unspecified (e.g., the cause of her fainting and her marital status in the end), the narrative amounts to a carefully framed three dots (O'Toole 1982: 107–10): the frames, which ironize each other, occupy, as it were, center stage, obtruding the view of that framed reality in the name of which they are created and subverted. "Life" takes place behind and in between the frames and clichés, so that the sense of genuine reality is created in a deliberately negative way—by omission and implication.

Emblematic of these strategies is the disembodied way in which the narrator relates his only but quite close encounter with the heroine. He dryly gives the facts, an evaluation, and a literary quote, but keeps out the physical and emotional details of the kiss. In fact, he omits a description he (or rather, Pushkin) had drafted of Dunia's "languid eyes, her suddenly disappearing smile, . . . the warmth of her breath and the fresh imprinting of her lips" (Pushkin 1937–49, 8: 644; the last word is *gubok*, "little lips"). Important for the narrator are Dunia's actions, which contribute to her characterization and foreshadow her moves in the main plot.

Similarly fabulaic is the role played by the pictures on the wall: together with the Karamzinian subtext, they form a false counterplot, a foil to the actual course of events. In the same spirit, the narrative design relies largely on chronological progression: the narrator's three visits to the station motivate the three installments (two of them successive flashbacks) of the sad story of the little man's gradual demise. The sum total of these fabulaic scripts and counterscripts spells out the message of "The Stationmaster": 'beware of clichés, or you may end up a prodigal father.' The parable is inverted, but the narrative remains within the confines of essentially parabolic discourse.

Pushkin's innovatively antithetic framing both reacted against and grew out of the organic design exemplified by "Poor Liza"'s almost exclusively "sorrowful sorrow." Karamzin's first-person narrator begins with a lengthy introduction about his love of "sad subjects," proceeds to relate his tearful *fabula* (practically without temporal shifts or suppression of information),[7] and closes the frame on his nostalgic reunion at the heroine's grave with the repentant protagonist. The sentimentalist 'love of sadness,' however, is a contradictory ideological position, and it is unwittingly taken to an absurd extreme (by the protagonist and the narrator-author alike) in Erast's "listen[ing] with unfeigned pleasure" (p. 61) to the sad story, told by Liza's mother, of her husband's death in her arms.

Moreover, the naive confirmation of sentimentalist values, which takes place in the frame, conflicts with their metaliterary critique in the *fabula*. Erast falls in love with Liza because she embodies his idyllic bookish fantasies: "He often read novels and idylls; he . . . transported himself mentally to those times (real or unreal) when, if we are to believe poets, all people wandered carefree across meadows . . . [etc.]. It seemed to him that in Liza he had found what his heart had been long seeking . . . and decided—for a while at least—to abandon high society." In the end, he becomes disenchanted partly for similar value-laden reasons—because "platonic love had given way to feelings of which he could not be *proud*." The italics are Karamzin's, highlighting reference to the fashionable discourse of the time (which is in accordance with Girard's [1965: 1–52] theory of 'mimetic love,' mediated by culture or other third parties).

The contradiction is patched over in the frame with the help of 'sadness': sentimentalism ends up feasible—if not as idyllic pastoral, then at least as graveyard elegy. Yet the seeds of metaliterary irony have been sown. Another major contradiction involves the treatment of the cultural motif of 'money.' Erast keeps trying to buy Liza's love and forgiveness and sells his own affections to the rich woman he marries. But the narrator has no part in this, and even Erast is brought to repent it in the unambiguously naive frame closure.

Pushkin's travesty of "Poor Liza" reacts to and inverts both of its 'cultural' strands: (1) it builds on Karamzin's mimetic view of love by inscribing it into the numerous frames and subtexts only to subvert it in the end (Liza and Minsky live happily ever after *despite* all sentimentalist expectations), and (2) it develops the mercantile theme in a similar way.

Pushkin makes money matters pervade the *fabula*, often in a clear echo of Karamzin's situations: Minsky generously overpays the services of the station-master, bribes the doctor to fake illness and stay at the house while he courts

Dunia, keeps Dunia in money and luxury, and tries to pay off her father's claims on her.

Moreover, Pushkin introduces financial considerations into the frame, where the primary narrator repeatedly mentions his disbursements. A. G. N. keeps track of paying the various drivers who bring him to the station—and the stationmaster himself—and what is more important, he "purchases" Vyrin's narrative with a glass of punch, just as in the end he "buys" the story's denouement from Van'ka.

A link between the framing and framed stories in this respect is provided by Dunia's kiss, "bought" by A. G. N. Thus, the "realistic" motif of 'acquisition for money' subsumes the *fabula* and the frame: Pushkin ironically transforms the Karamzinian narrative contract (between the narrator, characters, and readers), based on the aesthetic value of suffering, into a commercial one (both stories and beloveds can be bought).[8]

Pushkin's framing strategies are epitomized by the closing scene:

A red-haired, one-eyed little boy in tatters ran up and led me straight to the edge of the village. . . . We arrived at the graveyard, a bare place, exposed to the winds, strewn with wooden crosses, without a single sapling to shade it. I had never seen such a mournful cemetery.

"Here's the old stationmaster's grave," said the boy to me, jumping on a mound of sand with a black cross bearing a brass icon.

"And the lady came here, did she?" I asked.

"Aye, she did," replied Van'ka; "I watched her from afar. She threw herself on the grave and lay there for a long time. Then the lady came back to the village, sent for the priest, gave him some money, and went on her way, and to me she gave a silver five-kopeck piece—a wonderful lady!"

I too gave five kopecks to the urchin, and no longer regretted either the journey or the seven roubles spent on it. (Pushkin 1983: 102–3)

One protagonist's visit to the grave of the other is relayed to the reader by the limited primary narrator, who sees it through the eyes—indeed, the single eye—of a little peasant boy who had watched the scene earlier "from afar." This sighting is encased in and practically obscured by a fourfold framework of monetary transactions: between the priest and Dunia, Dunia and Van'ka, Van'ka and A. G. N., A. G. N. and the cabdriver.

This ending pointedly contrasts with that of "Poor Liza," in particular in the treatment of the 'graveyard witness' motif[9] and of 'nature.' The onetime visits of Dunia (a past farewell) and A. G. N. (a curiosity detour on one of his business trips), guided by the careless Van'ka, who "desecrates" the grave by his stomping, are in clear opposition to Erast's and the reliably authorial narrator's reverent commemoration of Liza's grave. In fact, even Liza herself is a definite, if figurative, presence there: according to the superstitious villagers, the wailing of the wind, to the accompaniment of which her story is being recalled, carries the groans of "poor Liza."

> This sad but effective union with a force of nature, underscored by the grave's location "by the pond, under a grim oak-tree," the narrator's favorite spot, caps Liza's consistent identification in the story with flowers and the natural. Erast and Liza meet outdoors. The "hand of her dear friend" plays with her hair together with "the zephyrs." Abandoned, she sheds her tears and heaves sighs in the woods. Her wailings merge with the plaintive voice of the sad she-dove, and so on. (Dunia is seen mostly in interiors.)

All this is starkly reversed in the final picture of the desolate and tree-less grave of the stationmaster—only to be curiously recycled in a graveyard story written some hundred years later.

Indeed, "Gentle Breathing" begins exactly where "Poor Liza" and "The Stationmaster" end—at the graveyard—and it manages an un-likely hybrid. A sophisticated distancing of *fabula* by frame manipulation à la Pushkin is combined with the posthumous veneration of a young victim through more organic framing reminiscent of Karam-zin. I will first explore the 'destructive' hypothesis proposed by Vygot-sky and then advance a more constructive reading of Bunin's narra-tive.

"Gentle Breathing": Destabilizing the Narrative Worldview

Temporal shifts dominate the composition of "Gentle Breathing," working both to subvert ("lighten") fabulaic suspense and to strengthen some of the narrative contrasts and emotional jolts (Wood-ward 1980: 153). Whimsical as these shifts are, they shuttle more or less regularly between the present and the past in a pattern that as such can help both to defeat and to build suspense: [10]

> from the present (at the grave) to the past (Olia's school years), which almost reaches the present (her murder and its investigation), back into the past (the

story of her fall), again into the present (the classmistress on the way to Olia's grave), into the past (of the classmistress), again into the present (the grave), into the past (the conversation about gentle breathing), into the present (windy cemetery).

But Bunin further unsettles the orderliness of the shifts by uneven and disproportionate duration. Some major past episodes are cursorily summarized, while less important ones are developed into detailed scenes. Two major "close-ups" are Olia's conversation with the school principal and her final monologue about gentle breathing, both of no real fabulaic consequence, whereas a chain of dramatic events is related in one almost absurdly long and compressed sentence:

And Olia Meshcherskaia's unthinkable confession, which had staggered the school principal, was completely confirmed: the officer stated to the coroner that Meshcherskaia had led him on, been intimate with him, promised to marry him, and then, on the day of the murder, at the station, while seeing him off to Novocherkassk, had suddenly told him that it had never entered her head to love him, that she had only been making fun of him with all that talk about marriage, and then let him read the page in her diary that concerned Maliutin.

There are similar disproportions at the intrasentential level. The "norms" of relative semantic weight of the syntactic constituents are repeatedly distorted, as in the sprawling sentence that "muffles" the fatal shot by dispensing with it literally in one word (Vygotsky 1971: 156): "And a month after this conversation, a Cossack officer, ungainly and of plebeian appearance, who had absolutely nothing in common with Olia Meshcherskaia's circle, shot her on the platform of the railway station, in a large crowd of people who had just arrived by train." A similar effect is achieved by the immediately following description of Olia's "last winter":

The winter was snowy, frosty, the sun would go down early behind the grove of tall fir-trees in the snowy school garden, [the sun being] unfailingly serene, radiant, promising frost and sunshine again tomorrow, more strolling along Cathedral Street, skating in the city park, a pink sunset, and that swarm of skaters perpetually moving in all directions, among whom Olia Meshcherskaia seemed to be the best-dressed, the most carefree, and the happiest.

The sequence of urban festivities that includes the depiction of the heroine and occupies two-thirds of the sentence is syntactically marginalized, shifted to a modal ("promised") tomorrow and tucked away in a participial phrase at the end of a series of absolute attributive constructions. As for Olia, she appears in a subordinate clause further down in this long participial phrase. In addition to thus violating the hierarchy of signification, the sentence also exhibits a characteristic temporal merging (of 'today' and 'tomorrow') and the Proustian technique of neutralizing the difference between recurrent and singular events by endowing the former[11] with the detailed uniqueness of the latter (Genette 1970).

The effect of temporal irregularity of the narrative is further enhanced by the heterogeneity of flashbacks, some of which comprise several temporal frames while others are onefold. Moreover, even had they been rearranged in linear order, the reported events would not cover Olia's biography without significant gaps. Conspicuously loose is its correlation with the life of the classmistress, so that the epiphanic conversation about gentle breathing remains unattached to the chronology of Olia's vagaries (before or after the fall? before or after the affair with the officer?). This loosening up of the narrative fits in nicely with the absence of a centralizing narrator-character of the kind used in "The Stationmaster."

Thus, whereas in Pushkin's story the flow of time in the frame organizes a similar progress in the *fabula*, in "Gentle Breathing" time is on the one hand stopped (at the graveyard) and on the other moves chaotically back and forth, with irregularities and interruptions, that is, is both transcended and energized. Suspense is not completely blunted either,[12] for advance information of Olia's death weakens interest in the denouement but not in the peripeties that will bring it about (Connolly 1982: 71). The suspense is even intensified by the way the story of Olia's fall is first skipped over, then interrupted (in the scene with the principal), and only after these retardations presented through her retrospectively introduced diary (Whalen 1986: 12–16).

Yet the traditional presentation of the *fabula* definitely is subverted in "Gentle Breathing." One innovative device consists in leaving a number of loose ends, i.e. omitting not so much the causes of events as their effects.

We never learn about the outcome of Olia's schoolmate Shenshin's attempted suicide, the ending of Olia's dramatic encounter with the principal, the subsequent development of Olia's and her parents' relations with her seducer and their friend Maliutin,[13] the resolution of Olia's despair after her fall ("There is only one way out for me now . . . I'll never get over this!"). At the same time, the narrator indulges in a detailed characterization of the fabulaically irrelevant classmistress and finds room for the completely peripheral Tolia (her brother?) and the "tall, plump Subbotina."

The fabulaic material that does get narrated lacks traditional narrative focus. Rather than telling the story of one fatal love (as in "Poor Liza" and "The Garnet Bracelet"), "Gentle Breathing" chronicles the heroine's interactions with various characters disparate in time and space. Even the participants in the main triangle (Olia, Maliutin, officer) are never brought together, and Maliutin's reactions, if any, remain unknown. In fact, the antideterminist, "pro-chance" principle of narration characteristic of the time (in particular of Chekhov's "incidentalist" narrative [Chudakov 1983]), is almost directly stated in "Gentle Breathing" on several occasions. For instance, Olia's beauty came to her "without a thought or an effort on her part," and "for some reason [pochemu-to] no one was more popular with the junior classes" than Olia, while her murderer "had absolutely nothing in common with Olia Meshcherskaia's circle."[14]

This centrifugal privileging of 'extraneous factors' returns us to the topic of manipulative framing. "Gentle Breathing" far outstrips "The Stationmaster" in filtering the *fabula* through various perspectives.

Namely: those of the impersonal omniscient narrator; city gossips; Olia's diary, later shown to the officer and mentioned in the story still later in the context of the trial; the classmistress; and Olia's favorite book. At every juncture, Bunin accentuates both the obliqueness inherent in framing (narrator, rumors, diary and the circumstances of its reading, daydreaming spinster, temporally distant conversation of two schoolgirls, "funny old book") and the immediacy of the embedded reality (e.g., Olia's emotions and other details of the seduction episode and her almost audible breathing in the end).

Thus Bunin moves away from Pushkin's ironic detachment and toward genuine sentimentality, as is especially clear in his treatment of the 'graveyard witness' figure. The fantasies of Olia's classmistress are unexpectedly endorsed by the narrator as the two voices subtly merge in the story's closing frame (Vygotsky 1971: 158).

"And now this gentle breath is dissipated again in the world, in this cloudy sky, in this cold spring wind." The main verb of this sentence, *rasseialos'* (lit. "has disseminated itself," also translated as "vanished . . . into" and "wafted through"), is a subtle pun, combining the semes of 'dispersing, disappearing' and 'spreading'; it also makes for a very oxymoronic closure: the story ends on the note of a (half-)opening to the world.

As is often the case, narrative framing is echoed by the use of framed pictures in the literal sense. One such picture appears in the opening sequence, describing Olia's grave:

A rather large, convex medallion made of porcelain has been let into the cross itself, and on the medallion is the photograph of a schoolgirl with joyous, wonderfully vivacious eyes.
It is Olia Meshcherskaia.

The theme of vitality's escape from confining frames (the grave, the cross, the medallion, the picture) is signaled by the immediacy of the heroine's coming alive in the flashback prompted by the medallion. This narrative resurrection[15] and transcendence of boundaries is triggered by that emblematic one-sentence paragraph—"It is Olia Meshcherskaia"—written in the present tense and without reference to the picture.

Another picture that comes alive in the story is the portrait of the "young Czar, painted full-length in a splendid hall," that hangs over the principal's desk. In fabulaic terms, the picture of the supreme authority serves to redouble the hostile oppressiveness of the school principal (Woodward 1980: 151–52). But Olia eludes the deterministic constraints of the *fabula*: she "like[s] it in the office" (more about this presently) and is accordingly shown "glanc[ing] at the young Czar" with pleasure, that is, obviating the intermediary of the frame.

The transcendence of frames, figurative and literal, is not confined to the sphere of discourse. In the *fabula* it takes the form of the repeated violation by the heroine of norms of behavior and physical boundaries. She dresses too boldly, defiantly talks back to the principal, and does not play by the rules with her suitors (Shenshin; the Cossack officer). And the silk handkerchief through which she is first kissed by Maliutin proves insufficient to keep her within permissible limits.

In sum, Vygotsky's schema covers much of the ground but not all. The fabulaic element is both lightened and activated—destabilized—while frames, rather than obstructing "reality," are overwhelmed by and fused with it. This calls for a reformulation of the text's dominant.

"Gentle Breathing": Shift of Focus

The generic theme of "Gentle Breathing" is the time-hallowed one of 'life and death,' with a none too original hint of 'bittersweet victory in defeat.' The life-death opposition underlies
— the narrative's 'graveyard' genre;
— the consistent juxtaposition of episodes bubbling with life and those bringing or symbolizing death;
— the character of the heroine, who is not only both vivacious and prematurely dead herself, but who influences others in the same way (provokes her schoolmate to attempt suicide, her fiancé to commit murder, and the classmistress to worship her death);[16]
— the set of other personages—all studies in hybridization of "sexy" vitality with lifelessness: the teenage suicide Shenshin; the "youngish, but gray-haired" principal; her brother, Maliutin, who is "fifty-six, but still very handsome"; the classmistress, "a girl no longer young [*nemolodaia devushka*], . . . living on . . . illusion . . . in the place of real life"; and her brother, who dies young;[17] and
— the details of the setting, which invariably combine pleasant and lively warmth, light, freshness, and so on with their mortifying opposites, a principle epitomized by the coupling, in the story's opening line, of "cemetery" and "cross" with such epithets as "fresh," "strong," and "smooth," and the leitmotif prominence in the text of lexemes denoting 'life,' 'death,' and 'killing.'

The new twist to this age-old topos is given by Bunin's very own and yet typically modernist treatment of 'transcendence.' Both in the *fabula* and the *siuzhet*, Olia easily transcends boundaries, challenging conventions, jumping the stages of the life cycle (from childhood to youth to womanhood to death), and escaping death itself. Like a butterfly, she flutters out of frames, ages, life, grave. Two related semes control the narrative embodiment of this dominant: 'lightness' (highlighted by Bunin and noted by Vygotsky) and 'overstepping.'

'Lightness.' The heroine and the narrative alike free themselves from the rigid determinism of moral and fabulaic constraints. Hence the choice of the story's title trope, which identifies the most spiritual of corporeal attributes; hence also the entire aesthetic of foregrounding discourse, memory, fantasy, style, and tropes. Yet the overall effect is far from one of disembodied flights of stylistic fancy, albeit counterbalanced by life's fabulaic 'troubled waters.' Such an alignment of values (proposed by Vygotsky as the story's thematic dominant) would ill agree with Bunin's keen appreciation of the material world. Bunin therefore performs an original tour de force in the handling of 'matter' itself, in accordance with the story's second dominant seme ('overstepping of boundaries') and the general artistic spirit of the epoch.

'Overstepping' is reified as a literal 'shift of focus' from everything pivotal and central to the contiguous, peripheral, and superficial. In the *fabula*, it spawns inclusion of previously irrelevant factors, in particular new ways of linking characters and plot with setting and physical detail. In the *siuzhet*, the shift means positive interaction with frames and privileging less important facts, subordinate clauses, linguistic texture, and synecdoches. Let us examine some of the displacements at work in Bunin's story.

The sentence about the shot is remarkable not only for its negative thrust, which can be summarized as 'muffling the usual with the extraneous,' but also for the positive panning to the "big picture"—the crowd at the railway station. In fact, this is one of the many scenes that show Olia as part of a crowd—in a characteristic anticipation of the Pasternakian poetics of contiguity, "the sense of being related to the beauty of the entire spectacle." [18]

> As a little schoolgirl, Olia is fully merged with the crowd; then she stands out from it as "the best-dressed, the most carefree, and the happiest," as in the description of her last winter, or is seen against its background, as when she delivers her monologue about gentle breathing "during the noon recess, while strolling in the school garden."
>
> The garden is Olia's typical "Pasternakian" background. The "sun . . . go[es] down early behind the . . . fir-trees in the snowy school garden." Olia strolls in the garden (as well as in the fields and woods) while expecting Maliutin, then together with him in the garden, which is (lit.) "flooded with sunlight." The cemetery is described as a "large low garden," reached by the classmistress after walking across various parts of the city and a field.

Other macroexteriors include the cityscape, skating rink, railway station, fields, woods, wind, sky, and finally "the world" (in the concluding sentence).

Nor are interiors, despite being enclosures, hostile to the heroine.

> Olia is at home in the hall, where she runs around with her schoolmates; the glassed-in veranda, where she "falls"; the "brilliant hall" in the czar's portrait. Especially telling is Olia's counterfabulaic enjoyment of the principal's

office—its cleanness and spaciousness, the warmth of the Dutch fireplace, the freshness of the lilies of the valley (incidentally, poor Liza's emblematic flowers), the youthfulness of the pictured czar, and even the smoothness of the part in the principal's hairdo.

In saying to Olia, "You will attend badly," the principal unwittingly formulates the story's narrative program: the heroine's attention is focused not on her fabulaic antagonist but on the setting. Olia is not so much in conflict with the principal as in love with the "young Czar" and the Dutch fireplace, which is almost personified (the Russian word *gollandka* can also mean "a Dutchwoman").

On the smallest scale, the change of narrative orientation results in highlighting the material manifestations of the setting and the characters' appearance. The world of "Gentle Breathing" (as, indeed, Bunin's world in general) is consistently, provocatively physical.

We can clearly see, hear, feel the smooth heaviness of the oakwood cross, the whistling of the wind through the china wreath, the outline of Olia's developing breasts, her disheveled hair and the baring of her knee by her running around, the principal's knitting rolling away on the floor, and so on. Every character has a distinct physical presence: the Cossack officer is *nekrasivyi*, "ungainly, ugly"; the classmistress, "a girl no longer young," "a little woman in mourning, in black kid gloves, and with an ebony sunshade"; even Subbotina, who appears only once, is "tall [and] plump."

A peak of 'physicalness' is attained in the description of the "fall." Penned by Olia herself, it lovingly details Maliutin's horses, clothes, beard, eyes, and his English cologne, "except [she] didn't like that cape he came in." Characteristically, in contrast to Leo Tolstoy, who understands but disapproves of Natasha Rostova's unexpected physical infatuation with Anatole, Bunin not only fails to condemn his heroine but actually rather relishes the shallowness of her emotions. Thus he pushes to an extreme something subtly implicit in Tolstoy, whose "natural" heroine acts out her frustration with the abstinence imposed on her by the rationalistic Bolkonskys, father and son. As the impressionist narrator of a contemporary French novella aptly put it, "For me, there is enough depth on the surface of things" (Jean Giraudoux 1955 [1911], 1: 134). Bunin's reluctance to morally judge his heroine is part and parcel of the turn-of-the-century culture's revision of the entire "traditional/positivist" chronotope and value system.

Attention to detail produces sequences where a general view is followed by a synecdochic close-up.

Thus, the picture of the "gray-haired" but "young-looking" principal and her office narrows down to the description of the "smooth part" in her hairdo. Incidentally, this close-up may go back to Afanasii Fet's poem "Tol'ko v mire i est', chto tenistyi . . ." ("In the World There Is Only the Shadowy . . ."; 1883), which begins with a picture of a garden and then gradually zooms in on the heroine's *probor*, "hair-part."

The *pars pro toto* principle is introduced earlier in Olia's biographical sketch, where she is part of "the noisy crowd of little brown uniforms," and even before that in the sentence that equates the heroine with her graveyard photo, to say nothing of the synecdochic title.

In fact, the title, as spelled out in the closure, is emblematic of the shift of compositional focus from the fabulaic relations among characters to the continuum that subsumes the fabric of their individual beings and the surrounding macroworld. Characteristically, the heroine's gentle breathing does not refer to her interactions with the other protagonists (unlike, for instance, the garnet bracelet in Kuprin's story); it links her to her reading, her self-image, the impression that lives on extrafabulaically in the memory of her classmistress, and to the cemetery wind. This latter effect is carefully prepared.

> The 'wind' motif appears in the very first framing scene and returns in the last, where it pervades the classmistress's visit to the cemetery. It is absent from the episodes of Olia's life, where it is tactfully replaced with its human-size counterparts—Olia's "whirlwind" (*vikhrem*) rushing and her "deep breath" (*glubokii vzdokh*)—and it reappears in the last sentence, where the micro- and macro-winds meet.

Several less conspicuous foreshadowings of the finale are insinuated through subliminal wordplay, thus bringing us to the activization of yet another "extraneous" element: language.

> Very early, Olia is referred to as *vetrena*, "flighty," lit. "windy"; the implied environmental connection is not only linguistic but intertextual and mythological: it goes back to Fedor Tiutchev's poetic line about "vetrenaia Geba," lit. "the windy Hebe," who combines anthropomorphic and meteorological features ("A Spring Storm," 1829).
>
> Later, Olia's love of the principal's office is subtly motivated by the wording of its description, which has "the office [*kabinet*, masculine] breathing so well . . . with [exuding or inhaling] the warmth of the shining Dutch oven [*gollandka*, feminine]," and thus encapsulates the overall pattern of the heroine's union with the respiration of the world at large. (The words for 'world' [*mir*] and 'wind' [*veter*] are masculine; the mediating 'breathing' [*dykhanie*], neuter.)

Furthermore, the root of the key word of this phrase, *dyshavshego*, "[that was] breathing," links it to several other lexemes prominent in the text of the story: *vzdokh*, "sigh, breath"; *dykhanie*, "breathing"; *vzdykhaiu*, "[I] am sighing, breathing"; *vozdukh*, "air." The entire cluster is foregrounded by the title and the concluding episode, where breathing is read about, discussed, demonstrated, and promoted to closural trope.

The key phrase *legkoe dykhanie* ("gentle, light breathing") itself is a minia-ture poem, subtly metered (´-- - ´--) and onomatopoetically alliterated (in -*kh*-).

The 'importance of the word' is clearly articulated in "Gentle Breath-ing."

Paradigmatically, it is overdetermined by the Old and New Testament equa-tion of what was "in the beginning": the Spirit/Wind that moved upon the waters (Genesis 1: 1–2) and the Word (John 1: 1).[19]

Quite early, the narrator employs the hackneyed romantic figure of doubt-ing the adequacy of human words to depict the heroine's physical charms: "all those [bodily] forms whose charm has never yet been expressed by ordinary human words."[20]

Olia's confrontation with the principal revolves around the semantic prob-lem of whether Olia is a "little girl" or a "woman"; and the classmistress wonders "how one can connect this pure gaze and the horror now linked with the name [!] of Olia Meshcherskaia."

The resolution of the tension between Word and Flesh defines the peripeties of the narrative. In the spirit of the Silver Age (of which Bunin was if not part at least a reluctant partner), with its replay of the romantic and Platonic primacy of Word and Idea over Life, reality is shown imitating, conversing with, and embracing the word.

Thus, the outcome of Olia's terminological discussion with the principal had been predetermined by the wording of her reaction to the summons—"the quick womanly movement, already a habit," with which she arranged her hair—while the disclosure of the fall is presented as a "confirmation" of Olia's previous "unthinkable confession."

Similarly, the culmination of the *fabula* is a self-fulfillment of Olia's fore-bodings and a result of the diary page being somewhat futuristically brought out into the world, into the midst of the railway commotion.[21]

The story concludes with a manifold demonstration of the power of the word. The control exercised over reality by the verbal portrait of ideal beauty in the "funny old book" is confirmed both by a cumulative finale and by its careful foreshadowings, recognized in retrospect.

As one reaches the description, one realizes that the recipe has all along been embodied in Olia, in particular, the prescribed "arms longer than usual" (reminiscent of Olia's consistent excessiveness) and "shell-pink knees" (referring back to Olia's knee bared as she rushes).

Then the portrait's breathing comes spectacularly alive. It merges with *this* breath drawn by the heroine and *this* wind blowing at *this* moment at the cemetery. To do so, the bookish 'breathing' has had to traverse numerous boundaries and frames: the covers of the old book, read long ago; the inset of Olia's conversation with her friend; that of the classmistress's recollections; and the major compositional distinction between a sentimental character and the "objective narrator."

The sentimental classmistress, whose fantasies thus get narratorial approval, is, as we remember, fabulaically unconnected with the heroine. Instead, she is attached to Olia's story by the essentially lyrical motif of 'memory,' especially characteristic of Acmeist poetry and Proustian prose. The role of memory as a cultural force combating time and death is stressed by Olia's recollection of a passage from the "funny old book"[22] and the classmistress's remembrance of Olia's quoting it in a relay that is then taken over by the narrator and the author, who place it in the most prominent final position. This in turn accentuates the numerous literary reminiscences in the text, some of them full-blown, others latent. To those already mentioned (from Tiutchev, Fet, probably Akhmatova) we may add Maliutin's direct reference to *Faust*, the inevitable interplay with Anna Karenina's "railroad" death, and the poetic connotations of two proper names.

The heroine's family name, insistently recurring throughout the story, brings to memory Derzhavin's poem "On the Death of Prince Meshcherskii" (1779), which treats the transitory nature of pleasures, beauty, love, and life itself. The name of Olia's suicidal schoolmate, Shenshin, coincides with the Russian surname of the poet Afanasii Fet. Fet was Bunin's favorite poet, and in *The Life of Arsen'ev* (1928–39),[23] his semiautobiographical protagonist defends Fet's notoriously "noncivic" poetry by "arguing that there is no nature separate from us, that every slightest movement of air is the movement of our own life [!]" (Bunin 1965–66, 6: 214).[24] In this context it seems likely that the title of the story has as its literary prototype a similar phrase from a famous Fet poem, "Shopot, *robkoe dykhan'e*, treli solov'ia" ("Whisper, *timid breathing*, nightingale's warbles," 1850).

Commentary and a Further Comparison: "Spring in Fialta"

It now becomes clear how the tenor of Bunin's manipulative framing differs from Pushkin's. In "The Stationmaster," the composition is ironic and negative, displacing the fabulaic reality so that it can barely be glimpsed through the cracks in the multilayered frames. In "Gentle Breathing," the compositional displacement is, rather, positive and inclusive as it widens the focus from just one aspect of real-life material, the fabulaic, to encompass its other, "contextual" aspects, fusing a variety of natural, physical, social, cultural, linguistic, and literary motifs into a strong aroma, which is brought up close to the reader. Bunin, so to speak, reclaims Dunia's kiss from the draft's limbo. Having distilled it into pure breathing and separated it from the *fabula* and his heroine's love life in general, he informs the entire narrative with its subliminal presence and lets it sweep the frame and the world itself in a replay of poor Liza's strong posthumous presence.

Pushkin too had "taken notice of" and spotlighted elements of setting. But when these (e.g., the prodigal-son pictures) came out almost literally of the woodwork in his story, they did not free themselves from their ironic framing and continued to function in a traditional, fabulaic manner. In short, if in Pushkin the frame became "fabulized," Bunin by contrast "pictorialized" the fabula (and its environs). This painterly approach anticipated the poetics of Pasternak, who in turn saw a kindred stylistic spirit in Bunin's senior contemporary:

Chekhov . . . inscribed man in a landscape on equal terms with trees and clouds; . . . as a dramatist he was against the over-rating of the social and the human; . . . the conversational texts of the plays are not written in obedience to any logic of interests, passion, characters, or plots . . . , the cues and speeches are . . . snatched out of the space and the air they were spoken [in], like spots and strokes of a forest or a meadow . . . to render the true simultaneous resemblance . . . to life in the far broader sense of a unique vast inhabited frame, . . . to life as a hidden mysterious principle of the whole. (Pasternak 1960: 4)

In general, Bunin's narrative art has much in common with a wide range of stylistic phenomena representative of his transitional epoch.

Especially significant are his affinities with metonymic writing (e.g., Belyi and Pasternak); lyrical, fragmentary, and ornamental prose; "cinematic" montage of heterogeneous narrative fragments; urbanist (and unanimist) depiction of crowds; Proustian play with time and memory; the art-into-life sensibility of the Symbolists; and the Acmeist cult of literary reminiscences.

This jumble of seemingly disparate features had an identifiable core: for all his modernist and aestheticizing tendencies, Bunin was a descendant of the Russian realist tradition, representing its late, naturalist/impressionist/prefuturist stage. The "contextual" shift of focus, which we found to be the narrative dominant of "Gentle Breathing," was as much a departure from the nineteenth-century obsession with life's plots as a continued and expanded scrutiny of reality. Thus, Bunin's poetics—incidentally, not unlike Pushkin's[25]—combined on an essentially conservative base several successive trends. And in his long life, which straddled both centuries, he could witness the emergence and passing of multiple "isms" as well as a post-Symbolist revindication of his pre-Symbolist position.

But these differences do not make the two framing strategies incompatible. Just as Bunin managed to loosen Pushkin's ironic grip on Karamzinian emotionalism (without slipping into Kuprin-like frameless Romanticism), a later modernist (and closet romantic), Nabokov, undertook what he might have seen as a reencasing of Bunin's gushingly open-framed narrative in stricter, more suspenseful Pushkinian forms. His "Spring in Fialta" (1936)[26] is a study in consummate synthesis of most of the narrative means discussed above.

In theme and plot, Nabokov's "Spring in Fialta" recycles the same old story, featuring a bold woman, kisses, love triangle, rejection, heroine's untimely death, and an organicist narrator ("Were I a writer, I should allow only my heart to have imagination, and for the rest rely upon memory, that long-drawn sunset shadow of one's personal truth," 299). Narratively, it is decentered enough to compete with "Gentle Breathing":

> Both of its main protagonists lead family lives that in no way interfere with their romance. The heroine has other lovers and does not always take the opportunity to make love with the narrator. They have repeatedly met by chance for years without any buildup of tension. And the heroine's death results from an accident (rather than murder, suicide, or alcoholic self-destruction).

The composition works in several directions at once. First of all, it helps tighten and dramatize the *fabula*. A major step in this direction is the choice of first-person narrator as the main protagonist: it is as if Nabokov had combined in one figure Pushkin's A. G. N. or Bunin's classmistress (observers and fantasizers) with Bunin's Cossack officer or Kuprin's Zheltkov (rejected lovers). In fact, the 'kiss-breathing' that was narratively stifled by A. G. N. and blown up by Bunin's classmistress is promoted in "Spring in Fialta" to the story's culmination, where the framed *fabula* (the chronicle of the protagonists' past meetings) and the frame (the current encounter) finally meet as the hero declares his love:

Nina, who stood on a higher ground, put a hand on my shoulder and smiled, and carefully, so as not to crumple her smile, kissed me. With an unbearable force, I relived (or so it now seems to me) all that ever had been between us, beginning with a similar kiss . . . , but something like a bat passed swiftly across her face, a quick, queer, almost ugly expression, and she . . . became embarrassed.

The compositional focus on the last meeting is coupled with perspectival and temporal enlargement, conferring suspenseful importance on what is fabulaically another inconclusive kiss that just happens to precede the heroine's death.

The dramatization of this nonstory is further enhanced by the parallel intercutting of the present moment (which lasts one morning and the length of the story) not only with flashbacks of the past (spanning some fifteen years) but also with as many foreshadowings of the heroine's imminent death (which follows an hour or so later and is reported in the next day's newspaper). Some of the foreshadowings are explicitly anachronistic flashforwards, while others take the hidden form of circus posters, seen by the narrator on every corner but ignored by the reader until the closural mention of the fatal collision with the circus's truck.

This compositional device combines Bunin's shift of focus to the setting, allowing it to intrude "accidentally" upon the main story (as in the picture of the czar in the principal's office or the "extraneous" shot at the railroad station) with Pushkin's fabulaic, albeit counterpredictive use of pictures. A major difference, however, is that Nabokov's ironic framing calls into play not the inset pictures but rather the 'liveliness' and 'mortality' that pervade "real" life, as, for instance, in the parting scene—where else but at a railway station—saturated with elaborate framing:

She . . . climbed into the vestibule, disappeared; and then I saw her through the glass settling herself in her compartment, having suddenly forgotten about us or passed into another world, and we all, our hands in our pockets, seemed to be spying upon an utterly unsuspecting life moving in that aquarium dimness, until she . . . raised her eyes, fumbling at the frame as if hanging a picture . . . and . . . leaned out, audible and real, beaming with pleasure.

In fact, the narrator comes close to formulating his role as a medium of heightened perception very early, when he compares himself to an eye opening in the middle of a street to "take in everything at once."[27]

But the multiple frames also serve to control and detach, like the train window that makes Nina look otherworldly. The dotted-line double exposure of the hero's romance and his married life, led "as if in a picture," further defuses the fabulaically unrealized potential conflict, turning it into a kind of game or artistic curio. On occasion, Nina is described through a quote from the book authored by her husband, about whose writing the narrator is very ambivalent. In fact, it is no chance that the two contenders for her love are professional authors, one a writer, the other a moviemaker. Moreover, there is a third quasi-authorial presence, "the Englishman of the solid exportable sort," a Nabokov look-alike, who appears at several focal points in the narrative to establish the equations between his eyes and the 'I/eye' of the narrator and between the heroine and the "furry moth [*nochnaia babochka*], which he deftly slipped into a pill-box" (309).[28] This 'encasing act' is emblematic of the entire narrative: the world is a circus, the kiss should not crumple the smile, the close-up of life and death is best framed by the narrator's final word.

Indeed, the ending of "Spring in Fialta" is a perfect instance of frame flooded by *fabula* yet containing the flood. On the one hand, there is the poignantly accidental death of the heroine, accompanied in the chronotope of the narrative by the miraculous and ungrammatical leap from the last farewell in Fialta to the moment when the narrator learns the tragic news at "the station platform [!] of Mlech [Milan, in the Russian version]."

We stood for a little longer by the stone parapet, and our romance was even more hopeless than it had ever been. But the stone was as warm as flesh, and suddenly I understood something I had been seeing without understanding—why a piece of tinfoil had sparkled so on the pavement . . . : somehow, by imperceptible degrees, the white sky above Fialta had got saturated with sunshine, . . . and this brimming white radiance grew broader and broader, all dissolved in it, . . . and I stood on the station platform of Mlech with a freshly bought newspaper, which told me that the yellow car . . . had suffered a crash beyond Fialta, having run at full speed into the truck of a traveling circus.

On the other hand, Nina's death is distanced by its occurrence "out there," in the framed *fabula*, rather than up front in the frame; by its being reported in a brief summary of what the narrator read in a newspaper; and, finally, by the abstract, almost Platonic, terms in which the concluding sentence recasts it: rather than merely dying, Nina has "turned out . . . mortal."[29]

As we have seen, manipulative framing of the *fabula* has more uses than one, and so cannot be responsible for the specific cumulative impact of the narrative. The expressive potential of framing comprises such effects as destruction or intensification of suspense, distancing of or close-up focus on facts, fabulaic comment on 'reality' or pictorial foregrounding of context, closure or open-endedness. These effects are not mutually incompatible. "Poor Liza" is framed in a suspenseful, fabulaic, close-up, closured way; "The Stationmaster" in a suspenseful, fabulaic, distancing, open-ended way. "The Garnet Bracelet" is frameless, fabulaic, suspenseful, close-up, closured; "Gentle Breathing," framed, unsuspenseful, close-up, open-ended, both fabulaic and "contextual"; "Spring in Fialta," framed, suspenseful, unfabulaic, closured, both close-up and distanced.

On balance, Vygotsky's reading ends up being an overinterpretation (boiled down to 'light breathing') of an incomplete structural analysis (that alleges 'purely antifabulaic framing'). Guided by the activist spirit of his epoch, Vygotsky seems to have read into "Gentle Breathing" more modernism than was warranted by Bunin's actual writing, and missed the less extremist but quite original part of its dominant (the 'shift of narrative focus'). In a more general sense, however, Vygotsky and his contemporaries the Formalists were in tune with the direction in which the modernist aesthetics was moving. It was this awareness, coupled with their activist approach to form, that made possible their major contributions to the theory of story and discourse,[30] as well as their powerful rereadings of Russian literary texts. The completion of the formalists' project by structuralists and the current poststructuralist climate set the stage for rereadings of their own work, having laid bare their assumptions, metaphors, and strategies.[31]

PART III

Lineage and Conversion

FIVE

De- and Re-Constructing a Classic: "I Loved You" by Joseph Brodsky

Joseph Brodsky is a versatile poet, metaliterary almost to a fault. Our argument, therefore, must
focus on establishing not so much the intertextual links, largely self-
evident, but the specific tenor of his rereadings. We will closely examine the Sixth of his "Twenty Sonnets to Mary, Queen of Scots"
(1977: 49–60/1988: 18–26). The "Sonnets" are pointedly intertextual,
permeated as they are with jocular references to Dante, Schiller, Pushkin, Gogol, Akhmatova, Russian proverbs and popular songs, Mozart,
Manet, a 1940 Nazi movie about Mary Queen of Scots (*Das Herz
einer Koenigin*, with Zarah Leander), Parisian architecture, and so on.
They also constitute mock exercises in the genre. The parodic mode
is especially pronounced in the Sixth sonnet, targeting one particular poem, Pushkin's "I Loved You" (hereafter abbreviated as ILY).
Compare Brodsky's 1974 sonnet:

> Ia vas liubil. Liubov' eshche (vozmozhno,
> chto prosto bol') sverlit moi mozgi.
> Vse razletelos' k chertu na kuski.
> Ia zastrelit'sia proboval, no slozhno

5   s oruzhiem. I dalee: viski:
v kotoryi vdarit'? Portila ne drozh', no
zadumchivost'. Chert! vse ne po-liudski!
Ia vas liubil tak sil'no, beznadezhno,
kak dai vam Bog drugimi—no ne dast!
10 On, buduchi na mnogoe gorazd,
ne sotvorit—po Parmenidu—dvazhdy
sei zhar v krovi, shirokokostnyi khrust,
chtob plomby v pasti plavilis' ot zhazhdy
kosnut'sia—"biust" zacherkivaiu—ust!

I loved you. Love still (it is possible
that [it is] just pain) drills my brains.
The whole thing is shattered into the devil's
    smithereens.
I tried shooting myself, but it is so complicated
5 with the weapons. And furthermore, the temples:
which one to whack? What spoiled it was not the
    trembling, but
pensiveness. Hell [Devil], what a mess!
I loved you so strongly, so hopelessly,
as God grant to you by others—but He won't!
10 He, being of many capabilities,
will not create—according to Parmenides—twice,
this fever in my blood, [this] broad-boned crackling,
[such] that the fillings would melt in my jaws [muzzle]
    out of the desire [thirst]
to touch—"[your] bust" I delete—[your] lips![1]

with the 1829 Pushkin original:

Ia vas liubil: liubov' eshche, byt' mozhet,
V dushe moei ugasla ne sovsem;
No pust' ona vas bol'she ne trevozhit;
Ia ne khochu pechalit' vas nichem.
5 Ia vas liubil bezmolvno, beznadezhno,
To robos'iu, to revnost'iu tomim;
Ia vas liubil tak iskrenno, tak nezhno,
Kak dai vam Bog liubimoi byt' drugim.

I loved you [once]; love still, perhaps,
In my soul is extinguished not completely;
But let it not disturb you any more;
I do not want to sadden you by anything.

5   I loved you speechlessly, hopelessly,
      Now by shyness, now by jealousy tormented;
      I loved you so sincerely, so tenderly,
      As God grant to you to be loved by another.

By writing "over" a venerable classic, Brodsky grafted his sonnet onto not only the original but also a long tradition of versifying
in its powerful vein. Our task is to see how the Sixth sonnet follows in the footsteps of the original, subverts it, and comes out as a
distinctly Brodskian text. This threefold enterprise differs from Riffaterre's (1978) bipartite 'expansion-conversion' procedure. In Riffaterre,
the first stage, 'expansion,' consists of replicating/developing a 'hypogram,' that is, some traditional paradigm; after that, 'conversion' turns
the results of 'expansion' into opposites. Thus, the second and final
stage of text production is basically a negative operation. As parody,
Brodsky's sonnet inevitably instantiates the two Riffaterrian steps; but
by being very much his own text, it offers a positive surplus (over
the 'expansion-conversion' schema), which can be accounted for in
terms of the author's invariant themes (Zholkovsky 1984a: esp. 63–
82; Shcheglov and Zholkovsky 1987). We will see Brodsky copying,
spoofing, and appropriating Pushkin.

    Brodsky's uncanny sense of poetic lineage manifests itself in his
very decision to "sonnetize" Pushkin's two-quatrain lyric, seizing on
its affinity, thematic and metrical, with the genre. Indeed, the Russian sonnet used iambic pentameter as one of its meters, and the
emergence of ILY was actually influenced by some French sonnets
(more precisely, by two sonnets and another poem of Joseph Delorme/
Sainte-Beuve [Vickery 1972]; see nos. 8–10 in the list of ILY's precursors in the Appendix to this chapter). Yet ILY's return to the sonnet
fold, administered by a modernist poet, has all the hallmarks of his
idiosyncratic style. To approach the two facets of the problem, similarity and difference, we will begin with a look at the intertextual web
that envelops both poems.

"I Loved You": A Map of Rewritings

ILY never lacked attention. One of Pushkin's most famous poems,
it has been repeatedly anthologized, set to music, and analyzed by
critics, including Roman Jakobson (1985 [1961]), who made it into a

test case of his "poetry of grammar."[2] If one needed an archetypal instance of anxiety of influence, Mikhail Lermontov's reception of a song to the words of ILY (as reported by E. Sushkova, with whom he had a controversial involvement) is one:

> When [M. L. Jakovlev] started singing: "I loved you: . . ."—Michel whispered to me that these words expressed clearly his feelings at the moment.—"But let it not disturb . . ."—Oh, no . . . , let it disturb, that's the surest way not to be forgotten. . . . I do not understand timidity and speechlessness . . . , and as for hopelessness, I leave it to women. . . . Th[e ending] has to be changed completely; is it natural to wish happiness to your beloved woman, and particularly with another? No, let her be unhappy. . . . All the same, it's a pity that I did not write this poem. . . . But there is a piece by Baratynsky which I like even more . . . , and he started reciting [Baratynsky's "Uverenie," no. 6 in the Appendix, 1829]. (See Eikhenbaum 1981: 43–44; Glasse 1979: 112)

Lermontov exhibits an entire paradigm of intertextual hard feelings, featuring a dominant predecessor, Pushkin, who is in control of the terrain (including song lyrics), and his strong follower, Lermontov, who cannot help admiring and identifying with him; both envy and the urge to shake oneself free; groping for a change in sensibility; and recourse to an alternative poetic authority, Pushkin's contemporary Evgeny Baratynsky.

The poetic resonance of ILY was felt immediately upon its publication in 1830. None other than a very young Lermontov responded to it (some eight years before his comments to Sushkova) with two rather pompous echoes culminating with two-liners patterned on ILY's ending: "Nobody could have loved you as I [did], / So flamingly and so pure-heartedly" (no. 23); "No! I must be content even with / Having seen you miss another!" (no. 24). Other late romantics followed suit, among them Benediktov, Ogarev, Grigor'ev, and Fet. The chain of variations on ILY stretched into the Silver Age and after.

However, to speak of a chain is an oversimplification, if only because the sonnet connection already creates a loop. The picture is complicated by another early source of ILY: the genre of elegiac album poetry of the 1810s–1820s, which treated, often in iambic pentameter (newly assimilated and very popular at the time; M. Gasparov 1984a: 116–17), unrequited love and similar melancholy topics. The genre was much cultivated by Pushkin, whose characteristic interest in the ambivalent interplay of 'passion' and 'restraint' (Zholkovsky 1984a: 159–78) it fitted so well.

About a dozen pre-1829 Pushkin lyrics testify to the gradual germination of ILY's thematic and stylistic makeup.

> As early as 1816, Pushkin wrote a poem (no. 11) that uses the trite metaphors
> of flames and the cooling of unhappy love; speaks of the soul, its sadness and
> humble restraint; juxtaposes the speaker's love with a rival's loving and being
> loved; underscores this contrast with a lexical parallelism ("I love alone—he
> loves and is loved!"); rhymes *drugim*, "another," with *liubim*, "[is] loved";
> expresses self-abnegation through a concessive phrase ("let . . .") and a ref-
> erence to the suffering speaker in the third person ("She will not smile at his
> [my] verses");[3] and ends on a sequence of *i* rhymes.

The same and other components of ILY's future finds would repeatedly emerge in various combinations—being rehearsed, as it were—
over the next decade[4] and keep recurring after 1829—for instance,
in "To ***" (no. 22): "And with my heart to wish her all the best in
life, . . . / Everything—even the happiness of the man chosen as her
spouse."

To complicate matters further, similar patterns were also tried out
by Pushkin's predecessors and contemporaries, notably Baratynsky.
Several of his poems contain the motif of '(nearly) extinct love.'

> His "To Alina" (no. 2) foreshadows ILY's vocabulary ("I loved . . . , was loved
> by you"; "in my soul . . ."—with the same inversion as in ILY: *v dushe moei*).
>   His "Avowal" (no. 5) anticipates ILY in many ways ("tenderness", "sad,"
> "be calm," "speechless," "another" [as a rhyme word], and the entire phrase
> "The flame of my love is extinguished in my soul"). Small wonder that Push-
> kin admired the poem to the point of contemplating an end to his own elegy
> writing (Pushkin 1937–49, 13: 84).

Pushkin may have especially appreciated Baratynsky's original treatment of the love triangle in "Avowal."

> The male speaker consoles his beloved as his love for her cools off, and he
> deliberately sets about marrying a woman he does not love. Remarkably, the
> poem's later (1835) version bears additional affinities with ILY (e.g., the words
> 'jealous' and 'weakening gradually').[5]

Thus, Baratynsky's "Avowal" can be counted among ILY's precursors
and its progeny.

Finally, Baratynsky's "To . . . O" (no. 3) anticipates the way the gesture of 'withdrawal in favor of another' is iconized, in ILY, by the 'love'
word's 'retreat' from the rhyming position. The icon consists of two
patterns: (1) 'Prediction': the sequence *liubil—tomim—liubil* (loved—

[was] tormented—loved) creates the expectation of *liubim* ([be] loved) as the final rhyme; and (2) 'concession': the expectation is simultaneously frustrated and fulfilled: *liubim* fails to appear as the closural rhyme but is retained, albeit in a more modest, pre-final position. Both patterns were anticipated in Baratynsky's and Pushkin's texts prior to ILY:

> Pushkin's nos. 14–15 combine the predictive pattern with a paradoxical twist at the end (but without a thematic 'withdrawal'). Baratynsky's no. 3 features separately a 'withdrawal' and a concessive pattern, while in two other poems he tries out variants of the predictive-concessive arrangement: "I was not the loved one; / You, perhaps, were loved by me" (no. 4); "Ah, I can still love, / Although I do not flatter myself to be loved" (no. 2).

If the emergence of ILY involves a network of sources (with some of the poem's most felicitous solutions resulting from conflations of multiple tributaries), no less is true of its progeny. Nor are pre-ILY links totally insulated from later processes. For instance, an Ogarev poem combines several obvious echoes of ILY with an ending cloned from one of Pushkin's pre-ILY experiments.[6] And the later the moment, the denser and wider spreads the web of intertextual links, sometimes bypassing ILY and then feeding into the progeny again.

Since ILY's structure casts long intertwining shadows in the poetic tradition, it can be envisaged as a strong intertextual prism—a cluster of thematic and formal features with a powerful capacity for self-reproduction. The mechanism of reproduction need not be specified: the intertextual affinities may be due to intentional or unwitting borrowing; to metrical or other formal constraints on vocabulary (of the "formulaic" type); or to other typological, generic, or expressive reasons. Be that as it may, the components that have coalesced into the ILY cluster tend to reappear in conjunction with one another.

For instance, Fet's "To the Muse" (no. 48) clearly resembles ILY.

> It features the iambic pentameter with alternating feminine and masculine rhymes; the motifs of 'continuation,' 'negation,' 'deity' (in the closure); the words *trevozhen* (disturbed) and *drugikh* (others) placed in rhyming positions; and the *o-e-i* shift in the rhyme scheme. Line 4 rings especially familiar: "To revnost'iu ne nizhe ia drugikh" (But in my zeal I am inferior to no other[s]).
>
> The striking similarities span the rhetoric of 'exceptionality' (the negation of 'others' in a two-line quip); vocabulary (*to; revnost'; drug-*); morphology (the instrumental of *revnost'*); phonetics and rhyming (the conflation of ILY's clausulas of ll. 6 and 8, rhyming in *i*).

The seemingly perfect match, however, is plagued by discrepancies at every juncture. Fet's addressee is his Muse, not his beloved; his *revnost'* is "zeal," not "jealousy"; his *to* means "then at least," not "now . . . , now . . ."; and the distich crowns the first stanza, not the poem.

The very mismatch seems to corroborate the self-reproductive power of the cluster, which can be said to assert itself against all odds, conjuring up such a line out of the thin—or rather, densely intertextual—air of the tradition.

What, then, is a 'cluster'? It consists of all the major features of the original tested continuously against the corpus of the supposed progeny so that the cluster both defines the progeny and is redefined by it in a feedback cycle. This means that we are looking for poems that treat similar themes and/or are in the same meter and/or have similar rhyme schemes and/or use similar patterns and vocabulary. In themselves, such groups of features are mutually independent: love triangles can very well be treated in meters other than iambic pentameter,[7] and the same goes for the rest of the co-occurrences. And yet the material yields quantitatively significant combinations of ILY's features, variously grouped and represented in each poem, but on the whole producing a corpus that bears the original's imprint in several respects.

> The cluster approach as outlined above differs methodologically from the Taranovsky-Gasparov study of meters' 'semantic haloes.' Rather than covering the evolution of a meter,[8] I focus on the progeny of one original but include the projections of (ideally) all aspects of its structure.
>
> In addition to explicating the intuitive sense of a gravitational field exuded by ILY, the cluster approach seems tailored to the task at hand. By supplementing the unique original with a corpus of its cognates, one can create a picture that is both fuzzier and more revealing. As in folkloristic and paroemiological studies, where no single version of a tale, myth, or proverb is in theory privileged over the others, what matters are the invariant categories underlying the variations. ILY's progeny can be envisaged as an ongoing and recorded mythologizing/proverbializing process.

The overview of the cluster that follows will provide the set of structural options explored by the many poetic hands between Pushkin and Brodsky.

The Cluster: Thematic and Formal Characteristics

ILY's famous thematic ambiguities ('love/indifference,' 'hypothetical other/actual rival,' 'God as mere idiom/real deity,' etc.) were kept in perfect balance. In the progeny, they developed in various directions that reflected the ideological predilections of the authors and their times. The thematic paradigm of ILY's progeny comprises three major motifs: 'love,' 'the world,' and 'discourse mode.'

LOVE

Many poems treat the 'other' as a figment of rhetoric, dispensing with the triangle in favor of various unhappy pairings. But even such a binary relationship seems to disintegrate in two texts from circa 1890, which while harking back to romanticism pave the way to decadence: by Fet (no. 50), where the speaker deliberately postpones the consummation of a happy love, and by Briusov (no. 62), where the speaker declares his inability to love "anybody at all in the world."

Some 1850s poems are as noncommittal about the existence of a specific 'other' as ILY,[9] whereas later on, explicit references to 'multiple others' appear.[10] A few poems do spell out the triangle, varying and dramatizing it in additional ways; for example, by having a discarded lover become the successful rival's best man at the wedding (Grigor'ev, no. 35). Some poems written after 1890 alter the original's gender cast in "decadent" ways, featuring 'two women and one man' (e.g., Briusov, nos. 60, 61) or a veiled homosexual male triangle (Gippius, nos. 55, 59, with a subtle twist added by the real author's female sex). Hidden homosexuality may also underlie those "regular" triangles where the more intense link is between persons of the same sex, as already broached by Lermontov and later recycled with a vengeance by Briusov.[11] At the turn of the century, strictly homosexual pairing becomes possible, but even then (e.g., in Kuzmin's 1907 poem no. 71), the reading has to rely on extratextual—biographical—information.

Another variable is the choice of the speaker, whose role in most cases is filled by the unhappy lover but sometimes by the smug rejecter, as in Briusov's no. 62, featuring a pair, and in Gippius's nos. 59 and 55, where, respectively, one or both of the two pretenders are rejected. Unusual perspectives also include sex-role reversals between the actual author and the speaker of the poem (male-to-female in Tiutchev's no. 51, female-to-male in Gippius, with Akhmatova's no. 74 forming an intermediate case);[12] a detached third-person description of a couple (Fet, 1847); speech addressed by the sufferer to a dog (Esenin, 1925); and speech from beyond the grave (Sluchevsky, no. 53; Blok, no. 67 [1913]; G. Ivanov, no. 81 [1921]).

Finally, in modernist times, the triangle has been expanded into a quadrangle with 'two others,' as in Tsvetaeva (1915, 1924).

THE WORLD

In ILY, the unhappy love is mediated by God: the speaker loses his beloved but finds himself on the good side of the divine forces and is thus reconciled with life. The impact of the appeal to God, however, is weakened by its being a linguistic cliché.

Many descendants maintain Pushkin's ambiguity, while others take God more literally. In a defiant twist, Lermontov (no. 25), addresses God rather than the cruel beloved, while Tsvetaeva's speaker goes him one better by identifying herself, in post-Nietzschean style, with God (no. 79: "God has been carved out of a slab / And—smashed to pieces").

In the rest of the poems, mediation takes place without God, who is replaced by (or supplemented with) his surrogates or other representations of the world order: fate, life, nature, the world as such.

> The gamut runs (chronologically) through "sunset," "heavens," "fate," "life, death, Creation," "mother nature," "great limitless intimacy," "the whole universe," "temple," "spring," "all-forgiving distance," "worlds, luminaries," "paradise," "earth," "silence in the church", "hallelujah," "air outside the window," "the helmsman," "star."

In fact, sometimes—beginning with Lermontov and later in Fet, Bal'mont, and Akhmatova—the relationship with 'God / the world' eclipses the issue of 'love.'

Another God surrogate is 'the art of poetry,' which offers the speaker a metaliterary way out of his or her emotional plight. Fet and Akhmatova are especially prominent in this respect.

> Some poems omit 'love' altogether, notably Fet's no. 44, which indeed can be read as a triangle formed by 'the poet,' 'the world' ("night"), and 'art' ("song"). In others, 'love' blends with or is compensated for by poetry (e.g., Benediktov's no. 26; Fet's nos. 43, 47, 49; and Akhmatova's nos. 72, 74). Sometimes,

finally, the poet is involved with the muse (or readers) rather than an earthly person (Fet, no. 48; Akhmatova, nos. 76, 77). An extreme position is, as usual, enunciated by Briusov, the decadent experimenter (no. 62), who relishes life's perverse defeat at the hands of art.

While 'God' offers a constructive mediation between love and rejection, the destructive path leads ultimately to 'death,' an option spelled out in many descendant poems. Pushing the resignation of ILY's lyrical hero to its extreme, the speaker may anticipate death as proof, reminder, dramatization, revenge, or a way out of his or her thwarted love. Death may be imminent, relished as a threat, or even invited by the speaker; sometimes the beloved's visit to the grave of the speaker is envisaged. In a triangle, the relative order of the (speaker's) death and the appearance of the 'other' is relevant.

In a negative inversion of the 'mediating world,' death may equal reunion with the Universe or be omnipresent in the air.

The more pronounced cases are Gippius's no. 54 ("Oh, my friend, it is pleasant to die") and Pasternak's no. 80 ("go on to others, . . . the air itself smells of death"). Fet, true to his metaliterary preoccupations, in his negative moments laments the loss not so much of love as of inspiration; Akhmatova (no. 76), on the contrary, wants to be completely forgotten by the public (i.e., to die a literary death). Among the more bizarre 'death' cases are Lermontov's oft-quoted "Gratitude" (no. 25), where the speaker tauntingly asks God for death in what seems the closest approximation to suicide in our corpus (another is Pasternak's no. 80), and Gippius's "Do You Love?" (no. 55), where death befalls not the speaker but one of the two unloved lovers.

DISCOURSE MODE

The subtle balance maintained in the original between various implicit modalities ('positive,' 'resigned,', 'negative,' etc.) can be either reproduced faithfully or tipped in various directions. Sometimes the outlook becomes negative or overlaps with invoking death. Other poems retain the negative pole as a mere rhetorical backdrop for a passionate affirmation of love and life. Finally, the balance may be given a 'perverse' twist.

Decadent attitudes become prevalent around the turn of the century, but they appear as early as in Benediktov's somewhat aggressive, if otherwise gushing, no. 26 ("And, as revenge for rejection, / One day, to spite the ruthless [beloved]") and in Lermontov's 1840 sadomasochistic and sacrilegious invitation of death. Fet's 1892 postponement of sexual consummation can be seen as transitional to Silver Age sensibility, which brings such flowers of evil as the enjoyment of dying in Gippius (no. 54); Briusov's bigamous possessiveness (nos. 60, 61); Bal'mont's triumphant vindictiveness (no. 63); Sologub's elaborately decadent mixture of love, ennui, malice, resignation, and solipsism (no. 70); Kuzmin's relishing of rejection (no. 71); and Tsvetaeva's glorification of a mismatched quadrangle (no. 78).

VERSIFICATION

Most poems in the corpus are in iambic pentameter, but they offer a picture of rhythmic diversity that follows the tendencies characteristic of the meter at large (the weakening of the caesura in the late nineteenth century [Gasparov 1984a: 229] and the changes in the relative strength of feet).

Stanzaic variation is also considerable. ILY's alternation of masculine-feminine rhymes is not always preserved. Along with quatrains, we find sonnets, octaves, terza rima, various five-line strophes, irregular repetitions of rhymes, and irregular unrhymed verses.

In quatrains, "deviations" from ILY proliferate too.

Some poems use only masculine (m) rhymes, others only feminine (f), while Esenin (1924) admixes dactylic clausulas. Different types of rhyming are combined (e.g., enclosing and alternate [mfmf mffm], as in Akhmatova's no. 74), and even the same type is varied within individual poems (as in Bunin's no. 68, with its two different enclosing patterns [fmmf mffm]). As we draw closer to the exact rhyme scheme of ILY, we encounter poems where the order of alternation is reversed (to mfmf).

One strategic parameter concerns the original's shift from the opening feminine to the concluding masculine clausula: f——m. In this respect, many otherwise "deviational" sequences may still resemble ILY, observing either the feminine opening, the masculine closure, or, ideally, both.

Finally, an important feature is poem length, with the closest approximation of ILY being two-quatrain poems.

LANGUAGE

Introduced in Jakobson's analysis of ILY, the concept of the 'poetry of grammar' proves highly relevant to its progeny. To list some of ILY's most frequently echoed structural characteristics:

—The 'relayed' repetition of a leitmotif root (as in ILY's l. 1: "loved [you]: love still," iconizing the idea of 'continuation [of love]') appears in the corpus with the same and other roots (e.g., "I breathe still . . . / I can breathe, but").

—The dismissive gesture ("let it not") is reproduced literally or varied through near synonyms and cognate phrases ("what for?", "enough," "so be it," etc.) and other means.

—The parallel construction, usually ending the line (as in "speechlessly, hopelessly"), recurs frequently, filled with various parts of speech: adverbs, prepositional phrases, gerunds, negated nouns, infinitives, and adjectives of all kinds.

—The alternating pattern ("now . . . , now") is varied lexically and grammatically: "now in anger, now in tears"; "The sounds will come alive—and die down again"; "I was full of love for both of you, / For you, and for her, and again and again for you."

—The emphatic-comparative construction ("so [much], as [God grant]") is represented by numerous linguistic variations and near synonyms: "Oh, what a . . . !"; "if only . . ."; "with the only one, with whom."

—The figure of exceptionality is reproduced throughout the corpus, often with exaggeration: "no other . . ."; "only once"; "never . . ."; "impossible without."

—The infinitive-imperative-passive construction ("God grant to [you] to be") appears in its entirety or in parts, with or without the original vocabulary (e.g., "as . . . it is only once given to the soul to love," "impossible to permit me to love."

—The 'retreat' of a key word from the final position was largely overlooked by Pushkin's followers, with only three notable exceptions.[13]

—The phonetic mimicking of the original involves mostly the clausulas, producing rhymes in *ozhet* and *im* and finales with one or more *i* syllables.

A poem's vocabulary is defined by its full-meaning words ('love,' 'extinguish,' etc.), as well as its quasi-grammatical lexemes ('perhaps,' 'anything'). These lexical parameters of the corpus are remarkably stable, sometimes varied by word derivation, forming groups like *tomit'* ("to torment"), *tomitel'nyi* ("tormenting," adj.), *tomnyi* ("languid," lit. "tormentful").

The Sixth Sonnet as Parody: Brodsky Rereading Pushkin

In a spoof of a recurrent Pushkinian motif (see Jakobson 1975), Brodsky's "Sonnets" are declarations of love addressed to a statue (Mary, Queen of Scots, in the Luxembourg Gardens in Paris). To identify the tenor of this spoofing stance—friendly? subversive? negative? ignoring?—we will now turn to the Sixth sonnet and observe Brodsky confronting the old master (cum progeny) face-to-face and line by line. The direct quotes are concentrated in lines 1 and 8–9, but the entire text is, of course, based on ILY, which Brodsky systematically exaggerates, vulgarizes, and deflates.

In plot, 'love' becomes both stronger and cruder, thanks to the emphasis on physiology (pain, fillings, bones). It is also inflated to the point of suicide, which itself is then deflated—bogged down with technical problems (weapons, temples) and considerations of prestige. Pushkin's putative rival is pointedly pluralized, a variation we know from ILY's progeny but which sounds like an innuendo in light of some other "Sonnets" ("The number of your lovers, Mary, went/ beyond the figure three, four, twent-/y-five"; Brodsky 1988: 19). The understated uniqueness of love is developed into a mock philosophical treatise, resurrecting ILY's inconspicuous God to His full powers (a move rehearsed in the progeny), only to curtail them "according to Parmenides." Pushkin's trite and half-extinct flames are fanned into a "heat" capable of melting metal, viz. dental fillings. Brodsky also crudely mimics Pushkin's final sublimation of libido by ostentatiously rechanneling it from breasts ("hips" in his own translation) to lips. But the feat is rendered meaningless since the object of passion is a sculpture (rather than a real woman) and its subject a purely literary 'I,' busy writing and deleting, rather than a hot-blooded lover. The splitting of the speaker's persona is consistent with the original, while the 'metaliterariness' harks back to the branch of the progeny that promoted 'art' over 'love' and 'God'; but the send-up is unmistakable.

Thematic exaggerations/deflations are accompanied by similar formal effects.

Brodsky blends archaic poeticisms (*buduchi, sotvorit, sei, zhar, kosnut'sia, ust*) with colloquial and even substandard forms (*chert, na kuski, ne po-liudski, vdarit'* [instead of *udarit'*]).

Stylistic downshifting is emphasized by a series of synonymous transformations (*dusha*, "soul"—*mozgi*, "brains"; *byt' mozhet—vozmozhno; tak*

iskrenno—a banal *tak sil'no*, etc.), culminating in the jarring minimal-pair substitution of the rhymed word *beznadEzhno* (early nineteenth-century pronun-
ciation) with the current *beznadĔzhno*.[14] In generic terms too, the original is
mockingly upgraded—turned into a sonnet, whose form is then vandalized by
enjambments that violate every structural boundary of the octet and sestet, the
quatrains, and the tercets.[15]

Brodsky also lays bare ILY's main compositional principle—covert
intensification of passion toward the end—by a feisty crescendo
crowned with a brief exposure of breasts, a happy-ending kiss (albeit
imaginary), and an exclamation mark.

Syntactically, the counterpoint of 'passion' and 'restraint' in ILY
takes the form of a gradual expansion hampered by numerous reservations ("perhaps," "not completely," etc.) and burdened in the end
with an accumulation of heavy constructions ("As God grant to you
to be loved by another"; subordinate clause + complex object + complete passive phrase). But this shroud of restraint is punctured by a
subtle anacoluthon: an imperative (*dai*, "grant"), inadmissible in a subordinate clause; also, the success of the difficult syntactic trick turns
the very 'heaviness' into 'dynamism.'

Brodsky easily outdoes Pushkin in sentence length and complexity.
His last five lines are one sentence, featuring hypotaxis, gerund and
infinitive constructions, and parenthetical expressions ("*chtob . . .*";
"*buduchi . . . , zhazhdy kosnut'sia*"; "*po Parmenidu*"; " '*biust' zacherkivaiu*"). As for adversative obstacles to passion, Brodsky increases their
number and places them in strategic positions, including his flashy
enjambments ("NO *slozhno / . . . * NE *drozh'*, NO"; "NE *po-liudski*," "NO
NE *dast . . . / * NE *sotvorit*"). The final substitution of "lips" for "breasts"
crudely bares the subtle 'retreat' of 'love' from ILY's final rhyme and
emblematizes Brodsky's mock sublimation.

Along with exaggeration and deflation, Brodsky uses two other
garbling techniques: 'interruption' and 'compression.'

Both Pushkin quotes are promptly cut short: by a parenthesis in line 1, by an
emphatic "but" in line 9.

The line and a half devoted to the second quote are crammed with lexical
material from an entire ILY stanza: "I loved you" from lines 5, 7; "hopelessly"
from line 5; "so" + parallel noun phrases from line 7; "as . . .", etc. from
line 8.

Also compressed is the rhyming material, which in ILY proceeds smoothly
from *ozh* to *em, ezh* to *im*, with the dramatism of the final *i* reinforced by the

supporting *g* (in *drugim*). Brodsky blends Pushkin's *ozhet* and *ezhno* into *ozhno* (thus achieving a perfect fusion of *mOzhet* and *beznadEzhno* in *beznadĒzhno*); he then alternates this clausula with *gi, ki* (in his *mozgi, viski*, etc.).

Having compressed Pushkin's foursome of rhymes into a pair, he spreads it, thinly, over the octet. Thus he both adheres to ILY's rhyming (like much of ILY's progeny) and spoofs it.

The combined effect of all these distortions—compression, interruption, exaggeration, and deflation—is not unlike Mayakovsky's condescending treatment of Pushkin (e.g., in "Iubileinoe" [1924], where Onegin's "Letter to Tatiana" is misquoted).

> Kak eto
> > u vas
> > > govarivala Ol'ga?
> Da ne Ol'ga!
> > > Iz pis'ma
> > > > Onegina k Tat'iane:
> —Deskat',
> > > muzh u vas
> > > > durak
> > > > > i staryi merin,
> > ia liubliu vas,
> > > bud'te obiazatel'no moia,
> > ia seichas zhe,
> > > > utrom dolzhen byt' uveren,
> chto s vami dnem uvizhus' ia.—

> What was it your Olga used to say?
> Oops, not Olga!—it's from Onegin's letter to Tat'iana:
> "Like, your husband is a fool and an old gelding,
> I love you, please be sure to be mine,
> I must right away, this very morning be certain
> of seeing you during the day."

And like Mayakovsky, Brodsky informs his rendition of Pushkin with his own personality. He has plenty of space for it too: the sonnet is a longer form; compression and interruption have made for additional room; and most interestingly, his distortions, rather than merely mocking the original, saturate the text with his favorite motifs. Let us therefore reread the sonnet in the context of the author's oeuvre.

The Sixth Sonnet as a Brodsky Anthology

LINES 2–3

'Pain' as the curse of all living flesh and the obverse side of passion is a recurrent motif in Brodsky, and the brain is a typical locus of love's sufferings:

> Sravni s soboi ili primer' na-glaz
> liubov'—i cherez bol'—istomu. . . .
> No laska ta, chto daleko ot ruk,
> streliaet v mozg, kogda ot verst opeshish',
> provornei ust: ved' nebosvod razluk
> nesokrushimei potolkov ubezhishch.

The motif cluster 'love-pain-brain' often involves 'separation,' 'mouth, lips,' 'bones,' 'temples,' and 'consolation by poetry,' sometimes even with the same rhyme, linking "brain" and "temple":

> V moem mozgu
> kakie-to kvadraty, daty,
> tvoia ili moia k visku
> prizhataia ladon'. . . .
> unizhennyi razlukoi mozg
> vozvysit'sia nevol'no khochet.

As for the pain's "drilling," it is based on a Russian idiom (*sverliashchaia bol'*), foreshadows the contemplated shooting, and echoes "the distant caress that shoots at the brain" in one of the cited examples.

Being "shattered into smithereens" represents 'disintegration and ruin,' also a recognizable Brodsky invariant. See "Chto-to vnutri, pokhozhe, sorvalos', raskololos'"; "v bestsvetnom pal'to, / ch'i zastezhki odni i spasali tebia ot raspada."

LINES 4–7

The idea of suicide, toyed with and rejected, is often associated in Brodsky with fear, mistakes, separation, blood, temples, teeth / jaws: "To li puliu v visok, slovno v mesto oshibki perstom"; and

> No ne ishchu sebe perekladiny. . . .
> . . . delo, dolzhno byt', v trusosti.
> V straxe. V tekhnicheskoi akta trudnosti.
> Eto vliian'e griadushchei trupnosti.

Despite complaints about technical problems with firearms, shooting too is often readily imagined; for example, in the mood of "a thirst to merge with God, as with the landscape" (note "God" and the formula "thirst" + infinitive).

Obsession with suicide / murder is a variation on the poet's thoroughly physical anticipation of 'imminent death and nothingness,' as in

> gangrene climbing up the thigh of the polar explorer; realization that one is doomed to feed one's eyes to ravens; death crawling all over the map; shadow of a can's silvery tin lying on the scales of a fish; envy of inanimate objects, unfamiliar with fear, even when they are on the brink of death; and so on.

Especially frequent is the motif of vividly imagined castration, which, in the "Sonnets" to a beheaded queen, naturally takes the form of 'dreaded decapitation.'

> Vo izbezhan'e rokovoi cherty,
> ia peresek druguiu—gorizonta,
> ch'e lezvie, Mari, ostrei nozha.
> Nad etoi veshch'iu golovu derzha, . . .
> gortan' togo . . . blagodarit sud'bu.

Another variation on the same theme, in "Bobo's Funeral," combines several parallels to the Sixth sonnet:

> Bobo mertva. Na kruglye glaza
> vid gorizonta deistvuet, kak nozh, no
> tebia, Bobo, Kiki ili Zaza
> im [i.e., to the eyes] ne zameniat. Eto nevozmozhno.

Note the motifs of the uniqueness of life; the metaphorical yet physically very concrete deadly weapon; the part of the head about to be hurt; and practically the same compound, function word, punning rhyme: *nozh, no— nevozmozhno* (knife, but—impossible).

A salient detail of the would-be suicide is the hesitation between temples. Brodsky likes to weigh 'alternative versions' of behavior, life, worldview, and sometimes accompanies the idea with other motifs present in the Sixth sonnet. For example:

> Chem eto bylo? . . .
> Samoubiistvom? Razryvom serdtsa
> v slishkom kholodnoi vode zaliva?
> Zhizn' pozvoliaet postavit' 'libo.' . . .

rizy Khrista il' chalma Allakha . . .
v dva varianta Edema dveri
nastezh' otkryty, smotria po vere
("Pamiati T. B.")

Note the probable suicide; alternative gods, Christ or Allah; the world according to a teaching; the metaliterary problem of word choice ("Life permits to
put 'either [. . . or]' ").

LINES 9–11

The word *dvazhdy*, "twice," is a Brodsky favorite; it can even be
found rhyming with *zhazhdy*, "[of] thirst," several times. One such
occasion—

Bednost' sikh strok—ot zhazhdy
Chto-to spriatat', sberech';
obernut'sia. No dvazhdy
V tu zhe postel' ne lech'

—shares with the sonnet also the archaic form *sikh* ([of] these; stylistically similar to words like 'thither'), a metapoetic discussion of
"these very lines," and the speaker's unparalleled passion, substan-
tiated by a reference to a Greek philosopher, this time Heraclitus,
whose famous dictum ("Everything flows; one cannot step into the
same water twice") underlies "One is not to lie in the same bed twice."

Invoking a philosophical authority, often in parentheses or dashes,
is itself one of Brodsky's invariants. The motif of 'the world according
to X'—Aristotle, Archimedes, Cato (on Carthage), Malevich ("white
on white"), and many others (see esp. "Letter in a Bottle")—conveys,
in a tone of intellectual banter, Brodsky's profound relativism. Other
'relativist' motifs include alternative versions of Being, the dependence of one's worldview on dreams and even individual dreamers,
"depending on who dreams," and the dubitability of the world "on a
gloomy day."

This relativism, however, is not absolute: Brodsky is certain of the
ultimate reality of death, the void, Nothing, as well as the fleeting,
unique quality of love, life, and all that is physical and doomed to
perish. Time and again he varies the motifs of transience and loss.

The irretrievable loss of beloved places and women; the impossibility of reaching them by phone, to wake up together, even after death; the sad necessity "to
unzip apart"; the absence of life on other planets; and so on. At the same time,

he is obsessed with the idea of return, repetition, recapturing the moment—as a possibility, a dream, by a mental operation or in another dimension.

Only art, poetry, word, and pen are recapturable in Brodsky's poetic universe.

'Irretrievability of contacts' and 'world according to X' often combine to produce references to Euclid, whose straight lines intersect at one point only, or never, if parallel ("Naschet parallel'nykh linii / vse okazalos' pravdoi i v kost' [!] odelos' "). Sometimes the dream of a reunion prompts various non-Euclidean, and in particular Lobachevskian solutions.

> Peremena imperii sviazana s gulom slov,
> s vydelen'em sliuny v rezul'tate rechi,
> s lobachevskoi summoi chuzhikh uglov,
> s vozrastan'em ispodvol' shansov vstrechi
> parallel'nykh linii . . .
> s zatverdevaiushchim pod orekh
> mozgom. . . .
> I zdes' pero
> rvetsia povedat' pro . . .
> ("Lullaby of Cape Cod")

As in the Sixth sonnet, the separation, dream of reunion, and 'world according to X' are associated here with the brain, saliva, hum of words, and the pen. In the sonnet, the role of Euclid = non-Lobachevsky is assumed by (non-)Parmenides = Heraclitus, according to whom, alas, nothing happens twice, which makes the passion all the more exceptional. The philosophical gloss is somewhat ambiguous, but this is in line with Brodsky's mock intellectualizing and 'alternativism.'

LINES 12–14

The linkage of passion, heat, blood, crackling, jaws (*past'*), bad teeth, and "obscene" breasts on the one hand and deliberations over the choice of word and rhyme on the other is also recurrent in Brodsky.

The decaying mouth and crackling bones appear in a fragment about the body's disavowal of past passions:

> The body repents its proclivities.
> All these singing, weeping, and snarled activities.
> As for my dental cave, its cavities

> rival old Troy on a rainy day.
> Joints cracking loud and breath like a sewer,
> I foul the mirror.   (1980: 63)

Rotten teeth, associated with love, separation, aging, brain, culture, and creativity, are almost an obsession; on one occasion "jaws" rhyme with "passion"; on another, with "part [of speech]" (*past'-strast'-chast' [rechi]*).

Similar motifs underlie the ending of the Sixth sonnet. Although they do not surface in its rhymes, a closely related complex does: the *khrust-biust-ust* sequence (crackling-bust-lips).

> The "lips"-"bust" (*ust-biust*) connection also recurs in Brodsky, indeed as a rhyming pair (e.g., in "Einem alten Architekten in Rom"), and other cognate associations appear elsewhere too, albeit without echoing the sonnet's rhymes; for example, the telling equation of "genre" and "heat": "*zhanra (pravil'nei—zhara)*" ("Mexican romancero").

Of the two alternative rhymes to *khrust—biust* and *ust*, the former is suppressed in the sonnet, ostensibly out of decency. However, elsewhere Brodsky obviously relishes juicy talk and obscenities, often pretending to conceal them but actually parading them in a display of authorial power. Such speech gestures share with the Sixth sonnet the use of parenthetic syntax, metalinguistic use of words in quotes, and the hesitant choice of words, all of which help to set the speaker's deliberateness in relief. For example,

> wriggling at night on the sheets—
> how is not specified at least—
> I puff up the pillow with a bellowing 'you'
>   ("Niotkuda")

> I am writing these lines, trying with my hand . . .
> to outstrip by a second the 'what the . . . ,'
> which is ready to fly off my lips
> any minute . . .   ("Lullaby of Cape Cod")

A still closer approximation of the sonnet's finale occurs in a poem ("Letter to General Z.") where a rhyme is chosen and then discarded as death fails to materialize.

> General! Ia vzial vas dlia rifmy k slovu
> 'umiral,' chto bylo so mnoiu, no
> Bog do kontsa ot zerna polovu
> ne otdelil [did not separate my soul from my body],

i seichas ee [the rhyme]
upotrebliat'—vran'e.

(Note also the punning clausula in *no*, "but.")

The existentialist gesture of gratuitous verbal power in response to the surrounding void resembles the defiant posturing of Mandelstam, for example, in the final couplet of "I Drink to the Military Asters" (1931): "I drink, but I have not yet imagined [*ne pridumal*], out of the two I choose one—/The merry Asti-Spumante or the wine of Château Neuf de Pape."[16] Also somewhat Mandelstamian is Brodsky's opting for lips, which emphasizes the presence of the author's poetic persona, as do Mandelstam's motifs of moving lips, lips smeared by emptiness, and the like. In other words, while the sonnet overtly features lips as the object of kisses, its intertextual halo (inside and outside Brodsky's oeuvre) suggests the reinterpretation of lips as the organ of poetry.

Brodsky likes to close a poem with the image of speaking-versifying lips, to juxtapose the lips' sexual and verbal functions,[17] or to devise a double reading.

> "When a book was slammed shut; and where once you sat/just two lips were remaining, like that vanished cat" ("Kellomiaki"). Here the ostensibly purely erotic lips involve manifold poetic connotations: the Cheshire cat from *Alice in Wonderland*; the transition from reading to lovemaking in Dante's story of Paolo and Francesca (probably via Pasternak's "Autumn" ["Ia dal raz ekhat'sia"], Blok's "She Came In" [Ona prishla s moroza], and Mayakovsky's "so that you'd be just lips through and through" ["A Cloud in Trousers"]).

The verb *kosnut'sia*, "to touch," used with the "lips," also invites a dual interpretation. The direct meaning is "to touch [with one's lips] the breasts [respectively, lips] of the addressee." But it is the same word used in Pushkin's textbook classics ("The Prophet," "The Poet") to describe the making of a poet—by a seraph or "divine verb" TOUCH-ING the poet's lips (eyes, ears): "Moikh zenits [in another stanza: "ushei"] kosnulsia on [the seraph]"; "I on k ustam moim prinik" ("Prorok"); "No lish' bozhestvennyi glagol/Do slukha chutkogo kosnetsia" ("Poet"). In fact, in another poem ("Razgovor s nebozhitelem," an overt variation on "The Prophet"), Brodsky deliberately plays with that Pushkin verb.

> He shifts it from the seraph to the budding prophet and contaminates it with the poem's other pivotal verb: "to burn / sear [the hearts of people with the Word]";

"uzhe ni v kom/ne vidia mesta, koego glagolom/kosnut'sia mog by . . ./sliu-noi kropia usta" (note the lips, saliva, and "not touching the [bodily] parts").

Moreover, the word *zhazhda*, "thirst," which governs the verb *kosnut'sia* in the sonnet, happens to be the same as the very first noun appearing in "The Prophet"—and in a pointedly "spiritual" sense too: "Dukhovnoi zhazhdoiu tomim." And indeed "The Prophet"'s opening line is another Brodsky favorite; compare, in another poem: "Snaiper, tomias' ot dukhovnoi zhazhdy,/ to li prikaz, to l' pis'mo zheny,/sidia na vetke, chitaet dvazhdy" ("Letter to General Z."). This fragment, featuring the rhyme *zhazhdy-dvazhdy*, the 'alter-nativist' motif ("is it . . .—or . . ."), and the ILY root *tom*, "languish, torment," offers additional evidence for "The Prophet"'s intertextual pertinence to the Sixth sonnet.

All in all, the common denominator with the sonnet ('heat-burn,' 'touch,' 'thirst,' 'lips') seems sufficiently rich to warrant considering "The Prophet" its second major subtext.[18]

Indeed, in Brodsky's version of "The Prophet" ("Razgovor s nebo-zhitelem"), the protagonist too fails to die, and not unlike the result in the sonnet, death is overcome with the help of "lips" (". . . i, szhav usta,/ . . ./idesh' na veshchi po vtoromu krugu,/soidia s kresta"). This, of course, is the prerogative of lips that speak rather than kiss— or even of the poetic Word, which exists without the lips: "When around [you]—there are only bricks and rubble, / [but] no objects, only words./But no lips. And chirping makes itself heard" ("Einem alten"), as in Mandelstam's famous "Perhaps the whisper was born before the lips" ("Vos'mistishiia").

The substitution of lips versifying for lips kissing and kissed is quite natural in a metapoetic text and a universe where the word alone can survive the transitory moment and the engulfing void:

"Only the word is repeatable—by another word"; the "beads of words [scribbled by the polar explorer dying of gangrene] cover the snapshot of his spouse and thus supersede both of them"; similarly,

> . . . there are no unfortunates,
> no living and no dead.
> All's just a march of consonants
> on crooked legs, instead. . . .
> True, the more the white's covered
> with the scatter of black,
> the less the species cares
> for its past, for its blank

future. And that they neighbor
just increases the speed
the pen picks up on the paper. . . .
But as long as forgiveness
and print endure, we're alive
("Strophes, XI–XII, XVIII,"
Brodsky 1980: 140, 142)

Pushkin à la Brodsky

THE STRUCTURE OF THE SIXTH SONNET

We have seen Brodsky spoof and rearrange Pushkin's original and permeate the text with his own invariants. What kind of composition does this result in? As we recall, the principal change in the original plot consisted in making explicit the (mock) passionate declaration of love, which formed the new finale. The necessary space was afforded by the sonnet's extra six lines and the liberties taken with ILY's text by techniques of interrupting and garbling.

Adherence to the original, however loose, ends in line 9, as Brodsky cuts Pushkin short literally in midsentence by his "—but He won't!"[19] The sense of interruption is reinforced by the way the two concluding lines of the original (ll. 8–9) are made to straddle the major boundary of the sonnet: *beznadëzhno* is the last rhyme of the octet, *ne dast*, the opening rhyme of the sestet. But Pushkin's loss is Brodsky's gain. The obverse of this straddling is the effect of fusing the octet and sestet into a long-winded whole, thanks to lines 8–14 being based on a tightly knit borrowing from the original ("so . . . / As . . .").[20]

Thus Pushkin is gradually pushed aside so that Brodsky can have his say, giving free rein to his convoluted oratory. Syntactically, the poem is divided into a parodic section and a serious one. To be sure, the syntax is typically Brodskian throughout (with self-interruptions reminiscent of Tsvetaeva), but in the first nine lines it still observes the moderate sentence length of the original. A similar pattern is observable in the deployment of the sonnet's vocabulary: toward the end, vulgarisms make room for the "high style": *k chertu, vdarit', chert!, tak sil'no*; and *Bog, buduchi, sotvorit, po Parmenidu, sei zhar, kosnut'sia, ust.* It is also in the sestet that Brodsky's rhyming (after a parodic compression of Pushkin's in the octet) comes into its own: *-ast-, -azhdy, -ust*. It uses new material and subtly links it to Pushkin's (via *-azhdy,* which is reminiscent of -*ozhet*, -*ezhno*). The sestet rhymes narrow down dramatically from the open and voiced -*azhdy* to the voiceless and restrained—'sublimated'—-*ust*.

> This final rhyme features the closed and gloomy *u* and the doubly voiceless *st*, a cluster twice repeated in the final line (*kosnUT'sia, biUST*) and foreshadowed by the -*st* of the preceding rhyme *dast-gorazd*. This and another sestet rhyme, -*azhdy*, repeatedly oppose a widely open *a* to the concluding *u*. The width and vocality even increase at first: from the masculine and voiceless -*ast* to the intensely voiced and open feminine -*azhdy*. Only after this maximum openness has been reached (in the penultimate line, which in addition has three stressed *a* vowels), does the rhyming abruptly narrow to -*ust*.[21]

However, even in adding on new rhymes and rhyming effects, Brodsky keeps, like many of ILY's progeny, the overall *f*——*m* design of the original.

A clear compositional pattern emerges at the thematic level. One important series is the physical motifs, brazenly thrust into Pushkin's (and ILY's progeny's) strictly incorporeal context, somewhat in the spirit of Nabokov's "warts, warts, warts."[22] They come in two batches, replacing the two curtailed stanzas of the original. The first ("pain," "drills," "brains," "shoot myself," "weapon," "temples," "whack," "trembling"), spread over five lines, harps on love's sufferings. The second ("heat," "blood," "broad-boned crackling," "fillings," "jaws," "thirst," "touch," "breasts," "lips"), concentrated in the last three lines, stresses the uniqueness of love and therefore its triumph of sorts.

The ironic transition from complaints to a boastful tirade proceeds, against the common background of negative states (involving physiology and even technology—weapons, fillings), as follows: The negative states first center on the brain and temples (they are 'cerebral'), then pass, via blood and bones, to the mouth, and finally evaporate through the lips in a poetic kiss/word. In the beginning, metal threatens the brain; in the end, passion melts the metal.

Another important series of Brodskian invariants consists of his 'alternativist' ideas; they too form a chain with a twist at the end. The chain begins with the alternative pair love-or-pain (derived from ILY's "perhaps") and continues with the Brodskian motifs of potential suicide, the choice of temple, the pair trembling-or-pensiveness, the plurality of possible worlds, created 'according to X,' the problem of 'twiceness,' and finally the options with rhymes and endings.

In the end, however, love's uniqueness and the deliberate authorial choices mark a turn from relativistic hesitation to a gratuitous—
relativist-existentialist—resolution.

> This motif chain begins, quite appropriately, with the garbling of ILY's first
> parenthetic expression: Brodsky's relativism is indeed a distant offspring of
> Pushkin's self-deprecation. In other words, the unceremonious cut-and-paste
> of the original does not aim either at parody for parody's sake or a clean break
> with the tradition but an extension, extremist as it is, of Pushkinian principles.

The new images brought in by Brodsky form a characteristic triad.
One series represents the undeniable physicality of existence, another
the metaphysical void that surrounds, undermines, and threatens it.
The two are contrapuntally superimposed at every juncture: cerebral
pain combines physical suffering with alternativist philosophizing;
love's uniqueness links the widening of metaphysical horizons (which
includes Parmenides, God, and Creation) with the ensuing concentration on bodily functions. Finally, in a dialectical synthesis, 'lips'
combine the physicality of kissing with the gratuitousness and spirituality of poetry. The Sixth sonnet is an archetypal Brodsky poem,
embodying a powerful passion at once carnal and rhetorical, miraculously upholding itself by its sheer energy—like the Mandelstamian
(originally Flaubertian) period, which "lish' na sobstvennoi tiage, /
Zazhmurivshis', derzhitsia sam."

VOICE IN THE VOID

The theme of perishable flesh and matter bordering on the incorporeal void and death has numerous variations in Brodsky:

—the encounter of the corporeal and incorporeal, form and form-
lessness, visibility and silence (the images of shadow, memory, butterfly, water assuming the shape of the container, white on white, darkness in the room enveloped by the darkness outside, and so on);

—scientific (often merely classroom) abstractions underlying and
transcending physical reality (humans enclosed in space, space in
time, and time in death and emptiness; the images of vector, triangle, wedge, subtraction, gravity, moon's impact on tide, telephone
wiring); and

—various detached perspectives (leaving rooms, relationships, life;
point of view from another continent, future, nowhere; the genres of
epistle, "in memoriam," epitaph).

These motifs are variously interconnected, forming an overdetermined whole: one guise of incorporeality is scientific abstraction, in particular the concept of geometric enclosure; abstractions lead beyond reality and thus can naturalize the view from nowhere, permitting one to see life as silent, incorporeal. One recurrent motif is the image of anonymous passion suspended in the void—for instance, the beloved's "Cheshire" lips and the subsequent programmatic lines (in "Kellomiaki") that lead to a disquisition about "us" and "the here" as a wedge that protrudes but only so far:

> It's irrelevant now to remember your name, or mine. . . .
> . . . anonymity truly becomes us, fits,
> as it does in the end all that's alive, that dwells,
> on this earth, till the aimless salvo of all one's cells. . . .
> And our claim on that piece of land-
> scape extended no farther than, should I say,
> the woodshed's sharp shadow, which, on a sunny day,
>
> wedged a snowpile . . .
> let's agree that that wedge can be simply seen
> as our common elbow, thrust outside.
>
> (Brodsky 1988: 103–4)

Salvation from the enveloping void comes, as we recall, through its dialectical acceptance, in the form of the poetic word, "the march of consonants on their crooked legs." The "beads of words" are consubstantial with the material world, the ghostly Great Nothing, and the authorial power. Having widened to an extreme the textbook Pushkinian gap between "the sounds [of poetry]" and "life" (*Eugene Onegin*, 1: 7), Brodsky is obsessed with producing their "mix:/a dinosaur's passions rendered/here in the Cyrillic marks" ("Strophes, XXI," Brodsky 1980: 143).

The Sixth sonnet is crowned by just such a hybrid. The emblematic last line sums it all up:

> hero and heroine; human body and stone statue; the object of carnal passion
> and the organ of poetry; happy-end kiss and literary editing; physical touch
> ing and inspirational reference to "The Prophet"; sublimation of passion à la
> Pushkin and closure on "Cheshire" lips; laying bare of Pushkin's retreat from
> the prepared rhyme and display of authorial power over choice of words;
> parenthetic syntax and phonetic preparation of the final word, *ust*.

That epiphanic word is delivered after a remarkable break that sets it off and apart from the preceding text: syntactically and visually by the parenthetic dash, semantically by the deletion of the preceding object (breasts), phonetically by the interruption of the chain of *u-s-t* clusters with the different-sounding *zacherkivaiu*. As a result, *ust* is opposed—graphically in every sense—to the long-winded period it caps, a contrast that is underscored by the brevity of the monosyllabic word and the voicelessness and narrowness of its sounds. An intense and ironically stilted tirade dissolves in a barely audible short expiration, in accordance with the Brodskian principle that "Euclid notwithstanding, by tapering off to a cone / the object acquires not zero, but Chronos." This structural embodiment of the poet's favorite 'geometric enclosure in a void' is also iconized phonetically: the only vowel in *ust* is not merely narrow; it is labial. The poem ends with the poet's lips protruding conically into the surrounding void. A similar thematic, physical, and phonetic gesture crowns the "Sonnets" as a whole (with the punch sound *u* preserved even in the translation):

> Vedia tu zhizn', kotoruiu vedu,
> ia blagodaren byvshim belosnezhnym
> listam bumagi, svernutym v dudu.

> Leading the life I lead, I am grateful to
> the sheaf of previously snow-white leaves
> of paper, rolled for blowing through.

When all is said, de- and re-constructed, what kind of poem and poetry is this? Taking off from, and on, a classic of classics, it is rich in intertextual underpinnings, traditional and modern. Its treatment of Pushkin relies on an assortment of twentieth-century attitudes: Mayakovsky's futuristic desacralization, Akhmatova's stoic coping with the human condition, Tsvetaeva's desperate passion and disrupted syntax, and Mandelstam's defiant posturing. The resulting mixture of dinosaur's passion with Cyrillics, however, is unmistakably Brodsky's own. It is neither more cynical nor less sincere than Nabokov's blending of pornography with romanticism in *Lolita*. The analysis of passion's extremes, characteristic of this century (Proust's *Swann in Love* or Limonov's *It's Me, Eddie!*), is hardly its monopoly; it goes back to *Madame Bovary, Manon Lescaut*, and as far as Catullus. What is new is the way the authors lay bare the literariness of their anatomy of "base" (animalistic, pathological, etc.) passions or even supplant it altogether with the anatomy of the poetic word.

That is exactly what Brodsky brings to Pushkin's original: the point-edly metaliterary love for the Muse, who coincides not with the Be-loved Woman but with the Beloved Medium, the Language (Brodsky 1990). A link between this metapoetic sensibility (typically Brodskian, inherited largely from Mandelstam) and ILY is provided by a similar, if less provocative, displacement of focus, from 'love' to 'poetry' in part of ILY's progeny (Fet, Briusov, Akhmatova). Thus, both in this respect and in the anatomy of human nature (portrayal of passion through the prism of impassivity, splitting the speaker's persona into a transient self and a divine poetic 'I,' lyrical digressions that "murder" the plot) Brodsky is ultramodern and yet true to the Pushkinian tradition—in its "lofty passion not to spare / life for the sake of sounds" (one that Onegin, not being a poet, lacked).

His sonnet is, so to speak, Pushkin's "Ia vas liubil" dedicated in all sincerity and tenderness by Humbert Humbertovich Mayakovsky to the portrait of Marilyn Stuart by Velasquez-Picasso-Warhol. To put it in more sober terms, while rereading parodically the Pushkin original (cum canon) and inscribing in it his own version of modernist sensi-bility, Brodsky pushes to an extreme, but in a sense does not exceed, the prescriptions of the progenitor.

Appendix

SOME ILY-RELATED LYRICS

I. PRECURSORS: *V. A. Zhukovsky.* 1. "Vospominanie" (1816). *E. A. Baratynsky.* 2. "K Aline" (1819). 3. "K . . . O." ("Primankoi . . . ," 1821–1823). 4. "Raz-molvka" (1823). 5. "Priznanie" (1824; 1835). 6. "Uverenie" (1829; 1835). *A. A. Del'vig.* 7. "Sonet" ("Zlatykh kudrei . . . ," 1822). *Joseph Delorme [Sainte-Beuve].* 8. "Premier Amour" (1829). 9–10. "A Madame . . ." [1, 2] (1829).

II. A. S. PUSHKIN: 11. "Liubov' odna . . ." (1816). 12. "Zhelanie" (1816). 13. "Kniaziu A. M. Gorchakovu" (1817). 14. "V al'bom Sosnitskoi" (1817–20). 15. "Bakuninoi" (1817–20). 16. "Prostish' li mne . . ." (1823). 17. "Vse kon-cheno . . ." (1824). 18. "Puskai uvenchannyi . . ." (1824). 19. "Zhelanie slavy" (1825). 20. "Schastliv, kto izbran . . ." (1828). 21. "Ia vas liubil . . ." (1829). 22. "K ***" ("Net, net, ne dolzhen ia . . . ," 1832).

III. LATE ROMANTICS: *M. Iu. Lermontov.* 23. "Smert'" (1830). 24. "K ***" ("O, ne skryvai . . . ," 1831). 25. "Blagodarnost'" (1840). *V. G. Benediktov.* 26. "Liubliu tebia" (1835). *N. P. Ogarev.* 27. "E. G. L[evashevoi]" (1839). 28. "Tebe ia schast'ia . . ." (1841). 29. "A vy menia zabyli! . ." (1842). 30. "Kak chasto ia . . ." (1842). 31. "A chasto ne khotel . . ." (1842). 32. "Ia proezzhal . . ." (1843). 33–34. "Podrazhanie Pushkinu" [1, 2] (1842). *Apollon Grigor'ev.* 35. "Net, za tebia molit'sia . . ." (1842). 36–40. "Bor'ba" [3, 10–12, 15] (1857–58). *A. A. Fet.* 41. "Ia znal ee . . ." (1847). 42. "Eshche vesna . . ." (1850). 43. "Poslednii zvuk . . ." (1855). 44. "Eshche maiskaia noch' . . ." (1857). 45. "Vchera ia shel . . ." (1858). 46. "Komu venets . . ." (1865). 47. "A. L. Brzheskoi" (1879). 48. "Muze" (1883). 49. "Khot' schastie sud'boi . . ." (1890). 50. "Ne otnesi k kholodnomu . . ." (1892). *F. I. Tiutchev.* 51. "Ne govori: menia . . ." (1851). *A. K. Tolstoy.* 52. "Minula strast' . . ." (1858). *K. S. Sluchevskii.* 53. "Segodnia den' . . ."

IV. SYMBOLISTS: *Zinaida Gippius.* 54. "Otrada" (1889). 55. "Ty liubish'?" (1896). 56. "Ia bol'she ne mogu . . ." (1918). 57. "Zhara" (1938). 58. "Byt' mozhet" (1938). 59. "Ia dolzhen i mogu . . ." (1943). *V. Ia Briusov.* 60–61. "Osen-nii den' " [7, 9] (1894). 62. "Vstrecha posle razluki" (1895). *K. D. Bal'mont.* 63. "Don-Zhuan" [3] (1897). *A. A. Blok.* 64. "Otrocheskie stikhi" [5] (1898). 65. "Ty daleka . . ." (1901). 66. "O doblestiakh . . ." (1908). 67. "O, net! ne raskol-duesh' . . ." (1913). *I. A. Bunin.* 68. "Spokoinyi vzor . . ." (1901). *I. F. Annenskii.*

69. "Sredi mirov" (1901). *Fedor Sologub*. 70. "Liubliu tebia, tvoi milyi smekh liubliu . . ."

V. POST-SYMBOLISTS: *M. A. Kuzmin*. 71. "O, byt' pokinutym . . ." (1907). *A. A. Akhmatova*. 72. "Tvoi belyi dom . . ." (1913). 73. "A ty teper' . . ." (1917). 74. "Skazal, chto u menia . . ." (1921). 75. "Zemnoi otradoi . . ." (1921). 76. "Mnogim" (1922). 77. "Boris Pasternak" (1936). *M. I. Tsvetaeva*. 78. "Mne nravitsia . . ." (1915). 79. "Popytka revnosti" (1924). *B. L. Pasternak*. 80. "Razryv" [9] ("Roial' drozhashchii . . . ," 1918). *Georgii Ivanov*. 81. "Pesnia Medory" (1921). *S. A. Esenin*. 82. "Pis'mo k zhenshchine" (1924). 83. "Sobake Kachalova" (1925). *I. A. Brodskii*. 84. "Dvadtsat' sonetov . . ." [6] (1974). 85. "Niotkuda s liubov'iu . . ." (1975).

BRODSKY'S TRANSLATION OF THE SIXTH SONNET
(with Peter France; Brodsky 1988: 20)

> I loved you. And my love of you (it seems
> it's only pain) still stabs me through the brain.
> The whole thing's shattered into smithereens.
> I tried to shoot myself—using a gun
> 5   is not so simple. And the temples: which one,
> the right or left? Reflection, not the twitching,
> kept me from acting. Jesus, what a mess!
> I loved you with such strength, such hopelessness!
> May God send you in others—not a chance!
> 10   He, capable of many things at once,
> won't—citing Parmenides—reinspire
> the bloodstream fire, the bone-crushing creeps,
> which melt the lead in fillings with desire
> to touch—"your hips," I must delete—your lips.

Intertextual *Malgré Lui*: The Case of Limonov

With regard to literariness, as in other respects, Eduard Limonov is an antipode of Brodsky,[1] to whose Mandelstam he can be said to play a Mayakovsky and Esenin persona wrapped in one. Whereas Brodsky reads like an ongoing "Acmeist" study in metapoetics, Limonov seems anxious to furnish an "avant-gardist" counterexample, illustrating, as it were, the question begged by all discussions of intertextuality, namely: What if there appeared a writer either totally unversed in literary tradition or resolutely set on ignoring it—how would that fit into our scheme of things? An obvious response is to invoke the systemic status, or 'objective presence,' of *inter*texts (as distinct from the genetic *sub*texts). Unregistered by the author, they are forever available to the reader— as a paradigm of choices, field of tensions, background for oppositions. Intertextuality subsumes *a*-version to traditional models as a particular case of their *sub*- and *con*-version. In fact, Limonov's defiantly 'anti-culture' and 'pro-reality' writing itself forms part of the cultural tradition (cf. Chapters 2, 3); it inevitably follows psychological, cultural, and literary archetypes, uses strategies evolved by earlier iconoclasts, and cannot help engaging specific texts.

As Limonov claims to shift his attention from Art to Life, denying textual origins and connections, our focus should be reoriented accordingly, in order to recuperate the dissimulated intertextuality. Reversing the order of presentation of Chapter 5, we will begin with close readings and only after that proceed to search for subtexts. If with Brodsky, underneath an obvious parody we found his own idiosyncrasies, with Limonov, on the contrary, we will first oblige him by examining, at appropriate length, his precious narcissistic self and then try to show where it comes from.

Like other Russian poets turned prosaists (including Pushkin and Lermontov), Limonov is known outside Russia for his prose if at all;[2] his poetry (see Limonov 1977b, 1979, 1980, 1981, 1986) has attracted virtually no attention, although many native readers agree on its power and originality. We will look at specimens of both modes: a lyrical poem from his Moscow period (1979 [1969]), and a short story written much later in emigration (1990).

The Beauty Mark and the 'I's of the Beholder ("I Will Hold Another Person in My Thoughts")

A NARCISSIST POEM

Text.   1   Ia v mysliakh poderzhu drugogo cheloveka
         2   Chut'-chut' na kratkii mig . . . i snova otpushchu
         3   I redko-redko est' takie liudi
         4   Chtob polchasa ikh v golove derzhat'

         5   Vse ostal'noe vremia ia est' sam
         6   Baiukaiu sebia—laskaiu—glazhu
         7   Dlia potseluia podnoshu
         8   I izdali soboi liubuius'

         9   I veshch' liubuiu na sebe
                          [10]   ia doskonal'no rassmotriu
        11   Rubashku
        11a   ia do shovchikov izlazhu
        12   i dazhe na spinu pytaius' zaglianut'
        13   Tianus' tianus'
        13a   no zerkalo pomozhet

14   vzaimodeistvuia dvumia
15   Uvizhu rodinku iskomuiu na kozhe
16   Davno uzh gladil ia ee liubia

17   Net polozhitel'no drugimi nevozmozhno
18   mne zaniatomu byt'.
18a   Nu chto drugoi?!
19   Skol'znul svoim litsom. vzmakhnul rukoi
20   I chto-to beloe kuda-to udalilos'
21   A ia vsegda s soboi   (1979: 52)

1   I will hold another person in my thoughts
2   A teeny-weeny bit for a brief moment . . .
              and [will] again let him go
3   And very-very rarely are there such people
4   So as to hold them in [your] head for a half-hour

5   All the rest of the time I am by [lit. I is] myself
6   [I] rock myself—caress—stroke
7   Bring [myself] up for a kiss
8   And admire myself from afar

9   And every thing on myself
                    [10]   will I exhaustively scrutinize
11   My shirt
11a   I will go over [it] down to the [last] little seams
12   and even try to peek over at my back
13   [I] stretch stretch
13a   but a mirror will help
14   manipulating [lit. interacting with] two [mirrors]
15   [I] will see the sought-after beauty mark on my skin
16   Long have I already stroked it loving[ly]

17   No positively [it is] impossible with others
18   for me to be occupied.
18a   After all what [is] another?!
19   [He has] glided by with his face. waved [with]
              his hand
20   And something white [has] disappeared into
              somewhere
21   While I [am] always with myself

Theme.   The poem is a serio-ironic display of the 'Narcissus complex,' whose dynamics Genette has defined as "the confirmation of the
Ego under the guise of the Other," and the corresponding aesthetic,

as "a baroque . . . Vertigo, but one that is very conscious and . . . well-organized" (1966: 28). Going back to the Greek myth of Narcissus,[3] the term 'narcissism' owes its current use to Freud's classic 1914 study (see Freud 1964 and its redefinition by Kohut [1978]).

> To sketch a composite portrait of narcissism, it results from developmental problems with self-cohesion, in particular, a lack of 'mirroring' approval by the mother. Withdrawing the libido from external objects, the subject concentrates it on his/her own body by gazing (with or without a mirror), fondling, and other forms of gratification in order to protect the body-self from (the fear of) fragmentation. The resulting enviable sense of omnipotence, self-sufficiency, and immortality is compensatory and thus precarious. Compensation involves a retreat into an archaic grandiose self and approval by a parent figure, imagined watching the childish self and speaking about it in the third person. The self-directed libido is virtually auto-erotic or homosexual; the feelings of omnipotence border on megalomania; while the archaic obsession with the body-self and material self-objects (clothes, skin, erogenous zones, genitals) tend toward exhibitionism and fetishism.

Inherent in the Narcissus complex is a wealth of artistic possibilities. Associating its major components with the patterns to which they predispose,[4] we obtain a cluster of motifs that bears a striking correspondence to Limonov's poem.

> The mirror calls for symmetries; withdrawal, for closure and centripetal composition; megalomania, for expansion; gazing and self-objects, for focus on detail; childish regression and dreams of immortality, for suspension of time; personality splits, for play with the grammatical category of person.

Different components proffer contradictory demands, but, then, 'reconciliation of opposites' is the stuff poems are made of, and Limonov's text is no exception. Indeed, it manages an oscillating mediation between the infantile pole of 'impropriety, irregularity, imbalance' and its parental counterpart (whose stamp of approval is being sought) the pole of 'propriety, correctness, organization.'

This master design is inscribed on the poem's major planes. Emplotted as an opposition between fragmentation and cohesion, grandiose delusions and adult control, it is echoed by the asymmetry/symmetry of the composition, irregularity/regularity of meter and rhyming, and subversion/observance of linguistic norms. Intertextually, therefore, one might expect some classical models to come up for simultaneous vandalization and appropriation.

FORMAL STRUCTURES: CHAOS AND SYMMETRIES

Versification. The seemingly uncouth text is well organized. The variation in the length of lines (from one foot to eight) is compensated by their iambic homogeneity and implicit length regularity, suggested by the syntax and rhyming: a "normalization" of lines yields only four to six iambs, plus the final trimeter (see my bracketed numbering). Rhythmical variation is modest, well motivated, and held together by recurrences.[5]

The rhyme structure emerges gradually out of an unrhymed chaos, reaches a maximum of regularity, and then founders again.

> In stanzas 1–2 there are occasional internal rhymes (*poderZHU—otpuSHCHU*) and assonances (*otpushchU, lIUdi*), which develop into approximate and primitive rhymes (*otpuSHCHU—podnoSHU—liubUius'—rassmotrIU*). The first exact rhyme (*gLAZHU—izLAZHU*) is inconspicuous, as it straddles stanzas; but, finally, a regular quatrain emerges (*pomOZHEt—dvUMIA—kOZHE—liUBIA*; ll. 13a–16).

Then rhyming peaks.[6] The poem ends on an uneasy truce between the two principles: the blank penultimate line subverts iconically the contacts with the "other"; the rhymed closure seals the speaker's self-sufficiency.

Composition. The poem's unevenness disguises a well-proportioned stanzaic structure, with a beginning, middle, and end: $4 + (4 + 8) + 5$. The two middle stanzas are devoted to the speaker's concentration on the self, the outer two to the rejection of others. The last line is again about the self, in a symmetrical reflection of the opening word ("I").

This pattern combines the urge for withdrawal with the interest in mirroring. 'Withdrawal' calls for a paradoxical 'introverted expansion,' i.e. a development that consists of an increasingly narrower focus on oneself. In a typical pattern of syntactic *amplificatio* (Riffaterre 1978: 49–51), the poem has to grow, gradually conquering the world and Russian grammar, but narcissism confines the speaker to his body-self. Projected onto the symmetrical ('mirror-like') A-B-A design, this makes B the main arena of struggle between expansion and contraction.

> Most of the longer lines (the "classical" hexameters and pentameters) and complex actant and sentence structures are in the outer stanzas, which deal with "others." In the middle, the syntax at first shrinks almost to monosyllables

(l. 6), but then rebuilds itself, to involve, by the end of stanza 3, four actants ("I," "two [mirrors]," "beauty mark," "skin") and to celebrate the culmination with a hexameter about the "I" (l. 15). The transitions are facilitated by ellipses and the equality of line lengths around stanza boundaries.

The climactic mirroring scene occurs in ll. 13–15, i.e. close to the golden section point; a mirror is implied also at the other golden point, in ll. 7–8. The 'mirroring' motif is supported by numerous other symmetries, among them:

—the reversed repetition of the content of the first stanza in the last: ll. 1–2 and 19–20 are about 'others' leaving the scene, ll. 3–4 and 17–18, about the impossibility of entertaining them even mentally;

—lexical repetitions and reduplications; and

—the accumulation of symmetries in the culmination zone, in particular, in l. 14 (*vzaimodeistvuia dvumia*, "manipulating two").

Here for the first time, the idea of 'doubling,' until now subliminally suggested by a crescendo of reduplications,[7] is called by its name (*dvumia*, "two"); this is accompanied by the only—and rhymed—reference to the mirrors, subtly highlighted by the ellipsis of the actual word for "mirrors". The 'binary' theme breeds linguistic icons:

—it is named twice, at first less explicitly, by an unstressed prefix *vzaimo-* (lit. "mutual-," "inter-");

—the two expressions symmetrically surround the verb of action (*-deistvuia*); and

—all three components echo one another phonetically in several ways, thanks to repetitions of consonants (*vzstv; mm; dd; tv—dv*) and vocalic hiatuses (*ai—ei—uia*).

To convey the suspenseful instability of the balancing act, symmetries are supplemented with asymmetrical patterns. The line is full of syntactic tension:

—it is a gerund construction preceding the main verb;

—it omits the object ("mirrors");

—its metrical rareness is reinforced by the lopsided division into words, the first twice as long as the second.

All three devices (inversion, ellipsis, topheaviness) serve also to propel the line forward. The anticipated resolution is achieved in the next line, which is the longest in stanza 3 (hexameter redux), placed at the peak of the rhyming structure, and punctuated with alliterations and assonances (*uvizнu rodiнкu iskoмuiu нa кozнe*).

Yet it is here that the unraveling begins. The strongest stresses fall on *uvizhu rodinku*, after which the tension flags. The relaxation continues in the last line of the stanza (l. 16), with its shorter length, weaker rhyme, postposition of the gerund phrase, past tense, and imperfective verbs.

PLOT: SPLITTING AND COHERING

Enacting the poem's narcissist tensions, the plot revolves around the opposition 'separation/union' and informs the persona's 'withdrawal from others' with the compositional pattern of expansion. The relations with others, treated in the framing stanzas, contrast with and echo the inside story, where proliferation of split-off selves is compensated by a parallel forging of bonds between them. Generically, the plot is cast in the mold of the meditative lyric.

Stanza 1. Cohesive touching and gazing and meditative contemplation overdetermine the poem's master trope of '(be)holding.' It is first tried out on the "other," in the form of 'mental holding/separation' ("hold . . . in my thoughts . . . ," "let him go," "to hold . . . in my head"). Once the exclusion of others has left the speaker in splendid isolation, the stage is set for *Ichspaltung*, which will reproduce the dichotomy within his persona.[8]

Stanza 2. The equation of / division into "I" and "myself" (*sam*, l. 5) is followed by more palpable forms of 'separation/union': one part of the persona, the parental self ("I"), starts variously handling the infantile body-self, which is in need of mirroring (ll. 6, 8). Ego-splitting is accompanied by a differentiation between physical and visual holding ("rock—caress—stroke" vs. "admire"); the intermediate states ("bring myself up for a kiss") and the common denominator, 'love,' help to unite all the actions.

The first, covert appearance of the mirror both enhances the separation (by introducing an external self-object) and inaugurates a new strategy of cohesion. Line 7 also evokes the image of a parent taking a baby in his/her arms and bringing it up for his/her or a third party's kiss, in a further multiplication of the persona's selves.

As the stanza dissolves into a summing-up mirror view "from afar" (l. 8), the last word, *liubuius'* ("admire"), encapsulates semantically, as well as paronomastically, the visual and amorous contacts with oneself that will span the next stanza (note the sequence: *liubuius*, "admire"—*liubuiu*, "every"—*liubia*, "lovingly").

Stanza 3. In this stanza the body-self, initially perceived as one piece, gradually ramifies into a variety of material self-objects (shirt, seams, back, mirrors, beauty mark). Fragmentation goes hand in hand with cohesive processes: the numerous 'touches' and 'gazes,' mediated by 'physical movements in service of looking.' The activities grow in intensity: visual inspection gives way to thorough tactile probing, then both unite in the tortuous search that leads, via mirror juggling, to the spectacular meeting of the reflected gaze with the previous touch on the hidden back / underside of the speaker's body and personality.

In relation to the bonding of the different selves, this is indeed an encounter with the infantile past (highlighted by the past tense and the word *davno*, lit. "since long ago"). *Rodinka*, "beauty mark, birthmark," has clearly childish connotations (the root is "birth," the suffix, quasi-diminutive), as does the interest in one's body, clothes, and physical exertions. The birthmark also provides the parent-child relationship with an archetypal underpinning, given the role of such marks in the motif of recognition of lost children in myth and literature.[9]

The recovered hidden self has feminine aspects (*rodinka* is a feminine noun). This invests the release of tension on reaching the desired but until then only secretly caressed point with an aura of autoerotic orgasm uniting the male persona with the hidden female self. The effect is reinforced by the pronouncedly amorous vocabulary ("caress," "stroke," "kiss," "lovingly"). Furthermore, the active persona's feminine posture—of a Venus with a mirror—infuses the scene with homosexual and androgynous overtones. Yet, in keeping with the meditative thrust of the poem, it is autovoyeurism that is presented as an exciting discovery, while physical caressing is taken for granted (it has been available all along).

To match the enhanced bonding, the syntactic structure must now 'hold' more self-objects.

> In a cross between the three-actant constructions from stanza 1 and the reflexive ones from 2, there appear predicates that fill their three slots with external self-objects: "I—every thing—on myself"; "I—seams—[of] the shirt"; "I—[something]—on the back"; "I—beauty mark—on the skin."

Yet, the persona's introversion shows through the expansion as the autonomous self-objects gradually come to blend back with the body-self. A notable exception is the mirror (or, rather, "the two," as the mirror, reifying its function, doubles), but this only dramatizes the rule. The mirror is an epitome of the ego split—an externalization both of the 'object of contemplation' (like the "other" and the various self-objects) and of the holding 'screen' (like "head," "skin," etc.). The mirror's autonomy is stressed by its promotion to grammatical subject (l. 13a); but its function is clearly a cohesive one: to return the action back to the 'I.'[10]

If syntactic complexity iconizes the 'span' of cohesive mirroring, the 'intensity' of self-concentration finds its formal expression in the enlargement—and endearment—of the ever more fragmentary self-objects.

—Line 9 is the first to use the singular number, so far of a class of objects ("every thing").

—A concrete singular object ("shirt") appears in l. 11 and promptly splits into details, plural but tenderly diminutive ("little seams").

—The next shot is of the singular "back," which is already part of the body itself, but rather big and emotionally neutral.

—Then follows a further detour via mirrors, first singular and then plural, and only after that

—the striking close-up of the tiny, singular, quasi-diminutive *rodinka* comes to occupy the entire dramatic l. 15 (and, in fact, the next one too).

Thus the many self-objects and types of (be)holding serve as props in developing a meager surface view of the body-self into a veritable minidrama, a baroque tour de force of vertiginous physical and linguistic acrobatics, converging on the blown-up beauty spot in a suggestive array of narcissist effects.

Stanza 4. Here the external frame returns to reconfirm the persona's self-sufficiency in the face of a larger world.

PERSPECTIVE: DETACHMENT AND NEUTERING

Point of view. In a counterpoint to the opening introspection ("thoughts," "in my head"), throughout the autovoyeuristic session the description remains on the surface of the speaker's body-self. The body is seen and touched, as it were, by an external observer—Freud's (1964: 95) 'idealized parent,' who mirrors the 'I' into cohesion and speaks about it in the third person: "I am / is alone" (l. 5).[11]

The speaker's detachment from the various described 'I'-selves begins with the use of the habitual tense in l. 1. This effect reaches a high point in l. 16: once the caressing is discovered to have gone on for quite a while unbeknownst to the gazing parental 'I,' the latter is dramatically proven not to coincide with the omniscient speaker.[12] In other words, even as the plot celebrates the spectacular parent-child reunion and culminates in its most epiphanic predicate, 'recognition,' it effectively reconfirms the detachment of the speaker, subverting the epiphany itself.

The separation continues in the closing stanza. The extravagant sentence in ll. 17–18 ("No, positively [it is] impossible with others / for me to be occupied") is a variation on ll. 3–4, but with a difference. The earlier statement ("And very-very rarely are there such people / As to hold them in [your] head for a half-hour") did not mention the "I": being predicated on "people" and an impersonal "head," it made "others" the only objectivized presence. The reformulation, however, places the "I" and the "others" on an equal—and equally peripheral— grammatical footing (in the dative and instrumental, respectively), beneath an omnipotent impersonal "it." In fact, the "I" is now subjected, at least putatively and technically, to the impact of "others" ("to be occupied" reads as the passive opposite of "to hold"). To be sure, this is no more than a negated possibility, and presently the "other" suffers a complete removal from the scene. Yet the persona's solipsism has been punctured: the "I" both is and is not the only important presence.

Gender. It is fitting that just as "others" make their definitive exit, a higher agency should take their place, albeit subliminally. The resolution of a lyrical plot is often mediated by God or his surrogates (Nature, Life, Fate, etc.),[13] but the specific form this takes here is related to the gender perspective of the poem. Assumed to be male, the "I" is accordingly marked for gender (ll. 5, 16, 18). His main partners are pointedly non-masculine:

> in the framing stanzas, the generic "other" slips from masculine to sexless plural and then to explicit neuter (l. 20); in the middle, grammatically feminine self-objects predominate ("thing," "shirt," "back," "beauty mark," "skin").

This schema is, however, subverted by the "I"'s ambiguous semipassivity,[14] the unmarkedness for sex/gender in the framing stanzas, and the subliminal androgyny/homosexuality in the middle. As a result, the various 'disembodied' categories of the last stanza—neuter, passive, impersonal, infinitive, negative, atemporal, verbless, etc.—not only echo the explicit neutering of the "other," but seem to cast a similar shadow on the sexual identity of the speaker, whose self-searching discourse they crown.

> The persona's slipping, along with the 'other,' into the neuter is foreshadowed by the previous parallels between the two and by the neuter gender of *zerkalo*, "mirror."
>
> The neutering effect is also supported by the multiple foregrounding, in ll. 17–21, of the neuter or neuterlike -*o*- endings (*polozhitel'no, nevozmozhno, chto, chto-to*); moreover, phonetically, they neutralize the opposition of the poem's main rhymes in -*u*- and -*a*-.

TIME AND TENSE: HABITUAL UNIQUENESS

Time is crucial to the narcissist dream of eternal childhood / youth / beauty, and the idea of 'eternalizing the moment' dominates the temporal perspective of the poem, punctuated with circumstances of time stressing the transience of the "other" and the permanence of the "I." Grammatically, this is echoed by an original patterning of tenses and aspects that accommodates three contradictory tendencies:

— to extend the moment and bring time to a standstill (conveyed by the present tense, imperfective aspect, omitted copula, and lexically stative or continuous verbs: *derzhat', est', liubuius', vzaimodeistvuia, zaniatomu byt'*);

— to achieve the climax (conveyed by the perfective aspect and the imperfective verbs of coming, reaching etc.: *tianus', pytaius'*);

— to ensure eternal recurrence of the precious moment (conveyed by the perfective future forms used in the habitual sense and by lexically iterative verbs: *rassmotriu, pomozhet, izlazhu, uvizhu; baiukaiu, laskaiu, glazhu, izlazhu, gladil*).

The general temporal frame is provided by the future perfective denoting habitual present. It contrasts with the past and negative forms, referring mostly to "others"; is interspersed with imperfective present forms of all three kinds (stative, inceptive, iterative); and ends up dissolving in a neutralized, eternally lasting, or eternally recurring verbless present. So juxtaposed, verb forms cross-fertilize one another with subtle semantic overtones. The overall effect is paradoxical: the persona's activities are presented both as unique, continuing, striving toward and attaining a goal (through the exceptional tour de force with mirrors) and as happening regularly in the past, present, and future.

The rhetorical figure of 'regular uniqueness' is an archetypal vehicle for the themes of memory and transcendence of time; it underlies, for instance, Proust's idiosyncratically detailed descriptions of childhood scenes in a habitual past tense (*imparfait*; see Genette 1970). Classic Russian parallels would be Derzhavin or Pushkin gradually slipping from habitual present to present continuous or future in detailing his usual pastimes.[15] In the tradition of the poetry of frozen time, Limonov turns his description of a present moment into a parade of Russian tenses.

Stanza 1 introduces the habitual perfective future and the ideas of lingering and transience (*POderzhu*, "will hold a little"), then moves into a very general present ("there are") and further into the abstractness of an infinitive ("to hold"). Stanza 2 stays mostly in the imperfective present. In stanza 3, habituality reasserts itself in the perfective future forms ("will scrutinize," etc.), which now refer to a stable concentration on oneself (instead of fleeting contacts with "others"), or rather to paradoxically repeated unique feats of such concentration. The effect is strengthened by the alternation of perfective and imperfective forms, which helps to protract the attainment of each successive result.[16] This slowing down of motion parallels the spatial closing in on the beauty mark. The climax is again the construction "manipulating . . . [I] will see," where the present imperfective gerund accumulates all the continuousness of the described activities while the future perfective main verb represents their punctuality and recurrence.

Line 16 ("Long have I caressed") paves the way for the past and indefinite present tenses of the next stanza and for the general flagging of tension. Rather than stopping the clock at the summit ("will see"), the text offers a flashback into an unclimactic past.

In stanza 4, the "other" returns—to shoulder the habitual perfectives, whose brief span and negativeness are now underscored by the past tense. "I," on the contrary, stays with the present indefinite, which acquires the abstract overtones of the infinitive ("impossible . . . to be") and the timelessness of the omitted copula. This atemporality, again, is first tried out on the other (*Nu chto drugoi?* appr. "Well, what about another?") and supported by the various 'neutering' effects and the overall closural dissolve.

STYLE: GRAPPLING WITH THE NORM

The persona's internal instability and child-parent split determine the oscillation between a 'faulty childish' tone and a 'proper high' one. The former dictates the baby-talk vocabulary and morphology (*baiu-kaiu, shovchiki, chut'-chut,' redko-redko*) and primitive, often asyndetic, parataxis; the latter determines the meditative posture, emblematized by hexameters. Childlike as the poem may seem, 'adult' attitudes permeate all levels of discourse.

The syntax sometimes becomes pointedly difficult.

The poem features gerunds; parenthetical, impersonal, and complex object constructions; and a subordinate clause defining a hypothetical class of objects introduced by the existential quantifier ("there are such . . . as to").

Many structures are redundantly complete, with every slot filled.

Note the dutifully included *ikh* in l. 4; such awkwardly accurate circumstances of place as "every thing on myself"; the convoluted structure in ll. 17–18 (with both a dative and an instrumental); and the two indefinite—uninformative—pronouns in l. 20 (*chto-to; kuda-to*).

The persona's 'adult credentials' include

—thoroughness: note the "down to" construction (l. 11a) and a variety of universal, existential, and numerical quantifiers ("all the rest of the time," "every thing," "always"; "there are such . . . ," "something," "somewhere"; "half-hour," "with the two [mirrors]");

—purposefulness and logic: "go over," "try," "will help," "manipulating"; "impossible," "such as to . . ."; "but," "after all, what . . . ?";

—partiality for archaisms (*kratkii mig, chtob*), businesslike colloquialisms (*polozhitel'no*), and bookish or professional terms (*vzaimodeistvuia, iskomuiu*).

The two poles usually appear in Janus-like combinations with each other. Duality underlies the general strategy of dwelling, in all seriousness and, moreover, in a classical meter, on childish trifles. The same combinatory principle—'adult pattern, infantile filling'—is at work when childish expressions (e.g., "teeny-weeny," "very-very rarely") are inserted into an otherwise lofty sentence.

In other cases, the effect of 'impropriety' is created by a general failure to maintain the 'high' standard rather than by a particular baby-talk item.

For example, the ungrammaticality of *ia est' sam*, "I is alone," results from trying to sound too solid or archaic (by *not* omitting the copula). The same ill-fated ponderousness undermines the melding of two very 'adult' constructions in ll. 17–18. On the one hand, the speaker reaches for the archaic double dative ("for me to be occupied"), which is possible only with a short adjective (e.g., *mne byt' zaniatu*; the full dative form was already marked as undesirable in this construction by Lomonosov [1958: 566]). On the other hand, he tries to use the modern pattern, where the full adjective is appropriate but must be in the instrumental (*mne byt' zaniatym*).

Still subtler stylistic fusion is achieved when the same element of discourse has two facets, a 'proper' and an 'improper'. Thus, the poem's concentration on detail combines the madness of childish self-absorption with the method of a meticulous grown-up, and the elliptical syntax can be construed as both primitive inner speech and brisk business communication.

SUBTEXT: GRAPPLING WITH A MODEL

Why Derzhavin? Our focus on the poem's intrinsic analysis has involved a host of intertexts of varying specificity: Narcissus (myth and complex), Venus (with mirror), 'recognition by birthmark' (motif), Oblomov (vs. 'others'), Derzhavin, Pushkin, and Proust ('regular uniqueness'), Khlebnikov (ungrammaticality), meditative lyric (genre), archaisms and hexameters (lofty connotations), and so on. Even such an avowedly antiliterary and self-sufficient narcissist as Limonov owes much to 'others' and the 'tradition': these constitute his indispensable foils, and their 'dismissal' the point, rather than premise, of his discourse. One may expect, therefore, these twin foils to have merged into some particular presence, authoritative and alien at the same time: a classical subtext.

To sum up Limonov's stylistic game, it is as if the speaker tried to sound Derzhavinian but constantly slipped into babytalk, "bad" writing, and doggerel.[17] But this very slippage is also reminiscent of Derzhavin, whose poetry Pushkin called a bad free translation from a marvelous Tatar original (13: 181–82) and whose stylistic irregularities echo the unconventionality of his lyrical persona. In a deliberate mixture of Lomonosov's "high," "middle," and "low" styles, Derzhavin conversed with czars about God "in cordial simplicity" and "an amusing Russian style," introducing into the psalm and ode his own earthly personality ("Such is, Felitsa, my debauched self!") and even elements of narcissism.

Not unlike Limonov's persona, he would refer to himself as

—resembling a pampered child in a cradle (*v liul'ke*);

—interested in clothes (*kaftan*) and body hygiene (attended to by his wife, "by means of whom" he looks for lice in his hair [the famous "To eiu v golove ishchusia"]);

—self-sufficient and grammatically reflexive, often with "Limo-novian" double reflexives ("And [I am] happy with my own self [*lish' soboi samim*]"; "[I] myself by my very self [*soboiu sam*] tilling the fields. . . . / My peace is in myself");

—lavish in poetic and personal self-praise ("Boast, boast of that, my lyre! . . . / I will be standing, with self-importance");

—dreaming of grandeur, immortality, identifying with monarchs and emulating God ("imagining I am a Sultan"; "Through you [the empress] I will become immortal myself"; "[the poet] through his inspiration / Has become a Czar—[has] competed with God himself");

—distanced from and disdainful of others ("And I don't give a damn for [*v grosh ne stavliu*] anybody").

In developing narcissist themes, Derzhavin inevitably turned to their archetypal literary embodiments: the motifs of 'monument' (his poetic legacy; his bust); 'double' (his lowly namesake, 'another,' with whom he should not be confused); and 'echo.'[18] In a poem entitled "Echo" (1811), the poet boldly identifies himself with Narcissus, and the responsive readers, who will ensure his resonance in the future generations, with the nymph Echo.[19]

To be sure, Derzhavin treated his mortal persona's grandiose claims with irony, but he kept indulging them, mostly through links to great external 'self-objects'—kings, God, and the Muses. The latter in particular can offer the poet his poetic immortality, exclusive of other, ordinary humans. But Derzhavin also held that man's value is in his unity with the Creator. This more universal argument is central to the ode "God" ("Bog," 1780–84), which constitutes a likely subtext of Limonov's ode to himself.

Converting "God." In Derzhavin's poem (the relevant fragments are cited in the Appendix to this chapter), the reasoning goes approximately like this: "You are great, I am nothing by comparison; but I believe that you exist, for if I exist, then certainly you do; you are reflected in me, therefore, I am at the center of things and a god myself." In this ostensibly pious but actually quite self-centered system of syllogisms, Limonov foregrounds the narcissistic equation I = God. He then literalizes it by eliminating God from the text and appropriating His self-sufficiency as well as the rhetoric, lexicon, and grammar of His laudation. In other words, where for Derzhavin, God is the external self-object, the Great Other, whose existence confirms the persona's own identity, Limonov redirects the libido to his body-self. Thus he performs a conversion that is all but invited by the Derzhavin hypogram.

A major opportunity for a narcissist rereading is provided by Derzhavin's insistence on the 'egocentric' "I . . . , I . . ." and "[your]self by [your]self" formulas.[20] Limonov also borrows, and turns around, many of the philosophical and rhetorical mainstays of Derzhavin's argument:

> The 'But what? . . . Nothing!' move; the focus on the predicates of existence and modality ("is," "impossible") and on universal quantifiers ("all," "every"); the other's reflection in the speaker's "thought"; and God's 'impersonality, facelessness' (cf. "without faces" and "glided by with his face . . . disappeared").

A remarkable linguistic link is the use of the triple-verb pattern:

> Compare Derzhavin's shift from "Envelops, founds, maintains," referring to God (l. 8), to "Ponders, thinks, reasons," referring to the speaker (l. 69), with Limonov's self-directed triple formula "Rock myself—caress—stroke."

Linguistic roots of Limonov's mock-archaic style can be found elsewhere in Derzhavin, often in conjunction with significant thematic parallels.[21]

As a result, Derzhavin's "But I myself could not be by myself" (l. 90) and "[Your]self consisting of [your]self" (l. 25) are conflated to yield Limonov's punchline "I am always with myself." The metamorphosis is performed in the spirit of the Nietzschean deification of the superman self, introduced into the Russian poetic tradition by the symbolists; see Zinaida Gippius's pioneering pronouncement "But I love myself like God" (1972 [1894]: 3). Thus, cultural precedents have joined hands with the psychological dynamics of narcissism in propelling Limonov to the Jacobean task of, to use a Derzhavin phrase, "competing with God himself"—a classicist forebear represented by his most divine text.

To conclude, the boldly unconventional theme yields an almost classical design; the retrogressive, primitive, anticultural attitude expresses itself in a play with time-hallowed genres and subtexts; the absorption in one's selves ends on a note of traditional self-irony. In a feat of mediation between these opposites, the poem succeeds in inscribing Limonov's idiosyncratic and 'improper' narcissism into the objective, 'proper' world of poetry.

Limonov at the Literary Olympics ("The Belle Who Used to Inspire the Poet")

TEXT AND INTERTEXTS: LIFE OVER CANON

Rivalry. From both his poetry and his prose, the life of Limonov's authorial persona emerges as a chain of victories, à la Balzac's Rastignac or Stendhal's Julien Sorel, over ever-higher-class rivals. He begins by surpassing, back home in the provincial city of Kharkov, the local poet Motrich (1969; see 1979: 59). Once in Moscow, he challenges, with mixed success, various official and unofficial celebrities. Then he turns his sights on the West, which he first conquers in the literary dreamworld of his "We, the National Hero" (1977b), a scenario he will find hard to live up to in actual emigration (since 1973).

The scope of Limonov's ambitions can be inferred from his contempt of the 1960s Thaw generation, sarcastic treatment of Brodsky (1984b), condescension to Pasternak, and only a qualified respect for Mayakovsky (1983: 64). He reserves his real admiration for Khlebnikov, the avant-gardist Chairman of the Globe (1985b). Proclaiming his exit from Russian literature (1984c: 219), Limonov tries to take one last step from the provincial ghetto forward and up, *dahin, dahin*, to the Olympus of world literature, in a clear-cut case of the Bloomean anxiety of influence: the urge to make room at the top for one's creativity by visiting symbolic violence on literary ancestors.

Indeed, the story in question (Limonov 1990) begins at a "Poetry Olympics" in London.

> The autobiographical narrator-hero outperforms several poetic heavyweights from the Western world and, since "the Soviet authorities, angry with the West over something or other, haven't delivered the usual gift items, E[vtushenko] and V[oznesensky]," wins the bronze, no mean achievement for a foreign-language contestant. On its strength he also gets the sexy tele-starlet Diana.

But this is, as it were, only a warm-up: the main event matches him up with no less an opponent than the reigning champion, Mandelstam.[22] And, improbable as it may seem, Eddie takes the upper hand—almost.

Narrative art has evolved a variety of stratagems for arranging the protagonist's encounter with a great literary forebear. Here are some brief examples of the paradigm.

In Boris Pasternak's "The Mark of Apelle" (1915), the narrator practically identifies with his inspired poet-hero, an anachronistic twentieth-century "Heinrich Heine," who wins a poetic-and-real-life combat with a challenger; the weapon and the prize is the other poet's beloved.

Ivan Bunin has a story, "Mr. Mikhol'skii's Vest" (1934), told by a corny character who believes Gogol once envied him his flashy vest.

In "The Chimes of Bréguet" ("Zvon bregeta," 1959) by Iurii Kazakov, the narrator chronicles one day in the life of his protagonist, Lermontov, who tries to approach Pushkin, but, alas, it is the day of the duel.

Andrei Bitov sends the literary scholar hero of his "Pushkin's Photograph (1799–2099)" into the past in a time machine; but, having failed to hit it off with Pushkin on an equal footing, the hero has to settle for the role of a Pushkinian "little man."

The narrator-hero of Isaac Babel's "Guy de Maupassant" (Babel 1955 [1932]: 328–38) sweeps off her feet a newly rich plump lady dabbling in literature; he does so by the artistry with which he translates a Maupassant story ("L'Aveu"), whose juicy plot he thus consummates in real life. Later on, reading about Maupassant's painful dying of progressive paralysis, the narrator supplements his focus on the classic's texts with a glimpse of his life.

In all these cases the encounter with the forebear takes place in the plot's "real life." But quite often, especially in our ultrametaliterary age, the meeting occurs on a purely textual territory—playing exclusively with the predecessor's text.

The story line of Jorge Luis Borges's "Pierre Ménard, Author of the Quixote" (1939), boils down to the protagonist's rewriting, verbatim and yet anew, the great Cervantes novel.

And in Woody Allen's madcap spoof of several genres, "The Kugelmass Episode" (1975), the 1960s hero has an affair with Madame Bovary and soon does not know how to get rid of her.

What does Limonov do? With his Chernyshevskian conviction that 'life' is more genuine than 'art,' he is bound to opt for a personal confrontation.[23] Limonov would not be interested in a purely literary attack on a Mandelstam text or in regurgitating the poet's biography or even sneaking into that biography in the guise of a real or fictional contemporary. Nor would he indulge in fantasy, committed as he is to writing "the truth." On the other hand, the idea of stealing not only the show but also the beloved of his literary rival would certainly appeal to him.

To meet the contradictory demands, Limonov has recourse to the motif of the 'Great Widow.' Elsewhere (e.g., in 1983: 64) he has shown off his friendship with Mayakovsky's two most famous loves, Lily Brik and Tatiana Iakovleva-Lieberman, by then in their senior years.[24] Thus it is that in the title role of his "belle" Limonov casts Mme. Salome (Salomeia Nikolaevna) Andronikova-Halpern (1889–1982), the addressee-heroine of Mandelstam's "Solominka" (lit. "Little straw," 1916), with whom the poet was secretly and unrequitedly in love in the early 1910s.[25]

> In London for the Poetry Olympics, Limonov is taken by Alla, a "professoress" (*professorsha*) of Russian literature, and their common friend, the sexy Diana, to visit Salome. A chemistry seems to work between Limonov and Salome, and over a glass of J&B (having read *It's Me, Eddie*, Salome remembers that it is his favorite drink), she tells him how she had paid no attention to that "runt" (*pliugavyi*) Mandelstam, preferring the brilliant aristocrats of the Guards Corps.

Thus Limonov, who in the first round has won the affections of Diana, ends up in the finals as a confidant of the once beautiful Salome. Put together, the saucy Diana and the authentic if old Salome approximately equal one young Solominka. Mandelstam, meanwhile, is left holding merely literary laurels.

Memento mori. Limonov's 'victory' distinguishes his text from most of the other encounters with literary greats, mostly written in a reverently conservative mode. "The Belle" is also different because it tackles the ultimate problems of the human condition and creativity. In both these respects it is similar to Babel's "Maupassant."

> There, the narrator-hero's foil is Kazantsev, a translator from Spanish who knows all the castles in Spain but has never been there, a hairless bookworm identifying with Don Quixote's idealism and Tolstoy's vegetarian homilies. The hero, on the contrary, sees art as a means of conquering life. By replicating with the fleshy Raisa the erotic denouement of the Maupassant story, he (albeit only symbolically) visits France, the sunny land of lovemaking.

Art, however, is an instrument not only of love but also of death. "Then I spoke of style, of the army of words, in which all kinds of weapons are on the march. No iron can enter the human heart so chillingly as a well-timed period." At close range, this dissertation on verbal weaponry helps the hero to pierce Raisa's soul and body, but its more distant aim is to foreshadow his punch-line response to the death agony of Maupassant: "My heart contracted. A foreboding of [the] truth touched me." The implied "truth" seems to be that although art has power over love and life, they in turn are inexorably fraught with death.

Not always is Babel so dead serious. His "Answer to an Inquiry" ("Spravka," 1964 [n.d.]: 16–20) is, in a sense, the same story, but on a deliberately cruder level and in reverse.

> The narrator-hero charms the prostitute Vera he has been lusting after with an invented tale of his martyrdom as an orphan male prostitute kept by rich old lechers and thus gains her passionate "sisterly" love, generously free of charge.

The happy ending is a perfect celebration of the Baudelairian equation / mating of literature and prostitution, but it would have been unlike Babel to leave death completely out.

> A church warden! . . . I filched that out of some book or other, an invention of a lazy mind. To make up, I thrust an asthma into the old man's yellow chest, fits of asthma, a coarse whistle of choking. The old man jumped out of his bed and wheezed into the kerosene Baku night. Before long he died. His relatives kicked me out.

Whereas in "Guy de Maupassant" death has the last word, in "Answer to an Inquiry," the narrator wards it off in advance by spoofing its kitschy fictionalization.[26] Still more cloudless is Pasternak's romantically modernist "Apelle."

Limonov, on the contrary, places 'death' at the very center of his composition, creating a symbolic effect of descent into the nether world.

> Invited to meet Salome, he says he does "not want to visit a corpse." Salome's apartment has many locks, is cold and dark, smells like a museum. The hostess is old, dressed in a man's overcoat, and walks with the support of a gnarled stick. To Limonov's tactless question about feeling old, Salome replies: "The most unpleasant thing is . . . that I still want, but cannot play all those naughty female tricks that I so loved to commit. . . . It is as if I were put inside a heavy, rusty diving suit. The suit has grafted itself onto my body; I live in it, move around and sleep in it. Heavy leaden legs, heavy head on a stiff neck." Earlier in the story it was said that the old woman's face "was in harmony with the

lacquered knottiness of her stick" and that Diana and Alla saw her as "a sort of iron woman."

This is, of course, reminiscent of the mythological image of the maiden grown one with her armor, from which the hero has to break her free with his sword in a first prewedding test (see Chapter 3), and of the fatal engagement with a female statue in Prosper Mérimée's "La Vénus d'Ille" (1837). The consequences of Salome's answer are no less ominous:

> Both Salome and Limonov become pensive, the sun abandons even the lawn outside her window, the guests leave, and as they drive across London, the two women chat in the front while Limonov broods sadly, alone in the backseat.

Limonov fancies "Hemingwayesque" open closures where the hero, having survived a traumatic experience with honor if not without loss, remains alone with his stoicism (see *Eddie*, "Love," "On the Wild Side" [1983, 1984, 1985]). In "The Belle," this psychological superstructure is placed on a solid archetypal foundation. One of the story's major intertexts is Pushkin's "The Queen of Spades" (1833).

> Salome is akin to Pushkin's old Countess (even before meeting her, Limonov feels "like a working man who had climbed into bed with a countess"), once famous in Paris as La Vénus Moscovite. They are about the same age: the Countess is eighty-seven, Salome ninety-one,[27] and as Limonov promptly announces, his grandmother is eighty-seven. In both texts, the heroines' longevity serves as a bridge to a long-gone era and its romantic liaisons, which form similar time-warp triangles (Hermann to Countess to Saint-Germain as Limonov to Salome to Mandelstam). The survivors also voice their opinions of today's writing (Pushkin's old lady comments on the literature of the 1830s, Limonov's on a novel by Limonov). Diana the starlet and Alla the professoress together fill the role of Pushkin's Lizaveta Ivanovna, the Countess's poor young ward.

For himself, Limonov reserves the role of Hermann, a Russian Rastignac, forerunner of Raskolnikov. Limonov flaunts his delinquent tendencies: "I was . . . brazen, like a petty criminal who had finally done a 'big job' "; "[I was] no damn writer, just a crook."[28] Limonov's criminality is aimed, among others, at decrepit mother figures (he has an urge "to get his hands under senior women's skirts"). Indeed, the earthly interest the protagonist, whether Pushkin's or Limonov's (Hermann; Limonov), may have in the young companion (Lizaveta; Diana) is but a step toward the existential rendezvous with the old mother figure (the Sphinx, Pythia, Death), the androgynous (in "a man's overcoat")[29] keeper of otherwordly mysteries. The 'diving-suit' motif submerges all this even deeper under the ground, or rather, under the water.[30]

Although on the surface of things the discussion of old age is painful for Salome, it deals an even deadlier blow to the protagonist, just as the death of the old Countess, involuntarily caused by Hermann, leads to Hermann's demise. On the whole, the antagonists are well matched.

> Limonov parades as a "criminal" and is "cruel" in his refusal "to come into a premature contact with another's old age . . . what's the rush, when my own awaits me." (To be sure, along with cruelty, this statement manifests the narrator's thinly disguised fear of aging, in a foreshadowing of what is to follow in the plot.)
>
> Salome, in turn, boasts of having been "villainously beautiful in [her] youth" and "cruel": she "tortured [her] lovers and [metaphorically] drank their blood."
>
> The narrator later concludes that "in all epochs, cruel Solominkas, Ligeias and Seraphitas" were cruel to weakling poets, but not to guardsmen, who in their turn, mistreated and "dumped their belles, slapped them, shook them like dolls, threw them into the mud."

Salome's parenthetical mention of 'blood sucking' is not a mere accident of purple prose; it subtly links the theme of cruelty with the story's other leitmotifs—in particular, its emphasis on corporeality and death. "A propos of my lines . . . about kissing the hands of the Russian Revolution, the journalist [covering the "Poetry Olympics"] snidely wondered, 'whether this nice little kiss had not left Mr. Limonoff's lips covered with blood.' "

In addition to its ideological provocativeness, the figurative bloody tryst with Revolution cast as yet another deadly mother figure[31] is an early foreshadowing of the fatal encounter with Salome's old age and her message almost from beyond the grave. After that encounter, Limonov becomes practically separated from Diana, although until then he kept programmatically groping under her skirt. From his initial self-congratulatory "brazenness," via a Dantesque or Orpheus-like descent into Hades, he arrives at a state of sad wisdom.

In light of these life-and-death issues, the 'victory' over Mandelstam is but a meager consolation.

> Early on, describing the Poetry Olympics, Limonov stresses the physical, corporeal nature of artistic success. "But the people were not trying to make out

every word. The words only provided the musical background of the show, while the principal action was performed, like in the ballet, with the help of one's body, facial muscles and, of course, of dress and accessories." In the closing passage, however, Limonov imagines Mandelstam as "a little dwarf" who has "lain down on the wet sand [on the beach] in his bowler hat and black suit," compares him with a photo of Kafka and with Charlie Chaplin, and wonders what it is exactly that makes the guardsmen so "brilliant" in the eyes of society beauties (could it be "the abundance of epaulets and buckles [*portupei*]?").

In other words, the narrator comes to sympathize with the poet rather than with the crude darlings of success, thus virtually siding with Professoress Alla, who idolizes poetry and poets and keeps wondering how Salome could possibly have rejected Mandelstam.[32] Thus, from fancying poetry as a winning dance he shifts to a rather Mandelstamian view of poetry as a vulnerable yet eternal Word. To put it in more striking terms, from a Salome (Herod's this time) he turns into a John the Baptist.[33]

The final scene, observed by Limonov from the automobile, is emblematic: "A tall impressive punk with a bright-red hairdo à la Iroquois was slapping [the face of] a pale tall girl in a leather jacket and black leotard. By the wall of a pharmacy stood a small young clerk in a three-piece suit, neck-tie and all, observing the scene, emotionally absorbed." The young girl corresponds to Diana and the other belles thrown into the mud; the clerk represents Mandelstam; the punk is a reincarnation of the guardsmen of the 1910s and, closer to home, of the two winners of the Olympics (and thus defeaters of Limonov): "The most obscene in appearance was a punk poet . . . , whose reckless head was decorated with bluish-pink tufts of hair. . . . The most obscene in content was . . . a reggae singer. . . . He chanted his short verses [*chastushki*] . . . with the refrain: 'England is a bitch.' "

With whom, then, does Limonov identify—the punk or the clerk? His sympathies split: as a man, he values life, strength, power, sex, but as a sensitive and adrogynous poetic personality, he is doomed to suffer, observe, and portray life, knowing, especially after the encounter with the Oracle, that it ends in old age and death.

SUBTEXTS: CANON REGAINED

The origins of a hybrid. Life's brevity leads poets to pin their hopes on the longevity of art, but for Limonov that would be a contradiction in terms, given life's and body's primacy over words. Yet the trust that "what has been penned down cannot be axed out" (a Russian proverb) and will thus "escape rot" (Derzhavin, Pushkin) forms the very premise of writing. Limonov permeates his text with aesthetic name-dropping.

> He begins by portraying his Olympic competitors and "the evergreen Evtu-shenko and Voznesensky"; sounds the theme of physical fragility with a remark about the lame poet Krivulin (a living poet); introduces Diana as "playing hysterical women in telefilms based on Maupassant, Dostoevsky, and Henry James"; enlists Rembrandt's help in capturing the ray of light piercing the dark room; dresses Salome's beach companions in striped suits borrowed from Henri Rousseau's Les Joueurs de Football; paints Mandelstam as a cross be-tween a shot of Charlie [Chaplin] and a photograph of Kafka; and displays his own novel (It's Me, Eddie) at prominent junctures.

To these explicit references by the narrator I have added my own list of typological intertexts. Remarkably, the two sets overlap. For instance, of the three great prosaists mentioned in connection with Diana, Dostoevsky evokes the hero's Raskolnikov complex, while Maupassant helps to refer us to the Babel story ("Guy de Maupas-sant"), whose affinities and contrasts with "The Belle" are, indeed, impressive.

Most of the intertexts center on an obsession with approaching either the Master Artist or Mother Death and wresting from them some Mysteries of Art or Life, respectively. Limonov's distinction lies in having effectively fused the two archeplots by means of the Great Widow motif. It is as if Pushkin-chasing (in Kazakov or Bitov) had merged with Countess-chasing (in "The Queen of Spades"). Babel comes close to this, short of creating the pivotal hybrid.

> His Raisa combines two roles: a servant of the Muses and a priestess of sex (assisted in the latter by the pagan atmosphere of her house, in particular her "high-breasted maid" in whose eyes "one saw a petrified lewdness"). Yet dis-pensing sacred wisdom is beyond her purview. The hero himself lectures her on the secrets of style, but as for "the truth" about death, it comes from Mau-passant himself, via his biographer Edouard de Maynial, and thus in a pointedly nonfictional mode (opposed to Maupassant's fictional story).

Limonov, on the other hand, has a single character, Salome, covering the entire cluster of functions. How innovative is he in this?

A century earlier, Henry James, the third name on Diana's résumé, wrote a novella, "The Aspern Papers" (James 1936 [1888]: 3–143; recently translated into Russian), that "brought his . . . particular concern with the literary life to a heritage . . . , pioneered by . . . Hawthorne and Poe [!], in which a supernatural happening . . . played a significant part" (Curtis 1984: 8). Substituting, in the Russian context, the author of "Queen of Spades" for the two eminent Americans, one is tempted to say that James offered a transposition of Pushkin's formula into a plot about a "woman who had inspired a great poet with immortal lines" ("The Aspern Papers," chap. 7)[34] and thus created a major precedent for Limonov's "The Belle."

> James's narrator-protagonist is a literary historian who tries to acquire the letters of the great (fictional) American romantic poet and ladies' man Jeffrey Aspern. The papers are closely guarded by his former mistress, Juliana Bordereau, living out her life in Venice in the company of a pathetic middle-aged niece, Tita. Assuming a false identity and hoping for Juliana's prompt death, the protagonist rents, at an exorbitant price, an apartment in the greedy Juliana's house, wins Tita's confidence and attachment, and is shown by Juliana a portrait of the poet painted by her artist father.
>
> When Juliana falls ill, he tries to break into her secretary but is surprised by the watchful old lady. He leaves town but returns to hear that Juliana has been buried. On her deathbed she tried to burn the papers, but Tita rescued them for the hero. He can come into their possession by marrying her. He refuses. The next day he has second thoughts, but by then, Tita has burned them. They part. Later on, she sends him Aspern's portrait. He pays her a handsome price, pretending to have sold it for her, but actually keeps it as a consolation prize for the loss of the papers.[35]

The affinities of "The Aspern Papers" with "The Queen of Spades" are striking and evident. We will therefore concentrate directly on the motifs in James's novella that anticipate "The Belle":

—old age/death: portrayal of Juliana as a corpse, skull, relic; her half-covered face and dark, cryptlike, cavelike house; Tita's having been cheated out of a life;

—aggressive vitality: Juliana's boldly perverse ways in her youth, her present willfulness and greed; her sense that it is "great to be alive"; the protagonist's criminality;

—"esoteric knowledge," the "riddle of the universe" invested in Juliana;

—'quadrangular' rivalry with the dead poet (Aspern—Juliana—narrator—Tita).

These shared motifs are treated differently. In part, they are simply varied in different ways:

For instance, James develops the 'criminal' element into a 'crime narrative,' which he compounds with the 'military' metaphor (the narrator speaks of his nom de guerre, the siege of the citadel, etc.) and a Satanic one (Tita is courted with an entire gardenful of flowers). Limonov, on the other hand, seconds 'criminality' with the 'athletic' metaphor.

But more often, the differences reflect the opposite underlying stances of the two authors—'pro-art' vs. 'pro-life.'

James painstakingly distances himself from the actual facts by fictionalizing them.

Thus, in his retrospective "Preface" to the novella (1936 [1908]: v–xxiv) James had to defend the plausibility, doubted by his critics, of an American Byron and an American Miss Clairmont. He developed his ambivalent 'distancing/approaching' stance into a short treatise on his "delight in a palpable, imaginable *visitable* past" (p. x; his italics). This formula, presupposing a generation gap of about sixty years, fits to a T such pairings as Pushkin and his Hermann vs Saint-Germain and Casanova (in "The Queen of Spades"); Balzac vs Swedenborg (in *Seraphita*); James vs Byron and Shelley; Babel vs Maupassant; and Limonov vs Mandelstam.

Limonov, on the contrary, insists on narrating the story as an autobiographical fact, concealing fictionalization where any exists.[36]

Where James experimented with having a "dim Shelley drama played out in the very theater of our own modernity" (1984: 30–31; Shelley, along with Byron, was a prototype of Aspern, see note 35), Limonov is bent on systematically undoing the Mandelstam–Silver Age mystique.

James's narrator identifies with and tries to emulate the late poet.

He wants to join him in a sort of "fraternity"; covets his memorabilia; insists on penetrating into the house, looking into the eyes and holding the hand of Juliana ("some esoteric knowledge has rubbed off on her"); and is eventually ready to marry into the documents. Yet he is clearly no match for his mentor (who, incidentally, "had treated [Juliana] badly"), for the various mythological figures of art/power (Juliana's painter father; Orpheus; the *condottiere* statue), or for the two women (in the end he is even rejected by Tita).

Limonov, on the contrary, prefers life.

He starts out by *not* wanting to visit Salome, does not care for the Mandelstam poem, and comes out even, if not victorious, in the end. His belle had mistreated the poet, while he, Limonov, earns her respect; and so on and so forth.

All these contrasts notwithstanding, the sad ending and message, to which the two stories arrive from opposite premises and via different but equally self-subverting routes, is much the same: life is not sacrificed to art, but art is the best and most lasting thing about life. Also similar is the key hybrid of Mother Death and Art's Witness: the Old Beauty who had once inspired the Poet. Moreover, even James's emulation of romantic models finds an unexpected but rather thinly veiled parallel in Limonov, as we are about to see.

Hidden in plain view. Despite all the panning of the literary canon and its cult figures, much in the story turns on the appreciation of Limonov's person and writing by Salome. The dual message is that he is simultaneously warned about Death and inducted into Literature's hall of fame. But Salome's canonizing authority derives primarily from her association with Mandelstam (the Jamesian "rubbing off"!), in particular from her being the addressee-heroine of his famous lyric. Let us then see what treatment Mandelstam's "Solominka" receives in Limonov's text.

Although mentioned several times, it is pointedly marginalized and just plain mangled. The "professoress" misquotes the line "Lenore, Solominka, Ligeiia, Seraphita," omitting the first of Poe's heroines, replacing the second with the classical Circe (*Tsirtseia*), and Russianizing the Balzacian name into *Serafima*.

To be sure, the *professorsha*'s function is to represent, and thereby subvert, the bookworm view of art, similar to that of Babel's Kasantsev.

> She worships Mandelstam, reveres Salome, and "in her house [Limonov] has counted up to twenty-three photographs of the fashionable poet Brodsky" (!). The irony of her genuflection before literature is strengthened by the counterpoint with her spectacular love life in the past: the scenes in what can be described as the 'Mandelstam museum' are interspersed with brief insets of a younger Alla's risky rushings back and forth between her black husband and black lover in the heart of Black Africa.

But neither is Salome too careful with the sacred text and the entire Mandelstam myth. She does not bother to remember either the famous poem about herself or the name of the poet's widow— Nadezhda Mandelstam, a major literary figure in her own right.[37] At the same time, the professoress, who supplies the correct name of the widow, keeps addressing Salome by a stupidly wrong patronymic.[38]

And yet the poem that is so ostentatiously shoved aside comes to haunt the story subtextually. In effect, three quarters of a century later Limonov—whether intentionally or not—has rewritten Mandelstam, in the sense of both altering the hypogram and adhering to it. The paradigm comprises the following common elements:

—the overall strategy of turning a virtual nonevent (failure to fall asleep, casual visit) into an epiphanic encounter with Death with the help of world-class intertexts;

—the image of Salome as a lonely woman buried alive in her apartment, and thus similar to the archetypal heroines who straddle the boundaries between the male and the female, the living and the dead;

—the motif of sepulchral solidity combined with underwater coldness; compare Salome's diving suit in the story with the mirror's deadly pond (*omut*), the icy and heavy Neva, flowing in the bedroom, and above all, the sarcophagus (obviously Ligeia's, as is the image of air movement in the room) in the poem;

—the vampiric motif of blood drinking, conspicuous already in the poem (where it is paronomastically associated with *Salomeia-Solominka*, "Salome, The Little Sipping Straw"): "You have drunk up all death"; "blue blood is flowing from the granite"; "In my blood lives a December Ligeia." [39]

Thus, the most relevant subtext of Limonov's story—Mandelstam's "Solominka"—is spurned only as part of the antiliterary, antiquotational game, and thus hidden in plain view. The story engages Mandelstam, pretends to ignore him, but actually follows him and other predecessors, in accordance with the Jamesian/Bloomian principle of replicating the prototypical Master. Where Mandelstam was busy learning the "blessed words," Limonov strove to shake loose of them and grasp life's "corporeal" object lesson. Where Mandelstam, like James, tried to put a distance between himself and the woman by enshrining her in a multilayered poetic sarcophagus, Limonov insisted on taking her out of all literary shells and facing her in the flesh. Yet all this could not but result in a new Tombstone Text, with which the belle, who in her youth had inspired the poet, having aged, inspired the prosaist.

The rhetorical tightropes walked by Limonov in the poem and in the story are essentially the same. Proclaiming loudly his own, shockingly self-promoting, body-centered, anticultural values ('narcissist,' 'survivalist'), he ends up joining the dreaded/coveted tradition that he has tried to beat and whose presence, whether tacit or negated, actually pervades his texts. Wrestling with such a formidable foe, one is bound to lose—but may be marked in the process and thus leave one's own mark on the medium.[40] In this fundamental sense, Limonov and Brodsky, so different on most counts, are alike.

Appendix

DERZHAVIN, FROM THE ODE "GOD"

3   Bez lits, v trekh litsakh bozhestva! . . .
7   Kto vse soboiu napolniaet,
8   Ob"emlet, zizhdet, sokhraniaet. . . .
18 Lish' mysl' k tebe vznestis' derzaet,—
19 V tvoem velich'i ischezaet,
20 Kak v vechnosti proshedshii mig. . . .
24 V sebe samom ty osnoval:
25 Sebia soboiu sostavliaia,
26 Soboiu iz sebia siiaia. . . .
30 Ty byl, ty est', ty budesh' vvek! . . .
53 No chto mnoi zrimaia vselenna?
54 I chto pered toboiu ia? . . .
60 A ia pered toboi nichto.
61 Nichto!—No ty vo mne siiaesh'. . . .
63 Vo mne sebia izobrazhaesh'. . . .
68 Tebia dusha moia byt' chaet,
69 Vnikaet, myslit, rassuzhdaet:
70 Ia esm'—konechno est' i ty! . . .
74 Ty est'—i ia uzh ne nichto! . . .
81 Ia sviaz' mirov povsiudu sushchikh. . . .
82–86 [Ia . . . , Ia . . . , Ia . . . , Ia . . . , Ia . . .],
87 Ia tsar'—ia rab—ia cherv'—ia bog! . . .
90 A sam soboi ia byt' ne mog. . . .
106 To slabym smertnym nevozmozhno
107 Tebia nichem inym pochtit'
(1958: 32–35)

3: Without faces, in the three persons of the deity! 7–8: Who fills everything with himself, / Envelops, founds, maintains. 18–20: Just as thought dares to soar toward you [lit. Thou]—/ [It] disappears in your greatness, / Like a past moment in eternity. 24–26: You have founded [it all] in your own self: / Yourself consisting of yourself, / Yourself shining from inside yourself. 30: You were,

you are, you shall be forever! 53–54: But what [is] the universe, visible to me? /
And what [am] I before you? 60–63: And I am nothing before you. / Nothing!
But you shine in me / . . . / Represent yourself in me. 68–70: My soul desires
you to be [= to exist], / Ponders, thinks, reasons: / I am [, therefore,] certainly
you are, too! 74: You are [therefore,] I am no longer nothing! 81–87: I am the
linkage of the omnipresent worlds, / I . . . / I . . . / I . . . / I . . . / I . . . / I am czar—
slave—worm—god! 90: But I myself could not have existed by myself. 106–7:
Then for the weak mortals it is impossible / To honor you in any other way.

MANDELSTAM, "SOLOMINKA"

1

Kogda, solominka, ne spish' v ogromnoi spal'ne
I zhdesh', bessonnaia, chtob, vazhen i vysok,
Spokoinoi tiazhest'iu—chto mozhet byt' pechal'nei—
Na veki chutkie spustilsia potolok,

Solomka zvonkaia, solominka sukhaia,
Vsiu smert' ty vypila i sdelalas' nezhnei,
Slomalas' milaia solomka nezhivaia,
Ne Salomeia, net, solominka skorei.

V chasy bessonnitsy predmety tiazhelee,
Kak budto men'she ikh—takaia tishina—
Mertsaiut v zerkale podushki, chut' beleia,
I v kruglom omute krovat' otrazhena.

Net, ne solominka v torzhestvennom atlase,
V ogromnoi komnate nad chernoiu Nevoi,
Dvenadtsat' mesiatsev poiut o smertnom chase,
Struitsia v vozdukhe led bledno-goluboi.

Dekabr' torzhestvennyi struit svoe dykhan'e,
Kak budto v komnate tiazhelaia Neva.
Net, ne Solominka, Ligeiia, umiran'e—
Ia nauchilsia vam, blazhennye slova.

2

Ia nauchilsia vam, blazhennye slova—
Lenor, Solominka, Ligeiia, Serafita.
V ogromnoi komnate tiazhelaia Neva
I golubaia krov' struitsia iz granita.

Dekabr' torzhestvennyi siiaet nad Nevoi.
Dvenadtsat' mesiatsev poiut o smertnom chase.

Net, ne Solominka v torzhestvennom atlase
Vkushaet medlennyi, tomitel'nyi pokoi.

V moei krovi zhivet dekabr'skaia Ligeiia,
Ch'ia v sarkofage spit blazhennaia liubov',
A ta Solominka, byt' mozhet, Salomeia,
Ubita zhalost'iu i ne vernetsia vnov'.

(1967–69, 1: 59–60)

1. When, a straw, you are not asleep in your huge bedroom / And wait, sleepless, for the ceiling, impressive and high, / With its calm heaviness— what can be sadder—/ To descend onto your sensitive eyelids. // Resonant straw, dry straw, / You have drunk up all death and become more tender. / Dear unliving straw broke, / Not a Salome, no, rather a straw. // In the hours of insomnia the objects are heavier, / It is as if they were fewer—such [is] the silence—/ The pillows glimmer in the mirror, white, barely visible, / And the bed is reflected in the round [deadly] pond. // No, not a straw in the solemn silk, / In the huge room over the black Neva, / The twelve months are singing about the hour of death, / Pale-blue ice flows in the air. // A solemn December exudes its breath, / As if the heavy Neva were in the room. / No, not Straw, [but rather] Ligeia, the dying—/ I have learned you, [oh,] blessed words.

2. I have learned you, [oh,] blessed words—/ Lenore, Straw, Ligeia, Sera-phita. / In the huge room [is] the heavy Neva / And blue blood is flowing from the granite. // A solemn December is shining over Neva. / The twelve months are singing about the hour of death. / No, [it is] not Straw in her solemn silks / [Who] is enjoying slow, tormenting rest. // In my blood lives a Decem-ber Ligeia, / Whose blessed love sleeps in a sarcophagus, / And that straw, perhaps, Salome, / Is killed by pity and will not return again.

PART IV

Texts in Dialogue

SEVEN

A Duet in Three Movements:
Bulgakov—Olesha—Bulgakov

So far, we have confined our attention to one-sided intertextuality, where later texts reread earlier ones and often enriched them in the process—without, however, giving them a chance to respond. In the two chapters that follow, we turn to dialogue proper, in the full sense of literary exchange. This calls for looking at contemporaries and would profit from bringing together the analytic concepts tested separately in preceding chapters: the interaction of entire oeuvres, conversion of subtexts, and variations on common structures and motifs.

Dialogism owes its current popularity to the work of Mikhail Bakhtin, which originated in the same period as the major part of the triptych we will be examining in this chapter. It has been suggested (Jensen 1979: 313) that Bakhtin's polyphonic reading of Dostoevsky (1984 [1929]) was influenced by the cultural heteroglossia that nurtured Pilnyak's collagelike prose and Mandelstam's intertextual poetics ("composing others' songs again/anew [snova]")[1] and quite possibly was directly inspired by their texts. Jensen also mentions Tynianov's contribution to the polylogical concept of literature, and it is from what can be described as a joint Bakhtinian-Tynianovian perspective[2] that we will try to trace one of the threads in the multi-colored tapestry of the epoch: an exchange between Mikhail Bulgakov and Iurii Olesha, the authors of *Heart of a Dog* (1925), *Envy* (1927), and *The Master and Margarita* (1928–40).

This dialogue has been obscured by the fact that owing to political censorship, neither of Bulgakov's two contributions appeared in print until decades after the time of writing.

> The manuscript of *Heart of a Dog*, prevented from publication and even temporarily confiscated by the secret police, was widely read in Moscow literary circles and could hardly have remained unknown to Olesha (it was first published in the West in 1968, and in the Soviet Union in 1987). *Envy* was a major sensation in the late 1920s, and Bulgakov must have been familiar with it. Olesha died (1960) before the publication of *The Master and Margarita* (censored 1967; complete 1973); whether he knew about it and what his reaction would have been remains an open question.[3]

That the dialogue might have gone on unwittingly is a theoretical possibility, but a rather unlikely one given the interlocutors' common fellow-traveler orientation and personal friendship. Yet even if the dialogue was recuperable only in hindsight and as a purely paradigmatic intertext or a 'quasi-dialogue' (Smirnov 1985, Zholkovsky 1988), it would deserve no less—perhaps more—attention: the three texts seem to be filling out a common questionnaire, giving different answers to the same questions, and thus to each other, in an almost perfect dialectical triad. In following its course, we will concentrate on the invariance of the thematic framework, on its modifications and conversions, and on the degree and direction of the discourse's carnivalization.

Heart of a Dog

LITERARY POLYPHONY AND A NEW KEY

Bulgakov's fantastic tale was a fitting invitation to a dialogue, combining as it did political topicality with consummate literariness and manipulation of intra- and intertextual voices. In his case history of a transplant (heart of a dog plus brain of a drunkard) that goes awry, producing an ordinary Soviet monster, and has to be remedied at the last moment by a reverse surgery, Bulgakov successfully crossbred several literary genres. A 'canine story' (about wise dogs mixing with/behaving like people)[4] finds itself superimposed on the genre of Christmas tale and the Christian legend in general (involving transfiguration, death, resurrection, divine father), or rather, on its Faustian-Frankensteinian perversion (laboratory creation of artificial homunculi, operating on corpses, the creature attacking the scientist).

The action takes place on the Chaste Virgin street (*Prechistenka*) at Christmas-time; Sharikov calls the Professor "daddy" (*papasha*); the names of Professor Preobrazhensky and of the street where Chugunkin's body is found, the Preo-brazhenskaia Gate, as well as Sharikov's appearance in new, all-leather clothes (chap. 9) conspicuously refer to "Transfiguration" and, in the Soviet-Faustian context, to 'transformation' (*preobrazovanie [mira]*) (Fusso 1989).

Through the intermediary of a cognate modern genre—the science-fiction utopia/dystopia (in the manner of H. G. Wells and A. A. Bogdanov), already tried out by Bulgakov in *Fatal Eggs* (1924)—this literary hybrid was placed in the service of the topical 'new man' theme. For naturalization, it relied on satiric play with Soviet realia (the pandemic denunciations, "general rack and ruin" [*razrukha*], self-consolidation of tenants [*samo-uplotnenie*], etc.) but above all with Bulgakov's principal target—the Soviet cultural scene, whose main, albeit camouflaged, spokesman in the tale is Mayakovsky.

Mayakovsky's poetic and personal identification with the 'dog' is well known, including the metamorphosis 'man–dog' (Smirnov 1978), and its subtextual relevance to Bulgakov's tale has also been discussed (Zholkovsky 1986c, Chu-dakova 1987, Fusso 1989). Like Mayakovsky's lyrical persona, Bulgakov's Sharik/Sharikov is full of angry desire to attack and bite, and he learns his alphabet from street signs (compare his *Glavryba* = *Abyrvalg* ["Fish Trust—Tsurt-hsif"] experience with Mayakovsky's "Na cheshue ogromnoi ryby / Pro-chel ia . . . ," in his early futurist manifesto, the poem "A vy mogli by?" [1913; "Could You?"], and a later retrospective summation: *obuchalsia azbuke s vyvesok*). The similarities are so many (including Mayakovsky's famous rhymed ad for the Soviet firm Mosselprom, ironized by the dog Sharik) that one is tempted to read, anachronistically, the flood perpetrated by Sharikov in the bathroom (chap. 6) as an echo of Mayakovsky's "Rasskaz liteishchika Ivana Kozyreva o vselenii v novuiu kvartiru" (1928). In fact, according to Chudakova (1987), a polemic with *Heart of a Dog* is implicit in *The Bedbug* (1928–29).

Such a focus accounts for the predominantly textual orientation of the tale. Mayakovsky's—and *agitprop's* in general—campaign for the remolding of old human material provides a constant alien-voice counterpoint to Professor Preobrazhensky's own verbal themes, as the (re)education of Sharikov triggers an all-encompassing play with culture and foregrounds the Word.

The Professor corrects the linguistic and social manners of the Bolshevik house committee (*domkom*), covers the walls with Soviet-style cultural command-ments ("No playing on musical instruments"), pronounces the reading of Soviet newspapers bad for digestion, defends professionalism in singing, and so on. Incorporated or reported in the text are the discussion of Sharikov's first read-ing matter (unexpectedly for Preobrazhensky, it is the Engels-Kautsky corre-spondence rather than *Robinson Crusoe*) and aesthetic preferences (balalaika and circus rather than opera or drama); fragments from *Aida* and from news-papers that print rumors and innuendoes about the goings-on in the apartment; Sharikov's denunciation (*donos*) of the Professor; the "safe conduct" obtained by Preobrazhensky from his commissar patient; the identification papers issued to Sharikov, accompanied in the narrative by the motifs of name-giving and book-burning; medical terminology; quotations and subtexts from literature; and other textual objects.

The storytelling deploys several perspectives. It shifts from the dog's internal monologue (chap. 1) to third-person narration from the dog's point of view (chaps. 1–4), to medical case history, recorded diary-style by Dr. Bormenthal (chap. 5), to an ironic third-person omni-scient perspective (chaps. 4 and 6 through the end). Defamiliarization of the human world through animal eyes has a venerable tradition, running from Apuleius's *The Golden Ass* through Swift's *Houyhnhnms* and the various canine stories to Tolstoy's "The Strider." Bulgakov's startling innovation was to have the dog's sensitive and intelligent internal speech make room, as the dog turns human, for a vulgar, cliché-ridden, demagogic political jargon.

This plethora of voices orchestrates the scandalous show taking place in the "obscene flat" (*pokhabnaia kvartirka*). The central dog-man metamorphosis, which is at the core of the general reversal of the 'normal order' of things, is supported by a cluster of carnivalesque motifs:

—the apocalyptic snowstorm in the spirit of Blok's "The Twelve" (1918) and Pilnyak's *The Naked Year* (1921);[5]

—the dog's point of view 'from below';

—the orgy of rejuvenations, which parades human follies, high-lighting the Bakhtinian grotesque 'lower bodily stratum' ("I will give you a monkey's ovaries, madam!");

—the mysterious zero-sum relationship between the 'doubles,' the Professor and his creature: the stronger the one, the weaker the other;
—the invasion of the cozy apartment by the postrevolutionary "rack and ruin" in the person of Sharikov, as a perversely carnivalesque consequence of the Professor's scientific success;
—the ambiguity of the Preobrazhensky character itself; and
—the open-endedness of the narrative (the epilogue features the Professor continuing his dangerous experiments).
On balance, no voice, not even the Professor's authoritative basso, has the final word, which sounds an overture rather than closure to a dialogue. What, then, are the principal lines of debate introduced by *Heart of a Dog*?

ADOPTION, FATHERING, BELONGING

The plot is set in motion by the motif of 'adoption.'

Dr. Preobrazhensky, a medical luminary of first magnitude, offers refuge and a new lease on life to a hungry and wounded stray dog (Sharik) and to a drunkard stabbed to death in a saloon brawl (Chugunkin). He needs them as raw material for his daring experiment in transplantation, which, however, opens his ancien-régime, typically Bulgakovian home (complete with lampshades, pretty maids, table talk and rituals, etc.) to Soviet-style communal squabbling.

The Professor is an imposing father figure. He is referred to as "benefactor" and "daddy" (by Sharik/Sharikov), "ancient prophet," "pagan priest," "magus," "deity." His 'parenthood' also encompasses his assistant, Dr. Bormenthal (to whom, then "a half-starved student," the Professor once "gave a place [*priiutil*] in the department"), in a symmetrical pattern that sets up a conflict between the two "sons."

Already, as a foundling dog, Sharik experiences the enviable sense of 'belonging.' He can now pass the doorman. He wears a collar (which "is just like a briefcase": it lights up "fierce envy in the eyes of all the dogs he met") and can even enter "the chief department of paradise, . . . the realm of the cook, Dar'ia Petrovna." As a 'new man,' however, his loyalties will soon be shifting.

CLASS STRUGGLE

The political equation is symmetrical. The Professor and his assistant treasure private property, privacy, law and order, culture, civility, science, and Westernism. Preobrazhensky has a scholarly reputation in Europe, looks like a "French knight" and an "ancient king," emphasizes Russia's lagging behind Europe by two hundred years, contemplates emigration. The two intellectuals are pitted against a 'proletarian underdog,' indeed a proletarian artist (Chugunkin, the donor of the hybrid's brain, had been "a balalaika player in bars") and his Communist mentor, Shvonder. The "remnants of a dog's nature" are not as dangerous ("the cats are the least of his sins") as his class instincts; in a prophetic anticipation of the great purges, the Professor sees that "Shvonder . . . does not understand that Sharikov is a far greater menace to him . . . ; if anyone should . . . sic him against Shvonder himself, nothing will be left of him."

The struggle assumes acute forms.

> The conservatives dream of shooting or hanging their opponents and subdue Sharikov with ether and at gunpoint. There are several fights between Sharikov and Bormenthal, the younger and more militant of the two intellectuals; indeed, he is the first to suggest the counteroperation. The Professor is quite aggressive too; according to Sharik (as yet the dog), "He is just like me . . . , he'll nip them in a second." Shvonder and Co., in turn, would like to arrest Preobrazhensky; they lodge a denunciation against him, and Sharikov arms himself with a revolver.

The outcome invented by Bulgakov is bold, both as a narrative tour de force and in its political symbolism. Sharikov's victory is thwarted only at the last moment by the nearly supernatural reverse surgery. The operation returns the rebel-turned-ruler to the state of the "delightful dog" he used to be, whose appropriate place is at his master's feet. In literary terms, this constitutes a unique case of antitotalitarian lobotomy, for usually such operations are performed on doubting intellectuals and individualists.

> Thus: the "extirpation of fantasy" in Zamiatin's We (and subsequent dystopias; see Chapter 9); the surgery-assassination of the Komandarm in Pilnyak's The Tale of the Unextinguished Moon (1926); and the caging of Prisypkin, for scientific purposes, in The Bedbug. The latter, in turn, echoes Pilnyak's Machines and Wolves (1924–25), where the wolf, an embodiment of the Scythian principle, is put in a cage and becomes "like a machine" (Jensen 1979: 252–53).

VIOLENCE

The problem of violence is at the core of the tale. On the level of values, Preobrazhensky is against violence: he professes kindness and education to be the proper tools of progress, and while in control, he adheres to these principles. "By kindness [*laskoi*]. The only method possible in dealing with living creatures. By terror you cannot get anywhere with an animal, no matter what its stage of development." "Nobody should be whipped. . . . Neither man, nor animal can be influenced by anything but sugestion." "Never attempt a crime. . . . You must reach old age with clean hands."[6]

Indeed, thanks to his professional stature and highly placed patients,[7] Preobrazhensky can afford a measure of independence and even some 'gratuitous gestures' (such as his defiant refusal to accede to Shvonder's demagogic demand to help German children). One of his peaceful levers of influence is 'food,' with which he attracts the dog in the first place and later keeps Sharikov in check, threatening an embargo.

Having exhausted all peaceful means, however, the two doctors resort to "crime" after all. To be sure, they justify it by Sharikov's aggressiveness, the impossibility "to wait until we succeed in turning this hoodlum into a man," and by his being the Professor's "own creature, the product of [his] experiment." But although violence is contrary to the Professor's beliefs, a hubristic flaw is already inherent in the surgical—Frankensteinian—feat he has performed, i. e., the original transplantation: "Instead of feeling [his] way and moving parallel to nature, [he] force[d] the question" and thus created, in Sharikov, his own nemesis.

Indeed, already the first operation is seen (and foreseen, by the dog) as "something nasty, evil, if not a real crime."

It is performed by a "[pagan] priest," who is clad in strange—ritual—garments (even the maid, Zina, is "suddenly wearing a smock that looks like a shroud") and hums the aria of *Aida*'s Radames getting ready for human sacrifice. The two doctors are described as "hurrying murderers," the Professor as "an inspired cutthroat" and "satiated vampire"; he shouts, "Knife!" and "becomes positively terrifying." The chapter abounds in phrases like "the knife leapt into his hands," "he slashed," "plunged the knife," "rushed in like a predator," "treacherously stuck the needle," "tore out," and in gory details of manipulation with the skull, brains, heart, and seminal glands.

This carnal-criminal mix has counterparts in other chapters.

The dog is from the start injured—burned by a cruel cook. When subjected to healing procedures, he bites, and he wreaks havoc in the apartment. Chugunkin is also a victim of violence ("Cause of death: struck with a knife in the heart"). In keeping with his murderous (especially antifeline) instincts, Sharikov is appointed exterminator of cats and other stray animals; his commissar-style leather jacket stinks accordingly ("we choked them and choked them cats yesterday"); the cats "will be used for coats [*na pol'ty poidut*]."

CARNIVAL DOUBLES AND FOOD

In a variation on the Ivan Karamazov–Smerdyakov pair, influential in Russian intellectual history, Sharikov's bloodthirsty zeal makes him a parodic version of the Professor's pagan ways and involvement in the surgical transformation of the world.* An important structural link between the two is forged by the carnivalesque motif of 'food' and another of Preobrazhensky's doubles, his cook.

The Professor is a carnivorous gourmet and likes to launch into scholarly disquisitions about nutrition and the suspect quality of Soviet foodstuffs, in particular the Mosselprom sausage, which is fit only for dog food. In this he is echoed by the dog, who disdains "the Normal Diet Cafeteria for the employees of the People's Central Economic Soviet" and Soviet cooks in general, who are thieving and cruel, unlike "the late Vlas . . . , the gentry's cook for the Counts Tolstoy."

In the Professor's apartment, food is symbolically illuminated by the infernal flames coming from the kitchen "realm of the cook Dar'ia Petrovna," the fleshy priestess of sexual and culinary orgies ("Dar'ia Petrovna's face burned with eternal fiery torment and unquenched passion. Her glossy face dripped fat"). She too acts "like a furious executioner," wielding a "sharp, narrow knife" with which she "chopped off the heads and claws of helpless grouse . . . tore the entrails out of chickens," and so on and so forth, while "Sharik was torturing a grouse head."

The animal/surgical connotations of Dar'ia's cooking are prominent in the orchestration of the dinner motif in chapter 4. The dinner ("turkey for the second course") is of keen interest to both Professor and dog, follows the Professor's fumbling in the convolutions of human brains, and is hastily served

---

* Smerdyakov anticipates Sharikov as a parricidal quasi son, semihuman ("You're not a human being. You grew from the mildew in the bathhouse"; Grigory in *The Brothers Karamazov*, III, 6), hanger of cats, corny dresser and musician, uneducated upstart critic of texts, and intellectual apprentice to a radical mentor (Ivan/Shvonder).

just before the arrival of the "evil smelling suitcase" with Chugunkin's corpse, leading to the operation. All this echoes the sausage from chapter 1, mentally referred to by the dog, Sharik, as "chopped mare" and "rotten horse" in a vintage Tolstoy defamiliarization.

The Tolstoyan overtones, uniting the 'food' and 'gore' motifs into a strong and subversive cluster, also include Sharik's sweet memories of the cook Vlas and the subtextual presence of Tolstoy's "Strider," mentioned above as an instance of 'animal narrative' and additionally relevant in the 'slaughterhouse' context.

> After Strider's death, "his skin, . . . flesh, . . . [and] bones were . . . of use" (unlike his former master's) to wolves and people (Tolstoy 1964: 417–18).

This defiantly positive, 'pro-nature' view of animal death had been recycled in a provocative way in Pilnyak's "Mother Earth" (1968 [1924–25]), where the two urban intellectual protagonists are shown to be out of touch with nature.

> The idealistic Commissar Nekul'ev falls out of love with Irina once he discovers that her characteristic smell comes from processing horse carcasses (cf. Sharikov's stench). After she leaves, her pet "wolf-pup" is picked up by the peasant Kuzia, who realizes it is a fox and skins it for a fur hat. Of particular interest is the very technical report on the "methods of utilizing" horse remnants (cf. Sharikov's *pol'ta* to be made of strangled cats), delivered by Irina to a stunned Nekul'ev (see below, "*Envy*").

To sum up Bulgakov's treatment of the 'doubles' motif, he gives it an original twist. On the one hand, the Professor, an attractive and eventually triumphant figure, is cast as a demonic Provocateur, an ironic philosopher interrogating the reigning order;[8] yet he is also a conservative, defender of the status quo. On the other hand, Sharikov, a clearly negative character, gets the star role of carnival clown, disrupter of order, civility, and culture. This paradoxical pairing reflects the peculiar historical moment when, right after the revolution, both the old regime and the new could be equally perceived as '*the* order,' that perennial target of carnivalesque subversion. It also reflects Bulgakov's preference for the former, 'eternal' order of things and his mistrust of Chaos brought on by Carnival's elemental forces.

Envy

POLYPHONY IN THE NEW KEY

Olesha's short novel boasts no less impressive an array of intertexts tapped as underpinnings for a new—Soviet—theme.[9] As in Bulgakov's fantastic tale, polyphony is built into the system of narrative voices.

> In part 1, the first-person narrator coincides with the foundling, only this time around he is an intellectual, who sees his benefactor both 'from below' and 'from above.' The second part is narrated by an "objective" third person, whose style, however, is close to Kavalerov's, so that the latter's fabulaic defeats continue being compensated by his discursive superiority.
>
> Incorporated in the text are also fantasy stories (told by the Provocateur Ivan Babichev), two letters (Makarov's and Kavalerov's), a dream (Kavalerov's nightmare), a fragment from a technical manual (proofread by Kavalerov), "Lenin-style" notes and resolutions (Andrei's), and verse couplets (Kavalerov's and Ivan's).

But the tenor is different from that of *Heart of a Dog*; it is virtually opposite. *Envy* already contains many seeds of its author's subsequent "surrender and demise" (Belinkov 1974). Olesha was one of the first to treat the officially commanded theme of industrialization and create the figure of a well-educated Soviet specialist (Andrei Babichev), superseding the 1925 models (Pilnyak's *Machines and Wolves* and Gladkov's *Cement*), where the Communist ideologues still have to fight for the souls of foreign specialists (Forst and Kleist, respectively).

In indicting his dissident (Kavalerov), Olesha followed the Soviet rhetoric of blaming the recalcitrant opponent for the problems he has with the human condition as such. The manipulative trick was to appropriate the full power of the attendant existential and social critique while dismissing the complexity of the problems, allegedly irrelevant to the New Man and Society.

> To recall the "trials of classical literary characters" popular in the 1920s,[10] Kavalerov is simultaneously tried for several mutually incompatible "crimes": as a superfluous (Oblomov-like) little (Akaky-like) underground man, a Rastignacian individualist, a failed superman (à la Raskolnikov), and a would-be Romantic artist. Furthermore, the discussion does not take place in a rarefied philosophical space, but under the dictatorship of the accusers. On occasion,

as we will see, the author stacks the deck, making Kavalerov weaker and in general worse than his average real-life prototype was.

Despite such "defeatist" bias, *Envy* is known for its relatively even-handed treatment of the opposite voices—a profound ambiguity that earned it attacks from both the Right and Left and a lasting place in literary history.

What, then, are *Envy*'s "replies" to *Heart of a Dog* and "leading questions" to *The Master and Margarita*?

ADOPTION, FATHERING, BELONGING, BARRIERS, ENVY

Here again:

An important paternal figure picks up his ideological opponent in the gutter: a younger and weaker character, a drunkard thrown out of a pub after a fight. He puts him up in his cozy flat (with lampshades and all) and provides him with food and work.

The foundling brings in disorder, dirt,[11] and squabbling over housing space and the "little sofa" he sleeps on. His love-hate of his patron ends in rebellion, and his scandalous defeat is triggered by the interception of his false denunciation.

The father figure is impressive, solid to the point of fatness. He is the master, teacher, savior, and protector of his two 'adoptive sons,' an elegant dresser, a "lord" (*barin*), and at the same time a prodigious worker. And he, like Bulgakov's Professor, tries to reform the foundling.

He also plays father to his niece Valia, protecting her from the pernicious influence of her real father, Ivan, and Kavalerov (not unlike Preobrazhensky rescuing the poor typist from the amorous/matrimonial clutches of Sharikov).

The similarities with *Heart of a Dog* only set in greater relief the conversion undergone by the common plot.

Now it is a Communist boss adopting a declassé old-time intellectual and artist (Kavalerov's profession is almost the same as Chugunkin's: "monologues and couplets for a variety team," while Kavalerov's senior double, Ivan, also earned money "in beer halls[, where] he drew portraits of those who wished"). A 'Communist lord' is a new and controversial phenomenon. Kavalerov reacts to it by interpreting the problems it poses for him in terms of confrontations between 'little man and Bronze Horseman' and between 'son and father.' As for his own father, Kavalerov both dislikes him and recognizes him in himself, as somebody "already done, finished [or completed] . . . there won't be anything more."[12]

Kavalerov's Oedipal paradigm also includes his sexual rivalry with Andrei (over Valia) and with Anechka's fatherlike first husband.

The break with Andrei sends Kavalerov seeking guidance and protection from Andrei's brother and opponent, Ivan, who plays a (mock) Christ to Kavalerov's disciple. In terms of *Heart of a Dog*, this makes Ivan a 'reverse Shvonder,' only given much more ideological and narrative prominence as *Envy's* chief Provocateur. Kavalerov's relationship with Ivan, like that with Andrei, ends in a humiliating sexual triangle.

The problem of '(non)belonging' (touched upon, but peripheral, in *Heart of a Dog*) now becomes a central theme. Kavalerov alternately relishes (albeit with ambivalence) his vicarious and servile (*kholuiskii*) participation in Andrei's official status and suffers from exclusion and the ubiquity of insurmountable barriers.

Brought to the airfield by Andrei (pt. 1, chap. 9), he later finds himself outside looking in, separated by a barrier and guards from the "we" in-group. The text clearly plays with the title of Zamiatin's then unpublished but famous novel: "We gathered at the air terminal. I say, 'we!' Really, I was something on the side. . . . 'You are not from there,'—the soldier said, smiling." Thus, Kavalerov's narrative clearly spells out the sense of his *neprinadlezhnost'*, 'nonbelonging.'[13]

Ivan, on the contrary, seems to succeed in 'transcending the barriers.'

In his wish-fulfilling "Tale" (pt. 2, chap. 6) about the inauguration-turned-destruction of Andrei's pet project, the *Chetvertak* (Two Bits) diner, Ivan "did venture to get over the rope guarding the approaches to the tribunal" and eventually onto the lectern itself.

Along with physical and social barriers, there is the impenetrable communication wall that fences out Kavalerov and Ivan. The new establishment can and does ignore the outsiders. Throughout the plot, Valia fails to notice Kavalerov. Andrei never looks at him, nor does he react to his innuendoes ("He is not listening. His indifference to me is insulting"). And Makarov barely responds to Ivan. An emblem of this 'figure of ignoring' is the recurrent motif of Andrei's 'unseeing gaze.'

Kavalerov perceives him as an "awesome, invincible idol with bulging eyes. . . . Only from the side do I see his eyes; when his face is turned in my direction his gaze isn't there: only the pince-nez sparkles, two blind, round plates" (1: 8). Similarly, Ivan, while arguing with Andrei, "didn't see his brother's eyes . . . only the sparkle of the lenses."[14] At the airfield, Andrei's blind face "turns toward [Kavalerov] on an immobile body," and in the ensuing chase at the construction site, Kavalerov can see only his nostrils, "as if . . . looking up from below at a monument."[15]

The stone-walling of the anti-heroes by the establishment breeds in them the title emotion of the novel. The Soviet "holiday . . . beckons" to Kavalerov, producing the negative, self-destructive 'envy' syndrome, based on the acceptance of the hostile value system that rejects him. In so portraying the intellectual (anti-)hero of his time, Olesha may have been somewhat unfair but not too wide of the mark: even Mandelstam would soon sound a similar note.

In a 1931 poem,[16] he regrets that it is beyond him to join "the youth" at Moscow's stadiums and "glass palaces on chicken feet." Even though written at a later and grimmer time, this attitude is instructive, coming as it does from the once worshipper of the "unshakable scale of values" (1914) and a future anti-Stalin epigrammatist (1933). The "stadiums" seem to refer to the football episode in *Envy* (2: 8–9); the "glass palaces" reactivate the (anti)utopian 'crystal palace' motif,[17] while the rhythm and syntax of the stanza echo an earlier nostalgia for "world culture,"[18] thereby poignantly certifying the sincerity of the new poem.

To be sure, in Olesha the envy syndrome is far more acute: a pathetic mixture of humility, hatred, desire for revenge (to "get Valia—as a prize—for everything: for the humiliations, . . . for my dog's [!] life"), and defiant but impotent rage ("to leave with a bang, slam the door, as they say, . . . take the young world down a peg [*sbit' spesi molodomu miru*]"; see also 1: 11).[19]

With remarkable symmetry, the 'envy/defiance' complex is reciprocated by the 'new men.'

Makarov wants to "organize a union, for the knocking down of the bourgeois world a few pegs [*po sbivaniiu spesi*]"; "many [young Communists] envy [him]" because he lives with Andrei (cf. the stray dogs envying Sharik), while in his own heart "envy toward the machine has taken hold! . . . We invented it, but it turned out much more ferocious than we."

The last element is also a variation on the 'hybrid creatures' motif.

If Sharikov is half man, half dog, Makarov is on his way to becoming a machine, while Ivan, on the contrary, has "corrupted" [or "debauched," *razvratil*]— and thus humanized—his ideal machine, Ophelia.[20] As a result, Ophelia ends up murdering him, in full accord with the Frankensteinian paradigm.[21]

An important component of 'envy' is the kind of narrative optics it promotes: a jealously attentive, voyeuristic contemplation, somewhat from below, of the fortunate object by the virtually invisible subject (in accord with the etymology of the words *zavist'* and 'envy' and their Latin prototype *invidia*, lit. "on-looking"). Inherent in this perspective (fundamentally akin to the Bloomean 'anxiety-of-influence' concept of writing) is a potent weapon that the 'envier' can use against his superior adversary: the power of observation, reporting, (re)interpreting, and distorting, stylistically and otherwise, the image of the 'envied.' These strategies, used to the full by the narrator, are Olesha's original contribution to the dialogue. In the next section, we will see how Bulgakov revisits and revises the topos once again.[22]

CLASS STRUGGLE, VIOLENCE, PRISON, PSYCHIATRIC WARD

The political equation in *Envy* is a mirror reversal of that in *Heart of a Dog*:

Two men representing the ancien régime are pitted against two prophets of the brave new world. In each pair, there is an older and a younger member, and in the Soviet pair, the younger (Makarov) is more aggressive and ideologically extremist than the older (Andrei), whom he finds too soft and is prepared to kill (1: 13; cf. Sharikov as a threat to Shvonder).[23]

Similarly reversed is the view of the West and Western values taken, with the author's imprimatur, by the doctors in *Heart of a Dog*.

Kavalerov's flawed individualistic ideals—his dreams of being born in France, achieving world fame, being immortalized as a waxwork figure (one more hybrid!)—are a collage of characters and quotations from Western literature and history of technology. Ivan Babichev openly parades as a new Mephistopheles. Makarov, naturally, opposes the bourgeois world, both philosophically and physically, as he confronts on the football field the embodiment of Western success, the celebrated German player Getzke. The narrator openly disapproves of the individualist aesthetics of this star ("the famous Getzke . . . strove only to show his skill [or art, *iskusstvo*]"), whose name sounds like a pejorative-diminutive version of Goethe.

Andrei's command of European culture is more of a surprise, especially when compared to Kavalerov's exaggerated ignorance.

Andrei Babichev has lived abroad (as a former revolutionary exile) and speaks German. Kavalerov does not, and is only able to guess, from the rhyme and the foreign guests' laughter, that Andrei "ended the conversation [in German] with a proverb." This is a characteristic pro-Soviet sleight of hand by the author, especially since elsewhere Kavalerov archly spoofs Babichev's primitive and at times ungrammatical Russian (befitting a Soviet apparatchik; cf., on the contrary, in *Heart of a Dog*, the two doctors' conspiratorial recourse to German— *vorsichtig, später, gut*—in the presence of the ignoramus Sharikov).

The struggle between the two camps is as acute as in *Heart of a Dog*. Both sides readily talk of violence and sometimes come down to fisticuffs.

> Kavalerov, goaded by Ivan and on his own, keeps planning the assassination of Andrei. Ivan threatens to strangle Valia. Makarov threatens to and does beat up Kavalerov. Both Andrei and Makarov speak of shooting Ivan. Makarov threatens, Frankenstein-style, to kill Andrei, while Ophelia is envisioned (in Kavalerov's dream) killing Ivan. Ivan foretells Andrei's death at the hands of Ophelia, while Kavalerov sees Valia's "collarbones flashing like daggers" in a foreshadowing of Ivan's destruction by Ophelia (which reinforces the important parallel between Valia and Ophelia).

Unlike the old-timers, the new masters also have the options of arresting the antagonists (see the confrontations of Andrei and Ivan and the GPU episode) or packing them off to the lunatic asylum. Even in Ivan's own "Tale" Andrei believes that Ivan is "seriously ill . . . delirious." The threat of psychiatric commitment corresponds to the dystopian lobotomy motif, reversed in the two medics' use of surgery in *Heart of a Dog*.

FOOD, SLAUGHTER, DOUBLES, AND SEX

Once again, 'food'—indeed, sausage—plays a central, well-nigh mythological role in the narrative.

> Andrei Babichev is a fat man, "a glutton and a gourmandizer" (while eating, "his eyes became bloodshot"). From his father he has inherited a gift for cooking. He likes to hold forth on the topic of food ("We don't know how to make sausages! . . . Real sausages should spatter"). "He is a mighty sausage-maker, confectioner, and cook."

But unlike Preobrazhensky and the dog Sharik, Andrei (along with Kavalerov and probably Olesha) takes the Soviet Breadtrust, the Supreme Soviet for National Economy, and the like seriously.

> "He [Andrei] heads everything that concerns glutting. . . . He would like to give birth to food. He gave birth to 'Two Bits' "—his crystal palace. Not only

does he want to 'father' food; he wants to 'marry' it:[24] "Like a bridegroom who has noticed how beautiful his young bride is," he blushes, proud of the "cooked, tea-time sausage: a fat, evenly rounded rod cut," "a tightly stuffed intestine," "a beauty!"

The 'pagan priest' metaphor is also prominent. Andrei's laughter is that of a *žhrec* (1: 3), and his negative double, Ivan, is described as a "priestlike [*kak zhrets*] devourer of crayfish" (2: 2). Andrei's other 'double' is, in a remarkable analogy to *Heart of a Dog*'s Dar'ia, the widow Anechka Prokopovich.

> She too gives Kavalerov shelter, bed, and nourishment. The parallel is reinforced by Andrei's androgynous traits, beginning with his plumpness and female surname (*baba* means "[folksy] woman"),[25] and the snoring habit they share.

But above all, Anechka shares with Andrei the leitmotif association with the kitchen, sausage, and slaughter.

> She "cooks dinner for the barbers' artel," is "fat, and flabby. You can squeeze her out like a liver sausage." And she is consistently shown at the kitchen stove. "She feeds cats. Silent, slender cats fly up after her hands with electrodynamic movements. She strews some sort of giblets to them. . . . Once I slipped, having stepped on something's heart [!]—small and tightly formed like a chestnut. She walks enmeshed in cats and the blood vessels of animals. A knife sparkles in her hand. She tears through intestines with her elbows like a princess through a cobweb."[26]

But then, according to Makarov, Andrei himself is a backward cook, too close to crude butchering, despite all his emphasis on industrialization that so upsets Kavalerov.

> "You are using primitive means. You are happy cutting up calves" (Makarov's letter to Andrei; 1: 13). "In the evening I proofread: 'The blood collected during slaughter may be processed either for food, for the preparation of sausage, or for the manufacture of light and dark albumin, glue, buttons, paints, fertilizers, and feed for cattle, fowl and fish. . . . The heads and hooves of sheep with the aid of spiral electric drills,[27] automatic-acting cleaning machines, gas-operated lathes, and scalding vats are processed for food products, industrial bone oil, the hair and bones for various articles.' "

Babichev's brochure reads like a variation on the 'technoslaughter' topos we have noted in connection with the transplantation surgery and cats-to-coats processing in *Heart of a Dog*.

Its direct subtext seems to be the following passage from chapter 3 of Pilnyak's "Mother Earth": "Arina began to speak in a matter-of-fact way . . . : 'The skin is used for leather, the fats are used in soap-making, we feed the proteins to the pigs. The bones and sinews go to the glue works. Then the bones are ground to make fertilizer. We waste nothing here [*U nas vse ispol'zyaetsia*].' Arina's hands were covered with blood" (1968: 57).

In a striking parallel to Pilnyak's line about waste, Kavalerov, parodying Andrei Babichev, uses a similarly broken verb form in a similar context: "You want to utilize her [Valia], as you utilize [*ispol'zovyvaete*] (I purposely employ your word) 'heads and hooves of sheep with the aid of . . . electric drills' " (1: 11).[28]

Associated with 'food,' in particular through its 'carnal' overtones, is the topos of 'love and sex,' bearing some resemblance to that of *Heart of a Dog*, notably to Sharikov's sexual harassment of the two women servants, his abortive marriage to the typist, and Dar'ia's powerful sexuality (supposedly quenched by her fireman boyfriend).[29] But in Olesha's novel it is much more prominent, forming a major theme and the source of narrative suspense. In this respect, *Envy* incorporates, compressed into a nutshell, elements of the novelistic tradition, with its families, triangles, rivalries, and (eventual) marriages—a repertoire to which it adds the modernist motifs of androgyny, homosexuality, sex *à trois*, and others. These genre differences correspond to the shift of thematic focus: from an all-out philosophical subversion of the 'new man' in *Heart of a Dog* (combining a surgically resolved sci-fi cum gothic plot with elements of a political tract) to a close, and painfully ambivalent, look at the 'new vs old' human emotions (as signaled by Olesha's very title).

Hence 'love-and-sex,' always provocatively linked to 'food,' are at the core of *Envy*'s plot.

Kavalerov dreams in his sleep of a "sweet young thing" (*prelestnaia devchonka*) whose love costs "just two bits" (the associations with Valia's looks, Anechka's venality, and Andrei's diner are unmistakable). Andrei is in love with his "beauty" the sausage, priced at only "thirty-five kopecks." The sausage exudes strong sexual fluids, both anal and phallic, in accordance with Andrei's own bisexual image. Kavalerov (who despite the manly ring of his surname, meaning something like "Mr. Beau" or "Mr. Knight," is obsessively insecure about his masculinity) has a grotesque attack of castration fear in connection with Andrei's sausage: having to take it across town, he "several times was ready to fling [it] over the railing . . . into the waves," much in the manner of

Gogol's barber carrying Kovalev's cut-off nose (!). On receiving the sausage, the addressee, another sausage expert, "congratulate[s Andrei] and want[s] to kiss [him]."

'Food,' 'sex,' and ideology also come together in the issue of *byt* ('everyday lifestyle,' esp. the 'food and lodging conditions').

Andrei wants to abolish the traditional family, sordid private kitchens, and the idea of privacy in general, replacing them with communal diners and other crystal palaces on a humankind scale ("We are not a family—we are humanity").

Ivan defends "native home—home, sweet home!" (cf. Preobrazhensky's pleas for the right "to dine in the dining room, and operate in the surgery!" chap. 2). As an emblem of home, family, and traditional human links and feelings, he carries a pillow; he brings it to his public confrontations with his daughter and his brother, claims that she used to sleep on it and that Andrei, crushed by Ophelia, will come to die on it.

In Kavalerov's case, the pillow is echoed by his strong identification with beds, sheets, and blankets (in both Andrei's and Anechka's apartments), symbolizing his infantilism and sexual anxieties.

The narrative's ambivalence vis-à-vis the world of flesh is also projected onto the portrayal of women, represented by two opposite but equally threatening and essentially castrating types, Gogol-style. The carnal, mother-earth figure of Anechka is opposed to the unattainable, ideal, sexless, adolescent, tomboyish, machine- and daggerlike Valia. Kavalerov and Ivan rush between the two, drawn to and angry at both,[30] while the 'new men' are indifferent to sex, proclaiming the demotion of family values and emancipation of women from homemaking and *byt*: Makarov and Valia plan to get married only four years later and not to kiss until the opening of the Two Bits diner.

This incorporeal rationalism in matters of love and marriage has a positive prototype in Chernyshevsky's family engineering in *What Is to Be Done?* and a negative one, in the Enlightenment-inspired attitude of the Bolkonsky father and son (*War and Peace*), who postpone and thus doom Andrei's and Natasha's wedding. At a more general level, Valia's cluster of asexual features is an original and successful combination of the traditional virginity of the novelistic heroine (who does not get married until the end) with the new technological, utopian, and sexual-revolutionary topoi.[31]

Valia is not given any distinct social role of her own and is dependent on the male parental figures (her disowned father and adoptive father/uncle); thus, she remains a typical romantic damsel waiting for prince charming, her newly acquired athletic ways being but a new version of Natasha Rostova's adolescent prankishness. On the other hand, her "soaring" over the ground (in Kavalerov's dream; 2: 11), her "daggerlike collarbones," and other affinities with the murderous Ophelia are a new hybrid of romantic (Gothic) and dystopian (machinistic) elements.

PROVOCATION AND CARNIVAL

The shift from carnal surgery to the sphere of feelings, prestige, and perceptions does not mean a renunciation of carnival. If anything, Olesha's novel is more carnivalesque than *Heart of a Dog*, with the difference that the focus is now on 'symbolic action.' Since the anti-heroes' major problem is their 'invisibility' to the new establishment, two principal counterstrategies are available to them: exploiting their powers of vision and maneuvering themselves into positions of visibility.[32] The former underlies much of the novel's 'invidious' narrative (as discussed earlier); the latter is put to provocative use by Kavalerov and Ivan Babichev through their mostly dreamed-of, wished-for, or otherwise symbolic actions. Both strategies, especially the latter, are by definition intimately connected, indeed, tend to merge with the creative—literary or theatrical—act itself.

Symbolic action compensating for real-life defeat is another name for 'gratuitous gestures' (as practiced by Professor Preobrazhensky). Olesha's anti-heroes engage in or threaten clowning, scandals, assasination, suicide.

> Kavalerov wants "to raise the barrier [!] with a big scandal . . . suddenly just go ahead and do something obviously absurd, to perpetrate some sort of ingenious prank [*genial'noe ozorstvo*, "a prank of genius"] and then to say: 'So that's the way you are, and this is the way I am.' To come out on a square and do no matter what, and exit bowing. . . . Suicide without any motive. Out of mischief. . . . [C]ommitting a disgusting malicious crime" [the assassination of Andrei].

Of paramount importance to this rhetoric (originating with Dostoevsky's underground man and ideological suicides like Kirillov) is the element of provocative 'publicity':

Kavalerov challenges a "troupe of monsters" in a beer hall. Ivan, who plans "to leave with a bang," organizes (real and imaginary) disputes and demonstrations, including his pet project—the "last conspiracy/parade of feelings."

This distinguishes *Envy* from *Heart of a Dog* (Preobrazhensky delivers his gratutious speeches in the privacy of his dining room, and only out of necessity and in self-defense—before the intruding officials) and foreshadows the public performances to be put on by Woland and his troupe.

Now that Order has become firmly associated with Soviet reality, the role of clowning provocateurs devolves to its rejected opponents.

Kavalerov repeatedly refers to himself as a "jester" and "clown," and Ivan deliberately poses as a carnival 'king of fools': his self-description, *korol' poshliakóv*, "king of vulgarians," is a rhyming echo of the carnivalesque phrase *korol' durakóv*. Even Andrei is endowed with clownish traits (fatness, gluttony, etc.), at least in the perceptions of Kavalerov and Ivan (especially in his "Tale of the Meeting of Two Brothers").

A major provocateurial cluster (anticipatory of *The Master and Margarita*) is based on a carnivalesque inversion of the Gospels.

Ivan is a "new preacher." He poses as a mock Christ, refers to his Calvary, gets himself arrested and interrogated by the GPU. His conversation with the anonymous Soviet Pontius Pilate is modeled on a similar episode in Ehrenburg's *Jurenito* (which, in turn, goes back to the Grand Inquisitor chapter of *Brothers Karamazov*), while his "reverse miracles" (wine to water, etc.) go back to Goethe's Mephistopheles. Ivan undertakes a Mephistophelian seduction of Kavalerov and at the same time playfully disclaims his satanism in his doggerel verses, in which he claims he is "no German hocus-poker" but a "modest, Soviet joker," a "modern sorcerer."

Ivan is not only Kavalerov's master but also his senior 'double' as far as his frustrated ambitions are concerned. As an artist of sorts (versifier, inventor, hypnotist, etc.), he talks of fusing his envy and the aesthetics of gratuitous gesture into a planned carnival of feelings that are spurned by the New Man, in a sort of modern *Walpurgisnacht* (the novel's draft actually mentions a witches' sabbath).[33]

For this, Ivan needs a "demonic woman, and [her] tragic lover. But where should one look for him? In Sklifosovsky Hospital?" (2: 3). "I dreamed of finding a woman who would blossom in this hole with an unprecedented feeling. . . . I found such a being . . . Valia" (2: 4). But as the New Men succeed in taking her away from him, he pins all his hopes on the imaginary, feminine and sinful, machine, Ophelia, whom he sends (in his wishful storytelling) to destroy the Two Bits diner.

The (future) celebration of the *Chetvertak*'s opening (of the kind usually reserved the culmination place in Soviet production novels, e.g., *Cement* [Clark 1981: 259]) is rewritten—or shall we say re-produced, re-performed?—by Ivan as its spectacularly theatrical destruction.

"They took [Andrei] for the master of ceremonies [*konferans'e*]"; "the public was switching its attention, ready to watch and listen to the actors"; when Andrei failed to stop Ivan, the "crowd screeched: . . . 'This is hypnosis!' " "And indeed the whole scene could have been taken for a performance. . . . After all, actors often appear out of the audience. And what's more, real actors were pouring out of the wooden shed. Yes, like nothing other than a butterfly, a ballerina fluttered out from behind the boards. A clown in a monkey vest was climbing onto the lectern" (2: 6).

As for Ivan, he "stood leaning on the rope, or rather half sat on the rope hanging his rear over it, and, not caring about what complete disorder would occur if the rope should break, imperturbably, apparently amused, swung himself on the rope." Later, he emerged on the lectern with a pillow in his hand, as a typical circus or carnival clown.

In a draft version, Ivan refers to himself as "a touring actor . . . giving a gala performance in the provinces" (Ingdahl 1984: 94). Kavalerov appears there barefoot and draped in his blanket as a mock Christ (a foreshadowing of this scene made it to the published text; 2: 11), anticipating Woland's attire: "a long, dirty, black nightshirt, patched on the left shoulder" (chap. 22) and the intermittently half- and undressed state of Ivan Bezdomny in *The Master and Margarita*.

Remarkable are also the German/magical origins of the machine Ophelia: Andrei's arguments against her/its existence ("Who is this she? . . . It was just the wind that knocked a lantern against a beam. . . . That's a shadow!" 2: 6) are patterned on the reassuring explanations given by the father to his child in Goethe's "Erlkönig."

On balance, the alignment of values and subversions in *Envy* is much closer to the archetypal Bakhtinian-Rabelaisian carnival than in *Heart of a Dog*. And yet despite all his ambiguities, Olesha too exhibits a measure of preference for monologic seriousness, anxious to distance himself from his clowns and to protect from them the representatives of Order—in his case, the triumphant Soviet establishment.

The Master and Margarita

POLYPHONY AND THE SOVIET THEME

In his last finished novel, Bulgakov continued his carnivalesque subversion of the Soviet system, especially its cultural scene. Focused on the problems of writing, a writer's life, and coping with the Truth, the novel is famous for deploying a panoply of cultural references[34] (often shared with *Heart of a Dog* and *Envy*) and foregrounding the multilayered Text.

> Regarding the narrative structure, the Moscow and Jerusalem subplots are told in different voices—a satirical and a more objective one, respectively. There are the historical, fictional, and fantastic planes. The text comprises dreams, framed stories, staged performances, telegrams, poems, songs, characters' memories, and so on.

These polyphonic techniques are echoed by a similar treatment of characterization.

> Characters literally split into several voices (e.g., Azazello talking to Annushka on the staircase landing; Ivan Bezdomny in the psychiatric hospital, as his 'old' and 'new' selves argue with each other); use double-talk (e.g., Pilate in his veiled instructions to Arthanius concerning the execution of Judas); and undergo drastic identity transformations, internal and/or external (Woland and his team of tricksters, Bezdomny, Margarita, Natasha, Varenukha).

The novel's various layers and splits are held together by numerous motific and textual correspondences, which include

—doubling of characters (the Master and Yeshua; Ivan and Levi Matthu; Woland and Arthanius);

—sharing of thoughts and intentions by different characters (e.g., Pilate and Levi Matthu);

—reification of tropes (e.g., of references, made "in vain," to the devil);

—inner voices and thoughts of characters, overheard and promptly responded to by others (mostly by the demonic/divine characters—Woland's team, Yeshua, but also Margarita).[35]

The interplay of polyphony and unity (i.e., essentially, monologism) is nowhere so evident as in the status of the Jerusalem subplot.

> It is presented as a collective or anonymous Absolute Text that belongs to many narrators (Woland; the Master: "Oh, how well I guessed it all!" [chap.

13]; Ivan Bezdomny; the [implied and real] author; and Reality itself) and is eventually read by its divine protagonist (Yeshua).

In other words, this time around, Bulgakov wraps his satirical monologism in an atmosphere of genuine Carnival. The dialogism is also enhanced by

—casting demonic clowns-provocateurs as officers of supreme justice;

—a total theatricalization of the plot;

—a dualistic juxtaposition of the two worlds;

—the imperfection of the hero (the Master); and

—the unfinishedness of the Pilate-Yeshua exchange.

A major dialogic dimension is added to all this by the position *The Master and Margarita* takes vis-à-vis *Envy* and *Heart of a Dog*.

APARTMENTS, EDUCATION, ENVY, BARRIERS, TRANSCENDENCE

The motifs of 'shelter' and 'communal squabbling' reemerge in *The Master and Margarita*, but in a radically modified version.

The Master acquires his own cozy flat with a table, lampshade, and sofa. Similarly, his disciple Bezdomny (lit. Homeless) is shown in the epilogue working by a lamp in his apartment. The Master's self-sufficiency is achieved by the Master only thanks to the sponsorship of higher powers, in the shape first of a lottery win and eventually of the "eternal refuge" granted him by Woland.[36]

Predictably, the first, this-worldly domestic idyll is soon undone by Soviet reality: the Master is denounced, evicted, and arrested, and becomes a "pauper" (cf. Kavalerov's similar self-perception). But unlike the situation in *Envy*, this is not the whole story.

The housing problem ends in the eviction of the evictor (Aloysius Mogarych), as part of Woland's denounce-and-punish campaign against the "Muscovites, soured by the housing shortage." Also unlike the situation in *Envy*, Margarita leaves her husband's spacious government-provided apartment; later, having turned into a witch, she wrecks a whole apartment building (owned by the members of the Soviet cultural establishment). Another house becomes the epicenter of Woland's pernicious activities, centering on apartment 50, which belongs to two Soviet nouveau bosses (Berlioz and Likhodeev), but undergoes a ruthless 'de-consolidation' (the bosses are evicted; cf. *Heart of a Dog*) and transformation into the devils' den (the title of chap. 7 refers to it as *nekhoroshaia kvartira*, reminiscent of the *pokhabnaia kvartirka* in *Heart of a Dog*).

This aesthetic of destruction is a characteristic new twist. In *Heart of a Dog*, the Professor defended order and the sanctity of home from Sharik/Sharikov's carnivalesque destructiveness. Similarly, in *Envy*, "things liked Andrei," not the clown Kavalerov. The other clown, Ivan, repeatedly created provocative disorder, and both of them ended up in the pathetic and slovenly abode of the widow Prokopovich.

In *The Master and Margarita*, however, the obsession with mundane comforts is an accusation leveled at typically Soviet people, who are then punished accordingly.

The likable clowns/provocateurs/wreckers, who mete out the punishments, take the side of the independent intellectuals, who this time do not mind wreaking havoc in somebody's bathroom on an even grander scale than Sharikov. The destruction befalls Latunsky's apartment, the currency shop, the Griboedov restaurant, the money and goods produced by "black magic" for the covetous Soviet audience.

Thus Bulgakov, having absorbed a measure of *Envy*'s 'disorder,' moves to a more carnivalesque position.

A new spin is also given to the motif of 'education/apprenticeship' (a cognate of 'adoption' and 'fathering').[37] It is central to the plot, involving such pairs of protagonists as Matthu and Yeshua, Ivan and the Master, Natasha and Margarita, the petty demons and Woland. The reeducation of the foundling (Ivan Bezdomny) meets with more success than in the two previous cases; its direction is the same as that in *Heart of a Dog* but opposite to that in *Envy*.

Sharikov had to be returned back to his canine state; Kavalerov remained unreformed by Andrei. Now Ivan Bezdomny, a loudmouthed Soviet literary hack, is transformed into a truth-seeking intellectual, while in *Envy* the "hack" label was stuck on Kavalerov (despite the indubitable talent evidenced by his narrative) and on Getzke, the self-centered artist of German soccer. One could also argue that Bezdomny's apprenticeship with the Master is a positive version of Kavalerov's apprenticeship with Ivan Babichev.

The official ideological dogma and way of life are also abandoned, in one way or another, by Margarita, the Master, Varenukha (who becomes a vampire), Natasha, Levi Matthu, Pilate. To those who will not desist, severe—sometimes capital—punishment is in store.

The 'envy' complex, too, undergoes a conversion. Now it is the members of the literary establishment (the MASSOLIT writers' union) who are envious of one another.

An eloquent passage, spiced with irony, is devoted to the title theme of Olesha's novel—and in connection with a restaurant, too ("Who will say anything in defense of envy?" chap. 5); and the remark "Lavrovich has six [rooms] to himself. . . . And his dining room is paneled in oak!" revisits, with a gloating wink, Shvonder's strictures against Professor Preobrazhensky's housing habits.

The antiestablishment characters, on the contrary, are free from this syndrome.

Ivan Bezdomny watches "without envy" the happy reunion of the Master and Margarita. As for the Master, who is denied entry to the writers' world, he feels not envy but disbelief and horror. Unlike Kavalerov, he does not crave fame (despite Margarita's initial prodding, which she comes to regret). Even Riukhin realizes that no fame short of Pushkin-scale glory is worth much, and a Pushkinian view of literary values is recognizable in the otherworldly rest (*pokoi*) reserved for the Master in the end (in a positive, indeed sublime version of Kavalerov's utter indifference at the end of *Envy*).[38]

As for the barriers set up by the new establishment (in *The Master and Margarita*, as in *Envy*), they now come to be magically transcended.

Behemoth's and Koroviev's favorite hobby consists of invading the Soviet bosses' offices and the elite's currency shop and restaurant, providing a triumphant sequel to the pranks of Ivan Babichev. Thus, Behemoth's kerosene primus and his wicked toppling of the chocolate pyramid are similar, respectively, to Ivan's pillow and his balancing on the rope fence. And in what reads like a literal vindication of Kavalerov's craving to participate in the Soviet feast of life, Margarita and the Master are invited to (and she presides over) the Satan's ball.

The protagonists' 'belonging,' and at the very top too, is underscored in both spatial and temporal terms. Contrary to Kavalerov's futile chase after the diabolically elusive Andrei, Woland's agents seek out the two antiestablishment heroes and decide, for their sake, "to prolong the festive midnight for a while."

CLASS STRUGGLE

The political equation is not as symmetrical as before: both the balance of power and the conflict's center of gravity are now different. The mirror symmetry, of the kind pervasive in *Heart of a Dog* and *Envy*, is replaced with a more complex pattern involving a third, Satanic force. This third force sides with but is quite separate from the positive heroes (the Master, Margarita, Yeshua), while in the two previous texts, the demonic element was distributed between the opponents (Sharikov and Preobrazhensky, Andrei and Ivan). Nor do the representatives of the official camp form neat pairs with their opponents. Rather, the 'officials' are many and secondary in narrative and spiritual stature; and they either reform (Bezdomny, Pilate) or are dispatched quite decisively by the combined forces of the satirical narrative, the (literally) devilish plot, and judgment in light of absolute values.

The 'absolutist' stance includes, among other things, a Westernism taken for granted (as in Azazello's view of Moscow: "I prefer Rome, Messire"; chap. 29) and a rhetorical shift from ideological arguments (which are from the start declared irrelevant: Christ just existed, and no proofs are needed) to specific accusations (of stealing, lying, cowardice, meanness) and appropriate punishments.

Still, the general framework of the struggle on the whole follows, and varies, the familiar paradigm: debate, arrest, psychiatric hospitalization, physical repression. Ideological confrontations are many, involving Woland and the two litterateurs (Berlioz and Bezdomny), the Master and his critics, Yeshua and Pilate, Levi Matthu and Pilate, and so on. But more than anything, the novel reads like a record of an epidemic of 1930s-style arrests, aggravated by the provocative participation of Woland and his team.

> Bezdomny's urge to deport Immanuel Kant to the Gulag for his proof of God's existence and to "sort out" Woland[39] is followed by numerous disappearances of major and minor characters, arrested not for "ten days," as in *Envy*, but for real. Some of the disappearances (e.g., the Master's) are arranged by the victims' colleagues and neighbors, others by the devils, provocatively engaging in Soviet-style denunciations. In many cases (e.g., Likhodeev's), Woland and his minions attend to the deporting themselves. The arrest of the Master is only hinted at (chap. 13), probably for Aesopian reasons, but this is compensated for by the fully elaborated martyrdom of Yeshua (which can also be seen as a reification of Ivan Babichev's largely imaginary Calvary in *Envy*). The interplay between the mystique of the Soviet secret police and the truly supernatural powers reaches its climax in the failed arrest of the devils—in one more materialization of Ivan Babichev's vindictive dream tales.

The psychiatric ward option, with which Makarov threatened Ivan Babichev, develops into the very real Stravinsky clinic, to which characters are hauled in droves.

> The hospital's role as an analog to the unmentionable Gulag is underscored by the exchange between the Master and Bezdomny in the psychiatric ward (chap.

13): *"Itak, sidim?"*—*"Sidim."* In the English version ("So, here we are?"—
"Here we are"), this Aesopian pun remains as innocent as it ostensibly is in
Russian, unless the second meaning of the verb *sidet'*, "to sit," is taken into
account: "to do time [in jail]."

In the high literary tradition, those pronounced insane (the Master,
Bezdomny, Woland) are, of course, much wiser than their "normal"
denunciators.

The topos has been defined by the 'madness' of Hamlet and Chatsky (in Griboedov's *Woe from Wit*), the compulsory lobotomy of fantasy in Zamyatin's *We*,
and Ilf and Petrov's dissidents seeking refuge from purges in Dr. Titanushkin's
psychiatric clinic (*The Golden Calf*, chap. 16, a likely source of Bulgakov's
episode).

The potent mix of police arrests with repressive medicine and outright devilry may seem—and is—idiosyncratically Bulgakovian, and
yet it too had been anticipated by Olesha.

The three elements, often appearing separately in *Envy*, come together in the
confrontation of the two antagonist brothers: " 'To the *GPU*!' [Andrei] said.
Hardly had the *magic* word been pronounced when everything came out of
its *lethargy*, rousing itself" (2: 3; italics added).

In a broader perspective, of course, these (and some other) features
of *The Master and Margarita* signal its kinship to modern dystopias.

In accordance with the dystopian masterplot (see Chapter 9), the novel centers on a protagonist who falls out of the system, becomes a truth seeker,
writer, and ailing man. His love relationship with a woman focuses on writing
and safeguarding his book, and they move beyond the boundaries of the system's space and time. The plot involves suprarealistic forces (this time around,
magical rather than the usual science-fictional) and so on.

But Bulgakov's optimistic tone and the protection extended by his
Provocateurs to the positive heroes clearly distinguish *The Master and
Margarita* from "regular" dystopias.

VIOLENCE, PROVOCATION, AND CARNIVAL

The reification of vicious metaphors results in an orgy of physical
violence, which for the most part is done to the representatives of
the new order by their victims or by the satanic tricksters acting on
their behalf. The great terror of the 1930s is implied, avenged, and
ambivalently replicated by the provocative desacralization of death in

—the provisional beheading of Bengalsky and the terminal executions of Berlioz and Baron Meigel;

—the cheerfully cruel disclosure of the date of the greedy bar manager's imminent death (chap. 18);

—the episode of "invalid shooting" (*nedeistvitel'noi strel'by*) in the course of the attempt to arrest the magic cat (chap. 27), which fitfully crowns the novel-long play with 'murder mania'; and

—Matthu's plan to kill Yeshua and Judas, Margarita's determination to poison Latunsky, and the execution of Judas by Pilate and Arthanius (chap. 13).

The fanciful cruelty of such scenes reflects the leitmotif of 'arbitrary gesture,' typical of the entire triptych.

> Besides visiting a well-motivated (but quite excessive and spectacular) vengeance upon the Master's nemesis, Latunsky, Margarita-turned-witch engages in pranks dictated by a distinctly arbitrary desire "to do something amusing and interesting as a way of saying good-bye." Implementing Ivan Babichev's program of a 'door-slamming exit,' Margarita undertakes such "unnecessary acts" as breaking a streetlamp to pieces.[40]

Indeed, in Margarita, who now speaks in a "criminal voice," Woland has found the "demonic woman" once sought by Olesha's provocateur for his "parade of feelings."

> Margarita's literary genealogy is similar to Ophelia's: her homonym prototype was to Faust what Ophelia's was to Hamlet. She too is a hybrid creature: woman and witch, a product of provocateurial corruption; and like Olesha's Ophelia (and Valia), she becomes airborne, a condition she uses to destroy the establishment's crystal palace—in her case, the Dramlit Building.
>
> Incidentally, as she stops by to soothe the little boy whose sleep has been disturbed by the noise, she does so in a way reminiscent of the same "Erlkönig" implied in the corresponding passage in *Envy*: to the boy's question "Where are you, auntie?" she replies, "Ia tebe snius'" (lit. "I am being dreamed by you"; chap. 21).

Bulgakov's (quasi-)historical and fantastic episodes confer the status of fictional 'reality' on what Olesha introduced under the proviso of dreams, metaphors, and figments of characters' imaginations. Reified in the primary narrator's text of *The Master and Margarita* are the vindictive designs of Olesha's antiestablishment protagonists, their conspiracy of feelings, and the mythological figures they identified with or pretended to become.

The Master and Margarita features, in flesh and blood, such figures as Jesus Christ, Pontius Pilate, Roman soldiers (cf. Ivan Babichev's childhood episode involving the Pharsalus battle), and Woland-Mephistopheles (i.e., in Ivan Babichev's words, a "German hocus-poker," "a modest Soviet joker," a "modern sorcerer").

The 'parade of old feelings' even takes place twice. The first time, it is a farce at the Variety theater (claimed, as in *Envy*, to be a mere case of collective hypnosis); the second time, a bona fide mysterial rite, the Satan's ball. The ball is, as it were, Kavalerov's waxwork hall of fame come alive, with the Master and Margarita living his dream of attained dignity while Woland and Abadonna carry out his fantasies of deadly vengeance.

LOVE AND FOOD

The Master is lucky in love. Bulgakov rehabilitates his weak superfluous man and romantic dreamer by having him conquer his traditional counterpart, the strong woman of Russian literature.

Contrary to Olesha's Valia,[41] Margarita leaves her highly placed Soviet husband to share the life and fate of the Master. It is Kavalerov's dream come true ("Not you—I'll get Valia. We'll thunder in Europe—there, where they love glory"; *Envy*, 1: 11). While Valia fails to notice Kavalerov at close range, Margarita meets the Master as she is out looking for him ("She said that she had come out with the yellow flowers that day so that I'd find her at last"; chap. 13).

In both cases, the encounter takes place in a small lane off Tverskaia Street (quite probably the same, to judge by the topographical clues). Both heroines are caught at the moment of an important transition. Both scenes involve 'flowers,' which are offered and rejected, foreshadowing the eventual tragedy. Kavalerov's perception of Valia's collarbones as "daggers" is echoed, with a difference, by the Master's description of his and Margarita's instant love as having "leaped out at us like a brigand with a switchblade knife."[42]

In another sense, however, Bulgakov's treatment of 'love and sex' is rather traditional—'absolutist,' as it were, and certainly less ambiguous than Olesha's. Despite the abundant carnivalesque display of naked female flesh (including Margarita's), the relationship between the title protagonists remains a romantically disembodied one.

'Food' is less than central to *The Master and Margarita*, but its treatment is consistent with the general dynamics of our dialogic triad.

The bleak view of Soviet reality is emblematized by Woland's axiom that the abolition of spiritual absolutes entails a shortage of foodstuffs: "How come, whatever one reaches for [*chego ni khvatish'sia*], it doesn't exist here?!"—be it God, Satan, or mineral water (chap. 3). Soviet food services are based on such "nonsense" as "sturgeon of the second freshness" (chap. 18); decent food can be obtained only in the crystal palaces of the new elite, closed to the public (the Griboedov restaurant, the currency store). It is these that Woland and his team subject to carnivalesque destruction or at least practical sarcasm. (Thus, the breakfast served by Woland to the baffled Likhodeev, featuring "sausages with tomato juice" [chap. 7], might have earned the appreciation of Andrei Babichev.)

Contrary to the two preceding texts, this time 'food' is not fraught with sacerdotal connotations, but its links with creativity are ironically reified in the elitist writers' restaurant's bearing a simultaneously literary and gastronomical name—Griboedov. Named after the famous Russian writer, whose surname literally means "mushroom eater," the club-restaurant is the object of envy of Moscow gourmets (chap. 5). In yet another probable shot at Olesha's misguided respect for the Soviet food industry, Bezdomny mentally refers to the psychiatric clinic as a "factory-kitchen" (*fabrika-kukhnia*, chap. 8). And finally, the Master's living quarters in the narrative's present, Dr. Stravinsky's clinic, read as a near-literal reification of Ivan Babichev's idea about where one should look for the contemporary romantic hero—"in Sklifosovsky hospital?!"

How can the (quasi) dialogue of the two authors be summarized? Each text is ambiguous and open, if not fully polyphonic, yet each has its own ideological bias. Bulgakov voices a center-right position; Olesha "responds" in an ambiguously collaborationist, left-of-center spirit. Reacting to it, Bulgakov moves even further to the right. But the common framework of the debate remains rather stable, even as its thematics and carnivalesque treatment gradually shift from sausage and carnality to a dialogic probing of more spiritual, in particular metaliterary, issues.

Bulgakov's 1925 semifantastic parable emphasizes the futility of revolutionary change and the importance of gradualness in the underdog's acculturation. The tale's bid for carnivalization is mitigated by the author's nostalgia for law and order.

Olesha inverts the plot equation of *Heart of a Dog*; plays up the motifs of nonbelonging, envy, doubles, hybrid creatures, romantic love; and introduces—mostly on the stylistic and metaphorical level and in an ambiguous, probably Aesopian manner—the themes of art, provocation, Calvary, revenge, and destruction. All this adds up to a generous measure of carnival chaos.

In *The Master and Margarita*, Bulgakov reifies Olesha's metaphors, once again inverting the political equation. The absolute fabulaic vindication of the provocative wishful thinking of *Envy*'s anti-heroes is one of the original moves underlying the structure of *The Master and Margarita*. For its implementation, the novel relies on a combination of modernist and realist solutions. The introduction of the mythological plane adds a twentieth-century feature, and its naturalization through a traditional plot roots the novel in time-hallowed narrative conventions.[43] Another mixed result of the lessons supposedly learned from Olesha concerns the heightened ambiguity of Bulgakov's last novel. On one hand, the author has more clearly identified with the forces of subversion; on the other, he has farmed out this carnivalesque task (and attendant sexcapades) to special demonic clowns (Margarita the part-time witch is a notable exception), reserving for his romantic Master a strictly monological noble role.[44]

The 'dialogue' we have been discussing, whether a historical reality or a retrospective construction, need not be seen exclusively as an external, Tynianovian relationship *between* the two writers. Intertextualizing each other through the common literary topoi, each carried on an internal debate with himself, in the spirit of his characters and of the Bakhtinian view of dialogism.

Olesha was famous for his prophetic perceptiveness and generosity with creative ideas. Thus, he practically foretold, in a conversation reported by Lev Slavin (1975: 15), Fadeev's suicide.

" 'He became timorous . . . [, Olesha said]. I pity him. There is in him a subliminal honesty. Like a powder keg. If it explodes, he will perish.' I recalled this conversation when X. shot himself." Fadeev is not named, but his identity is clear from the context. Slavin also notes Olesha's perspicacity in predicting that Kazakevich would become a soldier (1975: 13).

Olesha also invented the character with limited vocabulary who was to become Ilf and Petrov's Ellochka the cannibal (Slavin 1975: 12), and he started mentioning "the Dragon" long before Evgenii Shvarts wrote his startling eponymous play.

"A new figure should be introduced into chess. I have already thought of the name—dragon. . . . The dragon moves however it wants and takes whichever piece it chooses" (Ovchinnikov 1975: 52). "The dragon is a revolution in chess" (Kataev 1981: 193).

And he kept thinking of a film script that would feature a Black Man (*Chernyi chelovek*) uncannily similar to both Ivan Babichev and Woland.

The Black Man was to be "disposed against the world outlook of the new society." He would want to use death to confound the "optimistic views" of the new youth. The "Black Man is not a ghost, but a living being. With some profession . . . unusual, but quite legal. I could make him a chiromancer . . . [or] a graphologist." He would resemble Boris Karlov in the monster role of *Frankenstein* (Olesha admired the 1931 film) and "wear an old-fashioned raincoat with a velvet collar" (Gopp 1975: 151–53).

Olesha's tragic flaw was probably the one that Bulgakov's Yeshua considered the worst of vices. He was *afraid*—both ideologically and creatively—to draw from *Envy* the far-reaching conclusions that suggested themselves. "The difference was that, because of the make-up of his creative personality and social outlook, Bulgakov remained devoid [*chuzhd*] of that self-reflection which corrodes creativity and which, let us say, prevented Olesha from completing his projects" (Chudakova 1988: 535).

Bulgakov too was good at predicting. He foresaw that after his death the coffin with his body in it would hit, on the narrow staircase, the door of a neighbor playwright (Kataev 1981: 220). But then, Olesha had described in his "Liompa" (1928) the death of an intellectual whose coffin hits walls and doors on the way out. Which one of them had the last word? A month before dying a death imaged forth by Olesha a decade earlier, Bulgakov did finish the novel that Olesha dared not write and whose embryonic parts he had therefore tucked away in the dreams, fantasies, and stylistic fireworks of his anti-heroes.

EIGHT

The Dynamics of Adaptation:
Pasternak's Second Birth

The textual intercourse we will now examine is, on the surface, different from the Bulgakov-Olesha "duet," but, in a deeper sense, similar to it. Focusing on just one author, one period of his work, and one poem, we will be able to envision that poem as a product of the poet's "triadic" interaction with the environment. To spell out the underlying similarity with the Bulgakov-Olesha-Bulgakov exchange, we could say that Pasternak's 1920s persona became aware of the 'feedback' it received from the prevailing Soviet culture circa 1930 and 'responded' with the 1931 text. But the emphasis here, unlike Chapter 7, will fall on the third, 'synthetic' stage of the process: the results of the poet's internal change triggered by outside pressure.

Pasternak and the Early 1930s

A CONVERSATION ABOUT APARTMENTS

Pasternak's dialogue with the times and with himself did not occur in a vacuum. His 1931 'response' can be better understood as position-taking vis-à-vis not only the official establishment but other fellow travelers as well—in particular Mandelstam.

When in the fall of 1933 the Mandelstams finally moved into the writers' condominium, Pasternak was one of the first to visit.

> "As he was leaving, he lingered . . . , saying how wonderful it was: 'Now you have an apartment, you will be able to write poetry.' . . . 'Did you hear what he said?' M. asked me. He was furious," Mandelstam's widow remembers. It was "in response to [this] almost casual remark by Pasternak" that Mandelstam wrote his poem "beginning 'The apartment is quiet as paper.' "[1]

Developing her idea of the two poets as "antipodes," Nadezhda Mandelstam argues that their different attitudes toward apartments (and desks) were emblematic of more profound professional differences.

> Pasternak could not do without his writing table—he could only work with his pen in hand. M. composed his verse in his head, while walking, and only needed to sit down briefly to copy out the result. . . .
> Seeking for a stable life, particularly in the material sense, Pasternak knew that the path to it lay through literature, membership in the literary community. . . . M. always shied away. . . . [Pasternak] was a domesticated creature . . . attached to the comforts of home and his dacha. . . . [O]ur literary bigwigs understood him quite well and they would be glad to come to terms with him. . . . M. was a nomad, a wanderer, shunned by the very walls of Moscow houses. . . .
> Moscow had belonged to Pasternak from the time of his birth . . . and he remained in possession of his heritage. . . . Pasternak would have liked to erect a protective wall of the State between the intelligentsia and the people.[2] It was simply not in M.'s nature to bank . . . on the State with its miracles . . . he placed no hopes in its patronage.
> The world of literature treated them accordingly, smiling on Pasternak . . . and seeking . . . to destroy M. . . . As early as 1927 I . . . sa[id] to Pasternak: "Watch out, or they'll adopt you." . . . At the end of their lives both of them acted in ways quite at variance with . . . their previous stands. While Pasternak . . . put himself in open conflict with the Soviet literary world, M. was ready to seek rapprochement with it—only . . . too late.

But in the early 1930s, the two still found themselves in very different relations to Soviet reality. A grotesque variation on this triangle of forces was the famous telephone conversation (in June 1934) between Stalin and Pasternak about the arrested Mandelstam. Incidentally, it began with Pasternak's complaints about the noise in his communal apartment (N. Mandelstam 1976: 146; Fleishman 1990: 180).

According to his widow, Mandelstam's "The Apartment" was a
"rejoinder . . . occasioned only by . . . [the] unfinished conversation in the hallway"—unlike another poem "occasioned by some lines
of Pasternak's" in his book of verse *Second Birth* (1931–32).[3] But that
same collection contained a text that could indeed have served as the
starting point of the two poets' dialogue about apartments. The third
fragment of the longer poem *Waves*,[4] "I Want [to Go] Home, into the
Hugeness," read as follows:

I   1   Mne khochetsia domoi, v ogromnost'
          Kvartiry, navodiashchei grust'.
          Voidu, snimu pal'to, opomnius',
          Ogniami ulits ozarius'.

     2   Peregorodok tonkorebrost'
          Proidu naskvoz', proidu, kak svet.
          Proidu, kak obraz vkhodit v obraz,
          I kak predmet sechet predmet.

     3   Puskai pozhiznennost' zadachi,
          Vrastaiushchei v zavety dnei,
          Zovetsia zhizniiu sidiachei,—
          I po takoi grushchu po nei.

II   4   Opiat' znakomost'iu napeva
          Pakhnut derev'ia i doma.
          Opiat' napravo i nalevo
          Poidet khoziainichat' zima.

     5   Opiat' k obedu na progulke
          Nastupit temen', prosto strast'.
          Opiat' nauchit pereulki
          Okhulki na ruki ne klast'.

     6   Opiat' povaliat s neba vziatki,
          Opiat' ukroet k utru vikhr'
          Osin podsledstvennykh desiatki
          Suknom sugrobov snegovykh.

III 7   Opiat' opavshei serdtsa myshtsei
          Uslyshu i vlozhu v slova,
          Kak ty polzesh' i kak dymish'sia,
          Vstaesh' i stroish'sia, Moskva.

     8   I ia primu tebia, kak upriazh',
          Tekh radi budushchikh bezumstv,

Čto ty, kak stikh, menia zazubrish',
Kak byl', zapomnish' naizust'.

I   1   I want [to go] home, into the hugeness
         Of the apartment inducing sadness.
         I will go in, take off my coat, come to,
         Become illuminated by the lights of the streets.

     2   The thin-ribbedness of the partitions
         I will pass all through, pass, like light.
         I will pass, as an image penetrates an image
         And as an object cuts [cross-sects] an object.

     3   Let the lifetimeness of the task
         Growing into the testaments of the days
         Be called a sedentary life,—
         I long after it even the way it is.

II   4   Again, of the familiarity of their song
         The trees and houses will give off a smell.
         Again, right and left,
         Winter will start bossing around.

     5   Again, during a walk before dinner,
         Darkness will fall, real scary.
         Again it will teach the side streets
         To be no fools with their hands.

     6   Again, from the sky, bribes will start falling,
         Again, the whirlwind will cover, towards morning,
         Tens of asp-trees under investigation
         With the cloth of snowdrifts.

III 7   Again, with [my] heart's slumped/collapsed muscle
         I will hear and put into words
         How you crawl and how you send up smoke,
         Rise up and build yourself, Moscow.

     8   And I will accept you like a harness,
         For the sake of those future madnesses,
         That you will cram me, like a verse,
         Will learn me by heart like a true story.

"I Want to Go Home" (hereafter abbreviated as IWH) instantiates with remarkable completeness the 'adoptive complex' imputed to
Pasternak by Nadezhda Mandelstam. Beneath his love for his apart-

ment (albeit communal), the desk, and the Moscow cityscape, one discerns an acceptance of strict Socialist discipline in exchange for the recognition of contemporaries and history. Pasternak's stance becomes especially clear when compared with Mandelstam's, which underlies also that poet's other possible "rejoinder" to IWH, "Leningrad."[5] Compare:

Pasternak: IWH	Mandelstam: "Leningrad," "The Apartment"
home, into the hugeness of the apartment inducing sadness; again . . . the smell of familiarity	I came back to my city, familiar to the point of tears; hurry up, recognize; the apartment's . . . quiet
I will go in, . . . pass through	I will find the dead men's addresses
the lights of the streets	Leningrad river lamps
the thin-ribbedness of the partitions	I live on a black back staircase; the damned walls are thin
the lifetimeness . . . sedentary life	there's nowhere left to run to
growing into the testaments of the days; you . . . rise up and build yourself, Moscow	ration books; some honest traitor; comber of collective-farm flax
a walk before dinner	get busy and gulp down the fish oil . . . egg yolk
darkness . . . real scary, will teach the side streets to be no fools with their hands	a bell ripped out by the roots; a stream of old fear
winter; from the sky, bribes will start falling; the cloth of snowdrifts	this December day
thin-ribbedness; [my] heart's slumped muscle	stabs at my temple; such torturous malice; stream of . . . fear
I will hear and put into words . . . for the sake of . . . that you will cram me, like a verse	teaching executioners how to chirp

Moscow, . . . for the sake of those future . . .	Petersburg! I don't want to die, not yet; I will find the dead men's addresses
lifetimeness; under investigation; I will accept you like a harness	clanking the fetters of my door chains; and I, like an idiot, am forced to play tunes on a comb; it's time to stamp [your] boots

Pasternak does sound conciliatory vis-à-vis the 'harness/fetters' imposed by the Stalinist dictatorship, but his tone is hardly that of "some honest traitor," "some comber of collective-farm flax" of the kind scornfully dismissed by Mandelstam. Rather, IWH offers a poetic expression of a deliberately ambiguous position. Ambiguity, however dubious morally, has always been a staple fare of poetry. In what follows, we will see how IWH, remaining within the bounds of Pasternakian poetics, succeeds in reconciling the contradictory ideological demands of the moment and thus functions as Pasternak's response to new realities.

TEMPTATION

The *Second Birth* collection, as heralded by its title, marked a profound change in Pasternak's poetic self-image. Following the early period, characterized by the young persona's ecstatic fusion with the universe, and anticipating the self-sacrificial Christian tenor of his later poetry, the 1931 book reads in retrospect as a bridge between the two.[6] It implements a fellow traveler's honest endeavor to join the Socialist process[7] and his newly found readiness to lower his aesthetic standards. All this, the poet admits, is dictated by "the power of the same old temptation:/In the hope of glory and [common] good,/To look at things without fear."[8]

For a while I am going to write badly—from my previous point of view—until I get accustomed to the novelty of the themes and propositions. . . . For a while I shall write like a cobbler. Solely . . . in mediocrity's distorting mirror, . . . am [I] obliged . . . to reject Demyan Bedny. . . . I prefer him to most of you. (Pasternak 1990b: 176–78)[9]

Indeed, paving the way from pagan worship of earthly existence (characteristic of his first period) to the somewhat otherworldly emphasis on spiritual and ethical values (typical of the third), Pasternak in the early 1930s programmatically embraced the sociopolitical and cultural dictates of the times, in a gesture combining a *Realpolitik* interest in the affairs of this world with an emphasis on ideology. He simultaneously underwent a formal evolution from what he would later perceive as a whimsically modernist earlier style to the mature simplicity of his post-war poetry.

In his 1956 autobiography, Pasternak disowned his early poetics; he declared that his first autobiography, *Safe Conduct* (1929), "unfortunately . . . is spoilt by unnecessary mannerisms, the common fault of those years" and that "I do not like my style up to 1940" (1959b: 19, 81).

The period of transition—indeed of dialectical antithesis—was far from being unproblematically optimistic. Rather, the "change" in the persona's "strivings and mainstays," symbolized by the ebb and flow of the sea, "is sounded in a minor key" (*Oni shumiat v minore*).[10]

In 1925, responding to the questionnaire about the Party's still relatively liberal resolution concerning literature, Pasternak had written: "The presence of the proletarian dictatorship is not sufficient to affect culture. That would require a real organic domination that would speak through me . . . even against my will. I do not feel that. That that [condition] is not there objectively either is clear from the fact that the resolution has to call on me to resolve the themes it outlines" (1990b: 259–60).[11] The concept of "organic domination" invoked by the poet—that is, the miraculous power exercised by the whole of creation over "every last trifle"—is an invariant theme in Pasternak and one of the keystones of his philosophy and aesthetics, whose sources lie in, among others, Tolstoy and Goethe.[12] Pasternak's world is one of a magnificent play of forces, natural, yet miraculous, in which everything is in unity with everything else: small and great, home and the outdoors, this instant and eternity.[13] The confrontation of this harmonious worldview with the realities of ascendant Stalinist Socialism was bound to produce controversial results.

The dictatorship's "organic domination," still disputable in the mid-1920s, had to be recognized as a compelling fact of life by the early 1930s. The consolidation of Stalin's totalitarian regime spelled the end of all pluralism, political or literary, to the accompaniment of noisy propaganda of Socialist construction and the new, collectivist morality. Sadly, the dictatorship's combination of repressive stick with ideological carrot succeeded in favorably impressing many an honest intellectual of the 1930s, inside as well as outside the Soviet Union. Pasternak's texts of the time offer an instructive testimony to the internal workings of these ideological processes.

Pivotal to Pasternak's poetic acceptance of the emerging "Socialist" reality were several new strategies rooted in his previous stances. To outline these strategies, underlying *Second Birth*, I use Andrey Bely's method of 'composite quotation': a semi-prosaic summary of poems (with additional explanatory comments in brackets).

1. Voluntary and even enthusiastic submission to power:

The distant horizons (*dal'*) of Socialism—or is it "upcloseness' [*bliz'*, a Futurist-style neologism]?—are inevitably moving in, they are right here; the [Party's] General Plan resembles the steep Caucasus Ridge, whose heel tramples over the poet's prophesies; the strong New Man has already ridden over us in the Project's horse cart. The revolutionary will, ongoing executions, and a historical parallel with the inexorable but creative violence done [a century earlier] to the Caucasus by czarist troops, who took it the way one takes a woman (i.e., by a force mixed with love and independently of imperial Petersburg)[14]—all these suggest succumbing to power before one turns into a [saint's] relic and an object of pity.

2. Hope for positive changes and trust in collectivism:

One is witnessing a change of all the mainstays—a resettling, a transfiguration of the world: one can hope for glory and common good and should restrain one's own temporary caprices (*vremennuiu blazh'*). In spring one can hear the rustle of news and truths; ahead there lies an impregnable novelty, a life beyond gossip and slander; the future itself, along with the poet's beloved, invades his room. The [proletarian holiday of] May Day heralds the blossoming of songs, living mores [*zhivye nravy*], tilled land, various crafts and industries, and a spirit that has ripened and undergone a new fermentation and thus cannot help manifesting itself. The Soul is leaving the West; revolutionary will spells a relief in women's lot, a delivery from the pains of jealousy, and a happy future for children. The new way of life will involve the poet in the desired and legitimate collective labor (*so vsemi soobshcha i zaodno s pravoporiadkom*); it promises to eliminate the falsity of a litterateur's life and endow the poet with supernatural vision, unheard-of stylistic simplicity, accessibility to the people, and an ability to merge with the native tongue and landscape in the manner of Pushkin and Lermontov.

3. Reliance on tradition, with the new passed off as the familiar old:

Accounts of the generations that served a hundred years before us and inspire the revision of our mainstays; the experience of great artists, in particular

Pushkin (author of semicollaborationist "Stanzas" to Czar Nicholas I[15] and of *A Feast in the Time of the Plague*) and Chopin (who miraculously holds off the mob raping/crucifying him and his piano);[16] the consoling analogy with the beginnings of Peter the Great's glorious days; and the uninterrupted chain of vernal holidays, going from May Day back to Trinity's birch trees and the lights of Panathenaic festivals [in ancient Greece] and forward to the eventual blossoming of the Commune.

4. Socialism as part of the landscape:[17]

A master metaphor for the change is the succession of waves (*smena voln*) foaming/singing along the way [in a Pasternakian paronomasia of *pena/pen'e*]. The account of the previous generations is narrated by the woods; the novelty of the future is a sort of echo; the General Plan is likened to the Caucasus Mountains; Socialism is seen as distance (*dal'*), and it is there that the Second Five-Year Plan proffers the theses of the soul. The new mores and songs lie down quite literally "into" the space of the meadows, fields, and industries (*v luga i pashni i na promysla*), and the rushing streams receive the outskirts of construction sites "into" their creeks.

All four strategies for accepting the new are organically rooted in Pasternak's poetic world. 'Submission to power' is one of his favorite motifs. 'Hope' is in accord with the poet's ecstatic outlook. 'Changes and transfigurations' are a recurrent manifestation of the world's magnificent intensity. And 'collectivism' easily comes under the heading of unity and contact. In its turn, 'reliance on tradition' means equating the everyday (the present) with the great (the past and the future),[18] which results in feeling 'at home in the future.'[19] Finally, the treatment of 'Socialism as landscape' relies on the Pasternakian 'contact with nature.'

Adaptation to the new also encompasses the sphere of poetic language, resulting in

5. Stylistic simplification:

Pasternak streamlines his syntax and renounces lexical rarities and convoluted tropes. He also lets the 'I' of the speaker (and the human shape in general) emerge more distinctly from the background, with which it had been programmatically blended.[20]

Pasternak's search for poetic accessibility (which was to continue in later years) also came from his general belief in the magnificence of all things trivial, lowly, and provincial, manifested through a liberal mixing of stylistic registers, use of dialectisms and officialese, and so on. Paradoxically, in his earlier verse this tendency had resulted in density and obscurity; one wonders, therefore, what shape the striving for unheard-of simplicity (i.e., the art of "writing badly") would ultimately have taken were it not for the populist pressure exerted by the cultural situation of the 1930s.

SABOTAGE

The 'acceptance of the new' in *Second Birth* was, of course, far from wholehearted. Instead of embracing the extremes of the ruling ideology, Pasternak opted for compromise, welcoming Socialism on universal humanitarian grounds rather than those of class struggle. Accordingly, his tone is tinged with reservations. I will isolate three of his self-subversive strategies.

6. Qualified assertion of the new, premised on such modalities as suppositions, questions, and reservations:

> The meaning of the recent experience is not yet complete. In this book there will be arguments and litigations. Oh, would that the issue of Socialism were as graphic as the Caucasus Ridge!—in that case one could . . . ; please, do correct me, [you,] the distance/closeness of Socialism, but only you yourself— rather than the hollow verbosity (*pustozvonstvo*) of flatterers. The distance, however, is only vaguely visible through the smoke of theories (*Ty kurish'sia skvoz' dym teorii*). "Caucasus, oh, Caucasus, what shall I do?!" "Oh, had I known that this is what happens! . . ." So far, one can talk only of an eve's bud (*buton kanuna*): the May Day spirit will manifest itself only in the remote future; optimistic hopes are a temptation that can lead one to a dead end, and to succumb to it, one would need the consolation of historical parallels.

7. Accumulation of negative images:

> The waves sound in a minor key, number dark myriads [*t'ma* means both "darkness" and "myriad"], and envelop the entire range of the poet's nostalgia. The decline of the West is similar to a manor house without owners and spells the decline of living merits [*zhivykh dostoinstv*]. The Caucasus landscape is rife with excesses of figurative and literal evil (pain, fear, ruthlessness, anger, backbiting, stutterer scared by the wet nurse, defeats, captivities, ineluctable violence, brigandry, clangor of daggers, [poison] gas attack, salvoes of shooting, throats of the beheaded). The scenes of Moscow life abound in images of
>   —hardship: consolidation (*uplotnenie*) of apartments, fuel shortages, decline of domestic comforts;[21]
>   —emotional disarray: sterility, deception, cerebral fictions resembling rot-

ten fish heads, the hour of sadness; something in us is weeping: oh, have mercy; last year's despondency and guilt will again sting the poet;

— pain: the heavy heaviness of illness, with all my weakness, feeling like a cripple, ripping the soft flesh [of the fingertips] until it bleeds [*i miakot' v krov' poria*, about Chopin's piano playing];

— death: mutinies and executions, death of a poet (Mayakovsky), completely perishing in earnest, the passing of a major musician, a dead city; the road heading, with an absolute straightforwardness, for the crematorium; to freeze as a crucifix of pianofortes; verses will gush through the throat and kill the poet; a pill will not save one from death; the sequence of days has snapped; we are at Plato's symposium/feast in the time of the plague ("i poniali my,/ Chto my na piru v vekovom prototipe—/Na pire Platona vo vremia chumy"; "Leto" ["Irpen'"]).

Stylistically, these forms of ideological sabotage are seconded by a characteristic Aesopian device:

8. Exaggerated use of political officialese, dry to the point of absurdity; for example:

> I tak kak s malykh detskikh let
> Ia ranen zhenskoi dolei . . .
> I tak kak ia lish' ei zadet
> I ei u nas razdol'e,
> To ves' ia rad soiti na net
> V revoliuts'onnoi vole.

> And since from my tender childhood years
> I have been wounded by the plight of women . . .
> And since I am affected only by it
> And in our country it is in full swing,
> Therefore, I am glad to shrink away completely
> In the revolutionary will.

The strategies of sabotage also proceed from Pasternak's invariants. His 'qualifications' regarding Socialism thrive on the rich rhetorical soil of his poetic discourse as he literalizes his tropes and thus restores them to their full face value. As a result, his favorite similes, interrogative and conditional moods, subjunctive constructions with *by*, and other nonfactual modalities become the tools of questioning the allegedly unquestionable 'new.'

Compare, for instance, the questions that genuinely torment the speaker of the *Second Birth* ("The distance? . . . Or is it the up-closeness? . . . Oh, only if . . . then . . . I would") with the similarly structured but purely rhetorical questions in *My Sister Life*, brimming with enthusiastic assurance ("Where shall I put my joy? . . . When else did? . . . When, if not: In the Beginning?").

The 'negative' motifs (pain, destruction, etc.) undergo a similar re-interpretation:

> If previously they were used as the rhetorical reverse of the world's overwhelming magnificence, in *Second Birth* they tend to become the focus of attention, threatening to topple the magnificent balance of 'overwhelming power' and 'overwhelmed powerlessness.'

Finally, the use of 'dry officialese,' pushing as it were to its logical extreme the democratization of poetic language, brings Pasternak full circle back to obscurity, this time of the Soviet-bureaucratic rather than subjective-lyrical sort. The deliberate arduousness of these flights of quasi-official rhetoric iconizes the jarring difficulty of the new reality and thus both celebrates it (in a futurist vein) and subverts it by exposing its unnaturalness.

Such deviations from the Party line on how a fellow traveler should go about becoming one with socialism did not pass unnoticed. Suffice it to say that Pasternak's ambiguous rewrite of Pushkin's "Stanzas" was barred from *Second Birth* for three decades after 1934, the year the First Congress of Soviet Writers inaugurated the reign of Socialist Realism.

"I Want to Go Home": Themes and Strategies

THEME: A POLYVALENT CLUSTER

The core of IWH's message is informed by an interplay of several thematic complexes.

First, and in the most immediate sense, IWH expresses the speaker's 'nostalgia for his Moscow home.' Openly stated from the start, this theme defines the fragment's place within the longer poem: the anticipated return to the familiar apartment interrupts the poet's impressions of the Caucasus.[22]

Second, as a representative of *Second Birth*, IWH implements the 'acceptance of the Socialist new' and to do so, deploys the contrasting strategies of 'adaptation' and 'sabotage.'

Third, IWH is, in a widening circle, an instance of the all-Pasternakian magnificence and unity of existence. Even a cursory glance at the text yields a wealth of "Pasternakisms," for instance:

Importance of the small ("the hugeness of the apartment," risks of a predinner walk); extreme states ("right and left," "by heart"); intense motions ("pass all through," "cuts [cross-sects]," "rise up," *zazubrish'* [a punning combination of "cramming" and "denting"]); powerful-sinister emotions ("darkness real scary,"[23] slumping of the heart's muscle, "future madnesses"); and the grand scale of the categories involved ("like light," "lifetimeness," "testaments," the future).

As usual, these 'magnificent' motifs are combined with manifestations of the world's 'unity':

Itineraries connecting the in- and outdoors; situations of illuminating, passing through, growing into, covering, enveloping, exchanging (of favors: "I will accept you . . . for the sake of . . . that you will"), and strong emotional reactions (verging on a heart attack).

Fourth, in still wider, extra-Pasternakian, intertextual terms, IWH is a poem on the time-hallowed topic of the 'role of art,' in the tradition inaugurated in Russia by Pushkin's "The Prophet." That poem is a major presence in IWH, and not just in the sense of 'genre memory.'

Both texts are about the rebirth of the poet. The transformation is accompanied by returning from another place (the desert in Pushkin, the Caucasus in Pasternak) and assuming an important social responsibility (to stride over the earth, searing human hearts with words, in Pushkin; to put into words Moscow's growth, in Pasternak).

In Pushkin's poem, the rebirth follows a symbolic death ("Like a corpse, in the desert did I lie") and magical surgery, performed by the six-winged seraph on the eyes, ears, mouth (lips and tongue), and heart of the nascent prophet. In IWH, the upsurge of poetic energy (in stanza 7) is preceded by the snow-shrouded landscape and begins, paradoxically, with another deadening downward move, the slumping/collapse of the heart.

As the heart's muscle, together with the speaker's hearing, eyesight, and speech, proceeds to create poetry, it seems to hark back to "The Prophet" in (1) its synesthetic magic, partly foreshadowed in stanza 4, where the speaker smells the song of the visible landscape, and (2) its spatial organization: Pasternak's triadic image of Moscow crawling, sending up smoke, and vertically growing replicates the Prophet's alertness to the goings-on in the air, on land, and under water ("And I took in . . . / The on-high flight of the angels, / The growing of the valley vine, / and the underwater movement of sea monsters").

The image of cutting/cross-secting (*sechet*, in stanza 2) recalls the seraph's cleaving/cutting up (*rassek*) the prophet's breast. Such an anatomic literalization of Pasternak's cubist image is reinforced by the lexically ambiguous "thin-ribbedness of the partitions, passed through as if by light," overtly referring to the partitions installed in consolidated apartments to accommodate additional tenants but also connoting X-ray pictures. This double exposure of the 'apartment / rib cage' anticipates the eventual harnessing of the sick heart (in stanzas 7–8) and echoes the painful imagery elsewhere in *Second Birth*,[24] while X rays offer a technological counterpart to Pushkin's image of the world magically penetrable to the prophet.

All this is in tune with Pasternak's reorientation in *Second Birth* from the romantic tradition of Lermontov (which was so important for *My Sister—Life*) to that of Pushkin qua national poet. In fact, Pushkin, thrown overboard from the steamship of modernity by the futurists, would be touted from the 1930s on as the great forebear of the official culture and quite earnestly used as a literary model by such disparate figures as Pasternak and, say, Zoshchenko.[25]

In 1923 Pasternak wrote an overt, and pointedly romantic-futurist, variation on "The Prophet" ("Mchalis' zvezdy, v more mylis' mysy") focusing on the poet's supernatural contact with the entire world, at whose center it placed the writing of the Pushkin poem. Eight years later, Pasternak's accent had shifted from the self-indulgent celebration of poetry as such to the necessity of pressing its power in service of superior goals (in Pushkin, God's voice bids the newly born prophet to "be filled with My will").

Finally, in yet another intertextual affiliation, IWH is a treatise on the vital issue of 'the poet's apartment.' The portrayal of living space has long been an ideologically laden topos in Russian literature.

A major strand of this tradition runs through Chernyshevsky's *What Is to Be Done?* and Dostoevsky's *Crime and Punishment* all the way to the Soviet period. Characteristic of this latter are new—avant-gardist and Socialist—views of private versus communal space and an acute shortage of housing, richly thematized in the prose of Zamyatin, Zoshchenko, Olesha, Bulgakov, Ilf and Petrov, Pasternak, and many others.[26]

In the lyric genre, the poet's lodgings often represent 'the locus of art,' and as the paradigms of 'poetry' and 'lodging' are superimposed on each other, the apartment's walls, windows, ceiling, furniture, and their relation to the outside world become metaphors-metonyms of the creative process.

Such is clearly the case in Mandelstam's "The Apartment Is Quiet as Paper" (signaled by its opening simile) and its two equimetrical sources: Alexander Blok's 1908 "To [My] Friends" (Druz'iam) and Vladislav Khodasevich's 1921 "Ballad" (Ballada).[27] All three share a dim view of the apartment as the embodiment of the staleness of the poetic profession and pin the hopes for change on an escape from its confining walls.[28]

> In Blok's poem, the alternative ("to bury oneself in fresh high grass") is aired only briefly and involves renouncing poetry and consciousness.[29]
>
> Mandelstam displays, against all formidable Stalinist odds, a defiant determination to start anew, even if it entails finding inspiration not in Hippocrene's spring but in "a stream of the old fear [that] / Shall burst into the slapdash walls / Of an evil Moscow flat."
>
> Mandelstam's reference to a classical emblem of poetry (Hippocrene's spring) may have been patterned on the concluding image of Khodasevich's "Ballad," whose speaker succeeds in transcending the walls of his squalid room without physically leaving it as he transforms himself through the magic of poetic creativity into that archetypal poet of all time, Orpheus. By the same token, Khodasevich transforms Blok's purely negative paradigm of the poet's lodgings by coupling it with the dialectic script of 'the rebirth of a poet'—in particular, with elements from Pushkin's "Prophet."[30]

The negative valorization of the apartment as opposed to outside space was in keeping with the romantic-symbolist tenet that 'life is elsewhere.' This is of course, quite contrary to Pasternak's positive view of both indoor and outdoor environments,[31] nor was such a position the only possible one among the symbolists. In fact, two poems by the symbolist-turned-pro-Communist Valerii Briusov—"At Home" (U sebia, 1902; Briusov 1961: 177–78) and "By the Kremlin" (U Kremlia, 1923; Briusov 1961: 471)—instantiating an alternative pattern of valorizations, may have shown Pasternak a way to mediate between the extremes of rejecting and embracing the harsh realities of Socialism.[32]

> In the earlier Briusov poem, the speaker has a residual attachment to his familiar surroundings, but finding that the flames there have grown cold and seeing his old self "as a snake [sees] the skin it has shed," he decides to leave his home "in search of new perfections."
>
> The second poem, written very much in the official Soviet vein,[33] pointedly revisits and revises the older one, indeed retraces backward the outbound journey begun there: the speaker is now shown returning from various exotic places to Moscow and "the Red Kremlin," which he declares to be both his "domestic world" and the center of the world's miracles.

In IWH, Pasternak combines, as it were, all of Briusov's itineraries (he comes back to his Moscow home from a remote exotic place, then goes out of the apartment into the rising capital) and value judgments (the familiar "domestic world" is both sad and desirable, Moscow the site of miracles). Thus, ironically, he comes to repeat, eight years later, Briusov's pro-Soviet move, which at the time he had considered a violence to the poet's genuine self.[34]

In sum, the traditional poetic topoi of the vatic artist and his lodgings qua locus of poetry are refracted in IWH through Pasternak's invariants—his overall vision of the world's magnificent unity and his 1930s meditations on the pros, as well as the cons, of accepting the new realities, triggered by the homesickness that seizes the speaker vacationing in the Caucasus. The subthemes that compose this thematic cluster exhibit, as we have seen, strong mutual affinities:

—'nostalgia,' 'poet's lodgings,' and 'home's unity with the macro-world' all center on the motif of 'home';

—the rebirth of the poet as prophet has been linked to the transcendence of the confining apartment;

—the adaptation to / sabotage of Socialism are formulated in idiosyncratically Pasternakian terms;

—the subversively 'negative emotions' can easily accommodate 'nostalgia'; and so on.

MEDIATION: A DUBIOUS ECSTASY

In implementing a complex theme, however, success depends not so much on the seamless fusion of its components as on the persuasiveness of the overall design that mediates the text's various voices and oppositions. IWH's rhetoric hinges on an ambiguous yet ecstatic acceptance of new, Socialist Moscow, seen as a stringent but necessary harness. This formulation raises several questions (as is only natural in view of the 'ambiguity'). How specific is the reference to 'Socialism'? How does 'harness' fit into the thematic cluster outlined above? By what Tolstoyan "labyrinth of couplings" is the transition achieved from the hugeness of the apartment to the acceptability of the harness?

Unlike some other poems of *Second Birth*, IWH never mentions Socialism by name. Rather, it looms behind such elliptical expressions as

—"growing into" (*vrastaiushchei*): a political slogan of circa 1930 that called for individual farmers to grow into Socialism;

—"testaments" (*zavety*): a current phrase that referred to the testaments of Il'ich, i.e. Lenin's legacy;

— "the task" (zadach[a]) is reminiscent of Party lexicon—in particular, the title of Lenin's essay ("Ocherednye zadachi sovetskoi vlasti");
— "you build yourself" (stroish'sia): the verb stroit' (build, construct) inevitably conjured up Socialism as its direct object in the propagandistic lingo of the times.

Thus, these allusions were sufficiently transparent for contemporary readers.

What is more, the portrayal of Moscow in the poem's finale seems to have been more or less directly borrowed from Mayakovsky, the number one herald of poetry's subjugation to the dictates of Socialist construction. His 1926 poem "Two Moscows" (1955–61, 7: 176–79) about the transformation of Russia's proverbial "big village" into an industrial Socialist capital, offers striking parallels to IWH.

> Mayakovsky has Moscow building itself; enthuses upon seeing it rock, rise, and straighten itself; opposes it to old-time hooliganism and rural darkness (cf. IWH, stanza 5); imagines the new city rushing the village [like a horse] at cord's end (cf. IWH's harness!); proclaims his kind of verse as fastening loose prose down with bolts (cf. the "cramming/denting" of verse in IWH, stanza 8); and declares that it does not take a visionary prophet (!) to see the Socialist future.

These images, putting down the traditional cult of the poet and glorifying technocratic violence done to life and literature in general and horses in particular were, of course, vintage Mayakovsky—a pro-technology futuristic persona, yet strongly identifying itself with dogs and horses, and very much in sync with the time's fixation on 'slaughter.'[35] A further crystallization of this thematic cluster appeared in Mayakovsky's "What Are You Complaining Of?" (predating his death by only one year and Second Birth by two), where the poet, a denizen of the skies, is called upon to discard his ancient mantles and fasten his muse with strong ties, like a horse, to the cart of everyday life.[36]

The 'horse/Muse taming' topos may have held several attractions for Pasternak. For one thing, he had his own biographical and poetic investment in the equine motif.[37] He had also been long involved with Mayakovsky's poetic posture, which he tried to emulate before distancing himself from it.[38] Therefore, having survived Mayakovsky's tragic death and pondering his own second birth into the Socialist 1930s, Pasternak would naturally be faced with the twofold challenge: on the one hand, to adopt Mayakovsky's program of stepping, for Socialism's sake, on the throat of his own song and hitching his poetry to the Project's cart, and yet, on the other, to do so on—and in—his own terms. Such may have been the underpinnings of Pasternak's feat of self-harnessing,[39] performed in an evasively ambiguous and thus almost natural, nonviolent, emotionally agreeable manner. How did he manage this tour de force?

STRATEGY: A MOMENTUM FOR ACCEPTANCE

Coming to grips with reality—reconciling with life and ultimately with death—is an eternal issue. Art has developed an array of strategies for its treatment and rhetorical resolution. In IWH, Pasternak resorts to one such figure, which is based on the principle of foreshadowing:[40] by placing the undesirable element at the end of a long sequence of its more acceptable versions, the poet creates a powerful momentum for its eventual acceptance.

In the theory of advertising, this figure—I will call it 'Acceptance by Momentum'—is known as "yes-response technique."

The canvasser rings the doorbell. The door is opened by a suspicious lady-of-the-house. The canvasser lifts his hat. "Would you like to buy an illustrated *History of the World*?" he asks. "No!" And the door slams. . . . Hence . . . we [must] start a person in the affirmative direction. A wiser canvasser rings the doorbell. . . . "This is Mrs. Armstrong?" Scowlingly—"Yes." "I understand, Mrs. Armstrong, that you have several children in school." Suspiciously—"Yes." "And, of course, they have much home work to do?" Almost with a sigh—"Yes." [And so on]. . . . That second canvasser is destined to go far! He has captured the secret of getting, at the outset, a number of "yes-responses." (Overstreet 1925: 16–17)

The analogy with advertising may seem crude,[41] but it offers a pertinent perspective on IWH as the poet's attempt to "sell" (to the reader and, more importantly, to himself) the new, tight, and unattractive harness of Socialism. Pasternak's "harness commercial" relies on a staggered process to make the critical transition almost imperceptible, if not welcome, by having it follow on the heels of steps that raise no objections; hence, incidentally, the poem's considerable length. But, of course, in adapting the 'Acceptance by Momentum' technique to his artistic goals, Pasternak deviates from its skeletal formula, enriching it in at least two respects.

First, his acceptance is circumscribed with reservations. Note the concessive phrase in stanza 3: "Puskai . . . I po takoi." The new Moscow is accepted in the spirit not so much of Pushkin's encomium to Petersburg in the introduction to *The Bronze Horseman* ("Liubliu tebia, Petra tvoren'e") as Lermontov's ambivalent "Motherland" ("Liubliu otchiznu ia, no strannoiu liubov'iu"). In other words, the yes-response technique becomes a yes-and-no-response technique.

> One characteristic manifestation of this ambivalence is the obsessive, if some-what obscure, use of expressions with ominously 'criminal' connotations ("life-timeness," "boss around," "to be no fools," "bribes," "under investigation"). All of these expressions are employed figuratively, but their cumulative effect is clearly negative. It is reinforced by the similarly ambiguous albeit 'ideologically positive' effect of the tongue-in-cheek officialese.

Second, Pasternak diversifies the technique by engaging simultaneously four aspects of the self-harnessing process—temporal, spatial, emotional, and stylistic—as the speaker comes to like something that is unfamiliar, confining, disagreeable, and altogether unpoetic. As a result, the poem's rhetorical design becomes more multifaceted and thus better naturalized—rather than stark and obvious. Added to the original length of its melodic line and its major-key/minor-key ambivalence is the polyphony of several levels of discourse.

The Four Reasons

TIME: NEW = OLD

This rhetorical equation is inherent in the very technique of affirmative responses, designed to smooth the transition from the earlier stages of a process to its payoff in the end. Such a technique should prove all the more relevant in the temporal sphere. Thus, the temptation to pass off the unfamiliar Socialist new for the familiar traditional old finds an iconic expression in the structural properties of the chosen compositional figure. This momentum (actually a familiarization device) also gets a boost from the 'homesickness' component of the theme: nostalgia by definition means looking forward to a return to the familiar past.

The rhetoric of familiarization pervades the text of IWH. In the manner of a fortune-teller who first gains the customer's trust by divining his past and only after that proceeds to predict his future, the path into the unknown future under construction is beaten, in IWH, through the familiar sites of Moscow's domestic life and landscape.

These scenes, composing three quarters of the entire text (stanzas 1–6), are saturated with 'habitual' motifs: homecoming, taking off one's coat, sedentary life, predinner constitutional, the cycle of day following night (5–6). In stanza 4, the theme is sounded openly: *"Again*, with the *familiarity* of their song"*; once announced, it begets the structural leitmotif of the "song" that will reverberate through to the end of the poem—the sequence of seven anaphoric repetitions of the retrospective "again" (*opiat'*).[42]

On the microrhythmical scale, this is echoed by the choice of meter in stanzas 4–6: they stress the familiarity of the Moscow cityscape in the most 'regular' forms of iambic tetrameter (the most frequent fourth form, with the unstressed third foot, and the most "normal," fully stressed first form). Thus the theme of familiarity is expressed even on the subliminal, "musical" level of the text, and what is more, Pasternak almost literally fulfills his promise "to write badly," namely, in the meters of a Demyan Bedny.

In fact, the entire text of IWH is a metrical compromise between the early Pasternak's modernist preference for the stress on the first foot and the more traditional statistical predominance of the second, favored by the Soviet literary Thermidorians, looking back to nineteenth-century classics (see M. Gasparov 1974: 94).[43]

The concerted action of the plot, lexicon, and rhythm is also joined by the "poetry of grammar," which, appropriately, takes the form of an original use of the future tense.[44] That tense would be, and is, quite in order in the poem's finale, which anticipates the imminent assumption of the Socialist harness and the poet's subsequent hard-earned passing into the memory of the generations to come. The future tense, however, makes its appearance in the text well ahead of time, as early as stanza 1; it pervades stanza 2, disappears briefly in 3, and is firmly back in control from 4 on. This grammatical device greatly facilitates the difficult task of "riding into the unknown":[45] the presentation of perfectly habitual situations (such as entering one's apartment, taking off one's coat, going for a walk before dinner, etc.) under the grammatical guise of future events desensitizes the reader to the distinction between present and future. The poet, as it were, repeatedly cries wolf at the slightest provocation, and when the "wolf" does appear, the vigilance has been lulled, and the Socialist harness gets accepted automatically, without alarm or objection.

SPACE: CONFINEMENT = EXPANSE

The poem's finale has Moscow both narrowed into a harness for the poet and expanded into the wide (and ever-widening) audience for his verses. This crucial neutralization of the largely spatial opposition crowns a series of much more attractive variations on the same theme.

The spatial plane of IWH is overdetermined by the treatment of Socialism as landscape, which in turn is based on the Pasternakian contact between indoor and outdoor space. The poem's nostalgic theme (whose spatial aspect consists of returning to one's native city and home) and the technique of 'Acceptance by Momentum' concur to produce a plot featuring a long chain of displacements and other spatial interactions. Moreover, from the start, an equation is established between being enclosed (in the apartment, at the desk) and being at large (in the apartment's hugeness, growing into the testaments of the days). As early as stanza 1, on entering the apartment, the poet is emblematically illuminated by streetlights. Furthermore, both the closed and the open spaces are (at least in part) positively valorized (as is characteristic of Pasternak's poetic world),[46] thus preparing eventual acceptance of the harness.

Another aspect of IWH's spatial ambiguity is its paradoxical dynamics of motion, combining at all times the opposites of mobility and slackness.

> While inside the apartment, the speaker, rather than remaining passive (as prompted by the spatial restrictions, as well as his sadness, and the reflexive-passive verbs in stanza 1), swings into active movement ("enter," "pass through," "cutting"). The momentum he thus acquires sends him coursing through the streets of Moscow, but this expanding movement is accompanied by a decrease in his activeness: stanzas 4–6 omit the first person from the narrative, turning the acting subject into an unmentioned (!) passive witness and emotional experiencer of the activities of the landscape and the elements.

The two concluding stanzas complete this symmetrical composition by an ambiguous fusion of confinement with expanse and energy with passivity.

> On the grammatical level, this is iconized by the equal distribution of the subject-object roles between the poet and Moscow ("[I] will put [lit. enclose!] into words—how you . . . build yourself"; "I will accept you—you will cram/memorize me"), thus illustrating the fairness and reciprocity of the contract.

Such is the spatial dynamics that leads to the emblematic image of Moscow-as-harness from its embryonic prototype—"the hugeness of the apartment."

FEELINGS: DESIRING THE UNPLEASANT

The emotional plane of the 'Acceptance by Momentum' technique consists of admixing some positive elements to the inevitably negative tonality of the poem and thus anticipating eventual self-harnessing, in a carefully dosed vaccination or medication with "a spoonful of sugar." This strategy draws naturally on Pasternakian admiration for the world, even at its saddest; the deliberate ambivalence of *Second Birth*'s rhetoric; and the bittersweet nature of the poem's nostalgia.

The pivotal find is the characterization of the longed-for apartment as "inducing sadness." Surely it would be more natural to long for joy and happiness, but then, the mood of grudging concession and acceptance ("Puskai . . . I po takoi"; "I ia primu") is best suited by the seemingly tautological while actually oxymoronic 'nostalgia for sadness.' And yet the sadness imparted by one's apartment is "one's own"—acceptable, familiar, sweet. The same goes for the speaker's voluntary confinement at the desk and the minor-key but 'passionate' involvement with the gloomy winter landscape, which, so to speak, immunizes him against the dangers to come.[47]

Having from the start slipped into a melancholy mood and sunk ever deeper into it as the poem unfolds, the poet and the reader develop a willingness—indeed, a sort of strained enthusiasm—for Socialism. To schematize the poem's emotional route, skipping the intermediate stages: "I want to go into . . . sadness . . . harness."

The emotional (as well as spatial) plot bridging the gap between the apartment and the harness is reinforced by the formal structures of the text. Thus, the narrative curve, leading from the sad enclosure of the first stanzas through the expansion and lightening in the middle to the dark and scary contraction in the end, is accompanied by a similar patterning of IWH's rhyme scheme.

The rhyming starts with closed vowels in closed syllables ending in voiceless consonants (*ogrOmnost'*, *grUst'*, *tonkorEbrost'*). Then the vowels widen and the syllables open up (*zadAchi*, *dnEi*, *napEva*). But in the dark alleyways there again appears the narrow U, and the syllables get blocked with consonant endings (*strast'*, *vikhr'*); still, a degree of wideness and openness is retained (strAst', MoskvA), coupled with the poignancy of the narrow, or rather, sharp I, punctuating the moment of creativity (vIkhr, mYshtsei). The poem ends on the gloomy chord of four rhymes, all featuring U followed by voiceless consonants (kak Upriazh'—bezUmstv— zazUbrish'— naizUst'). This brings us full circle back to the beginning (naizUst'—grUst'), emphasizing the link between the harness and the sad apartment.

AESTHETICS: SUBLIMATION OF HARNESS

In meeting the artistic challenge of poeticizing the utterly unpoetic harness, Pasternak had the support of two prestigious trends in Russian poetry: the realist, prose-oriented civic tradition (harking back to Nekrasov and even the later Pushkin), with its attention to the humble details of the life and work of everyman—in particular, the peasant—and the futurist promotion of real work—in particular, its tools—over art as such.[48] In a sadly ironic twist (mirroring the general irony of the populist revolution turned tyranny),[49] Pasternak's present task was to press this democratic/iconoclastic legacy into the service of oppression—by extolling, to paraphrase Pushkin, the charms of the harness.[50] For a means of naturalizing this difficult conceit, Pasternak could and did tap another honorable topos: the romantic image of poet as scapegoat, i.e., a sublime, yet trampled upon, sufferer.

How were these heterogeneous hypograms reconciled in Pasternak's own esthetic credo? Not only did it aim at mediating between high and low, at finding "poetry underfoot" (1985b: 173), and bearing witness to the "intercourse of rapture with the everyday" (1985b: 54); it also featured an appropriate figure of the poet: a human embodiment of the unity of 'pain, weakness, humility, trifling existence, overwhelmed passivity, and submission to one's duty' with 'supernatural powers of observation, flights of imagination, and contact with the world's vastness and eternity.' By the 1930s, the focus in this image had effectively shifted, to stress its self-sacrificial and obligational aspects.[51]

Regarding IWH's specific themes, an important aesthetic solution may have been prompted by the motif of 'homecoming.' Despite his many travels and paeans to exotic landcapes, Pasternak remained, and with time increasingly so, the poet of Moscow and its environs (poet-dachnik), behind whose tree trunks he was always able to discern the sea anyway.[52] In the 1930s, the modesty of such tastes acquired an additional meaning as a principled refusal to participate in the "creative trips" of official Soviet writers: "And what if, for instance, I was once captivated by the way Pushkin and Tiutchev journeyed and still do journey through their books and I have given up all the strength of my heart to the difficulty of *this* sort of journeying, which means neglecting the ease—all too deeply rooted among us nowadays—of stage-performance tours?" (1985b: 175). In this sense, the poet's voluntary confinement at home, by the writing desk, in IWH is another ambiguous, Aesopian mixture of 'collaborationist' and 'dissident' stances.

The "encounter of rapture with the everyday" overdetermines the symbolic significance of most images in IWH; for example:

the painful ecstasies of the *passe-muraille* poet; the lifetime task of penetrating the future without leaving the desk; susceptibility to (Christ's?) passions in the vicinity of home; heart collapsing in an enthusiastic response to Moscow's upsurge.

The peak of this high-wire aesthetic act is reached in the last stanza.

First comes the acceptance of the harness, proclaimed with self-sacrificial sublimity: the verb *prinimat'* means both "accept" and "assume," as in the assumption of responsibility, chastisement (*kara*), monastic vows (*postrig*), and the way of the cross. Then follows the jarringly bureaucratic and elevatedly archaic phrase (*Tekh radi*), which is made even more cumbersome by the inverted word order and extrametrical stress (on *Tekh*), to seal the bartering of self-imposed harness for future poetic madnesses.

In accordance with IWH's master figure and in a feat of iconic showcasing of the high/low aesthetic, the climactic harnessing sweeps in on the crest of a powerful momentum generated from the quotidian/negative material of stanzas 4–6. On the plot level, the modest details are whipped up into an ominous condensation of darkness, passions, and 'subjugation':

The winter's relatively mild *khoziainichat'*, "to keep house, boss around" (in stanza 4), leads all the way to *podsledstvennykh*, "under investigation" (6), while the rather placid horizontal movements, "right and left" (4) and "during a walk" (5), give way to more dramatic—and submerging!—vertical ones: "start falling from the sky" and "cover" (6); this downward plunge is then followed by the climactic counterpoint of 'collapsing' and 'rising' (7).

On the level of poetic syntax, this is echoed by the crescendo resulting from a skillful manipulation of the ostensibly monotonous repetition of the anaphoric *opiat'*, "again" (itself emblematic of life's routine). The incidence of the anaphoras combines with the variations in sentence length and structure to yield the impression of a simultaneous expansion of the lungs and quickening of the pulse.

> On one hand, after anaphoric regularity has been established, the word *opiat'* occurring in every other line (stanzas 4, 5), the interval suddenly contracts (6), an effect that is enhanced by the alliterative mimicking of *opiat'* in the very next word, *povaliat,* "will start falling" (6: 1).
>
> On the other hand, the sentences that begin with *opiat'* gradually merge, becoming longer and more complex: from two separate two-line sentences (6) to two two-line sentences with a common subject ("darkness," 5) to two separate sentences with the expanding one-plus-three pattern (6) to four-line complex sentences with subordinate clauses (7, 8). Just as the maximum sentence length and complexity are attained (in 7), the acceleration of the *opiat'* occurrences peaks. After a poignant reconfirmation, as *opiat'* is once again phonetically replicated by the next word (*opavshei,* "slumped"; 7: 1),[53] *opiat'* disappears from the text.

Thus, launched by the 'low' yet highly energized trifles, the poem develops the impetus that transports it into the lofty celebration of the down-to-earth and demeaning Socialist harness.

What is, on balance, the dialogic nature of IWH? Pasternak, who had shortly before declared that he "was not born to look three times differently in the eyes" of history,[54] was indeed changing with the times—experiencing a "second birth." Steering his ambiguously 'adaptive/subversive' course between the Scylla of Mayakovsky's extreme pro-Bolshevism and the Charybdis of Mandelstam's extreme defiance (both of which led to tragic premature deaths), he was able to survive. Indeed, he lived to undergo a third major transformation of his literary identity (manifested in *Doctor Zhivago* and the later poetry) and become a harbinger of post-Stalin dissidence. The secret of Pasternak's "miraculous" survival (which may well have been due to sheer luck—or Stalin's inexplicable personal liking) can be related, on the literary level, to the very "organic" and "soft" way he tackled the harsh challenges that faced him, prefiguring his eventual embrace of Christianity.[55]

Rather than a mere Aesopian compromise with the powers that be, IWH (and *Second Birth* as a whole) exhibits a profoundly idiosyncratic and consummately artistic treatment of the 'collaborationist' theme and engages in a multidimensional poetic intercourse with predecessors and contemporaries (Pushkin, Briusov, Mayakovsky, Mandelstam, the 'apartment topos,' etc.). That is probably what accounts for the puzzling hybrid of a truly great poem with a conduit for such Orwellian equations as 'Sadness is Joy,' 'Ugly is Beautiful,' 'Confinement = Freedom.' To quote another major contemporary, Anna Akhmatova: "If only you knew, out of what trash, / Verses grow, unfamiliar with shame." Akhmatova's 'pro-low' aesthetic credo expressed in these famous lines from "Tvorchestvo" (1940) is very much akin to Pasternak's views. All the more pertinent, if sad, is the irony of their unexpectedly provocative applicability to IWH (and the poetics of *Second Birth* in general) in the ideological sense. In blander—theoretical—terms, however, "I Want to Go Home" can be summed up as a case study in intertextual approaches to evolution: we actually see the poet change in response—that is, by responding—to the master discourse of his epoch.

PART V

Multiple Readings

NINE

A Dystopian "Newdream" Fivefold:
Analyzing Ilf and Petrov's
Closet Monarchist

Ilf and Petrov and Pluralist Reading

The problem of multiple readings is intertwined with that of an intrinsic vs. extrinsic approach. Structuralism, and the New Criticism before it, summarily indicted nowadays for their fixation on the intrinsic, actually broached the subject of multiplicity. They did so by splitting the analysis into different levels, which were to be read according to respective universal (i.e., external) codes, or sets of rules. At the same time, however, structuralism posited the principle of a more or less harmonious isomorphism of levels, thus placing a severe constraint on potential interpretive pluralism. An important decentralizing step was taken by Roland Barthes, who in *S/Z* (1974 [1970]) explicitly related the five levels of his essentially structural analysis to the corresponding codes and renounced the integration of the resulting partial readings into a single Message. This inaugurated current poststructuralist permissiveness, welcoming any number of conflicting interpretations and misreadings.

Conceding *in abstracto* the merits of an "infinite play of signifiers," one feels reluctant, however, to lose sight of the more limited pluralism of those meanings projected into the text by the specifically relevant historical, generic, or authorial sign systems. Contrary to *S/Z*, they can be fully fledged thematic readings, but as in *S/Z* and contrary to some structuralist and New Criticism analyses, there can be more than just two (forming some sort of polar opposition), for instance, five or more. This makes accounting for the complex mode of their coexistence an interesting theoretical and practical challenge. Generally speaking, both extremes—discordant polylogue and total thematic subordination—are possible, as are all the intermediate shades of ambiguity. The critic's focus should be on stating the various codes according to which the text is being read, the typical patterns of interplay among the readings, and the specifics of the resulting interpretive picture.

It is in this spirit that I will concentrate on a short episode from Ilia Ilf and Evgenii Petrov's widely popular Ostap Bender saga. This satirical saga comprises two novels, *Dvenadtsat' stul'ev* (*The Twelve Chairs*, or *Diamonds to Sit On*, 1928) and *Zolotoi telenok* (*The Golden Calf*, 1931), whose plot revolves around the adventures of a witty confidence man, the "Grand Schemer," *Velikii Kombinator*, Ostap Bender, hunting for individual treasure in his collectivist land. In the tradition of travelogue narrative,[1] threading the main story through a series of vignettes, every chapter plays the leitmotif of the itinerant hero against those of the episodic characters representing the social milieu. This syntagmatic linkage emplots the fundamental paradigmatic similarity of the two juxtaposed (arche)characters: both Bender and his variable partner embody the theme of 'adaptation,' central to the novels. As a rule, the episodic character represents a pathetically slavish or unsuccessful version of adjustment to Soviet ways, while the Grand Kombinator subverts the very idea of conformity by artistically aping the official clichés and idiosyncratic manias of the "maladjusters" he encounters in his picaro's progress.

The episode with the hapless dreamer, Khvorob'ev (*The Golden Calf*, chap. 8; see Ilf and Petrov 1966: 87–97), is no exception.

Fearing arrest for their antics, Ostap Bender and his team of petty thugs decide to paint their car another color in the barn belonging to Khvorob'ev, an old education official and unreformed monarchist. Out of exasperation with the "new order," Khvorob'ev has retired from his job and moved to a house in the country, but reality catches up with him, haunting his very dreams with Soviet scenes and slogans. His hopes of having a good old prerevolutionary dream are repeatedly dashed. It is by claiming to have precisely such dreams that Bender gains his confidence. (For a more detailed rendering of the episode, see the table in the Appendix to this chapter.)

Bender's mocking conmanship provides the familiar musical accompaniment to which Khvorob'ev's grotesque theme is played, reverberating with manifold literary, cultural, and ideological overtones. This contrapuntal structure is further enriched by Bender's (and the narrator's) double-voiced treatment of the conventions and value systems involved.

The degree of Ilf and Petrov's polyphonism has been debated. Treasured, along with Zoshchenko, during the Stalin years as the most subversive authors available, they have now lost some of their luster to the rediscovered Bulgakov, Platonov, Nabokov, and some others in the ongoing post-Stalin revision of the modern literary canon. When the two satirists do receive critical attention, the focus invariably turns on the ambiguity of their message, pro-Soviet yet provocative, and their ostentatious literariness—qualities that in their case, for extra-artistic reasons, are seen as evidence of moral compromise and stylistic shallowness.[2] In reading the multicode score of the Khvorob'ev episode, we begin with the 'Ostap theme' as the least extrinsic one.

The Bender Act

The script underlying Ostap Bender's behavior has been distilled into a set of invariant patterns (Shcheglov 1986c: 93–104; 1990, 1: 41–46). Ostap desacralizes and defeats his episodic antagonist by means of three main stratagems, which emphasize his own uninvolved posture (he is carnivalistically both superior and inferior to the partner) and an objectifying (re)definition of the other person.

Bender starts with Recognition: he promptly reduces his new acquaintance to a formula, identifying the appropriate set of stereotypes for manipulating him. From the arrogant position of a jaundiced observer of human folly, he catches on to his partner's game in mid-sentence and chimes in with parodic Mimicry of his enthusiasm and characteristic discourse. Acting both 'from below' and 'from above' (the motivation is trivial, but the performance is con brio), Bender coldly feigns solidarity and juggles the corresponding sacred clichés, playfully adapting them to alien stylistic contexts and frivolous circumstances. Thus, he reproduces in a light key the same labors of adaptation that the others go through in earnest and with tormenting anguish: his sloppy bricolage of clichés is merely a hyperbolic mirror image of the clumsy originals. Recognition and Mimicry set the stage for cynical Exploitation, whereby Bender channels his partner's preoccupations or idealistic beliefs into the service of his own "base" needs. All three operations express a common theme ('desacralization of stereotypes') and are usually employed in conjunction with each other.

The outlined triptych is amply evident in our episode:

—First comes Recognition (in part already mixed with Mimicry): Bender secretly watches Khvorob'ev, listens to his complaints about "the same cursed dreams," waits for the "results of the mysterious trial" as Khvorob'ev decides "to try once more," embraces the distressed dreamer, declares sympathy, and ventures a close guess by claiming to have dreamed of the Mikado.

—Then Mimicry takes over: guided by Khvorob'ev's eager responses, Bender zeroes in on his target, inventing enviable monarchistic dreams, is invited in and told the story of Khvorob'ev's plight.

—Exploitation rounds off the episode: Bender offers help, hastily diagnoses the problem, and prescribes the cure in an improbable jumble of Freudian and Marxist terms:

Since, as the saying goes, "Existence determines [the nature of] consciousness," therefore, inasmuch as you live in a Soviet land your dreams are bound to be Sovietic. . . . I have had occasion to treat some of my acquaintances according to Freud. . . . The main thing is to remove the cause of the dream . . . [i.e.] the very existence of the Soviet power. As soon as there is no more Soviet power you will somehow feel better." (1966: 91–92)

He promises to effect the recovery "on [his] way back," meanwhile keeping his car in the barn of his newly acquired patient, is gratefully granted permission, and leaves Khvorob'ev shuffling after him in a state of hopeful trepidation.

The Dream Genre

Bender's quack diagnosis echoes an equally loose patchwork of symptoms that make up Khvorob'ev's case. Dreams are a venerable and well-researched literary tradition (see Gershenzon 1926, Remizov 1977, Katz 1984), and the episode under analysis is intertextual to a fault. This means, however, that Khvorob'ev and his dreams are made of the same stuff as the rest of the book, which is a carnival of quotations mimicking and deflating one another.

Some intertexts are invoked quite openly. For instance, the refrain that punctuates Khvorob'ev's lamentations is unashamedly borrowed from Grigorii, the future Pretender, in an early scene from Pushkin's *Boris Godunov*: "The very same dream!" (Vse tot zhe son!).

> The link is corroborated, laid bare, and rendered absurd as the narrator forthwith compares Khvorob'ev to Grigorii's antagonist, Czar Boris Godunov, only this time from the Mussorgsky opera, or rather, in a completely metatextual gesture, to the famous basso Chaliapin himself. The Boris connection is then strengthened by Khvorob'ev's line "Not a minute of rest!" ("Ni minuty otdykha!") and the narrator's statement "Nor could his proud soul find any solace at home" ("No i doma [Khvorob'ev] ne nakhodil uspokoeniia svoei gordoi dushe"). These two go back to Boris's soliloquy "Shestoi uzh god ia tsarstvuiu spokoino, / No schast'ia net moei dushe" ("For over five years have I reigned calmly [in peace], but there is no happiness for my soul"), but also admix with it one more troubled operatic monarch, Borodin's *Prince Igor*: "Neither sleep, nor rest is there for [my] tormented soul" ("Ni sna, ni otdykha izmuchennoi dushe").
>
> Further scrutiny yields a Pushkin subtext also for the sentence "He wanted to run, but he couldn't" ("On khochet bezhat' i ne mozhet"), lifted almost verbatim from the description of Petrusha Grinev's dream haunted by Pugachev, yet another classic Russian pretender (*Captain's Daughter*, chap. 2).

The last quote is probably not intended for exact attribution but rather for promoting the general atmosphere of literariness. Among other virtual subtexts are:

—the title of Fedor Sologub's novel *Tiazhelye sny* (*Nightmares*, lit. *Heavy Dreams*); compare *Odurevshii ot tiazhelykh snov monarkhist* ("The monarchist, befuddled by his nightmares");

—the line in *Evgenii Onegin* (4: 36–37) about the hero's rural way of life: "Onegin zhil anakhoretom" ("Onegin lived anchoretically"; Pushkin 1964, 1: 199); compare "I davno vy zhivete takim anakhoretom?—

sprosil Ostap" ("And have you lived long so anchoretically?" Ostap asked);

—and the old prince Bolkonskii's exclamation "V svoem dome ni minuty pokoia!" ("Not a moment's peace in my own house!" *War and Peace*, Tolstoy 1966: 599); compare Khvorob'ev's similar predicament and language (see also Shcheglov 1991, 2: 482).

In a still more abstract sense, the entire episode is highly intertextual: a variation on the nightmare genre, whose parameters are familiar to the Russian reader from the works of Pushkin, Gogol, Tolstoy, Dostoevsky, and others. The generic dream usually serves to characterize the dreamer and express the text's overall theme; can provoke an appeal to God, who is responsible for sending dreams; is told to a listener in exchange for interpretation; corresponds in one way or another to surrounding fictional reality, as narrative foreshadowing, wish fulfillment, fixation on a role model, philosophical parable, and so on; tends to recur, terrify, replace waking life, or deceptively blend with it; can be invented, shared by different characters, and so on; is seen as an analog to art (e.g., narrative), hence used as a framed story.

The Khvorob'ev episode easily meets all these requirements. It portrays Khvorob'ev as an ill-adapted monarchist (note the obsessive 'royalism' of the intertexts) lost in the world of Soviet clichés. Khvorob'ev repeatedly invokes God and even addresses a bureaucratized supplication to Him. "Khvorob'ev . . . woke up, . . . prayed to God, pointing out to him that there apparently had been a regrettable hitch, as a result of which a dream intended for a high-placed and trusted comrade was sent to a wrong address. As for him, Khvorob'ev, he would like to see His Majesty the Czar's issue from the Cathedral of the Assumption of the Holy Virgin." The dreams are told to a "sympathetic" Bender, who both soothingly dismisses them as insignificant and offers a solid scientific interpretation. Khvorob'ev's actual dreams mirror reality, whereas the ones he desires are an escapist idyll, displaying a fixation on dubious royalty. The nightmares recur incessantly, are the dreamer's only activity, and blend with reality by being indistinguishable from it. Bender fakes dreams that exactly match Khvorob'ev's frustrated tastes. And the dreams are not only told and traded like stories but are ordered by Khvorob'ev as if from a magic hypnotheque or, to put it in today's terms, from a video store.

The analogy between dreams and mass media is explicitly stated in the text, as Ostap Bender claims to have dreamed "a mélange. The sort of thing that the newspapers call 'News from Everywhere,' and in the cinemas, 'Topics of the Day,' . . . the Mikado's funeral," and so on.

The authors pointedly vandalize the dream genre by creating a modernist pileup of its standard features, exaggerated and clashing with one another. The "wandering dreams of alien bards" (Mandelstam) are inflicted on Khvorob'ev in a way that explodes the tradition while purporting to follow it. Indeed, a "genuine" dream can hardly be so openly intertextual, especially with the quotations so felicitously picked from mutually exclusive sources. Contradictions and absurdities also plague Bender's interpretation (which in addition to its other aspects is a spoof of a medic's bedside babble in the manner of Molière), while the divine origin of dreams is debased by stylistic mongrelization. Perhaps the most flagrant deviation involves the "dream = art" parallel, which is repeatedly pushed to an extreme (orders are placed for customized dreams) and just as regularly subjected to dramatic failure (Khvorob'ev gets the opposite of what he ordered). These and other ungrammaticalities disqualify the episode qua "the same old" traditional dream, stimulating the reader to seek other avenues of interpretation—in accordance with the theory that ungrammaticality signals a lack calling for 'conversion' to crown the reading process.[3]

The problem of remodeling a tired genre is both directly and indirectly posed in the text under analysis: the chapter is given a pointedly meta-aesthetic title—"A Genre in Crisis."[4]

> This title derives from the chapter's other episode: a spoof of the small-town community of traditional artists trying desperately to compete with an avant-gardist who "works" his portraits of the town's Party dignitaries in bolts, nuts, oats, and other unconventional but topical materials. However, when viewed side by side, the two episodes exhibit common thematic concerns.
>
> Once the juxtaposition has been made, they read as a bipartite treatise on official portraiture: avant-gardist portrayal of Soviet leaders in the one case and traditionalist court painting/photography in the other. Remarkably, all that Khvorob'ev wants to see in his dreams (and Bender claims to have seen in his) are the czar and his courtiers patterned on photographs in the official prerevolutionary press.

At a still deeper level, the 'genre-in-crisis' leitmotif can be taken to refer to the authors' own procedure in the chapter, especially in the Khvorob'ev episode, suggesting that it is written to be read as a conversion of the genre it appears to instance.

The Adaptation Game

One clue to a possible reinterpretation is furnished by the 'adaptation' problem, present here in the form of the drastic "rewriting" of Khvorob'ev's dream scripts by a higher office. Formulated in such terms, the situation reveals its further intertextual affinities. Indeed, adjustment to ideological censorship, as a metaliterary version of adaptation in general, figures prominently in all of Ilf and Petrov's oeuvre.

Among its classical examples in the novels are Nikifor Liapis-Valois's ideologically correct and universally adaptable poem *The Gavriliad* (*The Twelve Chairs*, chap. 29); the plight of the old rebus composer Sinitskii, whose innocent craft suffers from the invasion of Soviet slogans ("Ideology has got me [Ideologiia zaela]," he complains; *The Golden Calf*, chap. 9); or "The Complete Celebrator" kit, invented by Bender to help streamline the work of his "colleagues," the Soviet writers (*The Golden Calf*, chap. 28).

The same theme pervades Ilf and Petrov's feuilletons and short stories, for example, such classics as "Kak sozdavalsia Robinzon" (How [the Soviet] Robinson Crusoe was created) and "Ikh bin s golovy do nog" (Ich bin from head to feet).[5] The common plot that underlies the last two pieces offers instructive parallels to our episode, shedding light on the dynamics of Ilf-and-Petrovian 'adaptation.'

In both cases, a creative artist (a writer; a circus performer) is pitted against a censoring body (the editor of a youth journal; Repertkom, or the Repertory Committee). The artist is encouraged to produce and contributes his own fresh and unofficial creation, which turns out to represent a different, alien— 'foreign'—artistic convention and system of values (a Robinson Crusoe–like adventure story; a German performing dog that says, "Ich liebe! Ich sterbe!"). But then the censoring body gradually forces the artist, over his objections, arguments, and pleas, to expunge everything non-Soviet (the individualism of Robinson Crusoe; the "abstract humanism" of the dog's repertoire) and to conform fully to Soviet clichés. The metamorphosis passes through a stage of compromise, breeding preposterous hybrids (Robinson becomes a social activist, Soviet-style; the dog is to deliver a lengthy propaganda piece). Eventually, the utter inflexibility of the alien artistic creature (Robinson is an "eternal" classic; the dog is, after all, only canine) dooms it to total demise (Robinson Crusoe is thrown out of "his" story; "The dog's traces [footprints] were lost" [Sledy sobaki zaterialis']).

Precisely the same happens, mutatis mutandis, to Khvorob'ev. He too has a pet project (of personalized dreams) stemming from an un-

Soviet cultural tradition (monarchist). He submits it to a higher authority (represented, ironically, by "God") but is rebuffed (has strictly Soviet dreams). He protests in vain, then knuckles under and is ready to compromise (e.g., to dream of the leader of Constitutional Democrats in the prerevolutionary Russian Parliament, Pavel Miliukov, who is, after all, "a university man and a monarchist at heart"), only to be told (this time by Bender, about which later) that the surrender to conformity must be complete ("Inasmuch as you live in a Soviet land, your dreams are bound to be Soviet").

On the whole, the Khvorob'ev story offers a rather harsh version of the artist/censorship confrontation.

> Khvorob'ev is one of Ilf and Petrov's most principled nonconformists—on a par with the dissidents seeking refuge in the lunatic asylum (*The Golden Calf*, chap. 16), with whom, incidentally, he also shares the motif of mental disorder. Sticking to his personal code, he consistently rejects the Soviet way of life and has a long and consistent track record of internal emigration.
>
> The treatment he receives is equally uncompromising: Soviet culture implacably invades first his office hours, then his solitary promenades, and finally the dreams he believes sacrosanct and hopes to enjoy in his countryside retreat (" 'The Soviet power took everything away from me. . . . It has even replaced my thoughts. But there is one sphere where the Bolsheviks cannot penetrate: the dreams that are sent down to us by God' ").
>
> The lines of conflict are drawn so clearly that they practically exclude the hybridization of Soviet and "alien" elements so beloved by Ilf and Petrov. In the story line, the sole exception is the consent to edit in Miliukov, and perhaps on the level of style, the prayer in bureaucratese.

The Dystopian Masterplot

Ilf and Petrov's mythopoetics of adaptation did not simply result from an idiosyncratic obsession but was developed in response to a central issue of Soviet ideology and culture. The Khvorob'ev episode in particular seems to be the authors' variation on the so-called antiutopian theme, introduced into Soviet literature by Zamiatin's *We* (1954 [1924]) and Ehrenburg's *Julio Jurenito* (1922; esp. chap. 27, "The Grand Inquisitor Outside the Legend," expurgated until recently from later Soviet editions). The genre of antiutopia (Morson 1981: 115–41), which had had a long history of subverting its utopian twin, was infused with new meaning in the twentieth century as totalitarianism claimed

to be utopia come true. It was also strongly influenced by Dostoevsky's antiutopian discourse in "Notes from the Underground," *The
Possessed*, and "The Legend of the Grand Inquisitor," and by the subsequent Kafkaesque exploration of the human condition in modern
society. It is at the intersection of the antiutopian tradition, sociopolitical reality, and modernist-existential writing that the new genre
of 'dystopia' crystallized over a period of several decades: "a type of
anti-utopia that discredits utopias by portraying the likely effects of
their realization, in contrast to other anti-utopias, which discredit the
possibility of their realization or expose the folly and inadequacy of
their proponents' assumptions or logic" (Morson 1981: 116).

A comparative study of six dystopian classics written before, parallel with, and after *The Golden Calf* yields a rather stable masterplot,
which can serve as our next frame of reference for the Khvorob'ev episode. The six are Evgenii Zamiatin's *We* (1954 [1924]), Aldous Huxley's
Brave New World (1950 [1932]), Vladimir Nabokov's *Invitation to a Beheading* (1959 [1938]), George Orwell's *1984* (1949), Ray Bradbury's *Fahrenheit 451°* (1967 [1950]), and Anthony Burgess's *A Clockwork Orange*
(1963 [1962]). For brevity's sake, I concentrate on the common denominator of these texts without trying to do justice to variations, which at
best are mentioned parenthetically (for more detail, see Zholkovsky
1986g: 190–98).

> The action of a dystopia takes place in a "rational" society, which, having
> traded God and the freedom of will for universal harmony and happiness,
> decrees total uniformity of thinking and abolishes privacy, repressing all that
> is unpredictable and rooted outside the spatial, temporal, or epistemological
> boundaries of the System. This dictatorship of the political superego results
> not in the promised harmony but in a personality split, which reveals itself
> as the Protagonist embarks on his dissident Quest. Gradually abandoning his
> allegiance to the system, he comes within reach of a perfect synthesis of the
> traditional opposites—Nature/Culture, Reason/Emotion, Man/Woman, Child/
> Adult—all in one way or another suppressed by the system and therefore
> united in resisting it. But the quest ends in the defeat of the protagonist or even
> his reverse metamorphosis into a conforming vegetable.
>
> The protagonist is usually a common and commonsensical man, an intel-
> lectual functionary of the system; for example, Zamiatin's constructor of the
> Integral supermachine; Huxley's technicians of hypnopaedia and poetic pro-
> paganda; Orwell's official of the Ministry of Truth engaged in updating the
> past; and Bradbury's fireman burning forbidden books.

The system looks after the protagonist as if he were a Child, and as such he is inherently natural, spontaneous, disobedient, socially unintegrated—marginal. These centrifugal tendencies are activated in the course of the quest as the protagonist acquires also the characteristics of an Old and Ailing Man, which combine inferiority and dependence on the system with links to the preutopian past and other borderline and sacral states of mind. To complete the set of peripheral roles, the protagonist meets a Woman, and their natural, free, and individual Love challenges the system and is eventually destroyed by it. The protagonist's other roles—child, old man, ailing man—can also be played by separate characters.

The hero's antagonist is the Inquisitor, who in his dual role of utopian thinker and experienced practical ruler displays Omniscient Understanding of and Provisional Identification with the protagonist's quest but then engages in a sophisticated and provocatively cynical Apology of the system ushered in by the Revolution.

Like the protagonist, the Inquisitor can be split into more than one character. Thus, his grotesque sophistry may be entrusted to the Provocateur, who has no stake in the state's power and clowningly apes the perverse logic of its defense. Such, for instance, is the role played by Julio Jurenito as he interviews, in an imitation of Ivan Karamazov's Christ, the "important Communist" (alias the Inquisitor, alias a thinly fictionalized Lenin). The Provocateur is an important fixture in fellow-traveler writing, as evidenced by the figures of Jurenito, Babel's Benia Krik, Olesha's Ivan Babichev, Bulgakov's Woland and retinue, and, of course, Ostap Bender himself. Along with other Dostoevskian Inquisitors/Provocateurs, Ostap's genealogy also features Peter Verkhovensky.[6]

The Inquisitor has at his disposal the Apparatus of Power, often based on state-of-the-art technology and comprising the means of enforcement proper and those of brainwashing (the boundary between the two is sometimes pointedly obfuscated). The Inquisitor's seat is the Ministry, where the protagonist too is kept, as a worker, patient, or convict. The protagonist starts out living in semi-public quarters, transparent to technology and/or informers, but the quest and the woman bring him to the Old House.

The Old House goes back to the pastoral Hut (opposed to sentimentalism's corrupt City), to the abandoned/haunted Castle of the gothic, and to "progressive" nineteenth-century writing (e.g., Conan Doyle). Now it also becomes a repository of Culture and the antipode to utopian phalansters.

In the Old House or elsewhere, the protagonist comes into contact with the Outside World, Nature, the Past, its forbidden Culture (including God), and the Book. The reading/writing and hiding of the book (often the protagonist's diary) forms a core element of the masterplot (Morson 1981: 141). The antonym of the Book is the obligatory official Anti-Book and various brainwashing media. Among its synonyms are other forms of cultural memory and windows onto the last stronghold of resistance to censorship: the Irrational—in particular, Dreams.

It is to the dystopian treatment of dreams that I now turn, leaving the masterplot transcription of the Khvorob'ev story till the end of the next section.

The "Newdream"

The dreaming motif is one of the nerve centers of dystopia, its relevance to the genre being overdetermined in several ways. 'Dreaming' is naturally associated with the philosophical problematic of cognition (in the spirit of Plato's cave, Calderón's *La vida es sueño*, etc.), eminently germane to the utopian substitution of universal good for truth. The "nationalization" of dreams by the state is of course the archetypal dystopian nightmare. Also, dreams mesh well with the protagonist's abandoning the role of a healthy member of the system to become an ailing man (see esp. Zamiatin), spending much time in Bed and slipping into prophetic states.

Generalized from the six subplots (see Appendix, "Summaries"), the dream segment of the dystopian masterplot features the following invariant situations:

In a predictable recycling of the traditional Desired Dream, found in all six dystopias, the protagonist has (has always had, wants to have, or acquires in the course of the quest) his own Desired Dreams, which are his Sanctuary from the all-pervasive system. However, these dreams—indeed all dreams—are either Forbidden by the state or just Not Dreamed by the citizens (Zamiatin, Nabokov, Bradbury). Instead, Obligatory Dreams (or Obligatory Dreamlessness) are induced by a variety of Manipulation Techniques: lobotomy (Zamiatin), drugs (Huxley, Bradbury), hypnopaedia (Huxley, Burgess), or more sophisticated combinations of physiological and psychological treatment (Orwell, Burgess).

In this atmosphere of Dream Control, the characters develop strategies for Ordering[7] and/or Faking their Desired Dreams. The protagonist does so to protect himself. For example, Winston Smith's epiphanic decision to "dream right" (*1984*, 3: 4) replaces his earlier line of defense: "Confession is not betrayal . . . only feelings matter. . . . They could lay bare . . . everything you had done or said or thought; but the inner heart, whose workings were mysterious even to yourself, remained impregnable" (2: 7). The Inquisitor orders/fakes dreams to win his Intellectual Combat with the protagonist (Bradbury), which commonly features the latter Prostrate in Bed at the mercy of the Inquisitor and/or in his Embrace.

The Khvorob'ev episode, written rather early in the history of the dystopian genre (1931), exhibits remarkable affinities with the masterplot in general and its Newdream aspect in particular. It dramatizes an escalating invasion of the system into the protagonist's life and his very dreams: "The Soviet regime . . . invaded even the dreams of the monarchist."

At first the protagonist is a normal member of society, but then he leaves his job in the Ministry (of Public Instruction [!]) and embarks on his antiestablishment quest. In this he suffers setbacks and soon succumbs to ailing, as symbolized by his very name (*khvoroba* means "ailment, disease").[8] He is an old man, a leftover of the prerevolutionary era[9] residing in an old house located outside the city—in nature, hung with portraits representing cultural memory. Khvorob'ev hates the new anticulture with its obligatory dreams, anti-language (*khamskii iazyk*, cf. Orwell's Newspeak), and anti-books (note the mention of Vsevolod Ivanov's *Armored Train 14-69*).

A linguistic remark in the text invokes the utopian obsession with mathematics (targeted by generations of anti-utopians from Swift down to Zamiatin and his followers): Khvorob'ev reports to work at "the Methodological and Pedagogical Sector. . . . Oh, that sector! Never did [Khvorob'ev], who treasured all things elegant, including geometry, suppose that this beautiful mathematical concept, denoting a part of the area of a curvilinear figure, could be so banalized."

Khvorob'ev tries to commune with God and retreat into the sanctuary of dreams, which he insists on ordering but finds effectively forbidden, while the Inquisitor-Provocateur Bender displays faked dreams and promises to countermanipulate Khvorob'ev's nightmares with the help of the Book (Freud). Bender shows a total understanding and provisional identification with Khvorob'ev's predicament and refers to the official Anti-Book (Marx) in his apology of the system. Their combat takes place in the proximity of the bed (which is "in disorder, presenting convincing evidence that its owner spent there the most restless hours of his life") and culminates in Bender's powerful embrace, accentuating in Khvorob'ev the child and ailing man, doomed to ultimate defeat.

In several respects, however, Ilf and Petrov's episode deviates from the masterplot. Conspicuously absent are the Inquisitor proper and his apparatus of power and manipulation techniques, replaced by the phantasmagoria of self-inducing obligatory dreams and the Bender figure (the latter accumulates three roles: Bender's usual self as manipulative Kombinator, the dream genre's listener-interpreter, and dystopia's Provocateur). This may have been dictated by Aesopian reasons and also accords with the ambiguous, grotesquely modernist tone of the episode.

Another difference is the irony of Khvorob'ev's cherishing as his private, antiestablishment values similar bureaucratic clichés, but of a previous culture, in a natural consequence of the cruel ambivalence with which Ilf and Petrov, along with Bender, treat their episodic protagonist. Khvorob'ev is thus degraded to the level of the performing dog whose "own" text is none other than a stereotypical love song. This is in line with the two satirists' general tendency in most of their stories and the treatment of the novels' episodic characters to play clichés against clichés rather than clichés against a Truly Free Individual, a role reserved for the Grand Kombinator alone.[10] To humiliate Khvorob'ev further, the authors make him irreversibly old and pathetic and do not provide him with a Woman.

Among Ilf and Petrov's contributions to the dystopian masterplot are some of the absurdities resulting naturally from the episode's other components. Especially interesting are the combination of Faked Dreams with Shared Dreams in Bender; the motif of Misaddressed Dream in Khvorob'ev, a whimsical variation on the theme of dream control; and the whole business of repeatedly Ordered, Forbidden, and Obligatorily experienced dreams. These innovations, however, are not without parallels in the dream-genre tradition and modern writing.

Dream Genre Revisited

Most of the characteristic irregularities that first led us away from the genre of the literary dream and now bring us back to it serve the dominant dystopian theme of invaded privacy. Such is one of the effects of crowding Khvorob'ev's dreamscape with references to Grigorii, Boris, Igor, and Grinev, aggravated by Bender's second-guessing and faking

Khvorob'ev's dreams. And of course the same theme is responsible for inflicting on Khvorob'ev the recurrent obligatory nightmares, while a cognate dystopian motif, countermanipulation of dreams, underlies Khvorob'ev's insistent ordering of desirable visions. All these effects build on properties inherent in the dream genre by amplifying, transforming, or recombining them, and they do so in ways characteristic of other modernist texts, prosaic and poetic.

Sharing dreams, usually with mystical or ominous connotations, was used in nineteenth-century literature (see "A Terrible Vengeance," *Anna Karenina*, *The Brothers Karamazov*, Lermontov's poem "A Dream," etc.). The reverse side of the mystical transcendence of the boundaries of self is this motif's potential for conveying the theme of invaded privacy. It was naturally seized upon and put to dystopian and other modernist uses by many contemporary authors, among them Anthony Burgess (see Appendix, "Summaries," 6) and Vasilii Aksenov.

> In Aksenov's *Surplus Tare of Barrels* (1968), all the characters have dreams. Their dreams are numbered, in a probable spoof of Chernyshevsky's *What Is to Be Done?* They all dream of The Good Man, each his or her own. The driver's dreaming ends in an actual accident. And gradually, as the characters are drawn closer to one another in their common love for the mysterious "tare of barrels," their individual visions incorporate more and more details characteristic of the others' dreams.

Faking dreams, in its turn, was already practiced by the child narrator of Tolstoy's *Childhood*.

> In the very first chapter, he claims to have dreamed of his mother's death. When his *gouverneur* tries to console him, he starts crying and half believes his own invention. From then on, the dream is accepted as having taken place, and later it actually comes true (Katz 1984: 114).

A much less innocent form of Faking appears in Platonov's *The Foundation Pit* (1930):

> There, the upwardly mobile toady Kozlov declares that "he had seen in his night dreams the chief of the Central Administration of Social Security, Comrade Romanov, and a varied society of people dressed in clean clothes," which he so wants to join (Platonov 1973: 53).

The character who invents dreams behaves in an authorial way or, to put it the other way around, serves as the author's excuse for his or her fictions. Indeed, the attempts at deliberate control, manipulation, and countermanipulation of dreams have their roots not only in the desirability of traditional idyllic visions but also in the arbitrariness, sanctioned by the literary convention, with which authors ascribe to their characters whatever dreams they need for narrative or thematic reasons.

> Such is the function, for instance, of the chapter-long dreams in Goncharov's *Oblomov* and Chernyshevsky's *What Is to Be Done?* and a shorter but programmatic dream at the end of *Crime and Punishment* where Dostoevsky sends Raskol'nikov a prophetic dream to seal his eventual salvation.

In the twentieth century, the infliction of dreams on characters—by the author, narrator, speaker of a poem, and even other characters—becomes much more self-conscious, assuming various functions, among them the dystopian.[11]

While testifying to the richness of our episode's intertextual background, these parallels differ from the avowed sources (*Boris Godunov, Captain's Daughter, Prince Igor*) in that they rely on the paradigmatic features of the dream genre rather than specific textual references. In the artistic economy of converting the ungrammatical jumble of overtly invoked literary nightmares into an innovative Newdream structure, the former function as "false leads."[12] The paradigmatic intertexts, on the other hand, indicate the general direction in which the episode's deeper significance may lie, albeit without offering specific textual clues. Theoretically, such intertextual blandness in administering conversion is possible, but for such past masters of quotation as Ilf and Petrov, would be rather unlikely. Indeed, a closer scrutiny of the dream genre yields several texts that seem to contain direct textual foreshadowings of the most salient, dystopian aspects of the Khvorob'ev episode.

Gogol's "Nevsky Prospekt" offers a classical model of the deliberate ordering of dreams.

> Piskarev repeatedly tries to dream of the prostitute he has fallen in love with, is repeatedly frustrated, several times dreams of some officials instead (!), and finally sees her in the idealized guise of an elegant lady; "dreams become his life." On realizing, however, that reality cannot live up to the dreams (the girl *is* a prostitute), Piskarev commits suicide.[13]

Relevant in even more ways is Dostoevsky's *The Village of Stepanchikovo*, as will become clear from the transcription of one of its episodes in terms of the dystopian masterplot. Dostoevsky, along with other classics, looms large as a subtextual presence in the Bender novels. Notably, motifs from Dostoevsky's letters to his wife (Dostoevsky 1926, a recent publication at the time of Ilf and Petrov's writing) form one of the major strands woven into Father Fedor's (!) travels and letters to his wife in *The Twelve Chairs* (Shcheglov 1990, 1: 255). *Stepanchikovo* centers on the figure of Foma Fomich Opiskin, a "buffoon who has become the unlimited despot on . . . [the] estate, . . . a carnival king" and "anticipates in many ways the future heroes of Dostoevsky" (Bakhtin 1984: 163). In Chapter 6,

> Foma Fomich Opiskin plays a clownish Inquisitor to the serf boy Falalei's dystopian Protagonist, who also displays the characteristics of Child, Natural Man and Woman: "He had a girl's features—the features of a village beauty. . . . He was so naive, so guileless and simple-hearted, that one could easily have taken him for a simpleton . . . as innocent and gentle as a lamb, happy and carefree as a child. . . . Foma Fomich . . . decided to become Falalei's benefactor" (Dostoevsky 1983: 99).
>
> Opiskin decides to enlighten Falalei by teaching him French and good manners in the teeth of the boy's inability to learn and the opposition of the old man, the trusted valet Gavrila. Gavrila tries to protect the boy, but is punished by Foma, who subjects him to reeducation, forcing the old servant himself to study French (i.e., a Newspeak of sorts): "Old Gavrila . . . had the temerity openly to dispute the advantage of knowing the French language anyway. . . . Foma . . . ordered the fractious Gavrila himself to take up the study of French as a punishment" (100).
>
> As for good manners, Falalei makes a habit of telling Foma his recurrent dream of the white bull. Foma declares this vulgar dream forbidden and enjoins Falalei to have nobler dreams. Falalei complies, tries ordering dreams about elegant ladies, resorts to prayers, but fails: "Falalei . . . was strictly forbidden to have any more such uncouth peasant's dreams. . . . 'His dreams are every bit as bad as his day-time thoughts [Kakovy mysli, takovy i sny]. . . . Could you not dream of something refined, delicate, edifying, some scene out of polite society—say, gentlemen playing cards or ladies promenading in a fine park?' Falalei solemnly promised. . . . Before returning to bed Falalei, in tears, beseeched God for help and thought for a long time how he could possibly avoid dreaming of the accursed white bull. But . . . all through the night he dreamt of the hated white bull . . . and not a glimpse of a single lady promenading in a fine park" (101–2).
>
> Foma claims that the forbidden dream has been faked to spite him, and others try to persuade the innocent Falalei to fake the obligatory dream: "Foma Fomich categorically refused to believe in the possibility of such a repetition

of dreams, and declared that Falalei must deliberately have been worked upon
by a member of the household . . . expressly to annoy him, Foma. . . . It never
occured to Falalei to tell a lie, . . . that, instead of the white bull, he had seen
a carriageful of ladies with Foma in their midst" (102).

Foma is then distracted by other events and leaves Falalei alone until the
final scene of general reconcilation, only to find him stuck with the dream of
the white bull: " 'Falalei, what did you dream of last night?' . . . 'Of your virt . . .
of the white b-bull!' . . . 'At least I appreciate your honesty, Falalei. . . . I forgive
you!' " (228).

The dystopian manipulation of dreams fails for the nonce, but only
after its many ominous manifestations have been spelled out in full,
prefiguring in great detail the Khvorob'ev episode. In addition to the
already noted thematic motifs, the parallels include such specific features as

—the absurd monotony of repeatedly unsuccessful attempts at
having dreams made to order;[14]

—the 'nobleness' of the ordered obligatory dream about high society;[15]

—the narrative pause, allowing for the development of other subplots;

—the final vignette, emphasizing the ineluctability of the recurrent
dream; and even

—the phrasing of the Inquisitor's omniscient diagnosis: Foma's
"Kakovy mysli, takovy i sny" (best translated as "Like thoughts, like
dreams") seems to prefigure Bender's "Inasmuch as you live in a
Soviet land your dreams are bound to be Soviet."

A decisive step in the conversion of the traditional dream genre
into its twentieth-century counterpart was marked by Olesha's *Envy*
(1927). An episode from Ivan Babichev's childhood (2: 1) combines
elements of the authorial infliction of necessary dreams on characters,
a character's (Piskarev's) successful ordering of desired dreams for
himself, and one character's (Foma's) futile attempts at manipulating
the dreams of another.

The episode features little Ivan with what he claims is a dream-control device:
"As a twelve-year-old boy he demonstrated in the family circle an apparatus
of strange appearance, . . . and stated that with the aid of his apparatus it was
possible to evoke in anyone—by order—any dream" (1: 1).

His father challenges him by ordering a dream about the Battle of Pharsalus. When the boy's effort fails, he is about to punish Ivan. Then the mother

intercedes, faking the by now obligatory dream and arguing that it was misaddressed: "The mother . . . shouted: 'Don't beat him. . . . He made a mistake. . . . So what if you didn't dream? [It] . . . took off in another direction. . . . I, I saw the battle of Pharsalus! . . .' 'Don't lie,' said the director."

The father denounces her and whips Ivan, only to discover that someone (the maid Frosia) did have the misaddressed dream; later on, he dreams it himself.

The similarities with the Khvorob'ev story are striking, especially in the idiosyncratic motif of 'misaddressed dream.' Given the close chronological, thematic, and stylistic ties between the two works (as well as personal ones between their authors), one is inclined to suppose direct borrowing.

An interesting parallel/problem is also offered by the provocateurial child figure. The father, a stern school principal, teacher of Latin, guardian of 'right dreaming,' and enforcer of order, makes a plausible Inquisitor; the mother, a Woman; and the little Vania, a child Protagonist on a Quest. As for the role reversal in Dream Manipulation (the protagonist manipulates the Inquisitor), it constitutes an original but legitimate variation on the masterplot: it combines the protagonist's familiar attempts at Countermanipulation (as in Zamiatin, Bradbury, and Burgess) with the duplication by the Provocateurs of the state's machinery with their own mock structures (as in Bender's Office for the Collection of Horns and Hoofs versus The Hercules and in Ivan's Ophelia versus Chetvertak [the Two Bits diner]). Thus, the protagonist acquires some features of the Provocateur. An additional twist projects this combination into the protagonist's childhood, endowing it with some prankish plausibility.

The Score

The manifold structure, analyzed above voice by voice, so to speak, can be summarized now as an integral whole in a five-column table (see Appendix). Each column is filled out in its own metalanguage, that is, features motifs that are characteristic of the corresponding corpus of texts as variations on the dominant theme of that corpus.

Column 1 labels the events in terms of Bender's 'desacralizing behavior,' invariant in both novels. The second column rewrites the same material as a generic literary dream, centering on the opposition 'dreams versus reality,' and also provides actual subtexts. In the next column, the episode is categorized as a case of 'ambivalent conformism,' a theme varied throughout Ilf and Petrov's works. Column 4 uses the archetypal motifs and character roles of dystopia to chronicle 'an individual's quest in the totalitarian world,' and the last column lists the typical means of 'dream control,' elaborated in modern dystopian writing and earlier texts. (Incidentally, the contents of columns 2 and 5 could each be split into abstract generic features and concrete subtextual references, yielding a sevenfold description and underscoring the arbitrariness of code counts.)

The five codes (columns) are in varying degrees extrinsic to the episode itself and variously overlap with one another. The first represents the macroplot of the entire Bender saga; the second, the memory of the episode's traditional genre; the third, an invariant of the authors' oeuvre; the fourth, the masterplot of a modern genre; and the fifth, an original cross between the memory of the old genre and the demands of the new one. It is this modernist conversion, or rereading, of the tradition that constitutes the innovative crux of the episode, resolving the issue emblematically posed by the chapter's title ("A Genre in Crisis").

This central effect is supported by the episode's entire structure. Indeed, the five components of its reading form a remarkably coherent cluster, as if they "naturally" belonged together. Bender (column 1) sets the general ambiguous-parodic tone, spoofing the episodic character's fixation on personal dreams (column 2), which are, of course, least susceptible to adaptation. The adaptation game (column 3) is the authors' version of life in a dystopia (column 4), where even dreams are subject to control (column 5). In its turn, the new dream genre (column 5) is only a transformation of the old one (column 2) and has prophetic subtexts in Russian literature (column 5). It is this particular well-motivated clustering of voices, which overdetermine and naturalize each other, that can be said to define the theme of the episode— its single cumulative interpretation.

But the secret of the episode's effectiveness can be ascribed only in part to this general thematic outline and the potential for structural unity it generates. No less important are the original new combinations that successfully fuse the five components into a tight whole. Three such deep-level superpositions are pivotal:

—the one that confers on Bender the desacralizer (column 1) some inquisitorial functions (columns 4, 5), a possibility explored in Ehrenburg's *Jurenito*;

—the one that turns the traditional desired dreams (column 2) into dystopian ordered or obligatory dreams (column 5), in a radical inversion determined by Utopia's grim transformation into its opposite; and

—the one that reinterprets the familiar notions of dreams' divine origin and opposition to reality (column 2) as dream control and invasion of privacy (columns 4, 5), once the state has appropriated and relativized reality itself.

As a result of these equations, every one of the horizontal cross-sections of the "score" reads as an exercise in multiple discourse. Thus, for example, Khvorob'ev's lamentations (horizontal segment 3), which for Bender's purposes present the emotional involvement of his future dupe (column 1), are caused in terms of the dream genre by recurrent nightmares with a specific fixation and described in a jumble of corresponding quotations (column 2). The fixation on dubious czars serves as an ideological epitome of the episodic character's personal code (column 3), and the operatic source of quotations provides a stylistic expression of that code (a taste for ponderous old-regime clichés). In the dystopian context, however, this reads (column 4) as an ailing old man's links to the old culture (and its gods, especially if we take Khvorob'ev's "Avaunt! Don't touch me! Avaunt! [Chur menia, chur!]" in its literal, exorcist sense). Finally, from the perspective of New-dream (column 5), this segment is an early manifestation of obligatory dreams and futile attempts at countermanipulation by ordering (cf. segment 2), disguised so far as mere recurrent nightmares (column 2).

On the whole, the five-code format and the actual interpretation it helped formulate seem to have significant explanatory power and open the way for further analysis. In particular, one can proceed now to compare the contents of the columns with the repertoire of the corresponding genres (and other discourse types) to study the significant omissions from and additions to that repertoire. Also, expanding the format, one could try to account for the narrative rhetoric of each one of the five simultaneously unfolding vertical subplots, the artistic economy of horizontal combinations, and the overall strategy of the score's polyphonic development. Such an expressive analysis would have to take into consideration the immediate wider context of the chapter as a whole, whose other episode also involves the problematic of official art (see "Ilf and Petrov and Pluralist Reading," this chapter).

Premising these and similar avenues of study on the proposed format should not exclude the possibility of modifying or revising it. The format implements an approach that envisages intertexts as a given text's links to 'clusters of relevant features'[16] through the intermediary of which the other texts (e.g., *Village of Stepanchikovo*) are actually or potentially invoked. The cluster principle is supposed to limit the unbridled reading into the text of just any meanings. But there is no reason why the list of relevant planes / codes / contexts should not vary from text to text or why the particular set applied to a text should not be expanded with additional plausible contexts. For instance, it would be interesting to see how our reading of the Khvorob'ev episode would be affected by the adduction of Kafka's *The Trial*.

The above presentation clearly aimed at and accordingly produced a rather unified interpretation, polyphonic in the musical, not Bakhtinian, sense. It seems to be in agreement with the purport and tenor of Ilf and Petrov's writing and certainly with my theoretical preferences. These latter call for as much thematic integration as the text and its contexts will accommodate and admitting disparate pluralism only where the different voices can be shown to defy reconciliation effectively. This is a far cry from insisting on one right format and one right reading—something one would hardly think of doing in a chapter devoted to the horrors of "dreaming right."

Appendix

TABLE

The table that begins overleaf presents a series of passages from chapter 8, "A Genre in Crisis," of *The Golden Calf*. The arrangement of elements and their meanings are explained in text, pp.259–62.

SUMMARIES OF SIX NEWDREAM SUBPLOTS

1. Zamiatin, *We*. 'Dreams' are a symptom of the protagonist's infatuation with the woman, who comes from "the land of dreams" because she is "incalculable." "He never saw dreams before" and now dreams some "mortally sweet horror." While "not to sleep is criminal," "dreaming is a serious mental disease," the "ancient disease of dream seeing," along with such diseases as soul and fancy. Dreams are associated with the Ancient House (Zamiatin's coinage!), the "delirious world of the ancients," and the protagonist's diary records, which he calls "absurd dreams" resembling "a fantastic novel." The "dream sickness" (*snobolezn'*) is finally cured by the obligatory surgical Operation of "extirpating the [center for] fancy."

2. Huxley, *Brave New World*. The system relies for repression on the spraying of soma, which tranquilizes people by plunging them into pleasant dreams, and soma pills are willingly taken by citizens at the slightest threat of facing life's problems. Another powerful dream technique is obligatory caste-specific hypnopaedia undergone at a tender age by everybody on an incubatorlike assembly line to ensure that members of each caste are completely satisfied with their place in society. The protagonist, Mr. Savage (!), who has bypassed hypnopaedia and avoids soma, is able to face the prospect of death, about which he thinks in terms of dreaming and in the words of the forbidden book: "To sleep. Perchance to dream."

3. Nabokov, *Invitation to a Beheading*. The protagonist is imprisoned from the beginning, and dreams, especially erotic ones, are forbidden: "The inmate should not have at all, or . . . immediately . . . suppress nocturnal dreams whose content might be incompatible with the . . . status of the prisoner,

(*continued on p. 268*)

The Golden Calf (chap. 8)	1. BENDER ACT Desacralization of a Mania
1. "Outside the city limits, . . . Ostap . . . beheld a crooked little log house with little windows reflecting the blue of the river . . . [and] a barn that seemed appropriate shelter for Antelope . . . [and] pondered upon the pretext for entering the little house and befriending its inhabitants."	Exploitation
2. "The door of the house burst open and out dashed an honorable gentleman" in his underwear and with the sideburns of a nineteenth-century privy councillor, who "mumbled . . . , stretching his hands to the rising sun: 'God! God! . . . The very same dreams!' . . ." Having circled his little house in a shuffle, "the strange gentleman . . . , sighing, 'I'll go and try again,' disappeared through the door. . . . Wait[ing for] . . . the results of [the] mysterious trial [proby]" did not take Ostap long.	Emotional Involvement, Recognition
3. "Backing out like Boris Godunov in the last act of Mussorgsky's opera, the old man stumbled out onto the porch. 'Avaunt! Don't touch me! Avaunt!' he exclaimed with Chaliapinesque intonations in his voice. 'That curs'd dream again!' "	Emotional Involvement
4. "The Grand Schemer . . . seized the owner of the sideburns in a mighty embrace." He declares his sympathy with the old man's plight and generously shares with him the monarchist dreams he invents on the spot and claims to have dreamed ("A melange. The sort of thing that the newspapers call 'News from Everywhere,' and in the cinemas, 'Topics of the Day,' . . . the Mikado's funeral, . . . the Anniversary of the Sushchevsk fire department . . . , His Majesty's entry into the city of Kostroma, . . . Count Frederiks, the Minister of the Court, if you know what I mean?").	Feigned Involvement, Recognition and Mimicry
5. The old man believes Bender, envies him, asks him in ("The walls were covered with portraits of gentlemen in formal attire, . . . officials in the Ministry of Public Instruction. The bed was in disorder, presenting convincing evidence that its owner spent there the most restless hours of his life") and tells him his story.	Emotional Involvement (through the end)
6. "Khvorob'ev hated Soviet power. He, who had once been the District Inspector of Schools, was flung to the depths of a chairmanship of the Methodological and Pedagogical Sector in the local Proletcult." "He shivered in disgust at the thought of the vulgar comrades, . . . shock brigades, . . . the word 'sector.' "	Hearing Out (here and on)
7. "Nor could his proud soul find any solace at home." There, too, are "the wall newspapers, [state] loans, socialist competition," conversations about "month-long campaigns for the benefit of children and about the social significance of the play *Armored Train 14-69*. On his lonely walks he was haunted by the same realia and slogans."	

LITERARY [D]REAMS [D]ream vs Reality	3. ADAPTATION Ambivalent Conformism	4. DYSTOPIA Individual vs New Order	5. "NEWDREAM" Dream Control
	Escape	Old House, Nature	
[R]ecurrent Nightmares, [G]rigorii, Divine Origin [a]nd Prayer	Personal Code (here and on)	Old and Ailing Man, Bed, Nature, Culture, God	Ordering Dreams (Gogol, Dostoevsky, Olesha)
[B]oris (Pushkin and [M]ussorgsky), Chaliapin [a]ctor), Fixation on [t]zars, Grigorii		Old and Ailing Man, Culture, God	Forbidden and Obligatory Dreams (Dostoevsky, Zamiatin, Olesha, Nabokov)
[I]nvented and Shared [D]reams		Inquisitor, Prostration and Embrace, Omniscience and Identification w/Hero	Faked Dreams (Dostoevsky, Bradbury, Olesha)
[S]leep and Dreams		Old House, Culture, Bed, Ailing Man	
[N]arrating Dreams [here and on)	Resistance, Compromise	Functionary, Ministry, Quest, Culture, Anti-Culture and Anti-Book	
[B]oris Godunov, [P]rince Igor	Escape, Resistance		

	1. BENDER ACT
The Golden Calf	Desacralization
(chap. 8)	of a Mania

8. "With disgust he managed to persuade the Commissariat of Education . . . to grant him an old-age pension . . . and retired outside the city, . . . and tried thinking of pleasant things: Te Deums on the occasion of some august person's nameday. . . . But his thoughts immediately jumped to something Soviet, unpleasant, . . . May Day, as well as November demonstrations, . . . [or] the biannual balancing of the Methodological sector's accounts."

9. " 'Soviet power took everything away from me. . . . But there is one sphere where the Bolsheviks cannot penetrate: the dreams that are sent down to us by God.' " But then he dreamed that "any minute now he was about to be expelled from [the sector's] governing body," and that he "was to be given an additional load [of social work]. . . . He wanted to run, but he couldn't."

10. "Khvorob'ev . . . woke up, . . . prayed to God, pointing out to him that there apparently had been a regrettable hitch, as a result of which a dream intended for a high-placed and trusted comrade was sent to a wrong address. As for him, Khvorob'ev, he would like to see His Majesty the Czar's issue from the Cathedral of the Assumption of the Holy Virgin. . . . But every night he was visited . . . by perfectly correct Soviet dreams. . . . The Soviet regime had invaded even the dreams of the monarchist."	Hearing Out

11. Bender offers to help. But he explains that, since, "as the saying goes, 'Existence determines [the nature of] consciousness,' therefore, inasmuch as you live in a Soviet land your dreams are bound to be Soviet." Khvorob'ev is " 'ready for anything. Let's say, if I can't have [the extreme right deputy of the Duma] Purishkevich, that's OK. Let me have at least Miliukov. He is at least a university man and a monarchist at heart. But, no! Just these Soviet Anti-Christs!' "	Feigned Involvement, Mockery

12. Bender mentions treatment " 'according to Freud. The dream itself is no problem. The main thing is to remove the cause of the dream . . . [i.e.,] the very existence of Soviet power. But, for the present, I cannot remove it. I simply haven't the time. . . . I have to . . . roll [my automobile] into your barn. As for the cause, . . . I'll remove it on my way back.' . . . 'So there is hope?' Khvorob'ev asked, shuffling after his . . . visitor."	Exploitation (here and on)

13. The action then switches to the chapter's other episode (with the artists), after which it returns to the painting of the car Antelope, followed by the team's departure, secret from Khvorob'ev. " 'I did not have the heart to awaken him. Perhaps . . . he is dreaming the long-awaited dream. . . .' But at that very minute . . . issued the heartrending sobs. . . . 'That very same dream! . . . God! God!' 'Apparently he did not dream of the Metropolitan . . . , but of an extended plenum of the literary group "The Smithy and the Manor." ' "	Emotional Involvement, Defeat

| . LITERARY DREAMS | 3. ADAPTATION | 4. DYSTOPIA | 5. "NEWDREAM" |
Dream vs Reality	Ambivalent Conformism	Individual vs New Order	Dream Control
	Conformity	Old House, Nature, Culture, Anti-Culture	
Divine Origin, Dreams and Reality, Desired and Actual Dreams, Grinev	Escape, Conformity	Irrational, God, Quest, Invasion of Privacy (here and on)	Dreams as Sanctuary (Gogol, Zamiatin, Nabokov)
Divine Origin and Prayer, Recurrent Nightmares, Desired and Actual Dreams	Resistance, Compromise, Conformity (here and on)		Misaddressed Dreams (Olesha), Forbidden and Obligatory Dreams, and Ordering Dreams (here and on)
Interpretation of Dreams, Desired Dreams	Compromise	Inquisitor, Omniscience, Apology of Regime, Anti-Book, Culture	Manipulation of Dreams
Dreams and Reality	Resistance	Quest, Book	Countermanipulation of Dreams (Dostoevsky, Olesha, Orwell, Burgess)
Desired Dreams vs. Recurrent Nightmares, Dreams and Reality, Grigorii	Escape, Personal Code, Conformity	Invasion of Privacy, Irrational, Anti-Book	Ordering Dreams, Forbidden and Obligatory Dreams

such as: . . . sexual intercourse with persons who in real life . . . would not suffer said individual to come near, which individual will therefore be considered . . . guilty of rape." Yet Cincinnatus has them anyway—an "ennobled . . . semi-reality, more genuine reality than our waking life." Besides, the boundary between dreams and reality is blurred throughout the text. Most likely, the entire cardboard world of the novel is a ghostly nightmare, complete with its stylized characters and the statue of Captain Somnus (in the Russian original, Sonnyi, lit. "Sleepy"), which crumbles at the end, while death will be an awakening to genuine life. The protagonist's dreams intertwine with his writing (of the book), and the modernist arbitrariness of the narrative as a whole reserves the status of indisputable reality only for Nabokov's text itself. The protagonist's emblematic alter ego is the butterfly napping in his cell and like his soul, successfully eluding the jailers.

4. Orwell, *1984*. "Doublethink" presupposes (metaphorical) centralized hypnosis and self-hypnosis. The protagonist, Winston Smith, even believes that his former wife's frigidity was caused by "the hypnotic power of the Party." People are often arrested for what they have said in their sleep; therefore, one "must not only think right; [one] must feel right, dream right." That is the conclusion to which the prostrate protagonist (having passed through the stage of failure to distinguish between dreams and reality) is driven in the end by his Inquisitor, who knows more about his dreams (in particular, about the fear of rats that is hidden but discernible in his nightmares) than the dreamer himself. The protagonist has a whole suite of dreams: the Inquisitor telling him in the dark that they will meet where there is no darkness; his drowning mother and sister and the guilt he feels toward them; his mother shielding his kid sister with a helpless but loving gesture; the wall of darkness behind which something terrible is hiding—rats, as becomes clear later; the Golden Meadow, which turns out to be the real scene of his first date with the woman. While in prison, he has a complex dream: all doubts are over, he has surrendered and is blissfully awaiting a bullet in his back; he believes he is in the prison's corridor but at the same time as if in a sunlit place, which becomes the Golden Meadow; the protagonist thinks of the woman he loves, calls her by name, and wakes up. His scream signals to the Inquisitor that deep down he still has not renounced himself and his lover; by unleashing rats on the protagonist's face, he induces him to wish to shield himself with the woman's body in a mental gesture opposite to his mother's and thus effectively to betray the woman, fall out of love with her and in love with Big Brother. In the end, Winston again blissfully dreams of the sunlit corridor of the prison and the expectation of the bullet, but without the sequel involving the Golden Meadow.

5. Bradbury, *Fahrenheit 451°*. The protagonist's wife spends a night on the borderline of sleeping and waking, washed over by oceans of sounds from her

headphones. She also inadvertently takes an overdose of sleeping pills. The protagonist has become a fireman "in his sleep," in the footsteps of his father and grandfather. As the protagonist switches off the TV "walls," addictively watched by his wife, they are compared to "the pale brows of sleeping giants, now empty of dreams." In the poem he reads (Matthew Arnold's "Dover Beach"), the world first resembles "a land of dreams, so various, so beautiful, so new," but turns out to have "neither joy, nor love, nor light, . . . nor help for pain," as "ignorant armies clash by night." Thus, all major threads of the plot converge on a 'book' about dreams. Dreams are also invoked by the Inquisitor as he tries to win the protagonist over by claiming to have dreamed of gaining the upper hand in a duel fought with literary quotations. The protagonist listens to him literally with one ear while lending the other to the Professor (Old Man and Book), who supplies him with counterarguments through a microreceiver. The professor also plans to use this radio for the hypnopaedic teaching of culture, in a rare instance of an AntiState alliance of technology with dreams and books. Toward the end, the protagonist dreams of an idyllic farm, Nature, and the beautiful woman.

6. Burgess, *A Clockwork Orange*. The protagonist repeatedly encounters his Inquisitors while bedridden or strapped into the armchair custom-designed for the brainwashing operation—a grotesque hybrid of Coercion, Medical Treatment, Art, and Dreaming. Repeated obligatory viewing (with eyelids fixed open) of films about violence, to Beethoven's Ninth Symphony and in combination with an emetic, effectively suppresses the protagonist's aggressive, sexual, and aesthetic impulses. The reeducation's success is demonstrated in a scene where the tamed protagonist is humiliated in front of the watching public. From these horrors he escapes into a "sleep . . . with no dreams at all" and wants "to snuff it . . . without pain." In fact, his dreams (among them, those shared with his father) had actually forecast trouble, and in two prophetic nightmares dreaming was joined by Music, which had turned against him. The link between dreams and art is made quite explicit: the protagonist defines a dream as "a film inside your gulliver [head], except that it is as though you could . . . be part of it," but redreaming a sequence from the film that had "cured" him makes him sick. Another violation of his privacy is perpetrated with the help of music, which "drag[s him] out of . . . sleep" and pushes him to suicide. Equally unceremonious is the reverse treatment with hypnopaedia. The protagonist experiences it in his sleep as a sort of internal washing out and then filling up, after which he resumes his healthily aggressive dreams and love of "the glorious Ninth of Ludwig van."

TEN

The Codes and Contexts of Platonov's "Fro"

U nlike that of the preceding chapter, our present subject is a self-contained entity—a specimen of consummate storytelling.

"Fro" was written and published in 1936, at the height of literary reaction, in an issue of the semischolarly *Literaturnyi kritik* (no. 8) under the Aesopian guise of providing material for literary analysis. It was largely spared the usual official anathema reserved for Platonov's work and has been repeatedly reprinted and anthologized ever since the start of the post-Stalin thaw. In the 1980s, its fame was eclipsed, in part because of its previous acceptability, by texts that had been banned because of their greater ideological and stylistic daring, such as "Doubting Makar" (1929), *The Foundation Pit* (1930), and *Chevengur* (1972 [1929?]).[1]

We will begin with an analysis of "Fro"'s internal structure, to be complemented later by several contextualizations. In fact, even close reading itself[2] is not so exclusively intrinsic as is usually and uncritically assumed. It too is a contextualizing operation, albeit an unspecific and limited one: unspecific in the sense that it reads the text according to the most universal, generic codes of literary reception, in the context, so to speak, of literature as a whole; limited because in its textual comparisons it deals with various components of the text (its parts, characters, planes, etc.) rather than external "co-texts."

Structure

The plot of "Fro" is, briefly, as follows:

The heroine, Efrosin'ia (or Frosia [i.e., Frossie] or Fro), missing her husband, who has left for a construction project in the Soviet Far East, engages in all kinds of magic to get him back. She tries to commune with the train that "would have met the express rushing on to the Far East . . . and been close to her husband after her," and when this fails, she joins the night shift "helping the transportation system" (*transportu pomogat'*) to establish symbolic contact with the traveling Fedor. She gets an amorous telegram from him, sniffs and puts away a strand of his hair, pours her yearning for him into the notes she takes in the classes in railroad communication, from which she then drops out: "In any event, science had become incomprehensible. . . . She lived at home, . . . fearing the mailman might bring and take Fedor's letter back" in her absence. To ensure direct access to the mail, she seeks a job at the post office; once in possession of Fedor's address, she gets her father to wire him that she is dying. Thus, having moved from a passive expectation and solicitation of news about her husband to more active measures and finally to outright manipulation of means of communication, Fro succeeds in performing a miracle: a train brings Fedor back. But after a two-week interlude he leaves for an even remoter spot ("to the Far East . . . even to China"), and Fro has to settle for the company of the little neighbor boy playing the harmonica.

Underlying the story are key value oppositions that are mediated in the denouement.

OPPOSITIONS: 'DISTANCE/CLOSENESS,' 'IRON/SOUL'

Both protagonists are enthralled by "the distance" (*dal'*), each with his own: the husband with the utopia of Revolution and Socialist production, the wife with her love for the ever-distant husband. 'Distance' is also the stuff her father Nefed's life is made of; he is a retired locomotive engineer who has reregistered for occasional service and is always either out driving a train or waiting for a call—at home or by the tracks, "his eyes bright with tears, watching the trains."

Fedor's departure makes Nefed think of the train's movement and itinerary, while at the moment of Fedor's dramatic return the father's attention is focused on the expert way "the engineer gently, tenderly put on the brake. Watching this thing, Nefed shed a tear, even forgetting the reason he had come." Yet he "liked to be with his daughter or with someone when a locomotive was not occupying all his thoughts and feelings." He was especially lonely since his retirement and the death of his wife, who used to "long for him," as she had been a "little bourgeois housewife" (*meshchanka*), one of "those alright women"; Frossie thinks she is different, but essentially resembles her.

But when her father attempts closeness, Fro pushes him away, obsessed with her distant love in a pattern that is recurrent in the story: 'One lonely person gravitates to another, that other, to somebody or something else, and so on.' Played in a sublime key between husband and wife, the pattern is replicated semi-farcically between father and daughter; in one scene, Nefed, rejected by Fro, "opened the oven door [and] put his head inside, weeping into the dish of macaroni," and then wiped his face with a straw broom.

In the dance episode at the club, the same pattern is deployed twice.

At first the partner pressed close to Frossie and insisted that she was a familiar person, the daughter of the engineer he knew, but "this hidden caress did not excite her, she loved her distant man" and claimed she was not Frossie, but "Fro! . . . not Russian . . . certainly not!" Later, however, she "leaned obliviously on his chest" and with the pressure of her head opening his shirtfront [*shirinka*, which also happens to mean "(pants') fly"], "moistened [with her tears] the "virile hair" on his chest, and it was now his turn to be afraid that his fiancée "might maim him for the intimacy [or "closeness," *blizost'*] with this Fro."

Similar 'triangular' relations are at play elsewhere in the plot—for example, in the story of Natasha Bukova.

Variations on the same theme are instanced by the numerous cases of Fro's 'failed contact' with various minor characters—for example, with the railroad station porter and cleaner; with Natasha, of whom she loses sight; with Natasha's husband, the lonely night watchman of "the storehouse—an official place." At one point Fro is said to have "fallen asleep alone, like an orphan." The sense of orphanhood also pervades the episodes involving the fourth major character, the little neighbor boy. "In her head the monotonous little song of his harmonica" sounded as follows: "Mother's washing, father's working, . . . it is lonely, lonely here." The overall impression created by the story is one of disparateness, gaping emptiness, the absence of a single center in which the characters fixated on their separate distant objects of desire might come together.

For the sake of 'distant values,' the characters readily sacrifice even the needs of their own bodies.

> Fedor "was uncannily able to sleep amid noise, to eat any food with complete indifference to whether it was tasty or tasteless," and "he had never had his photograph taken after childhood, for he was uninterested in himself and did not believe in the significance of his own face." Fro's father, while longing for locomotives, would forget about food, but "was afraid of having to go out on an empty stomach, unfueled. . . . He was careful of . . . his strength and digestion, for in his own estimation he was the mainstay of the railroad, a steel-hardened cadre." Similarly, Fro, once she concentrates on "longing for [her] husband here at home," stops caring for her personal hygiene, beauty, and sustenance; moreover, even when Fedor comes back, she cooks "careless of the taste . . . so as not to waste time on the material, irrelevant side of their love."

The central invariant underlying all these tensions is not strictly spatial, involving as it does an entire set of oppositions, such as:

distant	close, nearby, intimate
abstract	concrete
general, communal	individual, private
future	present
reason	feeling
technology	nature
machine	human
soul	body
masculine	feminine
adult	childlike

In each character these oppositions are realized in different, sometimes paradoxical ways. The men are obsessed with 'distance,' which for them is represented by geographical notions (the Far East, "the Southern Soviet China"), mileage figures, transportation terminology ("local service"), and scientific and philosophical concepts ("ionized air," "stratosphere," "the ancient dream of heaven").

But these 'male abstractions' have concrete and tangible counterparts, creating a mediational interplay of 'distance' and 'closeness' based on the topical 'man-machine' metaphor of the times.

> The father happily "hugged . . . the boiler, as the belly of the entire working mankind." Fedor "felt [the machines] with the precision of his own flesh. He

animated everything that he touched with his hands or his thought, . . . sensing directly . . . the suffering patient resistance of machines' bodily metal." He "presented to her the lively workings of the mysterious objects that for her were dead and the secret quality of their meticulous calculation by virtue of which machines live . . . ; she began to understand them and to cherish them in her mind like in her soul. . . . Embracing his wife, . . . Fedor himself turned into a microfarad or an eddy current. Frossie could almost see what before she . . . could not understand. They were objects as simple, natural and attractive as the motley grass in the fields."

Despite this successful, literally speaking, 'naturalization' of inanimate machines (which join in the loving embrace of husband and wife), the clash of values is unmistakable. Fro's version of 'distance' is her romantic yet quite earthly love for the absent husband, her leitmotif is 'an enamored soul.'

From its first occurrence in the text, 'soul' is opposed to 'iron' (Fro "ran her finger over the iron casting of the mailbox—it was strong, nobody's soul in a letter would be lost in it") and other 'male values' (e.g., Fedor's dreams about "a radical transformation of man's pathetic soul"). At first, Fro tries to master men's metallic code: she would entrust her soul to the mailbox, takes a course in railroad signalization, turns to "iron shovels," and addresses passing trains. But what she really needs is "for there to linger and grow inside her ordinary, dull soul a second cherished life," that is, sexual love and its product, a child, while the "iron cores [lit. "hearts," *serdechniki*] grew barren in her heart," making her quit the courses. Attempts at her reeducation will be renewed later, but only for the short duration of Fedor's stay and in a distinctly "dreamative" mood.

At 'close' range, soul is represented by the heart, which "bears no postponement" in pleasure because it is part of the 'body.'

The first reference to Fro in the text is a close-up view of her lower half. " 'Move aside, citizen[ness],' said the porter to the two lonely plump legs." This emblematic sentence introduces the motifs of 'closeness,' 'corporeality,' and 'social rejection.' Later, Fro's legs/feet are associated directly with the heart and sex: "Frossie . . . worked, hurrying to fatigue her feet in order to tire out her anguished heart." Her job provokes the addressees to ask gynecological questions and propose marriage.

Another 'close' manifestation of the soul is respiratory—physical and spiritual at the same time (additionally naturalized by the felicitous etymological-paronomastic affinities of *dukh, dusha, dyshat', dykhanie, vozdukh*).

The 'soul-breathing-air' cluster permeates such high points of the narrative as the shoveling in the slag pit ("breathing was not easy . . . but in her soul she felt better"; "the women . . . stopped to rest and breathe the air"), Fro's fainting ("breathing in her chest contracted . . . it was hard to bear her disappearing, empty breathing"), and the tragifarcical text of the telegram ("Frossie dying brink of death complication respiratory tract").

The heroine literally suffocates in the iron world.

The only succor she finds in her surroundings comes from the land-scape, which she negotiates in a natural way, on foot (and that with a heavy mailbag), unlike the two men in her life, who ride trains.[3] Both Fro and the narrator keep combining this human-scale percep-tion of 'the distance' with the men's industrial perspective, as, for instance, in the picture of the "free night, lit by stars and electricity," that she watches from the slag pit or in the description of the train with which she tries to communicate; it is seen through her eyes yet couched in 'masculine' terms: "The locomotive performed on cut-off steam, the engine battled to cover the space." The word 'space' (*pro-stranstvo*) is one of the story's *loci communes* (and a Platonov favorite), literally a meeting ground for the characters, who are so similar in their centrifugality and craving for broad horizons.

Fro's landscape surroundings—wind, sun, stars, sky, fields, grass, pine trees, cows, birds, grasshoppers—form her own 'distance,' re-mote yet intimate.

Nature warms Fro's heart and blood, sings to her, and promises "happiness, which from the outside penetrates inside the person." At a low point in the plot, the pathetic semi-industrial landscape anthropomorphically echoes the heroine's emotional state: "There grew some kind of grass, small, stiff, mean. Frossie . . . stood in anguish amid this petty world of undernourished grass, from where there seemed to stretch a distance of two kilometers to the stars" (i.e., they were not too far away, but were unattainable, and, moreover, the mileage is given, as in the male code). Fro faints in an urban environment and recovers only after "running off into the fields."

MEDIATORS: 'PEOPLE,' 'MUSIC,' 'CHILDHOOD'

Reaching out for support, Fro explores a wide range of social con-tacts. On the most abstract level, she joins her husband in addressing the impersonal 'humankind,' yet she needs an immediate, 'close' con-firmation of such a distant pledge: "Having talked and talked, they moved into each other's arms—they wanted to be happy at once, that very moment, before their future concentrated effort would yield results for their own personal and universal happiness."

On the middle scale, Fro enjoys the contacts she has with the work crew, at the club, and at the courses, which briefly relieve her "from happiness and anguish"; "love slept peacefully in her heart," letting her "listen to the music and hold others by the hand." More intimate still are her sisterly ties with Natasha (and Fro's 'twin,' "the other Efrosin'ia") and the potentially amorous contacts at the dance and on the mail delivery beat.

> "Some even offered her wine or a bite," and "a man who got the journal *Red Virgin Soil* proposed marriage," as a collectivist measure: "This is a journal, it comes out edited by an editorial board, they are . . . a group, not just one person, and there will be two of us, as well! But an unmarried girl, what good is that—somebody lonely, practically antisocial!"[4]

All these bonds, however, come to naught, often undermined by the characteristic 'figure of uncertainty':

> Marriage is proposed "on an experimental basis—let's see what happens"; similarly, Fedor "hoped that machines would transform the world to the greater welfare and delight of mankind, or for some such reason; his wife did not know what exactly." At the end, Fedor is not expected back until he "has all his work done. . . . I don't know . . . communism—isn't it—or something like that—whatever comes up!"

The culmination of Fro's unattachedness is marked by her words "Oh, Fro, Fro, if only somebody hugged you!" which combine the very personal angle ("Fro," "you") with an utterly impersonal one ("somebody"). It is after this that her brief and inconclusive reunion with Fedor takes place, which is then followed by the meeting with the little musician.

In fact, music functions from the story's start as a salutary mediator between the distant and the nearby, soul and body, nature and culture.

> "While dancing, Fro's . . . blood was roused by the tune" (as on other occasions by the sun), "her breathing coming fast." Later, this role is taken over by the sounds of nature: birdsong, the chirrup of crickets, the creaking of pine trees, and the tunes played on the boy's harmonica.

The music of nature and that of the little boy are linked in several ways: through consistent textual contiguity; through the similarity of

Fro's responses to the two; by direct association in the text; and by the shared seme of 'breathing, air, wind instrument.'

> The musical theme is introduced in the very first paragraph, together with its industrial opposite ("The locomotive . . . began to sing a song of parting"). This paradoxical link is soon spoofed in the scene at the club (the amateur comedians' singing: " 'Toot-toot-toot'—a locomotive") and subverted by the narrator's double pun (Fro forgets the "upper harmonics of current" and the "iron cores" [lit. hearts] for the boy's harmonica and her heart's troubles). The motif of the boy's piping accompanies Fro's emotional experiences in a dotted pattern, is dramatized through its conspicuous absence ("Why don't you play?"), and makes a definitive comeback at the moment of Fro's lonely awakening. The musical seme symbolically accompanies even Fro's fainting: "She cried out on a high, singing note."

Music is opposed to the 'male' means of communication: transportation, electrical signals, mail and telegraph, and the "cleverly worded sentences" that Fro had asked Fedor to teach her but then "saw through herself."[5] Music is capable of affecting body and soul directly. It is understood without words (the burden of the harmonica tune is immediately clear to Fro) and even partakes of corporeality, as the boy "wiped his music on the hem of his shirt" in a child's response to the false physicality of the male world as it were (cf. the soul in the iron mailbox, etc.).

The little boy bears a pointed resemblance to Fedor's childhood photo.

> Fedor: "In the yellowed photograph there stood a little boy with an infant's large head and wearing a poor shirt and cheap pants, barefoot; behind him grew magical trees, and in the distance there were a fountain and a palace. The little boy looked out attentively into a world as yet little known to him, without noticing the beautiful life in the photographer's cloth behind him. The beautiful life was within the boy himself with his broad, inspired and shy face, who held a green sprig instead of a toy and touched the ground with his trusting bare feet."
>
> The boy: "A log lay near the barn, and on it sat the barefoot little boy with a child's large head, playing on his lip music [gubnoi muzyke]."

Both are "little boys" with "large heads," "barefoot," and in touch with immediate, 'nearby,' nature (grass, twig, log). As a child, Fedor was attentive to himself and the world, uninterested in toys and magical settings. Similarly, the little musician "had not yet chosen some one thing in the entire world as the object of his eternal love; his heart beat empty and free, without stealing anything for itself alone." 'Emptiness and freedom' clearly oppose the little boy to the one-dimensional fixations of the adults.

> The father, "after having lived four days at liberty" (i.e., in retirement), returned to the locomotives. Fro, thanks to the collective work in the slag pit, "saw the huge, free night," and at the club she was "free from happiness and anguish"; but the sense of freedom gradually disappeared, while her mail carrier's experience showed that "nowhere did life have emptiness or peace."

In opting for the company of the little boy and renouncing her claims on the hopelessly remote Fedor, Fro chooses 'closeness' over 'distance.' Or, rather, she succeeds in mediating between these opposites. In a passage written in free indirect speech, fusing the narrator's voice with the heroine's, Fro (whose name at this point reverts to Frossie!) is said to "know how to turn two kopeks into two rubles." Fabulaically, this closure is matched by her eventual consent to replace Fedor with somebody or something else—after a series of rejections (of the father, courses, work, other men and women).

The mediation achieved in the finale works on several levels.

> Music, which until now was heard, as it were, from on high and from nature, comes down to the ground level ("The harmonica was not playing upstairs") and enters the room. Instead of abstract mankind and the yellowed photograph of the ideal husband, Fro is visited by their living incarnation in the person of the little boy (he "probably was that mankind about which Fedor used to talk to her in so many nice words"). By "taking the child's hands in hers," Fro repeats the gesture that had freed her from her longing for Fedor and gave her a sense of kinship with other people. Moreover, the union with the little orphanlike boy (a double, in this respect, of her father and herself) symbolizes a reconciliation between parents and children (earlier the father is said to "know that children are our enemies").

Figuratively, this union also stands for the idea of childbearing, which pervades the narrative.

> Thus, the foreman expected some of the women "to go dancing to the club, [others], to conceive babies." The father, taken aback by Fro's coldness, wondered: "How did I ever conceive her with my wife?" Fro walked around "carrying the heavy bag on her belly, like a pregnant woman," and while making love to Fedor, she "wanted to have children, she would raise them, they would grow up and finish the cause of their father, of communism and science."

Yet the closure remains unstable and problematic.

"Fro left her father and went into her room," so that both the husband and the father (entrusted by Fedor with taking care of Fro) are included in the finale only through the intermediary of the little boy. Especially ambiguous is the status of the husband ("Farewell, Fedor! You'll come back").

But the boy's presence is also temporary; his parents are away only during working hours. What is more, his symbolic alliance with Fro has incestuous overtones:

He resembles the husband he has now replaced. His childishness calls to mind the tune "My Baby" (!) to which Fro danced with the dispatcher. Finally, the closing mise-en-scène has a bedroom aura: Frossie, wearing a nightgown, "let the visitor in, sat down on the floor in front of him, and took his hand in hers."

Such is the overall thematic balance, precarious but quite distinctly spelled out, of the story's major voices and valorizations. Turning now to the extrinsic presences enlisted into this internal dialogue, I will divide them into two main groups—classical and contemporary.

Intertexts: Classical

In terms of the formalist, as well as Bloomian, metaphors of literary power play, the "grandfatherly" voices, that is, the remote classical intertexts, exert a less domineering pressure (that is to be contested by the nascent original discourse) than do the more immediate "fatherly" (and "elder-brotherly") contexts. The distant forebears are capable of providing authoritative support, even though they are subjected to willfully selective use and conversion. To cite an example from a previous chapter, the persuasive energy "After the Ball" draws from its archaic intertext outweighs by far the pagan view of marriage inherent in that substratum and pointedly revised by Tolstoy.

We will concentrate on two such intertexts of "Fro": one classical in the sense of the grand nineteenth-century tradition, the other in the sense of the universal folkloric-mythological stock. In each case, we choose one intertext from among several. Thus, in the Russian tradition, along with the Chekhov connection ("The Darling"), one could explore a Bunin text[6] and probably some others; the same goes for the mythological substrata.

A PROTOTYPE: "THE DARLING" (1899)

Essentially, "Fro" can be seen as a reworking of "Darling" (Chalmaev 1984: 182), especially if we discount the farcical tripling of the male partner by Chekhov.

In both cases, the man keeps going away. The heroine, from whose perspective the third-person narrative is told, longs for him, is attached to him, his work and ideas. In the end, she transfers her fixation to somebody else's son ("as though the boy had been her own child" [Chekhov 1979: 219]).

In "The Darling," the heroine's links to her home are opposed to the 'distant' orientation of her male partners.

They go away on business or to the other world. For Olenka, the boy's leaving for school is "as though he were about to set off on a long journey." The links to 'the distance' are colored negatively and rely on mail (e.g., the letters from the first husband, the telegram about his "funneral" [khokhorony], the fear of a telegram spelling the boy's recall). The two husbands' deaths bring to mind the (telegraphically faked) death of Fro and Fedor's "almost irrevocable" departure.

Moreover, like Fro,

Olenka lives with her father (whom she "had loved"), dreams of having children and "a love that would absorb her whole soul, . . . and would warm her old blood." Without the men, she cannot eat or sleep properly and feels "like a complete orphan." She too is associated with nature (represented, at the lowest point in the plot, by an empty courtyard and "wormwood") and music.

To generalize, the two stories share an ambiguous mediation between the 'natural female emptiness' and the 'cultural male element' needed to 'fill' it.

In "Fro," the ambiguity—is this a story of an individualist reeducated or of utopianism tested by the case of a concrete human being?—may have been a deliberate Aesopian ploy. Interestingly, somewhat similar divergences in reading greeted "The Darling," pitting its great author against its great reader and admirer Leo Tolstoy. According to Tolstoy, Chekhov "wanted to show what a woman should not be like," but despite his authorial intentions, "the Darling's soul is not funny but saintly, marvelous, for its ability to give all of its being to those she loves."[7] In both cases, the opposing interpretations are determined by the way the quandary of a 'female soul' in the 'male world' is dramatized by the exaggerated departures of the hero and the exaggerated demands of the heroine.

Fro wanted to steal Fedor for herself alone and "was sad that she was only a woman and could not feel like a microfarad." "The Darling" is a classical precedent for such an overidentification with the male partner. Olenka's addiction to her men's "opinions" involves a breakdown of interpersonal boundaries, subtly expressed by the play with the meaning of the story's pivotal "we" phrase.

> Olenka referred to her first two husbands as "Vanichka (resp. Vassichka) and I" (in Russian, lit. "we with Vanichka/Vassichka") only to be rebutted by her third partner (Volodichka), who insisted on the exclusive use of the first-person plural: "When we veterinary surgeons are talking among ourselves, please don't put your word in."

At a deeper level, the deaths of her two husbands and the centrifugal tendencies of the two subsequent partners (the veterinarian and his son) may be construed as resulting from the heroine's psychological vampirism. Note that while "Olenka grew stouter, and was always beaming with satisfaction, . . . Kukin grew thinner and yellower, and complained of terrible losses, although . . . he was not doing badly at all."

Incidentally, Olenka's plumpness (cf. Fro's plump legs) reifies the idea of the 'soul's corporeality.' The word *dusha*, "soul," recurs in the text several times, and the heroine's title nickname (Dushechka, a somewhat corny term of endearment, literally means "Soulie") is consistently associated with her healthy physicality and sexual attractiveness.

> Remarkably, Tolstoy, who punningly emphasized "the Soulie's soul" (*dushu Dushechki*), expurgated from his "popularized" redaction of the story (Tolstoy 1906, 1: 421–33) the two sentences that associate the heroine's soulful nickname with her curves: (1) "And when he had a closer view of her neck and her plump, fine shoulders, he threw up his hands, and said: 'You darling!' "; (2) "Men thought, 'Yes, not half bad!' "[8]

Parallels with "Fro" include even such details as holding hands with women. "Ladies could not refrain from seizing her hand, . . . exclaiming, 'You darling!' " (Tolstoy apparently had no problem with this.)

To what use, then, did Platonov put the Chekhovian subtext? While obviously drawing on its classical prestige as well as ambiguity, he certainly "rewrote" it in a new key. Not only did he modernize the story in several ways, but he definitely reinforced the narratorial identification with the heroine, tilting the balance, so to speak, in the direction of Tolstoy's reading. The dynamics of such a conversion will become clearer in light of the intertextualizations that follow.

AN ARCHETYPE: PSYCHE

The correspondent who informed Chekhov of Tolstoy's reader response to "The Darling" had slightly distorted the title, highlighting by his slip the story's implicit link to the eighteenth-century narrative poem by I. Bogdanovich "Dushen'ka."[9] Links with that poem —a rococo version of the Apuleius legend of "Cupid and Psyche" (borrowed through La Fontaine's *Psyché*)—place "Fro" in a new, mythological context. On Russian soil, it includes a group of Finist folktales: "Peryshko Finista iasna sokola" (The feather of Finist the bright falcon; Afanas'ev 1957, 2: 236–46, nos. 234–35) and its literary counterpart, "The Scarlet Flower" ("Alen'kii tsvetochek," as retold by S. T. Aksakov in his fictionalized memoirs of childhood, 1983 [1856]).

Platonov's mythopoeticity, as well as his use of folkloric style, has attracted the attention of critics—for example, S. Zalygin (1971) and N. Poltavtseva (1981). B. Paramonov (1987) has proposed Penelope as the master archetype of his oeuvre; E. Naiman privileges the Promethean mytheme (1987) and connects "Fro" with Orpheus (1988: 345); and S. Semenova (1988), discussing Platonov's 'soul' theme, mentions "the sufferings of the Russian psyche." Platonov's use of the Psyche myth, however, has not yet been explored.

> Incidentally, the link may have been quite deliberate. Sometimes Platonov overtly stressed his mythological sources; for instance, in "Aphrodite" (1945), a story considered cognate to "Fro." The case for "Fro" is strengthened by the circumstantial evidence of Platonov's interest in both the "Finist" tale (see his literary version [1970 (1947): 143–69]) and Apuleius's "Cupid and Psyche" (mentioned in his letter to his wife, April 5, 1934; see Platonov 1988: 560).

But irrespective of any evidence of borrowing, the Psyche myth seems typologically relevant to "Fro," and that is what I will focus on.

In folkloristic terms, this group of plots comes under tale type 425 in the Aarne-Thompson classification: "the search for the lost husband" (Thompson 1977: 98ff.), comprising the motifs of 'forgotten bride,' 'disobedient wife,' 'disenchanting the supernatural/monster husband,' and some others. On a deeper level, this archaic cluster

reflects the fear of exogamous marriage: the heroine is shown to over-
estimate her kinship ties (e.g., by her sisters, i.e., her other selves,
plotting against the marriage) and her own importance (e.g., beauty),
to underestimate the husband (seen as a monster), and to aim at a normalization of the marriage (through disenchantment). Let us briefly
state the common denominator, or archeplot, of this group of texts.

The *initial situation* includes the father and three daughters; the two elder ones
are either unmarried or have ordinary husbands. The younger daughter, the
father's favorite, is famous for her beauty, which brings her admirers but not
bridegrooms, and the envy of rivals (the sisters, Venus herself).

The heroine's *acquaintance* with her future husband either takes place directly (e.g., she is visited by the invisible Cupid, who is sent by Venus to marry
her off to a monster but falls in love with her) or is implicit in the gift that she
orders, which includes the bridegroom's attribute (a feather, a red flower) and
is obtained by the father in exchange for the promise of his daughter's hand.

The *engagement* is arranged by the father with the daughter's consent (overt
or covert). The bride either stays with her father and sisters and is visited there
by the bridegroom, who flies in, summoned by his attribute (displayed on
the windowsill), or she departs for the bridegroom's palace in a funerallike
ritual, performed by magic means (e.g., by being left at a mountaintop, whence
Zephyrus softly lowers her into the other kingdom).

In this *preliminary marriage*, the heroine enjoys the husband's love, company, and wealth, despite his supernatural / monstrous status (as a prince,
visible only at night and only to his bride, who flies away as a falcon at
daybreak, or the handsome but invisible Cupid, allegedly a monster).

The bride's *happiness is destroyed* by her envious sisters, who make use of
some condition included in the marriage contract (by arousing her mistrustful
curiosity, they get her to break the vow not to look at the husband, and as a
drop of lamp oil awakens him, he flies away; by fitting out her window with
sharp nails, they injure the falcon, who, unable to get in, disappears, leaving
feathers / blood [cf. his attributes] on the nails; by keeping the heroine from
returning to her husband or tampering with the clock, they ensure a delay that
proves almost fatal to the husband).

The search begins as, left alone (often in the fields), the heroine longs for
her husband, finds out (from the wind or the stars; from some itinerant donors,
e.g., Baba-Iaga or Ceres) where to look for him, and obtains magical means.
She must wear out three pairs of iron shoes and pass three tests stipulated by
a woman who represents an alien tribe and possesses the lost husband (by
Venus, the future mother-in-law; by the hero's new wife).

The decisive (third) test entails overcoming a *death sleep*. In "Cupid and
Psyche," the heroine, while procuring the secret of beauty from Proserpine,
mistress of the nether world, violates an interdiction (she uses the secret for her-

self) and is plunged into a deadly sleep (the secret of beauty is sleep), but Cupid comes in time to save her. In the three Afanas'ev tales, the heroine exchanges her magic objects for nights with the lost husband. Twice the new wife puts him to sleep, but the third time around the heroine succeeds in waking him up, and he recognizes her.

After the reunion, the spouses leave the house of the women rivals, the bridegroom is disenchanted or released from invisibility, the marriage is accepted by its opponents (the sisters, Venus), the definitive wedding takes place, and the heroine acquires new attributes (rich clothes, immortality).

In light of this archeplot, we can now reread Platonov's story anew, much as we did "After the Ball" in Chapter 3. Fro too remains semi-single (she even gets marriage proposals) and attached to her father's name and apartment, where Fedor comes to visit. The window (albeit without the castrating nails) figures in the scenes of abandonment and longing as well as in the final induction of the boy into the bedroom.

Fedor exhibits supernatural characteristics, including invisibility and fiery nature.

Unlike Fro, he was able to "change himself into a microfarad or an eddy current" (cf. in Aksakov's tale the monster's connections with lightning and other "technological" effects). The Russian name of the hero, Finist, a distorted form of 'phoenix,' as well as his nickname, the Bright (Falcon), signal a contamination with the myth of the phoenix and thus connection with sun and fire.[10] Fedor "was always warm, strange, uncannily able to sleep amid noise, . . . was never ill." Most of the time he is not there; nor does he believe in the value of his face, so that Fro (and the reader) have to settle for his childhood photo and his attributes (his hair, smell, and the Wheatstone bridges, etc.), which ensure her contact with him.

Fro almost succeeds in 'disenchanting' Fedor. She gets him to come back, and we finally see him "wearing a hat and a long blue raincoat, his deep-set eyes gleaming attentively." A symbolic disenchantment of Fedor occurs in the very end where he is reincarnated in the person of the boy, the double of his "normal," childhood self.

The courses of signalization and the other means of communication form an analogue to the magic palace,[11] and Fro's loneliness resembles Psyche's perception of Cupid's palace as a "luxurious prison." Fro's attempts to 'disenchant' Fedor (first by entering his world, then by drawing him away from his) are comparable with Psyche's spying on Cupid. Especially telling is the scene where Fro "drew her finger cautiously over his warm back."[12]

The many 'death' motifs of the folkloric cluster (the heroine's initial descent into the otherworldly valley; the bridegroom's disappearance, death, or sleep; the heroine's later descent into the underworld and her deathly sleep) are matched by corresponding details in "Fro."

> The very first sentence ("He had gone far off, and for a long time, almost irrevocably") foregrounds this theme, and as the story unfolds, Fro descends under the ground, fakes death, loses consciousness, and says to Fedor that she will die if he stops loving her (i.e., refuses to become a 'normal,' 'disenchanted' spouse).

Abandoned by her husband, Fro finds herself alone in the fields and tries interviewing the wind,[13] the stars, and—locomotives. Her mail delivery job is a modern form of searching for the lost bridegroom. The sequence of her jobs resembles a series of tests, and the iron shovel and carrying letters come closest to wearing off iron shoes. Just like Cupid, Fedor returns because of Fro's near death, and the love interlude that follows corresponds to the folkloric motif of spending the night with the lost and found husband.[14]

It is at this pivotal point that a radical conversion of the intertextual paradigm takes place: regained sexual intimacy results in the husband's *leaving the heroine* for his other attachments (in this case, the Scientific Utopia) rather than his rejoining her. This failure to retain the lost husband transforms the happy fairy-tale ending back into a serious mythological one,[15] aligning "Fro" with the myths of Orpheus (who at the last moment loses Eurydice to Hades) and Proserpine (who in the end is permitted only to shuttle back to earth for part of the annual cycle).

> The presence of Orpheus can be detected in the person of the little boy, who descends with his music to Fro's "hell" (downstairs) as her "husband." Naiman (1988: 345) stresses the anagrammatic link between Orpheus and Fro and the Dionysian element that opposes Fro and the boy to Fedor. In an intertextual curio, Chekhov's Darling and her first husband produce *Orpheus in the Underworld*.

In general, reading Fro as Psyche need not exclude alternative mythological, literary, and linguistic contextualizations. Some of the other relevant references include

> (1) Penelope: note, in light of Paramonov 1987, Fro's would-be husbands.
> (2) Aphrodite:[16] Fro's full name, Euphrosyne, meant "joyous" in Greek; it belonged to one of the three graces in Aphrodite's retinue (Vasil'ev 1982: 181),

but originally the three names were simply epithets in her title, Pasithea Cale Euphrosyne, "the Goddess of Joy who is beautiful to all." The three Graces rivaled Aphrodite's beauty (Graves 1983, 2: 14; cf. the rivalry between Psyche and her mother-in-law, Venus-Aphrodite). Fro's face is first introduced as she looks at her reflection in a hairdresser's window, in a modernized replay of Venus's typical pose with a mirror. And Fedor is comparable to Hephaestus, Aphrodite's blacksmith husband.

(3) Eve: the archetypal biblical seductress and family founder; Fro's illiterate 'double,' "another Efrosin'ia," signs her name "with three letters that looked like Eve."[17]

(4) Several interrelated Russian barbarisms: fru, "Mrs." (from Ibsen and Hamsun); frau, "Mrs.," freilein, froiliain, "Miss" (from German); fria, "a pretentious plebeian woman" (see Fasmer 1973, 4: 208); and last but not least,

(5) Fru-Fru, Vronsky's horse, whose death foreshadows Anna Karenina's (i.e., a woman's train-induced death in the male world). Tolstoy named her after his riding horse, whose previous owner had named her "after the heroine of the popular French play by Meilhac and Halévy Froufrou that appeared in 1870 and very soon came onto the Russian stage. . . . The story line of this play touches on that of Anna Karenina. This was of importance to Tolstoy" (Eikhenbaum 1982: 161). Thus, Fro's association with Fru-Fru is anthropomorphic.

For reasons of space, one major intertext of this kind, Psyche, will have to suffice.

Intertexts: Contemporary

Among the immediate contexts of "Fro"—those it is most intimately related to and most carefully distinguishes itself from—are the legacy of (post)symbolism and Platonov's oeuvre. I will project the story onto these two backgrounds, again without any claim to exclusiveness and with an awareness of at least one important omission: the code of Socialist Realism.[18]

THE AESTHETIC OF MIRACLE-WORKING

"Fro"'s complex involvement with the symbolist/postsymbolist mentality may have sprung from Platonov's reaction to a popular version of its "miracle-mindedness": Akesandr Grin's short novel *Crimson Sails* (*Alye parusa*, 1978 [1920]), reissued in 1937. Grin (1880–1932) wrote generically "foreign" adventure and science fiction, inspired by the example of R. L. Stevenson, Joseph Conrad, and H. G. Wells.

In *Crimson Sails*, Captain Gray, an English aristocrat, falls in love with a victimized poor girl, Assol. Learning of her conviction that one day a man will come for her in a ship with crimson sails, he outfits his ship accordingly, and sweeps Assol away.

Platonov's review (1980 [1938]: 72–78) of Grin's book sounds at times like a program for the writing of "Fro" (Chalmaev 1984: 75, 181).

> The happiness of two lovers cannot be based on purely animal satisfaction, divorced from the heroic efforts of the people and their hard everyday life. Miracles must grapple with the "abominable concreteness" of life; "when the ship took on board only Assol, the people remained on shore, along with the . . . great theme for a literary work that A. Grin would not or could not write." The problem was, how does one write about "an Assol from Morshansk," i.e. from a god-forsaken provincial town, rather than from a romantic never-never land?

The transformation Platonov seems to have performed on Grin's novel to produce "Fro" can be described as follows:

> To turn Assol into Fro, he made her a workingwoman, and in creating Fedor, he coupled Captain Gray's generous idealism with socially useful goals. Both protagonists remained utopian dreamers: Fro dreams of romantic love, Fedor of his machines and revolutions; both (especially Fedor) pay no attention to the minutiae of ordinary life while striving to bring their respective remote miracles closer, repainting reality the color of their dreams. Thus, not only Fedor but Fro, as she tries her voodoo magic on him, act in the spirit of Grin and the entire epoch, which bred, among others, Platonov (himself a lapsed utopianist, he could well say "Fro, c'est moi").

To all these changes in the setup the major conversion of the Grin hypogram corresponds: the hero leaves the heroine behind, and their miracles, rather than converging on a happy ever-after, face in different directions as the center falls out of their story.

> Incidentally, the comparison of the platform on which Fro is left standing (in the very first paragraph) to "the deck of a ship that has run aground" reads as a reference to *Crimson Sails*, anticipating the corresponding passage in the review.
>
> Similarly, the very self-appellation that Platonov's heroine chooses for herself (and Platonov for his title)—the short, mysteriously outlandish Fro—may well be a subtle send-up of the pen name Grin: a contraction of Grinevskii, the writer's real family name, Grin is the standard Russian rendering of Green, making the pseudonym sound even more "English." Recall that the heroine insists she is "Fro . . . not Russian, no," but in the end "settles" for Frossie.

Gray-Grin's handpainted sails looming crimson in the horizon are but a popularized version of the symbolists' constant expectation, conjuring up, and performing of miracles.

Zinaida Gippius's programmatic "Song" (1893) features a window, a sunset, and a promise "of that which is not there in the world." In Alexander Blok's famous poem "Incognita" (Neznakomka, 1906), the vision of the mysterious lady "in the misty window" helps establish *correspondances* with the "enchanted distance," "somebody's sun," and "the truth."

The symbolists' miracle mongering was not confined to their art, for they proclaimed the importance of "life creation" (*zhiznetvorchestvo;* see Grossman and Paperno 1994), in an activist spirit that was akin, in the broader perspective, to the world-remaking philosophies of Friedrich Nietzsche, Nikolai Fedorov, Vladimir Soloviev, N. G. Chernyshevsky, and Karl Marx. In 1910, discussing the "crisis of symbolism," Alexander Blok formulated the movement's history as a dialectical triad that reads almost like a summary of "Fro"'s plot (Blok 1974–80, 5: 425–36; Masing-Delic 1989):

Thesis: poet-child creates freely, in a magic unity of art and life.
Antithesis: poet-man subjects life to analysis, in alliance with the devil and in opposition to passive and amoral femininity, which lusts for passion, death, and a premature miracle.
Synthesis: the opposites are miraculously reconciled in an androgynous infant representing the new humankind.

Later on, symbolism's vaguely para-Marxian ideas led to the acceptance of the "music of the Revolution" (in Blok's famous formulation), and in the hands of the futurists and other avant-gardists and finally Socialist Realists, wonder working was translated into various myths of social engineering, with a growing insistence on unceremoniously forcing 'life' to obey the 'power of art.'

Characteristically, while in Blok's poem "somebody's sun" has been passively and impersonally "entrusted" (or "delivered," *vrucheno*) to the speaker, Mayakovsky (in his "The Unusual Adventure That Happened to the Poet Vladimir Mayakovsky at His Countryhouse," 1920) bosses the sun, making it stop by for some tea and a literary chat.

This 'victory over the sun' marked the height of utopian bravado, and soon a mood of disillusionment set in (not unlike the transition from the optimism of the Enlightenment to romanticism's postrevolutionary brooding to profound Flaubertian skepticism). To subject the storming of distances to doubt, various literary tools were now developed:

—the dystopian discourse and the character of the Grand Provocateur, desecrator of ideals—for example, in the works of Zamiatin, Ehrenburg, Ilf and Petrov, and Bulgakov (see Chapters 7, 9);

—the Zoshchenkovian mockery of the New Man's linguistic and cultural pretensions (see Chapters 2, 3); and

—the direct subversion of 'distance magic,' as for instance in Iurii Olesha's *Envy* (2: 1), where Ivan Babichev as a little boy claims to be able to turn a soap bubble into a huge aerostat looming over the horizon:

He invented a special soap compound and a special little pipe, using which, one could turn out an amazing soap bubble. This bubble would enlarge in flight . . . , and on, on, right up to the volume of an aerostat. . . . And when father Babichev was drinking tea on the balcony, suddenly . . . far away . . . , gleaming in the rays of the setting sun, appeared a large orange sphere. . . . "He was a dry man, my dad, small-minded, but inattentive. He didn't know that on that day the aeronaut, Ernst Vitollo, flew over the city. Magnificent posters had announced it." (Olesha 1975: 60)

It is among these grotesque spoofs of the 'manmade miracle' that we should place the literary strategies of Platonov, who had been reared on symbolism, Fedorov, and the technological utopianism of Bogdanov; started his literary career with variations on these ideas; but ended by subverting them. (An Aesopian subversion was there already in "The Epiphany Locks" [1927], and in *The Foundation Pit* [1930] it became so blatant that the novel had to remain unpublished during the author's lifetime.)[19]

Of particular relevance to Platonov's ambivalence about faraway goals is a Nietzschean connection. In *Thus Spake Zarathustra* (1: 16, "Neighbor Love"), the idea of 'love for the furthest and future ones . . . and phantoms' (1967: 55) is proclaimed—over the more natural and easy love of one's neighbor, typical of women. The Russian public was introduced to this notion in the enthusiastic exposition by S. Frank (1903), through whom, or through Fedorov (see Gunther 1982: 185), it must have reached Platonov. In fact, Platonov was to write a story entitled "The Love of the Distant" (1934) where the idea is already treated with irony.

The retreat from 'distance' was not, however, universal, even among the most serious and independent writers. An unexpectedly successful fulfillment of miracles, often in a semiofficial key, was characteristic of Pasternak. "You are close by, [you] the Socialist distance. / Or would you say—nearness?" he wrote in *Waves* (1931).[20] As early as 1924, Tynianov had noted Pasternak's "strange visual perspective . . . attentiveness to things close at hand, and, immediately behind them, infinite space."[21]

> Tynianov cites an example from "To the Memory of the Demon" (the hero of the eponymous Lermontov poem), whose ghostly presence is perceived only "a yard or so away from the window" (apparently in the form of raindrops) and in the "ice on the summits" and the "avalanches," with which the demon promises to return.

This seemingly idiosyncratic angle of vision signals what can be described as Pasternak's solution to the general problem of mastering and superseding symbolist perspective on 'distance.' It is made possible—naturalized—by the typically Pasternakian privileging of contiguity and metonymy (typical of narrative prose) over similarity and metaphor (typical of lyrical poetry, especially romantic and symbolist), in particular the tendency to involve a third, often distant partner in depictions of binary contacts that occur "here."[22] As a result, ideal distant entities are drawn into the immediate vicinity of everyday trivia, so that the miracles dreamed of by the symbolists, wrought by the futurists, and subverted by Platonov and others again come true in Pasternak's world:

> The demon, mountaintops, avalanches, and so on approach the window; trains and platforms mingle with the landscape; the horizon becomes the beloved's pen pal; the air and distance are addressed, like letters, to 'you'; lightnings and fireballs enter rooms, and so on.

One example of such successful "mingling" à la Pasternak sounds like a deliberate conversion of Mayakovsky's adventure with the sun.

> Solntse saditsia i p'ianitsei
> Izdali, s tsel'iu prozrachnoi,
> Cherez okonnitsu tianetsia
> K khlebu i riumke kon'iachnoi.
>
> The sun sets [sits down] and, like a drunkard
> From afar, with a transparent purpose,

Reaches across the windows
For bread and the brandy glass.
(Pasternak, "Zimnie prazdniki" [Winter holidays], 1959)

. . . chem tak, bez dela zakhodit',
ko mne na chai zashlo by!

. . . rather than set [stop by] just like that, uselessly,
you'd better stop by for tea at my place!
(Mayakovsky, "The Unusual Adventure," 1920)

Even the puns (on the 'sundown' verbs *sadit'sia* and *zakhodit'*) are similar, highlighting the difference of tenor: this time, the sun itself stealthily reaches from afar to join the poet at his kitchen table.

In "Fro," much as in Pasternak, "the evening sun shone all through the apartment and penetrated all the way to Frossie's body." And the pine trees, which "grew outside the window, having begun their straight journey into the serene vastness of the skies," seem to prefigure Pasternak's famous "Pine Trees" ("Sosny," 1941), where men and trees are happily immersed in the sky and the (metaphorical) sea.

The entire poetics of juxtaposing the near and the distant is essentially the same, and Tynianov's observations are applicable to the way the close-up of Fro's "two lonely plump legs" follows the panoramic view of the "open space" and the "ship that has run aground."[23]

On the whole, then, Platonov's gesture in "Fro" is subversive of the shriller utopian variants of miracle making (embodied in Fedor) and supportive of its milder, Pasternak-like version (represented by Frossie). In this sense, "Fro" may be described as part of the semiofficial postsymbolism of the 1930s.

The question of 'semiofficiality' is a delicate one, as is always the case with Aesopian discourse and other forms of fellow-traveler writing grudgingly accepted by the totalitarian establishment. While barely subsisting on the brink of Soviet literature, Platonov proclaimed his view of Grin (safely dead at the time) as insufficiently in tune with the interests of "the people."[24]

THE PLATONOV PARADIGM

The poetic world of an author has been defined elsewhere as a system of invariant motifs—ideological, fabulaic, stylistic, intertextual—

unified by an overarching central theme (Zholkovsky 1984a, Shche-glov and Zholkovsky 1987). Briefly, Platonov's world seems driven by 'an urge to transcend the spatial, energetic, and existential limits of immediate reality.'[25] Hence such idiosyncratic oppositions as 'saving energy and matter in a world of shortage versus performing energy miracles'; 'solitude versus contacts,' 'closeness versus distance,' 'kinship versus alienness,' 'attachment, one-sidedness versus freedom, emptiness,' and some others. All these are often treated with ambiguity ("bipolarity," Naiman 1987: 194ff.), even within one text. These major oppositions, in turn, underlie what can be called Platonov's archediscourse about the world, which I will lay out in four installments, dealing, respectively, with the human being, his or her surroundings, family life, and existential drama.[26]

The *human being* consists of reason, oriented toward distance; soul, located in the throat and connected with breathing and air; and a body, with its physical needs. The body is dismemberable—in particular, divisible into the spiritual top and physical bottom. Reason tends to ignore the 'close' needs of body and soul, which experience cold, longing, and dessication as a result. Their warming is achieved through the food, joy, and heat that come from the outside, with which successful close contact is therefore necessary. Inside an ideal human being (child, parent, Bolshevik) exists an empty space where everybody/everything can be placed, this emptiness being connected with breathing/air and holes/graves.[27]

The *surrounding world* is composed of nature, technology, and society, which have 'distant' and 'close-by' manifestations. Men relate mostly to technology, women to nature, but not necessarily. Sometimes technology is identified with the soul, body, people, family, animals, nature. In Platonov one may encounter "rough people and tender locomotives" (Bocharov 1985: 262). Nature is both a challenge (storm, snowfall, lightning) and a source of support (sun, wind), and its representatives (flowers, butterflies, birds, animals) often figure as quasi-human protagonists. On the social plane, the oscillation is between underestimation of interpersonal relations (a leader's or thinker's indifference to real people; preference for technology over people) and their overestimation (in love, family).

Mediation often relies on means of communication (transportation, letters, mail, telegraph), sometimes with exaggerated 'immediacy' (getting around on foot, sending letters with friends rather than through the mail), and on art, especially music (violin, accordion, musical broadcasts). The "ethereal road" (the *efirnyi trakt* of the eponymous novella), which embodies a sci-fi solution to all the problems of technology and human existence, is actually nothing else than a total means of communication.

Family life is usually unhappy. Family members feel orphaned (because of death, inattention, abandonment, poverty, crowding). The spouses' (mostly the wife's) egoism and fixation on family, property, and sex remove them from broader contacts with the world, and sexual love wastes the energy needed for 'distant' deeds. Also destructive are (the wife's) jealous suspicions, which are often provoked by the 'distant' or asexual orientation of the husband and in turn lead to actual unfaithfulness and the breakdown of the family. These crises can be overcome by establishing 'additional links,' outside or inside the family: extrafamilially, by adopting a child, parent, or spouse (e.g., by absorbing an unfaithfulness or forming a sexually indefinite triple union); intra-familially, by upgrading the existing relationships (by a reconciliation of the spouses after an affair or even an alternative marriage; by a mutual adoption of children and parents; by a child's assumption of mediational, sometimes androgynous, functions; by a resurrection of the parents, restoration of their graves, or through rejoining them in death). Mediation often includes hand touching or other nonerotic ('brotherly') physical contacts.

The *meaning of life* lies in striving toward impossible goals: upward (e.g., up a mountain) or into the distance in search of lost/distant parents or be-cause of expulsion from home by unloving parents, on the whole, symbolically and archetypally, a departure for the "other" kingdom/world. This involves disdain for the nearby or on the contrary insistence on direct and immediate fulfillment of desires and ideas, challenging all natural and human limitations and living on the brink of death.

The death cluster includes real, near-complete, or simulated dying, some-times by suicide; a fall, descent underground into a pit, gravedigging; miracu-lous rescue, resurrection, reunion across or beyond the grave, cult of the grave; return, humble reconciliation, settling for the nearby or some other mediation between the distant and the close-by.

In a surprisingly comprehensive rendering of this paradigm, "Fro" seems to "have it all": a departure for the other world, attempts at an impossible remaking of the world, return, gravedigging, sym-bolic deaths, miraculous rescue, mediation between the 'distant' and the 'nearby,' streamlining distant lines of communication, repress-ing sexual claims on the husband, familial reconciliation by forging additional ties, overcoming orphanhood by a mutual reinforcement of links between parents and children.

But it is also true that "Fro" offers a rather moderate and benign version of the Platonov world, without real deaths, injuries, serious antagonisms or ruptures (in fact, Fedor is expected back, albeit in an indefinite future). Furthermore, its narrative follows (and very much identifies with) the heroine who stays 'here, nearby' rather than the hero who has embarked on a utopian quest (as, for instance, in the "Epiphany Locks"). There are in Platonov intermediate cases featuring as their 'protagonist on a quest' not a utopian dreamer/designer (usually a man) but rather an itinerant orphan (often a woman) whose 'distant goal' is more tangible and human. Yet, even compared to these (e.g., "At the Dawn of Misty Youth," 1938), "Fro" stands out in that its pointedly asocial heroine lays claims to her husband and personal happiness without incurring authorial disapproval (or having to counter it by heroic deeds). This lyrical tenor is reinforced by the Chekhovian subtext—both its presence per se and the direction in which it has been "reworked." Platonov continued with the rehabilitation of marital love in such stories as "The River Potudan" (1937), where the husband's centrifugal tendencies are for the first time in Platonov devoid of high social justification, and "The Homecoming" (1946), where they are definitively debunked.

From comparisons between "Fro" and the Platonov master discourse I have slipped into specific parallels with individual texts. A systematic survey of such parallels would have to begin with listing all the situations, narrative moves, and details in "Fro" that have been used by Platonov elsewhere.

> Compare, for instance, the wife summoning her husband back (from America) by a telegram about her alleged death ("The Ethereal Way," 1926); the top-bottom division of the body ("Chevengur," 1929; "Dzhan," 1934; "Dusty Wind," 1936); phrases like "Farewell—I'll welcome you back [*ia dozhdus'*]" ("The Ethereal Way"; "Takyr," 1934; "The Multicolored Butterfly").

"Fro" should also be correlated with whole plots that look like its close variants—some synonymous, others antonymous. This would involve what can be called Platonov's Socialist Realist cycle: "Love for a Distant One" (1934), "Amid Animals and Plants" (1936), "The Old Mechanic" (1940), "A Great Man" (1941), and in particular "Immortality," which appeared in *The Literary Critic* alongside "Fro" in a sort of "little dilogy" (Chalmaev 1984: 160–61). An intriguing problem also concerns the relation between "Fro" 's ostensibly "conformist" stylistic and Platonov's earlier overt surrealism, in a shift generally characteristic of the 1930s.[28]

Such comparisons, however, would far exceed the scope of this section, whose main point is that in "Fro," Platonov, although remaining generally true to the aesthetic of 'transcendence,' sounded a more "humane" note, toning down his earlier stridency.

The five decodings seem to yield the following results. Intrinsically, "Fro" reads as a cautious but definite emancipation of the heroine (who represents individual, human, female values) from 'distant' utopianism (Communist, technological, male). With respect to "The Darling," it is a modernization and what's more, lyricization, all the more surprising in the context of the Soviet production novel of the time. On the archetypal level, the story offers a dramatic conversion of fairy-tale optimism back to the seriousness of original myths. Vis-à-vis (post)symbolism, "Fro" marks a step toward the prosaization of miracles in the spirit of Pasternak's ambiguous, semi-idyllic acceptance of the official discourse. In Platonov's own terms, "Fro" is a milder version of his transcendence fixation.

One obvious consequence of such intertextual layering is a powerful effect of overdetermination. Every juncture of the plot proves to lie at the intersection of several forces; for instance, the episode of Frossie's shoveling work in the slag pit has a fourfold composition (the Chekhovian voice being practically inaudible):

> Structurally, this is one of several attempts at mediation between Fro's soul and the iron world of transportation, between her solitude and the collective, between nature and technology (from the pit she sees the "free night, lit by stars and electricity"). Mythopoetically, the scene represents a graphic descent into the underworld and an early intimation of death, so far rather innocuous. In the (post)symbolist perspective, the image is one of contact with a faraway sky, launched, so to speak, de profundis. And, of course, in terms of the author's oeuvre, it is an umpteenth instance of the 'pits, canals, holes, and graves' that Platonov's heroes seem forever so keen on digging.

The multiple superpositions enhance the narrative's coherence and persuasiveness by ensuring an effective mutual naturalization of the layers, grounded, respectively, in the rhetorical, Russian, archetypal, contemporary, and specifically Platonovian discourse modes, and coalescing into a well-motivated, meaningful whole. The theme of (Fro's) 'soul' finds its classical embodiment in the mytheme of Psyche, and the lyrical ambiguity, characteristic of Platonov's later work, draws on Chekhov's. On the other hand, the orientation toward nineteenth-century Russian tradition (and away from the avant-garde) is very much in the spirit of Soviet literature of the 1930s, as is, in fact, the orientation toward myth.[29] Such mutual agreement helps outbalance and thus sustain the contradictory tensions among voices. For instance, Fro's lyrical individualism is successfully played off against the officially prescribed collectivism, thanks to the reliance of the former on the classical, and therefore newly acceptable, Chekhov. Similarly, presented through (post)symbolist optics, topical Soviet material emerges both ennobled and subverted. On the whole, the mutual accommodation of the five different voices seems not to exceed the limits of a unified if ambiguous cumulative reading.

Afterword

In lieu of closure, here are several afterthoughts on the possible uses of this book.

To the general reader, it offers a set of reinterpretive superpositions of familiar texts, in the wishful hope that the rereadings will stick. That Tolstoy will stay mirrored in Zoshchenko. That from now on, *Selected Passages* will be enjoyed as a "Diary of a Madman"; a failed wedding test will remain inscribed, as a double exposure, in "After the Ball"; and Olesha's prophetic voice will reverberate through *The Master and Margarita*. That Khvorob'ev's nightmares will keep boasting a prestigious kinship with Dostoevsky and Orwell and that affinities with classics will have rubbed off on the programmatically lowly Limonov. In a word, that the texts will never be the same.

To literary theorists, the book reports on a series of experiments with such tools and concepts as motif cluster, masterplot, multiple reading, and various types of conversion and intertextuality. Into the hands of historians of Russian literature it hopes to place the categories of bad writing, adaptation art, 'Newdream,' the complex of 'non-belonging,' 'graveyard witness,' 'corpse versus culture,' 'slaughterhouse' motifs, and other characteristic topoi.

The ambitiousness of these claims stems in part from the vantage point afforded by the author's manifold intermediacy, which punctuates the relativity of cultural and scholarly "absolutes." But the preeminence of such a position is relative too, and this brings us to the question of the service the book performs for its specific author.

Briefly, it satisfies an interest in some literary texts, personalities, and problems that have long intrigued me. I have always been fascinated by the "eternal magic" of Pushkin's "I Loved You" and, for over a decade, by its reincarnation in Brodsky's sonnet. Very early on, I experienced a vague malaise over the deservedly famous *Envy* and "I Want to Go Home." A persistent challenge for my generation was to decipher the message addressed to us by Zoshchenko and Ilf and Petrov.

Some of my interests were strictly professional; others had a personal angle. In terms of practical criticism, I have wondered, for instance, whether Vygotsky's analysis of "Gentle Breathing" was really definitive. In theory, a contradiction gaped between the focus on 'the structure of the text' (Aristotle, Shklovsky, Eisenstein, the New Critics) and the idea (Tynianov's) that aesthetic effects are the property of such entities as entire literary processes, no less. This latter view entailed a ghostliness of the individual text (spectrally inhabited by the glimmer of other literary worlds) that corroborated Meyerhold's provocative claim concerning the unlimited malleability of the classics—that is, that any scene could be staged in a number of ways even without changing a word. In a personal vein, there were reasons to speculate about the possible links between my addiction to mirrors and my preoccupation with Limonov (and his with himself) or about those between my poor table manners (doubly conspicuous in emigration), my love of Zoshchenko, and the temptation to blame it all on Tolstoy, the foe of comme il faut.

Coming, like the questions, from the same variously circumscribed specimen of a particular culture, the answers to these questions were devised primarily for his own use. By referring to my limitations, I do not intend to disown my writing or plead with the reader for leniency. Rather, I am trying to furnish the book with a specific signature. To be sure, specific does not mean unique. Some problems I share with my generation. Others plague our entire profession. Inevitably remaining half science, half art form, literary criticism (practiced to a great extent by *écrivains manqués*) is in the business of competing with literature proper in the creation of "new works." To do so, it resorts to the only method available to it—reinterpretation. Hence the relentless pressure, stronger than in other trades, to produce innovation at any cost. Small wonder that the expansion of criticism (given full theoretical blessing by poststructuralism) resulted in a mass overproduction of merchandise—new readings.

More than a hundred years ago Tolstoy complained that "nine tenths of all that is printed is criticism," yet he recognized its usefulness in guiding readers through the literary "labyrinths of linkages." This book is both less and more than a road map—notes of an, alas, not so solitary traveler in the labyrinths of wandering dreams.

Reference Matter

Notes

INTRODUCTION

1. For an early self-assessment of formalism, see Eikhenbaum 1965 [1927], esp. pp. 134–36; the relevant Bloom texts are 1973, 1975.

2. Barthes's *S/Z* (1974a [1970]) is remarkable for the way a minute and comprehensive multilevel analysis of the text was combined with its principled release from teleological control.

3. See my account of these oscillations in Zholkovsky 1992e.

4. See Taranovsky 1976, Ronen 1983, Smirnov 1985, and Zholkovsky 1987f, 1988.

5. See also Culler 1981: 80–99.

6. This principle may prove useful in resolving a characteristic problem of intertextual reading. In establishing a 'dialogue' between two major writers, one is liable unwittingly to ignore their direct exchanges with their less-known contemporaries. Historically, i.e., genetically, this may be a distortion and yet make typological sense.

7. See Taranovsky 1963 (where the Russian iambic pentameter was shown to have the semantic halo of '[life's] journey,' inherited from Lermontov's "Vykhozhu odin ia na dorogu") and M. Gasparov 1976, 1979, 1982, 1983, 1984a.

8. See Bakhtin 1984 [1963] and Morson and Emerson 1990: 295–97.

9. See Propp 1971 [1928], Brooks 1975, Zholkovsky 1984a, Shcheglov and Zholkovsky 1987.

10. See Bloom, de Man, et al. 1987, de Man 1986, Harari 1979, Culler 1982, Leitch 1983.

11. On the striking affinities between the formalists and Bakhtin as theoretical mouthpieces of the democratic masses' advent to the cultural scene in the 1920s–1930s, see Mikhail Gasparov 1984b.

12. For a poststructuralist overview of Russian formalism, see Steiner 1984; for a revision of the theoretical heritage of the avant-garde, with special reference to Eisenstein's theory of art (and of my own earlier, generativist, reading of it, Zholkovsky 1984a [1964]: 35–52), see Zholkovsky 1992g; cf. also my rereading of Mayakovsky (Zholkovsky 1986c).

13. See, for instance, Jackson 1958, Debreczeny 1966, Maguire 1974.

ONE

1. Cf. the title of Ruth Sobel's monograph (1981).

2. In Fanger's (1979: 154) apt formulation, the narration there comes from all four directions at once—like the Petersburg wind described in the story.

3. Siniavsky-Terts (1975b: 12, 61) sees the author of *Selected Passages* as similar also to Akakii Akakievich, Chichikov, and other Gogolian "objects of slaps and mockery."

4. See *Selected Passages*, Letter 18 (3), pp. 104–5/294–95. All references to *Selected Passages* list the page numbers of the Zeldin translation (Gogol 1969; where necessary, the translation is emended) and after the slash, the pages in vol. 8 of the Russian edition (Gogol 1937–52).

5. Cf. also Siniavsky-Terts 1975b: 372–74 on the affinity between Gogol's stylistic propensity for accumulation of detail and the greediness of his characters, in particular Pliushkin.

6. Among such genres are also literary epigrams (sometimes collected into texts of epic proportions, like A. F. Voeikov's *Dom sumasshedhikh* [The madhouse, 1814–38]); literary epitaphs; Lermontov's "Death of a Poet" and its progeny; and others.

7. Even discounting its "skazzy" ambiguity, "Zhilet Pana Mikhol'skogo" is suggestive of the comic figure Gogol cuts in Russian literary mythology. Cf. L. I. Arnol'di's memoirs comparing Gogol, with his stock of unworn boots, to the anonymous episodic character in the last paragraph of chap. 7 of *Dead Souls*, who enjoyed trying on boots in the solitude of his room (*GVS*: 482); cf. also Gogol's thrifty ways of boot repair (*GVS*: 126–27) with those of the Bashmachkins.

8. Unfortunately, this colorful detail from P. V. Annenkov's memoirs (*GVS*:

263) does not seem to be borne out by the records of travelers, published in the *Moskovskie vedomosti* (see Iu. V. Mann's commentaries in Annenkov 1983: 560).

9. An intermediate stage of the characters' emancipation from Gogol's grip and their arrogation of equal authorial rights (making possible his eventual demotion in *Stepanchikovo*) is discussed by Bocharov (1985: 161–209) in connection with *Bednye liudi*.

10. On Gogol's homosexuality, see Karlinsky 1976 and Rancour-Laferriere 1982.

11. On Gogol's idea of writer-reader "coauthorship," see also Mann 1984: 240–52.

12. See Mashinskii's commentary to Aksakov's memoirs about Gogol (*GVS*: 620).

13. See their respective comments (*GVS*: 173, 333).

14. See S. T. Aksakov's letter to Gogol of July 3, 1842, where he reports a contemporary's opinion that the composition of the provincial society in *Dead Souls* is not accurate (*GVS*: 158) and Gogol's statement to the same effect in Letter 21 (124/311).

15. Dostoevsky was arrested for reading, at a meeting of the Petrashevsky circle (1849), Belinsky's forbidden "Letter to N. V. Gogol" (1847), the radical critic's attack on *Selected Passages* for what he saw as a betrayal of Gogol's previous, properly "civic" stand.

16. The positive view of *Selected Passages* has been canonized in that branch of Gogol scholarship influenced by the spiritual renaissance of the Silver Age and exemplified by the work of Mochul'skii (1976 [1934]) and Setchkarev (1965); see Sobel 1981: 6–8.

17. In this sense, even Chernyshevsky exhibits an unexpected affinity with Gogol. *What Is to Be Done?* is a classical case of bad but culturally influential writing (see Paperno 1988: 221; Zholkovsky 1992f), although the two utopias are very different in both content and style: where the ideologist Chernyshevsky is consistently, if naively, ironic, Gogol, the past master of *skaz*, is dead serious; on the utopianism of *Selected Passages*, see Gippius 1981: 183–84; Mochul'skii 1976: 99.

18. See Siniavsky-Terts (1975b: 321–24) on the origins of Gogol's "bad" prose in his bad poetry.

19. On the unsettling (even for a Bakhtin) aspects of the "Abject Hero"'s freedom from conventional wisdom, with reference to Horace, Rabelais, Diderot, Kierkegaard, Dostoevsky, Artaud, and Céline, see Bernstein 1981.

20. *Domostroi* (House orderer) was a sixteenth-century didactic work setting down the strict principles by which the head of the house is to rule his family.

21. Gogol went so far as to suggest that "the censor Nikitenko, if he ap-

proved the book, should be richly rewarded by the government" (Debreczeny 1966: 59).

22. The reverse of the same motif is Bobchinskii's desire that his name be made known to the emperor (*The Inspector General*).

23. On Gogol as the Grand Inquisitor, see Siniavsky-Terts 1975b: 69–70; cf. Morson: 115–41; on the dystopian progeny of Foma Fomich and the Grand Inquisitor, see also Chapter 9.

24. The "sympathetic" recycling of Stalin's image did not begin with the post-Soviet discourse, when demythologization had already run its course and could give place to reaestheticizing games, i.e., in the early 1980s émigré culture—in Komar and Melamid, Sokolov, and Siniavsky-Terts's 1983 novel *Spokoinoi nochi* (Good night). Elements of a grotesquely loving empathy with the "Kremlin hermit" can be traced as far back as Solzhenitsyn's underground late 1950s version of *First Circle* and Mikhail Bulgakov's oral tales about his imaginary "friendship" with Stalin (Chudakova 1988: 578–83; Paustovskii 1988: 106–8; Bulgakova 1990: 306–11). An interesting double exposure of the liberal rejection of Stalin and his retrospective aestheticization is found in Bulat Okudzhava's "Arbat Inspiration, or Memories of Childhood" (1986: 22–23). In that 1984 poem-song, the veteran of semiofficial dissidence looks back on his youthful love of Stalin and makes its authenticity credible by the use of the style and imagery that he usually reserves for such "alternative," un-Soviet heroes as Bach, Mozart, Pushkin, Pirosmani, etc. (Zholkovsky 1987d).

25. Cf. *Selected Passages*'s oft-quoted principle that love should be transmitted "up through the ranks" (*po nachal'stvu*; Letter 28, 194/366). In the letter to *gubernatorsha*, Gogol also mentions the infinite ladder of bribery (127/313).

26. Cf. Chernyshevsky's Vera Pavlovna (*What Is to Be Done?*) on carrying things over from the future into the present.

27. Typicality, that concept beloved of the contemporary critics, is also invoked regarding the choice of representative events and rumors to be recorded by the *gubernatorsha*.

28. Cf. this passage with the parody of Tolstoy's tautological periods in Chapter 2, note 16.

TWO

1. To be sure, the official command did not go unfulfilled. Appropriately baggy Soviet epics were indeed supplied, one even by a Tolstoy, the "red Count" Alexei Nikolaevich.

2. In fact, Zoshchenko had his own scores to settle with Turgenev, beginning with high school, where he "got One [i.e., an F] in Russian composition . . . on a Turgenev subject—'Liza Kalitina,' " and tried to kill himself as a result. "Beside the One, there was a remark written in red ink . . . :

'Drivel' [*Chepukha*]." The trauma inflicted by the belles lettres would not heal for decades, so that when Mikhail Kuzmin, in his capacity of the editor of *The Contemporary*, was to reject "five of my best little stories" as unfit for the "thick journal," "in my brain there flare[d] up the remark at the bottom of my gimnaziia composition: 'Drivel' " (Zoshchenko 1974: 30, 82).

3. This is a recurrent moral situation in Tolstoy; see Pierre's "conviction that all this had to be" in the episode of the inlaid portfolio (1966: 80) and similar thoughts of the protagonist of "After the Ball" (cf. Chapter 3).

4. Krupskaia remembers that at the end of 1915 in Berne "there was a performance of L. Tolstoy's 'A Living Corpse.' . . . Il'ich, who with all his heart hated all sorts of *meshchanstvo* [petty bourgeois mentality] and conventions, was agitated by the play" (Lenin 1969: 90). Lenin's disapprobation of the opera, in particular the Bolshoi theater ("Anyhow, it's a piece of the purely gentry culture"), led to his attempt to close it down altogether. In the polemic that ensued in November 1921, Lunacharsky prevailed, and the Bolshoi was saved (Chudakova 1988: 133–34). On the other hand, for Mikhail Bulgakov, "that same 'pompous' type of opera was an intimate part of the culture he had imbibed from childhood" (ibid. 134), which helps explain the treatment of opera in his *Heart of a Dog* (see below and Chapter 7).

5. The latter, according to Pushkin (and his own *Les Confessions*), "was unable to understand how the dignified Grimm / dared clean his nails in front of him," powder and rouge himself, thus in many ways falsifying his nature. Pushkin held that "the advocate of liberty and rights / was in the present case not right at all. / One can be an efficient man—/ and mind the beauty of one's nails: / why vainly argue with the age? / Custom is despot among men" (*Eugene Onegin*, 1: 24–25; see Pushkin 1964, 1: 107). The anxiety of "laboring on the nails" is prominent in the programmatic chap. 31, "Comme Il Faut," of Tolstoy's *Youth*. Cf. also *Anna Karenina*, 1: 5, 10.

6. Checking-in coats has been obligatory in Russian theaters (except for movie houses)—both a formal convention and a convenience, given the climate.

7. Zoshchenko quotes, without attribution, Nikolai Gumilev's poem "Dom" from his cycle of Chinese poems *Farforovyi pavil'on* (1918).

8. On Chekhov's narrative techniques in these two stories, see Chudakov 1983: 64–66; see also Ziolkowski 1983 on the genre of canine narrative in European and Russian literature.

9. Compare these tricks with the provocative visit of Koroviev and Begemoth to the hard-currency store in Bulgakov's *The Master and Margarita* (chap. 28).

10. The official Soviet view of the "old culture" was not always dim. Thus, Mikhail Lifshits (1934) discussed Kant's reflections on the inevitable "vices of culture" ("The more man develops, the more he becomes an actor" p. 43),

Engels's critique of the "plebeian asceticism" (p. 47), and Lenin's polemic against Klara Zetkin's praise of the proletarian illiteracy.

11. Zoshchenko "had the mischievous habit of giving his texts titles that already existed in literature. From Goethe he took the title 'Sufferings of the Young Werther,' from Dumas, 'Twenty Years Later,' from Rozanov, 'The Fallen Leaves,' from Blok, 'The Retribution', from Chekhov, 'Nervous People,' from Maupassant, 'Stronger Than Death' " (Chukovskii 1981: 66).

12. For a view to the contrary, see Skaftymov 1972: 401–2.

13. "Zoshchenko . . . told me in the middle of the 30s, that he was fascinated with the folk stories of Leo Tolstoy . . . their precise form and . . . linguistic perfection. But I believe that their didacticism was also relevant for him" (Dymshits 1981: 234). Incidentally, Zoshchenko's monkey may be a distant cousin of Tolstoy's ape in "The Leap" (on Tolstoy's children's stories, see Shcheglov and Zholkovsky 1987: 155–253).

14. Several chapters of *Before Sunrise* are reminiscent in various ways of Tolstoy's autobiographical trilogy and his children's stories. Moreover, Zoshchenko's search for his childhood traumas has a parallel in Tolstoy's "First Memories" (1878–92). Even some of the specific details are similar; cf. the negative images of water, hand, breast, and roar/thunderclap in *Before Sunrise* with the negative sensation of being bound up (in diapers) and the positive reactions to water (in a tub) and the hand (of the nanny) in Tolstoy. Finally, as noted by Kern (1974: 355), Zoshchenko "created in *Before Sunrise* a modern parallel to Tolstoy's *Confession*" (1882), which "begins by describing the author's youth, his quest for self-perfection and his inexplicable despair at the pinnacle of his fame. . . . But beyond this, the paths diverge. . . . Tolstoy uses reason to extinguish itself and ignite faith, whereas Zoshchenko . . . remains steadfastly with reason."

15. Note a similar rhetorical technique in the passing off of the narrator's perceptions as Natasha's in the Mlle. George episode, above.

16. See, for instance, the following by P. P[ilskii]:

Leo Tolstoy
The Kingdom of God Is Not in the Constitution

And that it was the constitution, i.e. that which nine tenths of the people that live on earth consider to be the only important and the only honorable thing, rather than the kingdom of God, i.e. that which is in reality the only important and the only useful thing, because only the divine, and not the human, or that which only appears to people to be human, is important and useful,—and that had been done by people, who, having gathered, several hundred thousand of them, on a small space of land, started killing one another, i.e. doing that which is called the constitution, because that which is called the constitution is what people consider to be the constitution. (Begak et al. 1980: 166)

17. Cf. Shklovsky's 1928 title "On Zoshchenko and Major Literature" (1976 [1928]). On Zoshchenko's "impossible form" as a sign of his "refusal to join . . . a compromised stylistic series," which "gave birth to some new, as yet unknown literary discourse," see Chudakova 1979: 88.

18. On Tolstoy as an "allegory of the Soviet power," especially in contrast to Dostoevsky the Bakhtinian "pluralist," fashionable in the Aesopian discourse of the Soviet dissident intelligentsia of the 1960s and 1970s, see M. Kaganskaia 1984: 152.

19. Cf. in this connection the Mayakovsky version of the cultural revolution, the Mayakovsky = Sharikov equation in Bulgakov's tale (see Chapter 7, first section), and Zoshchenko's interest in Mayakovsky the stylist (see below); on the 'equine' topos in Soviet literature of the 1920s, see also Chapter 7 and Zholkovsky 1992b.

20. See the novel *Narrenweisheit* (translated as *'Tis Folly to Be Wise*), where Jean-Jacques, after a lifetime of humiliation at the hands of his wife, is vindicated posthumously by the coming of the revolution he had foreseen.

21. The implied reference is to Lenin's phrase about the failure of War Communism ("a cavalry raid on capitalism") and to Tolstoy's "The Raid."

22. The equation "the Zoshchenko character = Sharikov = Zhdanov" has been formulated and emplotted by Aksyonov in *The Burn*, in the chapter appropriately entitled "The Evolution of the Type Discovered by Zoshchenko."

23. The grand imperial style (in particular, the system of military ranks) was restored by Stalin in the 1930s as part of his Bonapartist hijacking of the Revolution.

24. For an unexpectedly polyphonic rereading of Tolstoy, see Morson 1989; on "bad writing," see Chapters 1, 2, and Zholkovsky 1986f.

25. Lenin's statement, in his early work *The Development of Capitalism in Russia*, was about the lack of such a development. Zoshchenko's phrasing is strikingly similar: "The tragedy of human reason does not come from the high level of consciousness, but from its insufficiency" (1974: 173).

T H R E E

1. "After the Ball" was written in 1903 and published posthumously in 1911; see Tolstoy 1928–58, 34: 116–25 (commentary: 550–53). I am using (and sometimes amending) the Lesley Chamberlain translation (Richards 1981: 239–50); an alternative translation is by McDuff (Tolstoy 1985: 255–66).

2. More specifically, the old Count Rostov and Natasha may be ironically recycled here; see Natasha's keen identification with the count as he dances Daniel Cooper with Mar'ia Dmitrievna, and her Russian dancing in Otradnoe with the "Uncle" (Norton chaps. 1: 10 and 7: 7); for the negative connotations, see *papa* angrily replacing the uncouth Nikolen'ka in the mazurka in *Childhood* (chap. 22).

3. A similar emotional flooding takes place in "A Christmas Eve" (3: 53; Zhdanov 1971: 100). Ivan Vasil'evich's love for the father and the entire high society has parallels in Nikolai Rostov's feelings at Emperor Alexander's review of troops (2: 7). Both, as well as the debutante Natasha's feelings at her first ball (6: 9), are discussed as cases of "intoxicated consciousness" by Gustafson (1986: 362). See also the feelings of the title character of "Father Sergius" (1898, publ. 1912) as a young man toward Emperor Nicholas and the emphasis on the protagonist's integration into the society represented by his fiancée and the imperial father figure, both of whom he adores.

4. Cf. "Father Sergius": "He was particularly in love that day, but did not experience any sexual desire for her. On the contrary he regarded her with tender adoration as something unattainable" (Tolstoy 1968b: 304).

5. On plot reversals of the "Overdoing" type, see Shcheglov and Zholkovsky 1987: 137.

6. This acquiescence in the overruling power of conventions is reminiscent of Pierre's attitude toward the goings-on in the antechamber of the dying Count Bezukhov ("this all had to be"; 1966: 80); cf. Chapter 2, note 3.

7. "Brattsy, pomiloserduite"; the translation misses the subtle ungrammaticality of the verb form, conveying the Tatar's accent. Tolstoy's drafts show a hesitation between an even more pronounced garbling and the norm (Zhdanov 1971: 106, 250).

8. In "Father Sergius," the hero's leaving worldly life and military career to enter a monastery (upon his discovery of his fiancée's affair with the emperor; cf. Varen'ka's dancing with her father) has a less saintly motivation: success in whatever sphere.

9. Odintsov (1969) identified the techniques that set in relief the flogging scene. It is (1) presented in a sort of close-up, without references to the compositional frame (the aged protagonist's sharing his cautionary tale with the 1900s youth in a drawing room); (2) narrated as a single "perfective" event unfolding before the protagonist's eyes (as opposed to the sketch of a typical ball featuring imperfective verbs that connote recurrence); and in general (3) written in a more energetic, "main-verb" style.

10. "Dama s tsvetami": see Zoshchenko 1946: 45–52; a modified version, "Rassakaz pro damu s tsvetami," appeared in Golubaia kniga (The sky-blue book; 1934); see Zoshchenko 1987, 3: 250–55. There seems to be no English translation.

11. See Turgenev 1950: 681–751; the Russian title is "Zatish'e"; on Zoshchenko's special grudge against Turgenev, see Chapter 2, note 2.

12. This toponym, lit. "The Joyous," is not an innocent one: in addition to Natasha Rostova (see note 2), The Idiot's Nastas'ia Filippovna also has had some idyllic moments on an estate of that name.

13. This may be a jab at Blok's lines: "And I see a spell-bound shore / And a spell-bound distance" ("The Unknown Lady"); on Zoshchenko's Blok con-

nection, see Chapter 2; on the "uncrowning" of Blok's beautiful and unknown ladies by the young Zoshchenko, see also Vera Zoshchenko 1981: 84.

14. For attempts to interpret Zoshchenko's literary texts in light of his self-psychoanalysis, see Hanson 1989 and Zholkovsky 1987a, 1987b, 1989c.

15. See Ginzburg 1981: 119–25, 1985b [1977]: 99–106; for the first part of the memoirs, see Ginzburg 1985a, 1967.

16. Cf. the engineer's preoccupation with his childhood in "Lady with Flowers."

17. See *Anna Karenina*, 4: 13 (1968a: 361–62); for a semiotic reading of that episode, see Pomorska 1981: 389.

18. For the Russian text and literal translation, see Akhmatova 1990: 354–57. In the original, the poem (and the heroine's variation) are in trochaic tetrameters. On the structure of Akhmatova's poem, see Shcheglov 1986d: 175–203.

19. See his "Ty i Vy": "The empty *vy* with a cordial *ty*/She replaced in a slip of the tongue."

20. Cf. Sasha Sokolov's *Palisandria*, narrated by the absolute ruler of Russia (the ultimate *nachal'nik rezhima*) in the 'overcultured' style of the Silver Age, with corpses and necrophiliac loves galore.

21. In fact, "The Ephesus Widow" already exemplifies a contradiction between overt and covert meanings: in contrast to its explicit message, exposing the widow's 'anticultural' behavior, on the archetypal level the story enacts the culturally valuable carnivalesque equation of life and death, of the deceased husband and his living double, of sacrilege and ritualistic renewal (Freidenberg 1936).

22. See Graham: 364–85; for an analysis of the story, see O'Toole 1982: 11–20.

23. Without committing an intertextual version of the intentional fallacy, we may note Tolstoy's intimate working command of Russian folklore.

24. In what follows, I use the terms 'folktale,' 'fairy tale,' and 'magic tale' indiscriminately as equivalents of Propp's *volshebnaia skazka*.

25. Folklorists stress the bride's ambivalence and her links to the villain, as well as the cannibalism among the hero's future in-laws.

26. Shakespeare's *The Taming of the Shrew* goes back to the same archaic cluster (Freidenberg 1936).

27. See Elizarenkova and Syrkin 1964: 72 (wedding as murder); Baiburin and Levinton: 1972: 70–71 (phallic and punitive role of the bridegroom's whip and the best man's staff; marriage as violence done to the bride).

28. Levinton (1975a: 85–86) also notes the links between Sigurd's engagement to Brunhilde and their initiation into sacred omniscience, as well as between the falling-through of their marriage plans and Sigurd's intoxication with the treacherous wine of oblivion.

29. Cf. Levin's problems with the shirt that almost canceled the wed-

ding (*Anna Karenina*, 5: 3; 1968a: 408) and the 'gloves, etc.' motif in "After the Ball."

30. Publ. 1912 (with omissions), 1918 (in full); see Tolstoy 1928–58, 36: 59–74, commentary 584–89; Engl. version: Tolstoy 1935: 385–411.

31. Ivanov and Toporov 1974: 88–90. The blacksmith's affinity with poetry makes him a sort of authorial presence; cf., above, the narrator's triumph over the colonel.

32. Note that one of the underlying fairy-tale plots in "After the Ball" is Tale Type 410, "The Sleeping Beauty" (Thompson 1977: 96).

FOUR

1. "Legkoe dykhanie" (lit. "Light Breath[ing]") was first written and published in 1916 and slightly reedited in 1953 (see Bunin 1965–66, 4: 355–60, 464, 490). I use (and emend) the translations in Bunin 1922: 41–50 and Brown 1985: 59–65. Vygotsky wrote his analysis, "Bunin's 'Gentle Breath'" (1971: 145–65) in 1925 as chap. 7 of his *Psychology of Art*, which remained unpublished until 1965. His ideas have been developed in Connolly 1982, Kucherovskii 1980, Langleben 1991, Spain 1978, Whalen 1986, Woodward 1980.

2. Vygotsky used, respectively, the terms 'disposition' and 'composition'; for a modern systematization of these concepts, see Genette 1970, Chatman 1978. In these pages I will occasionally use the form 'fabulaic' as an adjectival reference to 'story.'

3. Characteristically, this approach was developed only toward the end of the following decade; see Eisenstein 1964 [1937]: 376–82.

4. For a presentation of Eisenstein's theory of art as a machine of pure persuasion, see Zholkovsky 1984a: 35–52; for a modification of that view, emphasizing the dependence of Eisenstein's theory on avant-gardist concepts and his own personal myths of power, see Zholkovsky 1992g.

5. Cf. Eisenstein's positive 'growing on' and 'looking up to' (his actual Russian terms are *vyrastanie*, "growing [up]," and *kolenopreklonenie*, "genuflection") with the rather subtractive freshness of perception owing to Shklovsky's defamiliarization (1965a [1917]), semantically close to 'lightness.'

6. Gershenzon's insights were developed by Bocharov (1974: 157–74), O'Toole (1982: 99–112), Debreczeny (1983: 119–37), and others.

7. One major exception is the story of Erast's marriage, which is given in retrospect during his last meeting with Liza; on the narrative structure of "Poor Liza," see Anderson 1974: 72–85, Hammarberg 1987.

8. An interesting European parallel is provided by the play with narrative and commercial contracts as emplotted in Balzac's contemporary story "Sarrazin" (1830) and analyzed by Roland Barthes (1974a: 212–13). In sociological terms, this can be connected with Pushkin's role and self-image as the

first professional writer; see his semijocular poetic maxim: "The inspiration is not for sale, / But one can sell the manuscript" ("A Dialogue Between a Book-Seller and a Poet," 1824). On the gradual transition among Russian literati from 'patronage' and 'familiar associations' to 'professionalism' and the place occupied in this process by Karamzin and Pushkin, see Todd 1986: 45–105.

As for the Balzac connection, note Pushkin's references to and near-quotations from his *Physiologie du mariage* (1829), mentioned by Akhmatova (1968 [1936]: 256), among them "in 'The Stationmaster': 'Dunia, odetaia so vsei roskosh'iu mody, sidela na ruchke ego kresel, kak naezdnitsa na svoem angliiskom sedle.' Cf. in Balzac: 'J'aperçus une jolie dame assise sur le bras d'un fauteuil, comme si elle eut monté un cheval anglais.'"

9. This motif is part of the topos of 'death' (see also Chapter 3) and of the sentimentalist canon in particular, beginning probably with Thomas Gray's "Elegy Written in a Country Churchyard" (1750; translated into Russian by Zhukovsky twice: 1802, 1839).

10. See below on Nabokov's "Spring in Fialta."

11. Note the imperfective *opuskalos'*, "[the sun] would descend."

12. That blunting is the centerpiece of Vygostky's reading, supported by parallels with Shklovsky's (1965b [1921]) concept of Sternian digressiveness (in *Tristram Shandy* and *Eugene Onegin*). For a view to the contrary and a formulation of an elaborate deep structure underlying "Gentle Breathing"'s chaotic surface plot, see Langleben 1991.

13. Olia's parents are mentioned only in passing and are absent during Maliutin's visit. Remarkably, before giving herself to Maliutin (a surrogate lecherous father figure), Olia "took a nap in Papa's study" (cf. Minsky's sleeping in the stationmaster's bed during his "illness"/courtship of Dunia). In archetypal terms, Olia's death reunites her with her absent parents, in particular the father, whose book turns out to have literally inspired her whole being and given meaning to her death.

14. Cf. in "Poor Liza," the narrator's programmatic love of "wandering about . . . without plan, without goal" (p. 53). According to a Soviet critic (Kucherovskii 1980: 235–37), however, the focal point of Bunin's sentence is the "plebeian appearance" of the murderer, signifying the historical demise of gentry culture.

15. According to Langleben (1991), at the deep structure level, "Gentle Breathing" (written for Easter in March 1916), is a story of death, resurrection, and transmigration of souls.

16. In this, Olia develops the "fatal" potential of poor Liza, who manages to "grab" Erast even from beyond the grave (on the links between Liza, Pushkin's mermaid, and Dostoevsky's Nastas'ia Filippovna, see Matich 1987). Equally traditional are the heroine's sexual boldness (Liza "threw herself into his arms," Dunia is a "little coquette," and so on, including Nabokov's Lolita

and his Nina, about whom see below) and her death, caused by her lover (Erast "considered himself Liza's murderer"; cf. the murder of Nastas'ia Filippovna). Woodward (1980: 152–53) goes so far as to see the motif of Parcae in the principal's jerking the ball of yarn she is knitting.

17. On the symmetries and contrasts between the two siblings as well as between Olia and the class mistress, see Langleben 1991.

18. This stress on the relation to the total picture distinguishes Pasternak's heroes' love from the romantic "blaze of passion" (*Doctor Zhivago*, 16: 15; Pasternak 1959a: 580/1958: 501) and is akin to his prosaic privileging of contiguity over similarity and metonymy over metaphor (as identified in Jakobson 1969).

19. Cf. Pasternak's treatment of wind in the eponymous poem from *Doctor Zhivago* (Zholkovsky 1983a).

20. Cf. the archetypal romantic poet Vasilii Zhukovsky's lines: "Imia gde dlia tebia? / Ne sil'no smertnykh iskusstvo / Vyrazit' prelest' tvoiu!" ("K nei").

21. The image of a printed, written, or drawn page struggling in the wind is a recurrent motif in Pasternak (Zholkovsky 1984a: 81); cf. also the introduction of the written word into the urbanistic collagelike compositions of Braque, Picasso, and their Russian counterparts.

22. The actual book could be the same as the one referred to in Bunin's short story "Grammatika liubvi" ("A Grammar of Love," 1915; see Kucherovskii 1980: 213; Blium 1978: 62)—a treatise on love (Mol'er 1831) translated from the French (Demolière 1829) at the time Pushkin wrote *The Tales of Belkin*.

23. See *Zhizn' Arsen'eva*, Bunin 1965–66, vol. 6. Its early version has been translated as *The Well of Days* (1933). The quotations that follow, however, are taken from the untranslated part (bk. 5, "Lika").

24. *Zhizn' Arsen'eva* is in many ways cognate to "Gentle Breathing." On literature's proper subject: "To write! Yes, one must write about the roofs, galoshes, [people's] backs, and not at all in order to 'fight against arbitrary rule and violence, defend the oppressed and deprived, typify vivid characters, paint broad pictures of modern public life, its moods and trends'! . . . Life is horrible! But is it strictly 'horrible'? Maybe it is something totally other than 'horror'? . . . I entered a cab-drivers' tea-room . . . looked at the meaty, ruddy faces, the red beards, the rusty, peeling tray, on which there sat before me the two white teapots with wet strings attached to their lids and handles. . . . Observing 'the people's way of life'? Wrong!—just this particular tray, this particular wet string!" (pp. 233–34).

On the power of place-names, which determine the hero's itineraries: "When I finally arrived in the real Polotsk, I . . . found it absolutely unlike the imagined one. And yet, even to this day there are in me two Polotsks: that imagined and the real. And this real one I also see now poetically: downtown it is boring, wet, cold, dark, and grim, while at the railroad station there is this warm big hall with large arched windows, lights are already on" (pp. 269–70).

25. Cf. Mirsky's (1958: 74) remarks about the confluence of classicism and romanticism in the poetry of the Golden Age.

26. See Nabokov 1978 (7–35) and Nabokov's own English translation in Richards 1981 (289–311).

27. This is especially pronounced in the Russian version. The recurrent attention to the eye focusing on Nina, as well as the narrator's professional connection with cinema and some other cinematic effects (e.g., the final "dissolve"), make doubly intriguing the temporal coincidence of "Spring in Fialta" (1936) and Eisenstein's analysis of Ermolova's picture (1937).

28. Perhaps Nabokov's favorite lepidopterological motif can be seen here as a reification of the 'butterfly' theme we have proposed for "Gentle Breathing"; then the two stories could be correlated with the myth of Psyche, whose name means "soul, breathing, butterfly" in Greek (on Psyche, see also Chapter 10).

29. On "Spring in Fialta," see also Saputelli 1988 and Zholkovsky 1991b.

30. These would be later generalized by Gerard Genette 1970 (see also Chatman 1978: 62–84).

31. See Steiner 1984; Zholkovsky 1992g; cf. to the contrary my earlier references to Eisenstein and Vygotsky as objective poetic "scientists" (see Shcheglov and Zholkovsky 1987: 84–86, 92–94, 288).

F I V E

1. In what follows, quotations from Brodsky are either in the original, in Brodsky's own translation (1988: 20, see Appendix to this chapter), or in my interlinear.

2. Further discussion of ILY's structure is based on that article and on Zholkovsky 1984a: 179–94.

3. On such splits in ILY and in Pushkin in general as manifestations of the 'passion/impassivity' opposition, see Zholkovsky 1984a: 188–89.

4. See nos. 12–20, especially 13 ("suffered alone, loved in speechlessness"); 16 ("now tender, now melancholy . . . , do not torment me . . . , so tender . . . , so flaming . . . , so sincere"); 17 ("I will not pursue you with my longing . . . you will be loved by many"); 19 ("You will not, do tell me, love another [woman] as me? . . . I . . . tormented by desire," with "tormented" [tomim] in the rhyme); 20 (speechlessness, flames of love, jealousy, a humble gesture, and acceptance of love for another—all within one quatrain).

5. For this observation, I am indebted to Professor Thomas Shaw.

6. Cf. Ogarev's "I was jealous, whilst I do not dare/Tell you how I love and how I suffer" (no. 29) with Pushkin's "You do not know, how strongly I love,/You do not know how hard I suffer" (no. 16).

7. Indeed, quite a few of ILY's forerunners, and descendants, are in iambic or trochaic tetrameters or hexameters or in heterosyllabic verses.

8. See M. Gasparov 1976; 1979; 1982; 1983; 1984a.

9. E.g. nos. 40 ("Oh, fall in love, if you can, again"); 52 ("even without jealousy . . . there remained the same old love").

10. Nos. 69 ("I languish [*tomlius'* !] with others"); 80 ("go on to others"); 74 ("[he] said that I had no rivals"). But '[many] others' appear as early as Pushkin's no. 17 and Baratynsky's nos. 3, 6.

11. See, resp., nos. 24 ("And I love him!"), and 60 ("you [a woman] caressed your [female] rival with love"). Such triangles can be interpreted in Freudian or 'mimetic desire' terms (see resp. [Rancour-]Laferrière 1978a: 48–77; Girard 1965: 1–52, Paperno 1994, Matich 1994).

12. There a female author/speaker reports the speech of the male partner (Pratt 1989).

13. See Tiutchev', no. 51, where the verb 'to live' relinquishes in the end the final position it occupied in an earlier stanza (". . . zhivu ia—/ . . ./ . . . zhit' uzh ne mogu"); Briusov's no. 62 (". . . ne liubliu ia,/ . . . liubit' ia ne mogu!"); and Akhmatova's no. 76, where the effect is traceable on the phonetic and grammatical level: ". . . liubit'/ . . ./ . . . zabytoi byt'."

14. Blending techniques also yield such high-low hybrids as *gorazd*, "capable," which sounds archaic in the context of *buduchi* and colloquial, in the context of *na mnogoe*.

15. The rhyming itself freely combines enclosing and alternating patterns (Abb Ab Ab Acc De De), a scheme already used by Pushkin, e.g., in "Madonna." Some other "Sonnets" take much greater liberties.

16. On Brodsky's existentialism, see Kreps 1980: 195–98; on the Mandelstam poem, Zholkovsky 1986a.

17. See, resp.: "ryba rvanoi guboiu/tshchetno dergaet slovo"; ". . . razomknut' usta/liubye. Otyskat' chernila/i vziat' pero"; "Tam est' mesta, gde pripadal ustami/tozhe k ustam i perom k listam."

18. The interplay may also involve Pasternak's variation on "Prorok"— "Mchalis' zvezdy."

19. Note the correspondence between this interruptive signifier and the negative signified ('God will NOT grant'). This spectacular interruption is first foreshadowed in line 1, where the Pushkin quote runs into a parenthesis, in an exaggeration of Pushkin's "braking" of passion by syntactic stops.

20. A sweeping "overflow" from octet to sestet is frequent in the "Sonnets." In the Sixth, it is prepared by the run-ons between the quatrains ("slozhno/s oruzhiem") and between lines 6 and 7 ("ne drozh', no/zadumchivost' ").

21. Brodsky, who likes comparing life to language, consistently sees the Russian *u* as narrow and opposed to the broad *a*: "na ploshchadiʌkh, kak 'proshchʌi,' shirokikh, / v ulitsakh uzkikh, kak zvuk 'liubliu' "; "i ulitsa vdaleke suzhaetsia v bukvu 'u'."

22. *Bend Sinister*; the pun is naturalized by Nabokov's hero's being a German Shakespearean scholar.

S I X

1. Note his critical attack on Brodsky (1984b).

2. On his sensational *It's Me, Eddie* (1983 [1979]), translated into many languages, see Kustarev 1983, Shukman 1983, Smirnov 1983, Carden 1984, Matich 1986a, variously focusing on the themes of emigration, alienation, megalomania, narcissism, androgyny, and "moral immoralism."

3. In brief: the gods promise Narcissus a long life, at the price of his not knowing himself; he rejects all lovers, among them Echo, who admires him and repeats his words; the gods punish him with an impossible love for his own reflection in a spring, which drives him to suicide.

4. On Limonov's narcissist structures, see Smirnov 1983; see also Genette 1966, Zholkovsky 1987a; on the expressive potential of thematic elements, see Zholkovsky 1984a: 26, 88–90.

5. For instance, a rare form of iambic tetrameter (stressing the second and fourth ictuses) recurs three times with similar—masculine—clausulas (in ll. 7, 10, 14).

6. The first line of stanza 4 continues, loosely, the feminine rhyming in ozh, to which then the triple masculine rhyme in oi is linked by its vowel, so that we are partly back to assonant and later on (l. 20) even unrhymed clausulas.

7. From a ready-made lexeme (*chut'-chut'*) to a looser emphatic doubling (*redko-redko*) to a free repetition of a main verb (*tianus' tianus'*); note also "half hour," connoting bisection.

8. A classic instance of the opposition 'I/Other' in Russian literature is Oblomov's indignation at being equated with "Other(s)." In another poem, Limonov's poetic persona is pictured lying on a sofa, Oblomov-style ("Kto lezhit tam na divane?"; 1979: 88–89). On ego-splitting in poetry see Rancour-Laferrière 1978a: 80–82, 102–4; 1978b: 65–75.

9. Remarkably, the eyeing of "a birthmark, a special hereditary, aristocratic birthmark . . . by which after decades mothers recognize their kidnapped children" is quite prominent in Olesha's *Envy* (pt. 1, chap. 3), a text which, due to its general popularity and the special affinities of its antihero (Kavalerov) with Limonov's autobiographical/lyrical persona, could hardly have escaped Limonov's notice.

10. To incorporate the mirrors, mere actant growth is supplemented with two gerund constructions and two quasi-hypotactic adversative conjunctions of sentences (contrasting with the parataxis of ll. 5–13).

11. Limonov often pushes such splits to ungrammatical extremes. Cf. "pridet li kto, a ia—lezhit" (whoever should stop by, I is lying [in bed]; 1979: 57).

12. Cf. the speaker's detachment from his own body/feelings conveyed by the play with the third person in Pushkin's "I Loved You" (see Chapter 5 and Zholkovsky 1984a: 72–75, 188–89) and Khlebnikov's systematic disruption of the traditional single-person perspective (Uspenskii 1973; cf. Zholkovsky 1986f); cf. also the following limerick: "A young man from the banks of the Po/Found his cock had elongated so,/That when he'd pee/It was not he/But only his neighbors who'd know" (Legman 1969: 45).

13. See Chapter 5, second section; cf. esp. the ending of Pushkin's "I Loved You" ("As God grant to you to be loved by another"), where God is invoked as the mediator, but grammatically it is "I" who lords it over "you," "another," and "God" (the last largely a proverbial fiction). Incidentally, Pushkin's closure is also intertextually relevant to Limonov's lines 17–18 as similar vocabulary and grammar are used to undermine mixing with "others" (see Zholkovsky 1984a: 267).

14. "I" is first semiactive in letting the other go; then both active and passive vis-à-vis himself; and finally, rather passive vis-à-vis the other and the grammatically active "it."

15. E.g., in Derzhavin's "Felitsa" (1782), "Evgeniiu. Zhizn' Zvanskaia" (1807), and Pushkin's "Osen'" (1833), which Limonov's poem resembles in the manipulation of tenses around the climactic perfective future verb (Limonov's *uvizhu*, Pushkin's *potekut*). On similar effects in Pasternak, see Zholkovsky 1992a.

16. *Izlazhu* [pf]—*pytaius'* [impf]—*zaglianut'* [pf]—*tianus' tianus'* [impf]—*pomozhet* [pf]—*vzaimodeistvuia* [impf]—*uvizhu* [pf].

17. For Limonov's interest in Derzhavin, see Limonov 1977a; on his links to the eighteenth century, see Titunik 1984; on bad writing, Chapters 1, 2.

18. See, resp.: (1) "Pamiatnik" (1795) and "Moi istukan" (1794); (2) "Privratniku" (1808); (3) "Lirnik" (1805), "Ekho" (1811), and its early foreshadowing, "Kliuch" (1779), complete with the poet, the echo, and the spring.

19. "O moi Evgenii! kol' Nartsissom/Toboi ia chtus', skaloi mne bud';/I kak pokroius' kiparisom,/O mne tverdit' ne pozabud'./. . ./Nartsiss zhil nimfy otvechan'em—/Chrez muz zhivut poety vvek/. . ./Potomstvo vozzvuchit s toboi." Derzhavin culled this accusatory simile from a letter by his friend Evgenii Bolkhovitinov (Derzhavin 1958: 516–17) and converted it to positive use.

20. In Russian, the latter construction (*sebia soboiu, sam soboi*, etc.) comprises only the self-reflexive forms, which facilitates the conversion from '[your]self' to '[my]self' and, therefore, from 'God' to 'Ego.'

21. Note, for instance, (1) rhetorical questions and exclamations ("Chto zhizn' nichtozhnaia?"; "Pochto zh semu bolvanu [i.e. the poet's bust]/Na svete mesto zanimat'?"; "Redka na svete dobrodetel'/I redok blag priamykh sodetel'./On redok! . . ."); (2) gerund phrases ("A ia, prospavshi do poludni,/ . . ./To, vozmechtav, chto ia sultan,/. . ./To vdrug, prel'shchaiasia nariadom . . ."); (3) complex adjective-infinitive constructions ("I byt' sebia on vechnym chaet"; "No byt' bogatym kupno sviatu/Tak trudno, kak . . ." [note the concatenation of the two forms that are mixed up in Limonov's *zaniatomu*]); and (4) habitual perfectives ("Byvalo, milye nauki/. . ./Pozavtrakat' ko mne pridut").

22. The choice of Mandelstam may have to do with his status as arguably the greatest Russian poet of this century; the only 'victim writer' who dared epigrammatize Stalin; an idol of the liberal intelligentsia; and, last but not least, Brodsky's mentor and namesake.

23. Limonov once said, in response to my query about what had influenced his poem "A Bandit's Wife" (1986: 6–7): "The bandit's wife did." In a telling contrast, Brodsky promotes the Language rather than the Beloved as the Poet's Muse (see Chapter 5, last section).

24. Cf. the protagonist's obsession with superannuated women in Sasha Sokolov's *Palisandriia* (1985) and the historical marriage of Vasilii Rozanov (one of Limonov's few acknowledged mentors) to Apollinariia Suslova, Dostoevsky's real-life *femme fatale*.

25. The text of the poem is cited in the Appendix; see Mandelstam 1967–69, 1: 59–60, 430–31; 1990, 1: 110–11, 475–76; Semmler-Vakareliyska 1985; the association with 'straw' is paronymic (*Salomeia* = *Solominka*).

26. The target of this parody could well have been *My Childhood* (1913) by Babel's mentor-guardian Maxim Gorky; on the "underdog" spin Gorky's autobiographical trilogy gives to his not-so-victimized childhood, see Wachtel 1990: 131–52.

27. This places the actual interview somewhere in 1980. Professor John Bowlt remembers visiting Mrs. Andronikova-Halpern in London in 1976. In discussing Vasilii Shukhaev's illustrations for the 1920 French edition of "La Dame de Pique" (Paris: Pleiade), she "paused, as if arrested by some vivid, yet distant thought, . . . not because she was recalling her friendship with Shukhaev, but rather as if, in some perverse manner, she was identifying herself with Shukhaev's image of the cold, aloof, and still powerful countess" (Bowlt's memo to me, March 10, 1992).

28. In this, Limonov is not all that different from the historical—rather

than his own, stylized—Mandelstam, who saw genuine literature as "created without permission" and downright criminal, "stolen air" (1990, 2: 92), and admired the poet-criminal François Villon.

29. Incidentally, the androgynous protagonist of Balzac's *Seraphita* (invoked in Mandelstam's "Solominka") is both young and "more than a hundred [years old]" (Balzac 1986: 36) and at home wears "his usual garment, which was as much like a woman's dressing gown as a man's overcoat" (32).

30. Underwater imagery was actively explored by the decadents-symbolists ca. 1900 (i.e., during Salome's formative years), in particular, in Balmont's 1894 sonnet "Underwater Plants" and Valerii Briusov's 1904 essay where he portrayed the decadent poets "walking under water in a diving bell, preserving a telephone link only with those . . . at the surface, where the sun shines" (in *Vesy*, 1904, no. 1: 50; quoted in Tsivian n.d.).

31. 'Revolution' is feminine in Russian, as are 'life,' 'love,' and 'death.'

32. Cf. a similar shift in the narrator's point of view in the end of "Gentle Breathing"; see Chapter 4.

33. The Salome–Saint John the Baptist myth originated in the Gospels (Matthew 14: 1–13; Mark 6: 14–29; for a recent analysis, see Girard 1984), had a long history in European painting, was recycled in Heinrich Heine's *Atta Troll*, and became the rage in the "decadent" era (Kuryluk 1987: 189–258; Meltzer 1984), into which Mandelstam's and Limonov's heroine was born. The Salome paradigm includes (1) the dance at a public gathering, leading to the decapitation of the prophet; (2) the prophet's blood-dripping severed head, cognate with that of Orpheus; (3) the kissing of bloody lips; decapitation as castration; (4) a castrating female, either a virgin (veiled, lunar, icelike) or a goddess of the underworld (Hecate, Venus); (5) a "doubles" relationship between precursor and follower (John and Jesus); and (6) the crushing of Salome (with the shields of Herod's soldiers). Mandelstam may have deliberately used some of these motifs (e.g., in Neva's icy invasion of the room and the ceiling's descending on Solominka's eyelids). Limonov's story, in its turn, features the following: a Salome; blood sucking; victimized, symbolically castrated poets; dancing; kissing the bloody lips of the Russian Revolution; a 'doubles' relation with Mandelstam; and, of course, a fateful meeting with an underworld figure. Whether this powerful interplay with the Salome topos is intentional is of secondary importance.

34. James may have been familiar with "The Queen of Spades" through Ivan Turgenev or even read it in an early English translation (by Antonio Melidori, in the series *Chamber's Papers for the People*, Edinburgh, vol. 38 [1850; 31 pp.]) or in Prosper Mérimée's French translation (1849). James liked Mérimée's work, in particular "La Vénus d'Ille," which he tried translating (Gale 1989: 676–79, 430–32). As early as 1874, he had read and praised Mérimée's translation of Pushkin's "The Shot" (in a Mérimée collection he reviewed; see

James 1957: 172). Tchaikovsky's opera (1890) postdates "The Aspern Papers." Limonov's familiarity with "The Aspern Papers" is another moot point. A possible mediating channel could have been *Aura*, by Carlos Fuentes (1962), who was familiar with both the Pushkin and James texts (as acknowledged in a conversation kindly reported to me by Gary Saul Morson).

35. The story fictionalizes several sets of facts. One of Lord Byron's inamoratas, Miss Jane (Clare) Clairmont (1798–1879), who had Byron's and Shelley's letters, lived in Florence. James learned about her only after her death but did not regret having "missed" her. But he knew somebody who did approach her and also knew a niece of Countess Teresa Guiccioli, who claimed to have burned one of his shocking letters. James moved the action to Venice, the scene of another famous affair, that of George Sand and Alfred Musset. Sand interested James very much as the "'supersensuous grandmother' of the affair" (Holland 1964: 133), a shrewd businesswoman, and a writer who divulged *privatissima* of her affairs in her fiction (Gale 1989: 110–11, 129–30, 582–86; Holland 1964: 130–38).

36. For instance, I have been informed that unlike "Alla," "Diana" was not present at the actual meeting.

37. On Nadezhda as an authority on Mandelstam and for that matter Pasternak, see Chapter 8.

38. Instead of Nikolaevna, she calls her Iraklievna, as if Salome were the daughter of the popular Soviet critic and TV personality Iraklii Andronikov. Cf. the mongrelization of Pushkin by Mayakovsky and Brodsky, discussed in Chapter 5.

39. Cf. also such common details as the reference to "bed(room)" in the very beginning of both texts and the "ceiling" later on (in the poem, the ceiling is to "descend upon the heroine's sensitive eyelids"); both ceilings may go back to Poe ("The ceiling, of gloomy-looking oak, was excessively lofty"; 1950 [1838]: 31) and/or to the 'crushing' of the heroine with shields in the finale of Oscar Wilde's *Salome*.

40. Remarkably, Balzac considered his *Seraphita* a "Jacobean effort" (1986: 7) in the sense of wrestling with the ghosts of his literary ancestors, notably that of Swedenborg, so insistently "visited" by the story. Another link to the 'Jacob' topos is the seraphic/angelic nature of Balzac's title protagonist.

SEVEN

1. "I snova skal'd chuzhuiu pesniu slozhit, / I kak svoiu ee proizneset" ("Ia ne slykhal rasskazov Ossiana," Mandelstam 1967–69 [1914], 1: 41). On Mandelstam's programmatic intertextualism, see Taranovsky 1976: esp. 1–7; Ronen 1983: esp. vii–xxi.

2. On Tynianov's "systemic" version of Russian Formalism, see Steiner

1984: 99–137. Once viewed through the prism of modernist writing, Dosto-evsky revealed to Bakhtin his inner dialogism and to Tynianov his external interplay with Gogol (see Tynianov 1977a [1921]).

3. L. E. Belozerskaia-Bulgakova explains the lack of reference to Bulgakov in Olesha's posthumous (1965) book *No Day Without a Line* "by the [evil] design of a hyper-subservient editor": "Of all people, Olesha should have been moved, by the logic of [their] mutual disposition, to recall Bulgakov" (1979: 106). On their closeness in the 1920s, see Chudakova 1988: 305.

4. The genre goes back to Lucian via Chekhov ("Kashtanka," 1887), Gogol ("Diary of a Madman," 1834), E. T. A. Hoffmann ("Account of the Most Recent Fortunes of the Dog Berganza," 1813), and Cervantes ("Colloquy of the Dogs," in his *Exemplary Tales*, 1613); see Ziolkowski 1983.

5. Sharik's onomatopoetic/paronomastic linking of *v'iuga* (snowstorm) to names of stores (*ga . . . stronomiia, Glavryba*) is based on Pilnyak's *Gviiu, gvaau . . . Gla-vbumm!* and mediated and narrativized by the barking sound *gau-gau*. The *Glavryba = Abyrvalg* palindrome harks back to some futuristic motifs in Andrei Bely's *Petersburg* (1915): the *Enfranshish = Shishnarfne* equation and the dissertation about the "Tatarism" of the letter ы, in particular, in the word *r-y-y-y-y-ba* (fish), consistently associated there with the ambivalent theme of 'revolution/provocation.'

6. Cf. Ostap Bender's proverbial reverence for the Criminal Code.

7. Cf. the motif of Evgraf Zhivago, his brother's well-connected guardian angel (eventually a general), in Pasternak's novel.

8. The Provocateur type—instanced by such characters as Julio Jurenito, Benia Krik, Ivan Babichev, Ostap Bender, and Woland cum retinue—emerged in the fellow-traveler writing as a result of cross-breeding Mephistopheles with traditional clowns and picaros, Sherlock Holmes–like intellectuals, and perversely enlightened Grand Inquisitors; see Chapter 9.

9. *The Bronze Horseman*, "The Overcoat," *Oblomov*, "Notes from the Underground"; the Christian legend, *Gulliver's Travels, Don Quixote, Faust, The Prince and the Pauper*; Rastignac, Quasimodo, Dick Whittington; H. G. Wells's *The War of the Worlds* and "The Door in the Wall"; *Julio Jurenito, We, Cement*; Pilnyak; Mayakovsky's and Gastev's utilitarianism; Lenin iconography; and many more; see Beaujour 1970, Barratt 1981. In turn, echoes of *Envy* reverberate in *The Egyptian Stamp* (1928), *The Golden Calf* (1931), Kataev's and Ehrenburg's Socialist-Realist novels, and elsewhere.

10. Incidentally, the future prophet of dialogism, Bakhtin, was famous as a brilliant counsel for the defense at such trials (Clark and Holquist 1984: 50).

11. "Things don't like" Kavalerov, and Makarov suspects that he "will bring lice"; cf. the "rack and ruin" brought by Sharikov and his fleas.

12. Note also Ivan Babichev's conflicts with his father, as well as Olesha's with his (Beaujour 1970: 96–97).

13. This motif, going back to Dostoevsky's "Notes from the Underground" and projected by Olesha onto Soviet exclusionary practices, was later developed in Ilf and Petrov's saga of Ostap Bender, who so brilliantly imitates Soviet ways and yet remains a total outsider; cf. the scene at the official opening of the railroad where he has to wait for Koreiko, a much more successful chameleon, "outside the fence" (*Golden Calf*, chap. 29); on the motif of '(non)belonging' in the Bender novels, see Shcheglov 1986c: 90–93.

14. Cf. Professor Preobrazhensky's eyes, which during the operation "glittered like the gold rims of his glasses," then became "piercing, prickly," while he "became awe-inspiring."

15. The little man chasing in vain a powerful idol is, of course, a conversion of the Bronze Horseman's pursuit of Evgenii; it is also akin to Gogol's "major" Kovalev's pursuit of his own nose turned state councillor, Mayakovsky's "Prozasedavshiesia" (1922), and Bulgakov's openly Gogolian "Diaboliad" (1923); and it anticipates Ostap Bender's search for Skumbrievich in the corridors of The Herkules (*Golden Calf*, chap. 18). The Soviet bosses' elusiveness due to their numerous functions was commented upon by Preobrazhensky, "an advocate of the division of labor. Let them sing at the Bolshoi, and I will operate." "Of course, if I began to skip around from meeting to meeting . . . , I would never manage to get anywhere" (*Heart of a Dog*, chap. 3).

16. "Segodnia mozhno sniat' dekal'komani" (Mandelstam 1967–69 [1931], 1: 189–90).

17. It goes back to *We*, "Notes from the Underground," *What Is to Be Done?* and is prompted by the new Le Corbusier building in Moscow (1990, 1: 517) and quite probably by Andrei Babichev's Two Bits diner in *Envy*.

18. See "Ia ne slykhal rasskazov Ossiana" (1914), "Ia ne uvizhu znamenitoi Fedry" (1915); for the discussion of the rhythmical-thematic formula "Ia ne . . . ," see Zholkovsky 1986a: 212.

19. Some of these postures, especially 'envy' and 'haughty airs' (*spes'*), are not alien to Mandelstam (cf. the 'envy' image in "Kantsona," 1931, and the realization that "it is time to stamp one's boots" in "Kvartira tikha," 1933); on Mandelstam's complex of 'unstable emotional postures,' see Zholkovsky 1986a: 211–13; on affinities with *Envy*, Zholkovsky 1992h.

20. Ivan "endowed [it] . . . with the most vulgar feelings," "on purpose, out of spite," like Dostoevsky's "ridiculous man," who had similarly "corrupted" the inhabitants of the utopian planet.

21. And more specifically, in the manner of the Martian from H. G. Wells' *The War of the Worlds*, who pins a man to the wall with his deadly needle of a nose. The motifs of man-machine hybrid and of blowing a "sorceress' soul" into a machine are also prominent in Pilnyak's *Machines and Wolves* (see Jensen 1979: 253–55).

22. On the visual effects in *Envy*, see Nilsson 1973; on the defusing of

threatening situations by perspectival manipulation, see Beaujour 1970: 38–58, esp. 53.

23. The next generation of the 'new world'—the machine—is even "more ferocious" than Makarov; on pairings in *Envy*, see Barratt 1981: 37–40.

24. Cf. the quasi-marital relationship between Gogol's Akaky and his overcoat.

25. On the sexual ambiguities in Andrei Babichev and *Envy* in general, see Harkins 1973.

26. The elbows may go back to the widow Pshenitsyna's in *Oblomov*, where they also emblematize the hero's eventual union with a kitchen-ridden simple woman instead of the romantic heroine (Olga Ilyinskaia, resp. Valia).

27. Cf. Anechka's "electrodynamic" cats.

28. A further echo of this topos is the lynching scene in Mandelstam's *The Egyptian Stamp* (1928), with its images of "entrails," "lungs," and "buttons . . . made of animal blood" and multiple links to 'slaughterhouse' and 'horse-torturing' motifs in Nekrasov, Mayakovsky, Babel, and others (Zholkovsky 1992b).

29. Note, however, the complete asexuality of the two doctors, resembling that of Sherlock Holmes and Dr. Watson and analyzable as crypto-homosexual and antiprocreative in the sense of various turn-of-the-century Russian utopian models (see Matich 1990).

30. Note Ivan's memories of the little girl who "set the step at the ball . . . was the queen," and "stole [his] show"; Ivan, "spoiled by worship, . . . couldn't stand it . . . gave her a thrashing [and] tore off her ribbons." The episode combines elements of the protagonists' quarrel in "The Shot" with a streak of misogyny typical of Lermontov's and Mayakovsky's personae (see Zholkovsky 1986c, 1992d): the envious rage is not so much *over* a girl as *directed at* her.

31. Cf. the antiprocreation models of love typical of the promiscuous 1920s (Matich 1990) and the puritanically sacred view of family in high Socialist Realism; cf. also note 29.

32. See Beaujour 1970 (56–57) on their "need to see their existence reflected onto the world" and "attempts to impose [their] vision on the Soviet world."

33. See Ingdahl's chapter "The Carnival of Feelings" (1984: 87–99), where Olesha's drafts are extensively quoted.

34. Among the most obvious are the Gospels, Roman history, *Faust*, Pushkin, Dostoevsky, Griboedov, Mayakovsky, Berlioz, Stravinsky; see B. Gasparov 1978. On the carnivalesque/polyphonic nature of Bulgakov's novel, see Proffer 1973: esp. 190–91.

35. Cf. the 'doubles' relationship between Kavalerov and Ivan, who repeatedly spells out the other's thoughts. The 'mind-reading' technique goes

back at least to Dostoevsky (e.g., the exchanges between Stavrogin and Liputin in chap. 2 of *The Possessed*).

36. Cf. the 'Evgraf' motif in *Heart of a Dog*.

37. In the 1930s, Bulgakov's treatment of 'education' meant a polemic with its use in Socialist Realism, which, in turn, had adopted it from the *Bildungsroman* tradition (Clark 1981: 17).

38. Cf. Pushkin's *pokoi i volia* in his " 'Tis time, my friend, 'tis time" (1834); on the motif of 'superior peace' in Pushkin, see Zholkovsky 1980a.

39. The verb *raz"iasnit'*, lit. "clarify, clear up," was a 1920s vulgar euphemism for "investigate and arrest"; cf. Sharik(ov)'s desire to "sort out" the dummy owl (chap. 2), promptly enacted by tearing it apart (chap. 3); the owl has not been forgotten in *The Master and Margarita*, where it is shot to pieces by the cat Behemoth (chap. 24).

40. Cf. the toast, proposed by Pasternak in 1935, to Bulgakov as "an illegitimate phenomenon" (Ianovskaia 1983: 304; Chudakova 1988: 560), and Mandelstam's concept of genuine literature as "created without permission" and downright criminal (Mandelstam 1990, 2: 92).

41. Valia ignores the old-style dreamers (her father, Ivan, and Kavalerov) and joins the men of action (Andrei and Makarov), following in the footsteps of an entire dynasty of Russian heroines (beginning with *Onegin*'s Tatiana, who married a general) and setting an example to a gallery of Soviet women (in Ilf and Petrov's *Golden Calf* [1931], Ehrenburg's *Out of Chaos* [*Den' vtoroi*; 1933], and many others).

42. In a follow-up to notes 29 and 31, let us note that the romantic and reciprocal love of the novel's two title heroes remains unprocreative, focused on the Master's manuscript as their only "child."

43. Cf., on one hand, the pointedly modernist narrative of Mandelstam's *The Egyptian Stamp* (1928) and Pasternak's *Safe Conduct* (1931), and on the other, the picaresque plot of Ilf and Petrov's Bender saga (1927–31). Incidentally, both mythologism and a strong fabula were in accord with the general "Thermidorian" style of the 1930s.

44. Similar 'romantic' treatment of the writer-protagonist figure (and the plot in general) in Nabokov's *The Gift* (1937) and Pasternak's *Doctor Zhivago* (1957), the two other major attempts at a modern Russian novel, seem to testify to the deep-seated conservatism of the Russian tradition.

EIGHT

1. "Kvartira tikha, kak bumaga," dated November 1933; see O. Mandelstam 1967–69, 1: 196–97, 508–9. The quotations in this section are from chap. 33, "The Antipodes," of N. Mandelstam's first book of memoirs (1976: 149–55).

2. N. Mandelstam cites the mysterious connections of Evgraf Zhivago; cf. Bulgakov's interest in figures of authority as desirable protectors of artists.

3. Namely, "Noch' na dvore" (1931), "a reply" to Pasternak's "Krasavitsa moia" (1931) and to its insistence on "the privileged social position of the poet."

4. *Volny* was written in the fall of 1931 and first published in early 1932 (see Pasternak 1990, 1: 488).

5. "Leningrad" was written in December of the same year, 1931, and published in 1932 (Mandelstam 1967–69, 1: 158–59, 486–87).

6. On Pasternak's three periods see Zholkovsky 1986b, 1990.

7. "Khotet', v otlich'e ot khlyshcha / V ego sushchestvovan'e kratkom, / Truda so vsemi soobshcha / I zaodno s pravoporiadkom" ("Stolet'e s lishnim— ne vchera"). Remarkably, an echo of these lines can be heard in Mandelstam's 1935 exilic "Stanzas," I: "Ia ne khochu, sred' iunoshei teplichnykh / Razmenivat' poslednii grosh dushi, / No, kak v kolkhoz idet edinolichnik, / Ia v mir vkhozhu, i liudi khoroshi." Moreover, in a still later (and only recently discovered, see Shveitser 1989), 1937 poem, significantly entitled "Stansy," probably his very last work, Mandelstam seems to continue his dialogue with IWH. The poem is written in the "Pasternakian" iambic tetrameter and attempts the acceptance of Socialism and Stalin by resorting to typically Pasternakian motifs, diction, grammar, and lexicon—including, at times, almost direct quotes: "vkhodit' v polia, vrastat' v lesa"; "zhizn' bez ukorizn"; "dozreiut novye plody"; "I ty prorvesh'sia, mozhet stat'sia, / Skvoz' chashchu prozvishch i imen." Pasternak by that time must have seemed to Mandelstam to be in possession of a magical secret of survival.

8. "Stolet'e s lishnim—ne vchera"; on this poem see note 15.

9. The Russian idiom *kak sapozhnik*, "like a cobbler," means "clumsily, poorly"; moreover, the cobbler image foreshadows the provocative promotion of Demyan Bedny to the status of "the Hans Sachs of our popular movement": the German poet "Sachs was a cobbler by trade" (see A. Livingstone's commentary on pp. 178, 281). On a still deeper level, however, the mention of *sapozhnik*, lit. "boot-maker," evokes the special value attached to *sapogi*, "boots," in Russian literature.

Boots were *the* emblematic synecdoche of the *raznochintsy* ("third-estate") intellectuals of the 1860s (note, in Mandelstam's "Kvartira," the allegiance to the democratic tradition of Nekrasov, expressed in "boot" terms: "Tebe, stariku i neriakhe, / Pora sapogami stuchat' "). The utilitarian Nihilist critics (Dmitrii Pisarev and others) claimed that boots were more valuable than "art for art's sake," e.g., than Pushkin. Dostoevsky ironized this in *The Possessed* ("sapogi nizhe Pushkina"; see commentaries in Dostoevsky 1972–90, 12: 284, 311–12, a reference kindly suggested by Marcus Levitt).

The Nihilists' program of producing 'useful art' was resurrected, in a new key, by the *Lef* futurists: "Such work gives the artist the right to stand along-side the other working groups of the Commune, with cobblers [!], carpenters, tailors . . ." (Brik 1919: 225–26); cf. also Mayakovsky's lines in *Oblako v shtanakh* (1914): "Chto mne do Fausta, feeriei raket / skol'ziashchego s Mefistofelem v nebesnom parkete! / Ia znaiu—gvozd' u menia v sapoge / koshmarnei, chem fantaziia u Gete."

10. On the thematics and stylistics of Pasternak's second period, see Siniavsky-Terts 1978: 107; Raevsky-Hughes 1974: 89–94.

11. On the 1925 Resolution, see Slonim 1977: 50; on Pasternak's reaction, Fleishman 1990: 133.

12. Pasternak's acknowledged indebtedness to and affinities with Tolstoy are well known, in particular from the second autobiography (1959b; see also 1985b: 195); on the Goethe connection, in particular on *sila*, "force, power," seen as the central principle in *Faust*, see Pasternak 1990b: 340–41; Kopelev 1979: 499–500.

13. Here and below, in characterizing Pasternak's invariants, I proceed, often without references, from my previous work (Zholkovsky 1976, 1980b, 1983a, 1983b, 1984a, 1984b, 1985a, 1985b, 1985c, 1986b, 1990, 1991a, 1992a), which owes much to and builds on Jakobson 1969 [1935], Nilsson 1978 [1959], Siniavsky-Terts 1978 [1965], and Lotman 1978 [1969].

14. Incidentally, 'rape' is a recurrent 'sinisterly magnificent' motif in Pasternak (Zholkovsky 1984b: 123): "Vo sne ia slyshal krik, i on. . . . / I zhenshchinoiu oskorblennoi, / Byt' mozhet, izdan byl vdali / . . . / Bol'shoi kanal s kosoi ukhmylkoi / Ogliadyvalsia, kak beglets" ("Venetsiia"); "V kontse zh, kak zhenshchina, otprianuv, / I chudom sderzhivaia pryt' / Vpot'makh pristavshikh gorlopanov . . ." ("Opiat' Shopen").

15. Pushkin's 1826 "Stanzas" ("V nadezhde slavy i dobra"), whitewash-ing Nicholas by likening him to Peter the Great, are an overt subtext of the programmatically analogous poem in *Second Birth*, "Stolet'e s lishnim—ne vchera" (A hundred years is not yesterday), where the 1930s are compared to the 1830s, and by implication, Stalin to Nicholas I and Peter the Great.

Pasternak's identification with Pushkin in his most problematic role as a "renegade" from his near-Decembrist 1820s self and a "collaborator" with the Nicholaevan regime may also underlie some essential similarities between the two authors' major prose works. Both *Doctor Zhivago* and *The Captain's Daughter* feature protagonists who find themselves now on one, now on the other side in a civil war, acting as involuntary traitors. On *The Captain's Daughter* in this respect, see Iakubovich 1939: 185–87; on *Doctor Zhivago*, Shcheglov 1990, 1: 47–49.

16. On the biographical and intertextual underpinnings of this image, see Pomorska 1975: 37–39.

17. In broader terms, this is a widely used figure of passing off some parti-

san ideology or special interest for something natural and universal; on such strategies, see Zholkovsky 1983b, 1985c.

18. E.g., "Eto poistine novoe chudo, / Eto, kak prezhde, snova vesna" ("Opiat' vesna").

19. "V ego ustakh zvuchalo 'zavtra,' / Kak na ustakh inykh 'vchera' " (1918–23); "V rodstve so vsem, chto est', uverias' / I znaias' s budushchim v bytu" (1931); "Ia vizhu . . . / Vsiu budushchuiu zhizn' naskvoz'. / Vse do mel'chaishei doli sotoi / V nei opravdalos' i sbylos' " (1958).

20. On the metonymic principle in Pasternak and its function in 'hiding' the speaker's persona in its surroundings, see Jakobson 1969, Nilsson 1978.

21. See "Ia komnatu brata zaimu. / V nei shum uplotnitelei tishe" ("Krugom semeniashcheisia vatoi"); "I okno po krestovine sdavit golod drovianoi" ("Nikogo ne budet v dome"; about this poem, see Zholkovsky 1980).

22. A draft version of "I Want to Go Home" (IWH) featured a link to the seascape of *Waves*: "Obrubki dnei, kak sakhar, khrupki, / I galek melko nakolov, / Znai skatyvaet more v trubki / Belok razorvannykh valov."

23. *Temen' prosto strast'* means literally "darkness to the point of passion" and connotes the passion of Christ on the cross.

24. Cf. the *grudnaia kletka* in a contemporaneous poem, "Borisu Pil'niaku," rhyming with *piatiletka* and symbolizing the speaker's gut conservatism.

25. On Zoshchenko's 1930s Pushkinism, see Reyfman 1992; on the conservative influence of the Socialist Realist canon on Bulgakov, see Chapter 7.

26. See Matich 1990; see also Chapter 7 on Olesha and Bulgakov, with a reference to Mayakovsky's poem "O vselenii rabochego Ivana Kozyreva v novuiu kvartiru," and Chapter 9 on the treatment of space in dystopias.

27. See Blok 1960–63, 3: 125–26; Khodasevich 1982–83, 1: 184–85. On these and other subtexts of Mandelstam's "Kvartira," see Ronen 1973: 385–87 and Freidin 1987: 239–41, 377; on Khodasevich's "Ballada," see Bethea 1985: 237–50.

28. On the conversion of the 'home' topos from positive to negative in Baudelaire's first "Spleen" and on attendant problems of poetic analysis, see Riffaterre 1978: 66–70.

29. "Zaryt'sia by v svezhem bur'iane, / Zabyt'sia by snom navsegda! / Molchite, prokliatye knigi! / Ia vas ne pisal nikogda!" Notably, Blok's complete renunciation is couched in the terms of Lermontov's "Vykhozhu odin ia na dorogu" (e.g., "Ia b khotel zabyt'sia i zasnut' "), which ends on the speaker's somewhat positive, if ambiguous, slumber under an evergreen oak, to the tune of nature's love songs.

30. Such as being pierced by a blade, rising above lifeless existence, reaching up to the skies and under the ground, acquiring a snake's vision, and being inspired by a superior agency: "I uzkoe, uzkoe, uskoe, / Pronzaet menia lezvie. / / Ia sam nad soboi vyrastaiu, / Nad mertvym vstaiu bytiem, / Stopami v

podzemnoe plamia, / V tekuchie zvezdy chelom. // I vizhu bol'shimi glazami, / Glazami, byt' mozhet, zmei—/ . . . // I kto-to tiazheluiu liru / Mne v ruki skvoz' veter daet"; in Pushkin's poem, the prophet is given a [she-]eagle's eyes and a snake's sting/tongue.

31. On the difference between symbolist and postsymbolist value systems see also Chapter 10, note 22. On the Pasternakian unity of the home and the macro-world, see Zholkovsky 1984a: 138–42; for a contrastive analysis of four poems (two by Pasternak, two by Okudzhava) treating a variation of the 'poet's apartment' topos ('the beloved's visit'), see Zholkovsky 1980c.

32. On IWH's numerous subtextual links with "At Home" (in light of symbolism's centrifugality), see Smirnov 1985: 80–82; the links with "By the Kremlin" were pointed out to me by S. I. Gindin (oral communication); see also Zholkovsky 1991c: 33–34. To quote some of Briusov's more striking parallels to IWH: "Tam vse poniatno i zhakomo, / . . . / . . . ia doma / . . . / Pust' . . . / . . . / I ne ischerpano blazhenstv, / No chuiu blesk inogo sveta, / Vosmozhnost' novykh sovershestv!" ("U sebia"); "Po snegu ten' . . . / No gorod-mif—moi mir domashnii, / Moi krov, kogda vne—burelom. / . . . / I—zov nad stonom, svetoch v temen'—/ S zemli do zvezd vstaet Moskva. / . . . / Polveka dum nas v tsep' spaiali, / . . . / Zdes' polnit pamiat' vse shagi mne, / I ia khranim, zvuk v ch'em-to gimne, / Moskva! v dymu tvoikh legend!" ("U Kremlia").

33. Briusov was one of the first to join the Soviet literary establishment. The poem in question was written for the celebration of his fiftieth birthday at the Bolshoi Theater, where Pasternak also read his dedication, "Valeriiu Briusovu." In that poem, Pasternak dwelt on the sad ambiguity of Briusov's position: "Chto mne skazat'? Chto Briusova gor'ka / Shiroko razbezhavshaiasia uchast'? . . . / Chto ne bezdelka—ulybat'sia, muchas'?" (cf. Grossman 1989).

34. See note 33. In fact, Briusov had proclaimed a similar defeatist attitude as early as 1905 in his "Griadushchie gunny": "No vas, kto menia unichtozhit, / Vstrechaiu privetstvennym gimnom"; incidentally, the word *gimn* appears in the penultimate rhyme of "U Kremlia" in what may be a deliberately grim self-irony. Pasternak later (in *Vysokaia bolezn'*, 1923–28) wryly portrayed such suicidal deference to "the people": "A szadi, v zareve legend, / Idealist-intelligent / Pisal i risoval plakaty / Pro radost' svoego zakata"; the rhyme *legend-intelligent* also echoes the concluding rhyme of Briusov's "U Kremlia": *aborigen* (Briusov's self-reference)–*legend*.

35. Cf. Mayakovsky's programmatic line "Kazhdyi iz nas po-svoemu loshad' " in his "Khoroshee otnoshenie k loshadiam" (1918); on his canine motifs and the 'slaughterhouse' theme in Bulgakov, Olesha, Babel, and Pilnyak and its links to the equine topos in Dostoevsky and Nekrasov, see Chapter 7 and Zholkovsky 1992b.

36. "Slezaite s neba, zaoblachnyi zhitel! / Snimaite mantii drevnosti! / Sil'neishimi uzami muzu vviazhite, / kak loshad',—v voz povsednevnosti!"

("Na chto zhaluetes'?" 1929; Mayakovsky 1955–61, 10: 143; the parallel with IWH was kindly suggested to me by Nataliia Rubinshtein.) In addition to the many obvious parallels with IWH, note the common motif of 'undressing' (see IWH, 1: 3) that accompanies rebirth.

37. On the role of horse and riding in Pasternak's personal mythology, see Fleishman 1977, Raevsky-Hughes 1989, Boris Gasparov 1990, and Zholkovsky 1991a.

38. On this episode of Bloomian anxiety of influence, see Pasternak 1985b: 137, Jakobson 1969: 149.

39. The genealogy of 'harness' probably also includes Nikolai Aseev's lines about the nightingale-poet's desire to share the yoke of the industrial plants ("solov'iu . . . zakhotelos' v odno iarmo / s gudiashchimi vslast' zavodami" in "O nem," 1922; Aseev 1967: 132). Aseev was Pasternak's favorite among Mayakovsky's futurist followers; he lived to revise his technocratic view of poetry (see "K drugu-stikhotvortsu," 1959; Aseev 1967: 278–79); Pasternak develops the 'art = yoke' metaphor in his "Bal'zak" (1928).

40. On foreshadowing, see Shcheglov and Zholkovsky 1987: 99–122; on "figures" as "artistic templates" (S. Eisenstein), or "objective correlatives" (T. S. Eliot), of emotions, see ibid.: 9, 13, 29–31, 273–82.

41. The study of advertising as an art form was broached by that consummate theorist of style, Leo Spitzer (1962). In fact, advertising qua art was actively promoted and practiced by the futurists, especially Mayakovsky; cf. note 9 on the topos 'boots' as an aesthetic object.

42. Both the 'again something new' motif and its anaphoric icon are Pasternakian invariants (see above), abounding, often in conjunction, in his texts before, during, and after the 1930s. E.g.: "Opiat' . . . / Proshlos' po lampam opakhalo . . . / Opiat' fregat poshel na travers. / Opiat' . . ." (Vysokaia bolezn', 1923–28); the seven "agains" in "Opiat' Shopen ne ishchet vygod" (Second Birth); "Ia na toi zhe ulitse starinnoi, / Kak togda . . . / Te zhe . . . / Tak zhe . . . / Tak zhe . . . / Ia opiat' . . . / I opiat' . . ." ("Ob'iasnenie," 1947).

43. On the "classicist" nature and orientation of Socialist Realism, see above and Siniavsky-Terts 1982 [1959]; Clark 1981.

44. On the concept of 'poetry of grammar,' see Jakobson 1985; on the trope-like manipulation of tense, with special reference to Proust, see Genette 1980: 113–14, 147 (cf. similar comments on Pushkin and Limonov in Chapter 6).

45. According to Mayakovsky's famous definition: "Poeziia—vsia!—ezda v neznaemoe!" ("Razgovor s fininspektorom o poezii," 1926).

46. The wide expanses, as well as routes that lead there, are consistently positive; but even closed, prisonlike enclosures are sometimes poeticized, with a bittersweet touch; e.g., "Kto eto, gadaet, glaza mne riumit / Tiuremnoi liudskoi dremoi" ("Devochka," 1922); "Dai zapru ia tvoiu krasotu / V temnom tereme stikhotvoren'ia" ("Bez nazvaniia," 1956). On Pasternak's positive use of the motif of 'law enforcement,' see Zholkovsky 1984b: 124–25.

47. Anna Akhmatova, in her metapoetic poem "Boris Pasternak" (1936), finds room for a paraphrase of IWH's stanza 6: "Kto zabludilsia v dvukh shagakh ot doma, / Gde sneg po poias i vsemu konets"; and her finale ("Za to, chto . . . / On nagrazhden") is patterned on the closure of IWH.

48. Cf. also the discussion of *sapogi* in note 9.

49. Pasternak coined an aphoristic image of this dialectic in *Spektorskii* (1925–30): "A starshii byl miatezhnik, to est' despot."

50. Pushkin epigrammatized Karamzin's *History of the Russian State*, which marked its formerly rather liberal author's turn to conservatism, with these lines: "In his *History*, elegance, simplicity / Demonstrate to us, without any partiality, / The necessity of autocracy / And the charms of the whip" (1818). Ironically again, Pushkin would live to undergo a similar evolution and thus set a precedent for Pasternak's (see above). Another irony, germane to the aesthetic issue at hand, is inherent in Pushkin's prescient linking of 'simplicity' with 'necessity,' 'autocracy,' and 'the knout.'

51. Cf. the ecstatic celebration of the poet (Pushkin) drinking the reflections of the stars from the beloved's kneecaps / cups (*chashechek kolennykh*) in "Tema" (1918; see Zholkovsky 1984a: 211–14) with the tragic image of Chopin in "Opiat' Shopen" (in *Second Birth*). On the Pasternakian motif of 'duty, indebtedness, tribute,' see Zholkovsky 1984b; it is prominent in the characterization of Balzac ("Bal'zak," 1928): "A ikh zadolzhnik i dolzhnik . . . / Chtob vykupit'sia iz iarma / Uzhasnogo zaimodavtsa, . . . / Zachem zhe bylo brat' v kredit / Parizh?"; see also the famous portrayal of the artist as "eternity's hostage held captive by the time" ("Noch'," 1956); on Pasternak's 'defeatist ecstasy,' see Zholkovsky 1991a.

52. "Chto gde-to za stvolami more, / Mereshchitsia vse vremia mne" ("Sosny," 1941). Note Pasternak's consistent siding with things 'marginal, provincial, second-rate,' to the point of stressing the "deliberate provinciality" of Jesus Christ in *Doctor Zhivago* (2: 10); poetry, accordingly, is defined as "a summer with a seat in a third-class suburban train car" ("Poeziia," 1922).

53. Paronomastic punctuation of *opiat'* sequences recurs in Pasternak (variously combined with beat acceleration); see the *opiat'-upast'* pairing in "Opiat' Shopen" and *opiat'-raspakhnutykh-opakhalo* in *Vysokaia bolezn'*.

54. "Ia ne rozhden, chtob tri raza / Smotret' po-raznomu v glaza" (*Vysokaia bolezn'*).

55. Note also the "survivalist" potential of Pasternak's metaphorical *Verdrängung* of 'sinister' motifs into nature's micro-world (flowers, raindrops, etc.); see Zholkovsky 1984b: 129–31.

NINE

1. The term is used here in a broad sense, covering such disparate cases as *The Divine Comedy*, the picaresque novel, *Don Quixote*, *Dead Souls*, and

Jaroslav Hašek's *The Good Soldier Schweik*; on the thematic relevance of such comparisons, see Shcheglov 1986c: 93–104; 1990, 1: 34–49.

2. For a survey of opinions, see Kurdiumov 1983: 9–34.

3. See Riffaterre 1978: esp. 3–5, 63–80; for the critical strategy of uncovering, underneath a parodic jumble, a positive thematic thrust, cf. the beginning of Chapter 5.

4. "Krizis zhanra." Malamuth's translation, "The Landscape Changes," completely misses this point, Richardson's "A Crisis in the Arts" is closer; see Ilf and Petrov 1966, 1962, respectively.

5. See, respectively, Ilf and Petrov 1961, 3: 193–97; 1935: 32–37; for English translations, see Guerney 1960: 397–407; my analysis is based on Shcheglov and Zholkovskii 1976: 220–22.

6. On the direct use of chap. 2: 7 of *The Possessed* ("U nashikh"), see Shcheglov 1990, 1: 217).

7. The word 'ordering' is used here in the sense of "calling up made-to-order dreams," as in "ordering a meal or a book" (and not "making dreams orderly").

8. This crippled condition is very much in the spirit of the times; cf. Pasternak's co-temporaneous statement: "My v budushchem, tverzhu ia im, kak vse, kto / Zhil v eti dni. A esli iz kalek [!], / To vse ravno: telegoiu proekta / Nas pereekhal novyi chelovek." (We are in the future, I keep telling them, like all, who / Have lived in these days. And if [we should prove to be] from among cripples, / It does not matter: With [his] cart of the Project / The new man has run over us) ("Kogda ia ustaiu ot pustozvonstva," 1931); cf. Chapter 8.

9. A similar figure is "substitute-chairman [*zits-predsedatel'*] Funt, . . . a man from the good old days," who did time (as the front for various shady companies) under several czars and revolutionary regimes. Funt is akin to the old railway worker Kordubailo in Solzhenitsyn's "An Incident at Krechetovka Station" (Pomorska 1971: 42–91), who has taken a military oath of allegiance to five consecutive regimes. A grim opposite case is provided, as usual, by Orwell, in the person of the anonymous old prole Winston Smith probes in vain for information about prerevolutionary times (*1984*, 1: 8).

10. Unlike Ilf and Petrov, the authors of most dystopias (with the possible exception of Burgess) are clearly in moral sympathy with the victimized protagonist, disillusioned as they are with the human condition.

11. For dream control in Akhmatova, Tsvetaeva, Zabolotskii, Mikhail Bulgakov, Thomas Mann ("Mario and the Magician"), and others, see Zholkovsky 1986g: 201–6.

12. Being "false" in this rhetorical sense, they are, of course, thematically overdetermined in other respects. Thus, they foreground Khvorob'ev's 'problematic monarchism,' which in turn provides an ironic counterpoint to the dystopian theme of total control.

13. Similar dreams and visions, including ordered ones, appear in Turgenev's "After Death (Klara Milich)."

14. Dostoevsky spoofs the traditional recurrence of "the same old dream" not only by iteration but also by the dream's very content: the Russian idiom *skazka pro belogo byka/bychka* ("a tale about the white bull") means "endless repetition of one and the same thing" (see the dictionary entry for *Belyi* ["White"], Chernyshev 1948: 379); an approximate English counterpart would be dreaming of a shaggy dog.

15. In the spirit of Tynianov's (1977a [1921]) analysis of Opiskin as a parody of Gogol's *Selected Passages from Correspondence with Friends*, the purported dream about elegant ladies cum Foma himself can be seen as an ironic combination of Piskarev's fixation on his prostitute qua lady and Gogol's own obsessive insistence in *Selected Passages* on the educational role of the company of beautiful ladies (esp. in chapters 2, "Zhenshchina v svete," and 21, "Chto takoe gubernatorsha"). Khvorob'ev echoes this only in the very general sense of yearning for dreams from court life. His one possible direct link with *Selected Passages* is in the mention of "Czar's issue from the Cathedral of the Assumption of the Holy Virgin," comparable with Gogol's praise of the book *Tsarskie vykhody* (Czars' issues): "It was as though I saw everywhere a Czar of olden times reverently going to evening services in all his antique imperial attire" (Letter 15, Gogol 1937–52, 8: 279; 1969: 86–87).

16. For the concept of intertextual clusters, see Chapter 5 and in more detail, Zholkovsky 1992c.

TEN

1. For the complete Russian text of "Fro," see Platonov 1971: 389–408; for an English rendering (by Helen Colaclides), see Pomorska 1971, 1: 183–202.

2. In the Russian critical tradition it is known as "slow" rather than "close," following M. Gershenzon (1919).

3. Cf. Marina Tsvetaeva's "An Ode to Walking on Foot" (1931).

4. Platonov foresees, as it were, the attacks to which "Fro" was to be subjected on the pages of that same journal by Gurvich (1938 [1937]). That article is remarkable for the way it grounds a Zhdanovite political denunciation in a perceptive and thorough analysis of Platonov's poetics. Platonov responded in *Literaturnaia gazeta* (1938).

5. Anticipating Yurii Zhivago, she "asked: 'But why does it follow that anyone should say B after saying A? What if . . . I don't want to?' " Cf. " 'Anyone who says *A* must say *B*.' . . . I'll say *A* but I won't say *B*—whatever you do" (Zhivago to Liberius; Pasternak 1958: 339). Both seem to go back to the Underground Man's rejection of the 2 + 2 = 4 principle.

6. "Fro" shares with Bunin's "Gentle Breathing" (about which see Chap-

ter 4) the 'soul-spirit-breathing-wind' cluster, and a direct influence is not improbable. Bocharov (in his article on Platonov, "The Stuff of Existence," 1985: 249–96) compares a 'breathing' passage from "Fro" with a similar one in "Aphrodite," which he shows to refer directly to "Gentle Breathing" (259–60).

7. Tolstoy 1928–58, 41: 375; see also Lakshin 1975: 81–97 (the chapter "Tolstoy's Favorite Story").

8. See Lakshin 1975: 96; for a complete list of Tolstoy's corrections, see Tolstoy 1975, 1 (2): 440.

9. I. I. Gorbunov-Posadov's letter of January 24, 1899, see Chekhov 1974–80, 10: 410. See also Poggioli 1957: 122–30 (repr. Chekhov 1979: 319–28) and Winner 1963.

10. The phoenix was a solar bird reborn in flames (Leach and Fried 1972: 868). This reconciles our reading of Fedor as an 'enchanted husband' with Naiman's "thematic mythology" (1987), in terms of which he is, of course, a Promethean character.

11. Cf. in Apuleius and Aksakov, the "technological" wonders permitting the heroine's communication with the invisible spouse: the magic music and voices, writings on the wall, immediately delivered letters, etc.

12. Cf. in some plots the disenchantment by kisses or by burning the animal skin of the monster husband; on a parallel to Psyche's spying on Cupid in *Anna Karenina* (7: 25), see Mandelker 1990: 63–64.

13. Her special links to the wind have Apuleian roots: Psyche is the Greek for "soul, breathing, butterfly," and Zephyrus is a "(westerly) wind."

14. In Platonov's "Finist," the heroine "leans down close to him, breathes one and the same breath with him" (162), very much in the spirit of Fro.

15. It is an accepted view that the folktale is a late, "sanitized," descendant of myth. For calculi of possible thematic and structural transmutations of the same plots, see Frye 1957 and Brémond 1973.

16. On Fro's affinities with the heroine of Platonov's "Aphrodite," see Tolstaia-Segal 1977: 202; Geller 1984: 363.

17. On this signature and the semanticization in Platonov of the characters' names, including Fro's, see Tolstaia-Segal 1977: 196–209.

18. On Platonov's relations with Socialist Realism, as well as its (post)-symbolist links, see Gunther 1982, Seifrid 1987, 1992.

19. On Platonov's links to Fedorov and Bogdanov, see Tolstaia-Segal 1981: 238–40; Geller 1984: 30–33; Teskey 1982.

20. On Pasternak's rhetoric of born-again Socialism, see Chapter 8.

21. See "Promezhutok" (Tynianov 1977b: 185); the section that deals with Pasternak is translated in Davie and Livingstone 1969 as "Pasternak's 'Mission'" (126–34; see 130–31).

22. See Jakobson 1969 [1935], Lotman 1978 [1969], Zholkovsky 1985b. The prosaic connection of such perspectives is illuminated by the literary origins

of the soap-bubble passage in *Envy*. Olesha admired Edgar Allan Poe's story "The Sphinx," where a man "who sat in front of an open window saw a fantastic monster moving across a distant hillside. . . . But it turned out . . . that it had been a most ordinary insect . . . crawling in a cobweb at a very short distance from the observing eye against the background of the distant hills" (Olesha, "In the World" [1937]; see 1956: 345). Poe had been a mentor of the French and subsequently Russian symbolist poets; remarkably, Olesha, a postsymbolist, turned to Poe's prose for a pointedly ironic naturalization of the mystical communion with 'the distance.' Since the symbolists focused on the "invisible to the eye," preferring to ignore "the crude bark of the matter" and "erase the occasional features" of things (in the classic formulations of Vladimir Solov'ev), it was up to the postsymbolists to reinvent "realistic," i.e., spatial and causal, links between nearby phenomena and faraway noumena (see also Bocharov 1985: 258).

23. The affinities between the two poetics extend into the linguistic realm, where the juxtaposition of the near and the distant, the concrete and the abstract, etc., is iconized by ungrammatical collocations; cf. Fedor "surrounded by Siberia" with such Pasternakian lines as "Smotrel otsiuda ia za krug Sibiri, / No drug i sam byl gorodom, kak Omsk/I Tomsk,—byl krugom voin i peremirii" (I looked from here beyond the circle of Siberia, / But [my] friend himself was a city, like Omsk/Or Tomsk,—[he] was a circle of wars and armistices), ("Okno, piupitr" [The window, the music stand], 1931). On the treatment of language in Platonov and Pasternak, see, respectively, Seifrid 1987, 1992, and Zholkovsky 1985b; on the analogies between the two, see Tolstaia-Segal 1981: 272.

24. On the problematic of adaptation to the official discourse, see Chapter 8.

25. Platonov's theme of 'overpowering' (*prevozmoganie*) is discussed by Vasil'ev (1982: 165).

26. I omit both the corresponding examples (superfluous for an informed Platonov reader) and an overview of the stylistic and intertextual motifs.

27. On the role of 'emptiness' in Platonov's worldview, see Tolstaia-Segal 1979: 246–47; 1981: 270; Naiman 1987; Epshtein 1989: 303–7; see also Podoroga 1991.

28. On Platonov's surrealism (and its links to Fedor Sologub), see Tolstaia-Segal 1979: 239.

29. Katerina Clark's view of the Socialist Realist novel as ritualistic is reflected in the subtitle of her 1981 book, *The Soviet Novel: History as Ritual*.

Works Cited

The following abbreviations are used in the Works Cited:

GVS   *Gogol' v vospominaniiax sovremennikov*: Mashinskii 1952
IJSLP   *International Journal of Slavic Linguistics and Poetics*
LO   *Literaturnoe obozrenie*
SEEJ   *Slavic and East European Journal*
SH   *Slavica Hierosolymitana*
SLIa   *Izvestiia AN SSSR. Seriia literatury i iazyka*
SR   *Slavic Review*
TZS   *Trudy po znakovym sistemam*
RL   *Russian Literature*
VL   *Voprosy literatury*
WSA   *Wiener Slawistischer Almanach*

Afanas'ev, A. N. 1957. *Narodnye russkie skazki*. 3 vols. Ed. V. Propp. Moscow: GIKhL.
Akhmatova, Anna. 1968 [1936]. "*Adol'f* Benzhamena Konstana v tvorchestve Pushkina." In her *Sochineniia*, ed. G. P. Struve and B. A. Filippov, 2: 223–56. Washington, D.C.: Inter-Language Literary Associates.
Aksakov, Sergei. 1983 [1856]. "The Scarlet Flower: A Fairy-Tale Told by Pelageya, the Housekeeper." Appendix to his *Years of Childhood*, trans. J. D. Duff, pp. 297–318. Oxford: Oxford University Press.

Alekseev, M. P. 1967. *Stikhotvorenie Pushkina "Ia pamiatnik sebe vozdvig . . .":* *Problemy ego izucheniia*. Leningrad: Nauka.

Al'fonsov, V. 1990. *Poeziia Borisa Pasternaka*. Leningrad: Sovetskii pisatel'.

Anderson, Roger. 1974. *N. M. Karamzin's Prose: The Teller in the Tale: A Study in Narrative Technique*. Houston: Cordovan Press.

Annenkov, P. V. 1983. *Literaturnye vospominaniia*. Ed. Iu. V. Mann. Moscow: Khudozhestvennaia literatura.

Aseev, Nikolai. 1967. *Stikhotvoreniia i poemy*. Leningrad: Sovetskii pisatel'.

Babel, Isaac. 1955. *The Collected Stories*. Ed. and trans. Walter Morrison. New York: Criterion.

———. 1964. *The Lonely Years: Unpublished Stories and Private Correspondence*. Ed. Nathalie Babel. New York: Farrar and Straus.

Baiburin, A., and G. Levinton. 1972. "Tezisy k probleme volshebnaia skazka i svad'ba." In *Qinquagenario. Sbornik statei molodykh filologov k piatidesiatiletiiu professora Iu. M. Lotmana*, pp. 67–85. Tartu: TGU.

Bakhtin, Mikhail. 1968 [1965]. *Rabelais and His World*. Trans. Hélène Izwolsky. Cambridge, Mass.: MIT Press.

———. 1984 [1963]. *Problems of Dostoevsky's Poetics*. Ed. and trans. Caryl Emerson. Minneapolis: University of Minnesota Press.

Balzac, Honoré de. 1986 [1835]. *Seraphita*. Blauvelt, N.Y.: Freedeeds Library.

Barnes, Christopher. 1990. *Boris Pasternak: A Literary Biography (1890–1928)*. Vol. 1. Cambridge, Eng.: Cambridge University Press.

Barratt, Andrew. 1981. *Yuri Olesha's "Envy."* Birmingham, Eng.: Birmingham Slavonic Monographs (no. 12).

———. 1987. *Between Two Worlds. A Criticial Introduction to "The Master and Margarita."* Oxford: Oxford University Press.

Bar-Sella, Zeev. 1982. "Tolkovaniia na." *Dvadtsat' dva* 23: 214–33.

———. 1984. "Vse tsvety rodstva." *Dvadtsat' dva* 37: 192–208.

Barthes, Roland. 1974a [1970]. *S/Z: An Essay*. New York: Hill and Wang.

———. 1974b [1973]. *The Pleasure of the Text*. New York: Hill and Wang.

Bayley, John. 1981. "Sophisticated Razzmatazz." *Parnassus: Poetry in Review* 9: 83–90.

Beaujour, Elizabeth K. 1970. *The Invisible Land. A Study in the Artistic Imagination of Iurii Olesha*. New York: Columbia University Press.

Begak, B., N. Kravtsov, and A. Morozov. 1980 [1930]. *Russkaia literaturnaia parodiia*. Ann Arbor, Mich.: Ardis.

Belinkov, A. 1976. *Sdacha i gibel' sovetskogo intelligenta. Iurii Olesha*. Madrid.

Belozerskaia-Bulgakova, L. E. 1979. *O, med vospominanii*. Ann Arbor, Mich.: Ardis.

Belyi, Andrei. 1934. *Masterstvo Gogolia. Issledovanie*. Moscow: OGIZ GIKhL.

Bernstein, Michael André. 1981. "When the Carnival Turns Bitter: Preliminary Reflections Upon the Abject Hero." In Gary Saul Morson, ed., *Bakh-*

tin: Essays and Dialogues on His Work, pp. 90–121. Chicago: University of Chicago Press.

Bethea, David. 1985. *Khodasevich. His Life and Art.* Princeton, N.J.: Princeton University Press.

Blium, A. 1970. " 'Grammatika liubvi.' " *Nauka i zhizn'* no. 9: 60–63.

Blok, Aleksandr. 1960–63. *Sobranie sochinenii.* 8 vols. Moscow: GIKhL.

———. 1962 [1910]. "O sovremennom sostoianii russkogo simvolizma." In his *Sobranie sochinenii*, 8 vols., 5: 425–36. Moscow: GIKhL.

Bloom, Harold. 1973. *Anxiety of Influence: A Theory of Poetry.* New York: Oxford University Press.

———. 1975. *A Map of Misreading.* New York: Oxford University Press.

Bloom, Harold, Paul de Man, Jacques Derrida, Geoffrey Hartman, and J. Hillis Miller. 1987. *Deconstruction and Criticism.* New York: Continuum.

Bocharov, S. G. 1974. *Poetika Pushkina. Ocherki.* Moscow: Nauka.

———. 1985. *O khudozhestvennykh mirakh.* Moscow: Sovetskaia Rossiia.

Bogojavlensky, Marianna. 1981. *On the Development of Gogol's Religious Thought: A Dissertation* (in Russian). Ann Arbor, Mich.: University Microfilms.

Bowlt, John. 1988. "The Presence of Absence: The Aesthetic of Transparency in Russian Modernism." *The Structurist* 27–28 (special issue on Transparency and Reflection): 15–22.

Bradbury, Ray. 1967 [1950]. *Fahrenheit 451°.* New York: Simon and Schuster.

Brémond, Claude. 1973. "Les bons récompensés et les méchants punis: morpholigie du conte merveilleux français." In Claude Chabrol, ed., *Sémiotique narrative et textuelle*, pp. 96–121. Paris: Librairie Larousse.

Brik, O. M. 1919. "Khudozhnik i Kommuna." *Izobrazitel'noe iskusstvo*, no. 1: 225–26.

Briusov, Valerii. 1961. *Stikhotvoreniia i poemy.* Leningrad: Sovetskii pisatel'.

Brodsky, Joseph. 1965. *Stikhotvoreniia i poemy.* Washington, D.C.: Inter-Language Literary Associates.

———. 1967. *Elegy to John Donne and Other Poems.* Trans. Nicholas Bethell. London: Longmans.

———. 1970. *Ostanovka v pustyne: Stikhotvoreniia i poemy.* New York: Chekhov.

———. 1973a. *Debut.* Trans. Carl Proffer. Ann Arbor, Mich.: Ardis.

———. 1973b. *Selected Poems.* Trans. George Kline. New York: Harper and Row.

———. 1977a. *Konets prekrasnoi epokhi.* Ann Arbor, Mich.: Ardis.

———. 1977b. *Chast' rechi.* Ann Arbor, Mich.: Ardis.

———. 1980. *A Part of Speech.* New York: Farrar, Straus and Giroux.

———. 1982. *Rimskie elegii.* New York: Russica.

———. 1983. *Novye stansy k Avguste.* Ann Arbor, Mich.: Ardis.

———. 1987. *Uraniia.* Ann Arbor, Mich.: Ardis.

———. 1988. *To Urania.* New York: Farrar, Straus and Giroux.

————. 1990. "The Poet, the Loved One, and the Muse." *Times Literary Supplement*, October 26–November 1, 1990: 1150, 1160.

Brooks, Cleanth. 1975. *The Well-Wrought Urn*. New York: Harcourt Brace Jovanovich.

Brown, Clarence, ed. 1985. *The Portable Twentieth-Century Russian Reader*. New York: Viking.

Brown, Edward J. (ed.). 1973. *Major Soviet Writers: Essays in Criticism*. London: Oxford University Press.

————. 1982. *Russian Literature Since the Revolution*. Cambridge, Mass.: Harvard University Press.

Bulgakov, Mikhail. 1967 [1940]. *The Master and Margarita*. Trans. Michael Glenny. New York: Harper and Row.

————. 1968 [1924]. *Heart of a Dog*. Trans. Mirra Ginsburg. New York: Grove Press.

Bulgakova, Elena. 1990. *Dnevnik Eleny Bulgakovoi*. Moscow: Knizhnaia palata.

Bunin, Ivan. 1922. *The Gentleman from San Francisco and Other Stories*. Trans. S. S. Koteliansky and Leonard Woolf. Paradise Road, Richmond, Eng.: (Published by Leonard and Virginia Woolf at) Hogarth Press.

————. 1965–66. *Sobranie sochinenii*. 9 vols. Moscow: Khudozhestvennaia literatura.

Burgess, Anthony. 1963 [1962]. *A Clockwork Orange*. New York: W. W. Norton.

Carden, Patricia. 1984. "Limonov's Coming Out." In Olga Matich and Michael Henry Heim, eds., *Russian Literature in Emigration: The Third Wave*, pp. 221–29. Ann Arbor, Mich.: Ardis.

Chalmaev, V. 1984. *Andrei Platonov. Ocherki zhizni i tvorchestva*. Voronezh: Tsentral'no-Chernozemnoe knizhnoe izdatel'stvo.

Chatman, Seymour. 1978. *Story and Discourse: Narrative Structure in Fiction and Film*. Ithaca, N.Y.: Cornell University Press.

Chekhov, Anton. 1959. *The Short Stories of Anton Chekhov*. Ed. and intro. Robert N. Linscott. New York: Modern Library.

————. 1974–80. *Polnoe sobranie sochinenii i pisem*. 30 vols. Moscow: Nauka.

————. 1979. *Anton Chekhov's Short Stories: Texts, Backgrounds, Criticism*. Ed. Ralph E. Matlaw. New York: W. W. Norton.

Chernyshev, V. I., comp. 1948. Vol. 1 of *Slovar' sovremennogo russkogo literaturnogo iazyka*, 17 vols. Moscow: AN SSSR.

Chudakov, A. P. 1983. *Chekhov's Poetics*. Ann Arbor, Mich.: Ardis.

Chudakova, M. O. 1972. *Masterstvo Iuriia Oleshi*. Moscow: Nauka.

————. 1979. *Poetika Mikhaila Zoshchenko*. Moscow: Nauka.

————. 1987. "Posleslovie" (afterword to *Heart of a Dog*). *Znamia*, no. 6: 135–41.

————. 1988. *Zhizneopisanie Mikhaila Bulgakova*. Moscow: Kniga.

Chukovskii, K. I. 1981. "Iz vospominanii." In Smolian and Iurgeneva, 1981, pp. 13–66.

Clark, Katerina. 1981. *The Soviet Novel: History as Ritual.* Chicago: University of Chicago Press.

Clark, Katerina, and Michael Holquist. 1984. *Mikhail Bakhtin.* Cambridge, Mass.: Harvard University Press.

Connolly, J. W. 1982. *Ivan Bunin.* Boston: Twayne.

Culler, Jonathan. 1975. *Structuralist Poetics: Structuralism, Linguistics, and the Study of Literature.* Ithaca, N.Y.: Cornell University Press.

———. 1981. *The Pursuit of Signs: Semiotics, Literature, Deconstruction.* Ithaca, N.Y.: Cornell University Press.

———. 1982. *On Deconstruction: Theory and Criticism after Structuralism.* Ithaca, N.Y.: Cornell University Press.

Curtis, Anthony. 1984. "Introduction." In James, 1984, pp. 7–25.

Davie, Donald, and Angela Livingstone, eds. 1969. *Pasternak: Modern Judgements.* Nashville, Tenn.: Aurora.

Debreczeny, Paul. 1966. "Nikolay Gogol and His Contemporary Critics." *Transactions of the American Philosophical Society* 56, no. 3: 5–68.

———. 1983. *The Other Pushkin.* Stanford, Calif.: Stanford University Press.

———. 1985. "Pushkin and Gogol: A Reassessment." Paper presented at the IV Pushkin Symposium at the New York University, Nov. 1985 (MS).

de Man, Paul. 1986. *The Resistance to Theory.* Vol. 33 of *Theory and History of Literature* series. Minneapolis: University of Minnesota Press.

Demolière, Gules. 1829. *Code de l'amour.* Paris.

Derzhavin, G. 1958. *Stikhotvoreniia.* Moscow: Khudozhestvennaia literatura.

Döring-Smirnov, J. Renate. 1989. "Tropen unter Tropen (Politische Allusion am Beispiel von Gedichten N. Zabolockijs)." *WSA* 22: 7–21.

Dostoevsky, Fedor. 1926. *Pis'ma k zhene.* Moscow: Gosizdat.

———. 1972–90. *Polnoe sobranie sochinenii.* 30 vols. Leningrad: Nauka.

———. 1983. *The Village of Stepanchikovo and Its Inhabitants.* Trans. Ignat Avsey. London: Angel Classics.

Dunham, Vera. 1976. *In Stalin's Time: Middle-Class Values in Soviet Fiction.* Cambridge, Eng.: Cambridge University Press.

Dymshits, A. 1981. "Chelovek, kotoryi ne smeialsia." In Smolian and Iurgeneva, 1981, pp. 232–41.

Edmunds, Lowell. 1975. *Oedipus: The Ancient Legend and Its Later Analogues.* Baltimore: Johns Hopkins University Press.

Eikhenbaum, Boris. 1965 [1927]. "The Theory of the 'Formal Method.'" In Lemon and Reis, 1965, pp. 102–39.

———. 1969. "Melodika russkogo liricheskogo stikha." In his *O poezii*, pp. 327–541. Leningrad: Sovetskii pisatel'.

————. 1974 [1919]. "How Gogol's 'Overcoat' Is Made." In Robert Maguire, ed., *Gogol from the Twentieth Century*, pp. 269–91. Princeton, N.J.: Princeton University Press.

————. 1981 [1924]. *Lermontov: A Study in Literary-Historical Evaluation*. Trans. Ray Parrott and Harry Weber. Ann Arbor, Mich.: Ardis.

————. 1982 [1960]. *Tolstoi in the Seventies*. Ann Arbor, Mich.: Ardis.

Eisenstein, Sergei. 1949. "The Structure of the Film." In his *Film Sense: Essays in Film Theory*, ed. and trans. Jay Leyda, pp. 150–78. New York: Harcourt Brace Jovanovich.

————. 1964 [1937]. "[Montazh (1937)]." In Eisenstein 1964–70, 2: 329–484.

————. 1964–70. *Izbrannye proizvedeniia*. 6 vols. Moscow: Iskusstvo.

Elizarenkova, T. Ia., and A. Ia. Syrkin. 1964. "K analizu indiiskogo svadebnogo gimna (Rigveda X. 85)." In Iu. M. Lotman, ed., *Programma i tezisy dokladov v letnei shkole po modeliruiushchim sistemam, 19–24 avgusta 1964 g.*, pp. 69–77. Tartu: TGU.

Epshtein, M. 1989. "Opyty v zhanre 'opytov.'" In A. P. Lavrin, ed., *Zerkala. Al'manakh. 1*, pp. 196–318. Moscow: Moskovskii rabochii.

Erlich, Victor. 1969. *Gogol*. New Haven, Conn.: Yale University Press.

————, ed. 1978. *Pasternak: A Collection of Critical Essays*. Englewood Cliffs, N.J.: Prentice-Hall.

Fanger, Donald. 1978. "Gogol and His Reader." In William Mills Todd III, ed., *Literature and Society in Imperial Russia, 1800–1914*, pp. 61–95. Stanford, Calif.: Stanford University Press.

————. 1979. *The Creation of Nikolai Gogol*. Cambridge, Mass.: Belknap Press, Harvard University Press.

Fasmer, M. 1973. *Etimologicheskii slovar' russkogo iazyka*. Trans. and suppl. O. N. Trubachev. 4 vols. Moscow: Progress.

Fet, A. 1956. *Stikhotvoreniia*. Moscow: Khudozhestvennaia literatura.

Fleishman, Lazar. 1970. "Avtobiograficheskoe i 'Avgust' Pasternaka." *SH* 1: 194–98.

————. 1984. *Boris Pasternak v tridtsatye gody*. Jerusalem: Hebrew University Magnes Press.

————. 1990. *Boris Pasternak: The Poet and His Politics*. Cambridge, Mass.: Harvard University Press.

Foucault, Michel. 1977. *Discipline and Punish: The Birth of the Prison*. New York: Pantheon.

Frank, S. L. 1903. "Fridrikh Nitsshe i etika 'liubvi k dal'nemu'." In P. I. Novgorodtsev, ed., *Problemy idealizma. Sbornik statei*, pp. 137–95. Moscow: Moskovskoe Psikhologicheskoe Obshchestvo.

————. 1977 [1909]. "The Ethic of Nihilism: A Characterization of the Russian Intelligentsia's Moral Outlook." In Boris Shragin and Albert Todd, eds.,

Marian Schwartz, trans., *Landmarks: A Collection of Essays on the Russian Intelligentsia—1909*, pp. 155–84. New York: Karz Howard.

Freidenberg, O. M. 1936. "Tri siuzheta, ili semantika odnogo." In her *Poetika siuzheta i zhanra*, pp. 335–61. Leningrad: GIKhL.

Freidin, Gregory. 1987. *A Coat of Many Colors: Osip Mandelstam and His Mythologies of Self-Presentation*. Berkeley: University of California Press.

Freud, Sigmund. 1964 [1914]. "On Narcissism: An Introduction." In vol. 14 of *Standard Edition of the Complete Psychological Works of Sigmund Freud*, trans. J. Strachey, 24 vols., pp. 69–102. London: Hogarth Press.

Frye, Northrop. 1957. *The Anatomy of Criticism*. Princeton, N.J.: Princeton University Press.

Fusso, Susanne. 1989. "Failures of Transformation in *Sobach'e serdtse*." *SEEJ* 33, no. 3: 386–99.

Gale, Robert L. 1989. *A Henry James Encyclopedia*. New York: Greenwood Press.

Gasparov, Boris. 1978. "Iz nabliudenii nad motivnoi strukturoi romana M. A. Bulgakova *Master i Margarita*." *SH* 3: 198–251.

———. 1990. "Ob odnom ritmiko-muzykal'nom motive v proze Pasternaka (Istoriia odnoi trioli)." Paper presented at the International Pasternak Symposium on Pasternak, Oxford, July 1990.

Gasparov, M. L. 1974. *Sovremennyi russkii stikh*. Moscow: Nauka.

———. 1976. "Metr i smysl: K semantike russkogo 3-st. khoreia." *SLIa* 35: 357–66.

———. 1979. "K semantike russkogo 3-st. iamba." In *Lingvistika i poetika*, pp. 282–308. Moscow: Nauka.

———. 1982. "Semanticheskii oreol 3-st. amfibrakhiia." In *Problemy strukturnoi lingvistiki—1980*, pp. 174–92. Moscow: Nauka.

———. 1983. " 'Spi, mladenets moi prekrasnyi': Semanticheskii oreol raznovidnosti stikhotvornogo razmera." In *Problemy strukturnoi lingvistiki—1981*, pp. 181–97. Moscow: Nauka.

———. 1984a. *Ocherk istorii russkogo stikha. Metrika. Ritmika. Rifma. Strofika.* Moscow: Nauka.

———. 1984b. "M. M. Bakhtin in Russian Culture of the Twentieth Century." Trans. Ann Shukman. *Studies in Twentieth Century Literature* 9, no. 1: 169–76.

Geller, M. 1982. *Andrei Platonov v poiskakh schast'ia*. Paris: YMCA Press.

Genette, Gerard. 1966. "Complexe de Narcisse." In his *Figures: I*, pp. 21–28. Paris: Seuil.

———. 1970. "Time and Narrative in *A la recherche du temps perdu*." In his *Aspects of Narrative*, ed. J. Hillis Miller, pp. 93–118. New York: Columbia University Press.

———. 1980. *Narrative Discourse: An Essay in Method*. Ithaca, N.Y.: Cornell University Press.

Gershenzon, M. O. 1919. " 'Stantsionnyi smotritel'.' " In his *Mudrost' Pushkina*, pp. 122–27. Moscow: Knigoizdatel'stvo pisatelei.

———. 1926. "Sny Pushkina." In his *Stat'i o Pushkine*, pp. 96–110. Moscow: GAKhN.

Ginzburg, Evgeniia. 1967. *Journey into the Whirlwind*. Trans. Ian Boland. New York: Harcourt Brace Jovanovich.

———. 1981. *Within the Whirlwind*. Trans. Ian Boland. New York: Harcourt Brace Jovanovich.

———. 1985a [1967]. *Krutoi marshrut. Kniga Pervaia*. New York: Possev-USA.

———. 1985b [1977]. *Krutoi marshrut. Kniga vtoraia*. New York: Possev-USA.

Ginzburg, L. Ia. 1989. *Chelovek za pis'mennym stolom*. Leningrad: Sovetskii pisatel'.

Gippius, V. V. 1981 [1924]. *Gogol*. Providence, R.I.: Brown University Press.

Gippius, Zinaida. 1972. *Stikhotvoreniia i poemy*. Vol. 1. Munich: Wilhelm Fink.

Girard, René. 1965. " 'Triangular Desire.' " In his *Deceit, Desire, and the Novel*, pp. 1–52. Baltimore: Johns Hopkins University Press.

———. 1972. *La violence et le sacré*. Paris: Bernard Grasset.

———. 1984. "Scandal and the Dance: Salome in the Gospel of Mark." *New Literary History* 15, no. 2: 311–24.

Giraudoux, Jean. 1955 [1911]. *Oeuvre romanesque*. 2 vols. Paris: Grasset.

Glasse, Antonia. 1979. "Lermontov i E. A. Sushkova." In M. P. Alekseev, ed., *Lermontov. Issledovaniia i materialy*, pp. 80–121. Leningrad: Nauka.

Gogol, N. V. 1937–52. *Polnoe sobranie sochinenii*. 14 vols. Moscow: AN SSSR.

———. 1969. *Selected Passages from Correspondence with Friends*. Trans. Jesse Zeldin. Nashville, Tenn.: Vanderbilt University Press.

Gopp, Filipp. 1975. ["Remembering Olesha"]. In Suok-Olesha and Pel'son, comps., 1975, pp. 149–154.

Gorky, Maxim. 1932. *Days with Lenin*. New York: International.

Graham, Stephen, ed. 1959. *Great Russian Short Stories*. London: Ernest Bennet.

Graves, Robert. 1983. *The Greek Myths*. 2 vols. Harmondsworth, Eng.: Penguin.

Grin, Alexander. 1978 [1920]. *Crimson Sails: A Fantasy*. In his *The Seeker of Adventure: Selected Stories*, pp. 19–93. Moscow: Progress.

Grossman, Joan D. 1989. "Variations on the Theme of Pushkin in Pasternak and Briusov." In Lazar Fleishman, ed., *Boris Pasternak and His Times: Selected Papers from the Second International Symposium on Pasternak*, pp. 121–40. Berkeley, Calif.: Berkeley Slavic Specialties.

Grossman, Joan D., and Irina Paperno, eds. 1994. *The Creation of Life: Aesthetic Utopias of Russian Modernism*. Stanford, Calif.: Stanford University Press.

Groys, Boris. 1987a. "Stalinizm kak esteticheskii fenomen." *Sintaksis* 17: 98–110.

————. 1987b. "Zhizn' kak utopiia i utopiia kak zhizn'." *Sintaksis* 18: 171–81.

————. 1988. *Gesamtkunstwerk Stalin*. Munich: Carl Hanser. (English trans.: *The Total Art of Stalinism*. Princeton, N.J.: Princeton University Press, 1992.)

Guerney, Bernard G., ed. and trans. 1960. *An Anthology of Russian Literature in the Soviet Period from Gorky to Pasternak*. New York: Random House.

Gunther, Hans. 1982. "Andrei Platonov und das sozialistisch-realistische Normensystem der 30er Jahre." *WSA* 9: 165–86.

Gurvich, A. 1938 [1937]. "Andrei Platonov." In his *V poiskakh geroia. Literaturno-kriticheskie stat'i*, pp. 57–113. Moscow: Iskusstvo (reprinted from *Krasnaia nov'*, 1937, no. 10).

Gustafson, Richard. 1986. *Leo Tolstoy: Resident and Stranger. A Study in Fiction and Theology*. Princeton, N.J.: Princeton University Press.

Hammarberg, Gitta. 1987. "Poor Liza, Poor Erast, Lucky Narrator." *SEEJ* 31, no. 3: 305–21.

Hanson, Krista. 1989. "*Kto vinovat?* Guilt and Rebellion in Zoshchenko's Accounts of Childhood." In Rancour-Laferrière, 1989, pp. 285–302.

Harari, Josue, ed. 1979. *Textual Strategies: Perspectives in Post-Structuralist Criticism*. Ithaca, N.Y.: Cornell University Press.

Harkins, William E. 1973. "The Theme of Sterility in Olesha's *Envy*." In Brown, 1973, pp. 280–94.

Holland, Laurence. 1964. *The Expense of Vision: Essays on the Craft of Henry James*. Princeton, N.J.: Princeton University Press.

Huxley, Aldous. 1950 [1932]. *Brave New World*. New York: Harper.

Iakubovich, D. P. 1939. "*Kapitanskaia dochka* i romany Val'ter Skotta." *Pushkin. Vremennik pushkinskoi komissii* 4: 165–97.

Ianovskaia, Lidiia. 1983. *Tvorcheskii put' Mikhaila Bulgakova*. Moscow: Sovetskii pisatel'.

Ilf, Ilya, and Evgenii Petrov. 1935. *Kak sozdavalsia Robinzon*. Moscow: Sovetskii pisatel'.

————. 1961. *Sobranie sochinenii*. 5 vols. Moscow: GIKhL.

————. 1962. *The Complete Adventures of Ostap Bender: The Twelve Chairs and The Golden Calf*. Trans. John H. C. Richardson. New York: Random House.

————. 1966. *The Little Golden Calf: A Satiric Novel*. Trans. Charles Malamuth. New York: Frederick Ungar.

Ingdahl, Kazimiera. 1984. *The Artist and the Creative Act: A Study of Iurii Olesha's Novel "Zavist'."* Stockholm: Almqvist and Wicksell.

Isenberg, Charles. 1986. *Substantial Proofs of Being: Osip Mandelstam's Literary Prose*. Columbus, Ohio: Slavica.

Ivanov, V. V., and V. N. Toporov. 1974. "Problema funktsii kuznetsa v svete semioticheskoi tipologii kul'tur." In Iu. M. Lotman, ed., *Materialy vsesoiuznogo simpoziuma po vtorichnym modeliruiushchim sistemam. I (5)*, pp. 87–90. Tartu: TGU.

Jackson, Robert Louis. 1958. *Dostoevsky's Underground Man in Russian Literature*. 'S-Gravenhage: Mouton.

Jakobson, Roman. 1969 [1935]. "The Prose of the Poet Pasternak." In Davie and Livingstone, 1969, pp. 135–51.

———. 1975 [1937]. "The Statue in Pushkin's Poetic Mythology." In his *Pushkin and His Sculptural Myth*, ed. and trans. John Burbank, pp. 1–44. The Hague: Mouton.

———. 1985. "Poetry of Grammar, Grammar of Poetry," "Two Poems by Pushkin." In his *Verbal Art, Verbal Sign, Verbal Time*, ed. Krystyna Pomorska, Stephen Rudy, and Brent Vine, pp. 37–58. Minneapolis: The University of Minnesota Press.

James, Henry. 1936 [1908]. *The Novels and Tales of Henry James. New York Edition*. Vol 12. New York: Scribner's.

———. 1957. *Literary Reviews and Essays on American, English, and French Literature*. Ed. Albert Mordell. New York: Twayne.

———. 1984. *The Aspern Papers and The Turn of the Screw*. Ed. and intro. Anthony Curtis. Harmondsworth, Eng.: Penguin.

Jensen, Peter Alberg. 1979. *Nature as Code: The Achievement of Boris Pilnyak (1915–1924)*. Copenhagen: Rosenkilde and Bagger.

Kaganskaia, M. 1984. "Shutovskoi khorovod." *Sintaksis* 12: 139–90.

Kaganskaia, M., and Zeev Bar-Sella. 1984. *Master Gambs i Margarita*. Tel-Aviv: Milev.

Karabchievskii, Iurii. 1985. *Voskresenie Maiakovskogo*. Munich: Strana i mir.

Karlinsky, Simon. 1976. *The Sexual Labyrinth of Nikolai Gogol*. Cambridge, Mass.: Harvard University Press.

Kataev, Valentin. 1981 [1975–77]. *Almaznyi moi venets*. In his *Almaznyi moi venets. Povesti*, pp. 5–224. Moscow: Sovetskii pisatel'.

Kaverin, Veniamin. 1981. "Molodoi Zoshchenko." In Smolian and Iurgeneva, 1981, pp. 91–109.

Katz, Michael R. 1984. *Dreams and the Unconscious in Nineteenth-Century Russian Fiction*. Hanover, N.H.: University Press of New England.

Kazanskii, B. V., and Iu. N. Tynianov, eds. 1928. *Mikhail Zoshchenko. Stat'i i materialy*. Leningrad: Academia.

Kern, Gary. 1974. "After the Afterword: The Genesis, Art and Theory of *Before Sunrise*." In Zoshchenko, 1974, pp. 345–76.

Khodasevich, Vladislav. 1982–83. *Sobranie stikhov*. 2 vols. Paris: La Presse Libre.

Kohut, Heinz. 1978. "Thoughts on Narcissism and Narcissistic Rage." In his *The Search for the Self*, 2: 615–59. New York: International Universities Press.

Komar, V., and A. Melamid. 1982. "Comrade Stalin and the Muses" (painting reproduction). *Artforum* 20, no. 8: 38.

Kopelev, Lev. 1979. "Faustovskii mir Pasternaka." In Michel Aucouturier, ed.,

Boris Pasternak 1890–1960: Colloque de Cérisy-la-Salle, 1975, pp. 491–514. Paris: Institut d'Études Slaves.

Korolenko, V. G. 1978. "Velikii piligrim." In N. M. Fortunatova, ed., *L. N. Tolstoy v vospominaniiakh sovremennikov*, pp. 244–46. Moscow: Khudozhestvennaia literatura.

Kreps, Mikhail. 1980. *O poezii Iosifa Brodskogo*. Ann Arbor, Mich.: Ardis.

Kucherovskii, N. M. 1980. *I. Bunin i ego proza (1887–1917)*. Tula: Priokskoe knizhnoe izdatel'stvo.

Kurdiumov, A. A. 1983. *V kraiu nepuganykh idiotov. Kniga ob Il'fe i Petrove*. Paris: La Presse Libre.

Kuryluk, Ewa. 1987. *Salome and Judas in the Cave of Sex: The Grotesque: Origins, Iconography, Techniques*. Evanston, Ill.: Northwestern University Press.

Kustarev, O. 1983. "Eduard, Edik i Edichka." *Dvadtsat' dva* 31: 191–205.

Lakshin, V. 1975. *Tolstoy i Chekhov*. Moscow: Sovetskii pisatel'.

Langleben, Maria. 1991. " 'Light Breathing' by I. A. Bunin: Structure and Interpretation" (unpubl. MS).

Leach, Maria, and Jerome Fried, eds. 1972. *Funk and Wagnalls Standard Dictionary of Folklore, Mythology, and Legend*. San Francisco: Harper and Row.

Legman, Gershon, ed. 1969. *The Limerick*. New York: Bell.

Leitch, Vincent. 1983. *Deconstructive Criticism: An Advanced Introduction*. New York: Columbia University Press.

Lemon, Lee T., and Marion J. Reis, eds. and trans. 1965. *Russian Formalist Criticism: Four Essays*. Lincoln: University of Nebraska Press.

Lenin, V. I. 1967. *On Literature and Art*. Moscow: Progress.

———. 1969. *O Tolstom*. Ed. S. M. Breitburt. Moscow: Khudozhestvennaia literatura.

Levinton, G. A. 1970a. "Nekotorye obshchie voprosy izucheniia svadebnogo obriada." In Iu. M. Lotman, ed., *Tezisy dokladov letnei shkoly po vtorichnym modeliruiushchim sistemam. 4*, pp. 27–30. Tartu: TGU.

———. 1970b. "Svadebnyi obriad v sopostavlenii s drugimi." In Iu. M. Lotman, ed., *Tezisy dokladov letnei shkoly po vtorichnym modeliruiushchim sistemam, 4*, pp. 30–35. Tartu: TGU.

———. 1975a. "Zamechaniia k probleme 'literatura i fol'klor'." *TZS* 7: 76–87.

———. 1975b. "K probleme izucheniia povestvovatel'nogo fol'klora." In E. M. Meletinsky and S. Iu. Nekliudov, eds., *Tipologicheskie issledovaniia po fol'kloru. Sbornik statei pamiati V. Ia. Proppa (1895–1970)*, pp. 303–19. Moscow: Nauka.

Lifshits, Mikhail. 1934. "O kul'ture i ee porokakh." *Literaturnyi kritik*, no. 11: 39–55.

Limonov, Eduard. 1977a. "Gruppa 'Konkret.' " In Shemiakin, 1977, pp. 43–46.

———. 1977b. "My—natsional'nyi geroi [and a selection of poems]." In Shemiakin, 1977, pp. 57–64.

348   Works Cited

———. 1979. *Russkoe*. Ann Arbor, Mich.: Ardis.

———. 1980. "Iz novykh stikhov." *Ekho* 1: 71–74.

———. 1981. "Moi otritsatel'nyi geroi." In K. Kuzminskii, A. Tsvetkov, and E. Limonov, *Troe. Ne razmykaia ust*, pp. 42–81. Los Angeles: Almanac Press.

———. 1983 [1979]. *It's Me, Eddie: A Fictional Memoir*. Trans. S. L. Campbell. New York: Grove Press.

———. 1984a. "Love, Love, Love." Trans. J. Rosengrant. *Humanities in Society* (University of Southern California) 7, nos. 3–4: 183–94.

———. 1984b. "Poet-bukhgalter." In Tolstyi, ed., *Muleta A*, pp. 133–35. Paris: Vivrisme.

———. 1984c. "Limonov o sebe." In Olga Matich and Michael Henry Heim, eds., *Russian Literature in Emigration: The Third Wave*, pp. 219–20. Ann Arbor, Mich.: Ardis.

———. 1985a. "On the Wild Side." In Tolstyi, ed., *Muleta B*, pp. 212–39. Paris: Vivrisme.

———. 1985b. "Neskol'ko myslei po povodu Khlebnikova." In Tolstyi, ed., *Muleta XOO*, pp. 35–38. Paris: Vivrisme.

———. 1986. ["Poems"]. *Sintaksis* 15: 3–15.

———. 1990. "Krasavitsa, vdokhnovliavshaia poeta." *Sintaksis* 29: 139–49. Also in E. Limonov, *Kon'iak "Napoleon." Rasskazy*, pp. 144–156. Tel-Aviv: M. Michelson and Nina.

Lindstrom, Thais. 1974. *Nikolay Gogol*. New York: Twayne.

Livingstone, Angela. 1978. "Pasternak's Last Poetry." In Erlich, 1978, pp. 166–75.

Lomonosov, M. 1958. *Polnoe Sobranie Sochinenii*. Vol. 7. Moscow: AN SSSR.

Loseff, Lev. 1984. *On the Beneficence of Censorship: Aesopian Language in Modern Russian Literature*. Munich: Otto Sagner.

Lotman, Iu. M. 1968. "Problema kudozhestvennogo prostranstva v proze Gogolia." *Uchenye zapiski Tartusskogo Gosudarstvennogo Universiteta* 209, *Trudy po russkoi i slavianskoi filologii. Literaturovedenie* 11: 4–50.

———. 1975. "O Khlestakove." *Uchenye zapiski Tartusskogo Gosudarstvennogo Universiteta* 361; *Trudy po russkoi i slavianskoi filologii. Literaturovedenie* 26: 19–53.

———. 1978 [1969]. "Language and Reality in Early Pasternak." In Erlich, 1978, pp. 1–20.

Lotman, Iu., L. Ginsburg, and B. Uspenskii. 1985. *The Semiotics of Russian Cultural History*. Ed. Alexander Nakhimovsky and Alice Stone Nakhimovsky. Ithaca, N.Y.: Cornell University Press.

Mandelker, Amy. 1990. "The Woman with a Shadow: Fables of 'Demon' and 'Psyche' in 'Anna Karenina.'" *Novel: A Forum on Fiction* 24, no. 1: 48–68.

Mandelstam, Nadezhda. 1976 [1970]. *Hope Against Hope: A Memoir*. Trans. Max Hayward. New York: Atheneum.

Mandelstam, Osip. 1967–69. *Sobranie sochinenii*. Ed. G. P. Struve and B. A. Filippov. 3 vols. Washington, D.C.: Inter-Language Associates.

———. 1990. *Sochineniia*. Comp. P. M. Nerler, intro. S. S. Averintsev. 2 vols. Moscow: Khudozhestvennaia literatura.

Mann, Iu. 1984. *V poiskakh zhivoi dushi*. Moscow: Kniga.

Mashinskii, S., ed. 1952. *Gogol' v vospominaniiakh sovremennikov*. Moscow: Goslitizdat.

Masing-Delic, Irene. 1980. "Biology, Reason and Literature in Zoshchenko's 'Pered vosxodom solnca.'" *RL* 8: 77–101.

———. 1989. "The Symbolist Crisis Revisited: Blok's View." In J. Douglas Clayton, ed., *Issues in Russian Literature Before 1917*, pp. 216–27. Columbus, Ohio: Slavica.

Matich, Olga. 1986a. "The Moral Immoralist: Edward Limonov's *Eto ia— Edichka*." *SEEJ* 30, no. 4: 526–40.

———. 1986b. "Sasha Sokolov's *Palisandriia*: History and Myth." *Russian Review* 45, no. 3: 415–26.

———. 1987. "What's to Be Done about Poor Nastia: Nastas'ia Filippovna's Literary Prototypes." *WSA* 19: 47–64.

———. 1990. "Polemic About the Bed in the Russian Avant-Garde." Paper presented at the *Russian Avant-Garde* conference, Los Angeles, Nov. 1990 (MS); Russian version: "Sueta vokrug krovati. Utopicheskaia organizatsiia byta i russkii avangard." *LO*, 1991, no. 11: 80–84.

———. 1994. "The Meaning of Love: Symbolist Theories of Life Practice." In Grossman and Paperno 1994.

Mayakovsky, Vladimir. 1955–61. *Polnoe sobranie sochinenii*. 13 vols. Moscow: GIKhL.

Meletinsky, E. M. 1958. *Geroi volshebnoi skazki*. Moscow: Izdatel'stvo Vostochnoi Literatury.

———. 1970. "Die Ehe im Zaubermärchen." *Acta Ethnographica Academiae Scientiarum Hungaricae* 19: 1–4.

Meletinsky, E. M., S. Iu. Nekliudov, E. S. Novik, and D. M. Segal. 1969. "Problemy strukturnogo opisaniia volshebnoi skazki." *TZS* 4: 86–135.

Meltzer, Françoise. 1987. "Salome and the Dance of Writing." In her *Salome and the Dance of Writing: Portraits of Mimesis in Literature*, pp. 13–46. Chicago: Chicago University Press.

Merezhkovskii, D. S. 1976 [1906]. *Gogol' i chort*. Letchworth-Herts, Eng.: Prideaux Press.

Mirsky, D. S. 1958. *A History of Russian Literature: From the Beginnings to 1900*. New York: Random House.

Mochul'skii, K. 1976. *Dukhovnyi put' Gogolia*. Paris: YMCA Press.

Mol'er. 1831. *Grammatika liubvi, ili iskusstvo liubit' i byt' vzaimno liubimym*. Trans. S. Sh. M. Moscow.

Morson, Gary Saul. 1981. *The Boundaries of Genre: Dostoevsky's 'Diary of a Writer' and the Traditions of Literary Utopia.* Austin: University of Texas Press.

————. 1988. *Hidden in Plain View: Narrative and Creative Potentials of "War and Peace."* Stanford, Calif.: Stanford University Press.

Morson, Gary Saul, and Caryl Emerson. 1990. *Mikhail Bakhtin. Creation of Prosaics.* Stanford, Calif.: Stanford University Press.

Nabokov, Vladimir. 1947. *Nikolai Gogol.* London: Editions Poetry.

————. 1959 [1938]. *Invitation to a Beheading.* Trans. Dmitri Nabokov and author. New York: G. P. Putnam.

————. 1978. *Vesna v Fial'te.* Ann Arbor, Mich.: Ardis.

Naiman, Eric. 1987. "The Thematic Mythology of Andrei Platonov." *RL* 21: 189–216.

————. 1988. "Andrei Platonov and the Inadmissibility of Desire." *RL* 23: 319–66.

Nietzsche, Friedrich. 1967 [1883]. *Thus Spake Zarathustra.* Trans. Thomas Common. New York: Heritage Press.

Nilsson, Nils Ake. 1973. "Through the Wrong End of Binoculars: An Introduction to Iurii Olesha." In Brown, 1973, pp. 254–79.

————. 1978 [1959]. "Life as Ecstasy and Sacrifice: Two Poems by Boris Pasternak." In Erlich, 1978, pp. 51–67.

————. 1982. "Isaac Babel's Story 'Guy de Maupassant.' " In Nils Ake Nilsson, ed., *Studies in 20th Century Russian Prose,* pp. 212–27. Stockholm: Almqvist & Wicksell International.

Odintsov, V. 1969. "Poetika rasskaza L. N. Tolstogo 'Posle bala.' " *Russkii iazyk v shkole,* no. 4: 14–19.

Okudzhava, Bulat. 1986. *Songs.* Vol. 2. Ed. Vladimir Frumkin. Ann Arbor, Mich.: Ardis.

Olesha, Iurii. 1956. *Izbrannye sochineniia.* Moscow: GIKhL.

————. 1975 [1927]. *Envy.* Trans. T. S. Berczynski. Ann Arbor, Mich.: Ardis.

Orwell, George. 1949. *Nineteen Eighty-Four.* New York: Harcourt Brace Jovanovich.

O'Toole, L. M. 1982. *Structure, Style and Interpretation in the Russian Short Story.* New Haven, Conn.: Yale University Press.

Ovchinnikov, I. 1975 [1962]. ["Remembering Olesha"]. In Suok-Olesha and Pel'son, 1975, pp. 43–54.

Overstreet, H. A. 1925. *Influencing Human Behavior.* New York: W. W. Norton.

Paperno, Irina. 1988. *Chernyshevsky and the Age of Realism: A Study in the Semiotics of Behavior.* Stanford, Calif.: Stanford University Press.

————. 1994. Introduction to Grossman and Paperno 1994.

Paramonov, B. 1987. "*Chevengur* i okrestnosti." *Kontinent* 54: 337–72.

Pasternak, Boris. 1958 [1957]. *Doctor Zhivago.* Trans. Max Hayward and Manya Harari. New York: Harcourt, Brace and World.

————. 1959a. *Doktor Zhivago*. Société d'Edition et d'Impression Mondiale.

————. 1959b. *I Remember: Sketch for an Autobiography*. Trans. David Magarshack. New York: Pantheon.

————. 1960. "Three Letters." *Encounter* 15: 3–6.

————. 1965. *Stikhotvoreniia i poemy*. Moscow: Sovetskii pisatel'.

————. 1985a. *Izbrannoe*. 2 vols. Moscow: Khudozhestvennaia literatura.

————. 1985b. *Pasternak on Art and Creativity*. Ed. Angela Livingstone. Cambridge, Eng.: Cambridge University Press.

————. 1989. *Sobranie sochinenii*. 5 vols. Moscow: Khudozhestvennaia literatura.

————. 1990a. *Stikhotvoreniia i poemy*. 2 vols. Leningrad: Sovetskii pisatel'.

————. 1990b. *Boris Pasternak ob iskusstve*. *"Okhrannaia gramota" i zametki o khudozhestvennom tvorchestve*. Comps. E. B. and E. V. Pasternak. Moscow: Iskusstvo.

Paustovskii, K. 1988. "Bulgakov." In E. S. Bulgakova and S. A. Liandres, comps., *Vospominaniia o Mikhaile Bulgakove*, pp. 93–108. Moscow: Sovetskii pisatel'.

Pilnyak, Boris. 1968. *Mother Earth and Other Stories*. Trans. Vera T. Beck and Michael Green. New York: Praeger.

Platonov, Andrei. 1938. "Vozrazhenie bez samozashchity. Po povodu stat'i A. Gurvicha 'Andrei Platonov.'" *Literaturnaia gazeta*, no. 69 (Dec. 20).

————. 1970. *Volshebnoe kol'tso*. *Russkie skazki*. Rendered by A. Platonov. Ed. M. Sholokhov. Moscow: Sovetskaia Rossiia.

————. 1971. *Techenie vremeni*. *Povesti, rasskazy*. Moscow: Moskovskii rabochii.

————. 1973. *The Foundation Pit: Kotlovan*. Bilingual ed.; trans. T. Whitney, preface by Joseph Brodsky. Ann Arbor, Mich.: Ardis.

————. 1980 [1938]. "Rasskazy A. Grina." In his *Razmyshleniia chitatelia*, pp. 72–78. Moscow: Sovremennik (repr. from *Literaturnoe obozrenie* 1938, no. 4).

————. 1988. *Gosudarstvennyi zhitel'*. Moscow: Sovetskii pisatel'.

Podoroga, Valerii. 1991. "The Eunuch of the Soul: Positions of Reading and the World of Platonov." *South Atlantic Quarterly* 90, no. 2: 357–408.

Poe, Edgar Allan. 1950. *Selected Prose and Poetry*. Ed. and intro. W. H. Auden. New York: Rinehart.

Poggioli, Renato. 1957. *The Phoenix and the Spider*. Cambridge, Mass.: Harvard University Press.

Poltavtseva, N. G. 1981. *Filosofskaia proza Andreia Platonova*. Rostov-na-Donu: Izdatel'stvo Rostovskogo Gosudarstvennogo Universiteta.

Pomorska, Krystyna (ed.). 1971. *Fifty Years of Russian Prose: From Pasternak to Solzhenitsyn*. 2 vols. Cambridge, Mass.: MIT Press.

————. 1975. *Themes and Variations in Pasternak's Poetics*. Lisse: Peter de Ridder Press.

————. 1982. "Tolstoy—contra semiosis." *IJSLP* 25–26: 383–90.

Pratt, Sarah. 1989. "The Obverse of Self: Gender Shifts in Poems by Tiutchev and Akhmatova." In Rancour-Laferrière, 1989, pp. 229–44.

Proffer, Carl, ed. 1969. *From Karamzin to Bunin: An Anthology of Russian Short Stories.* Bloomington: Indiana University Press.

Proffer, Ellendea. 1973. "*The Master and Margarita.*" In Brown, 1973, pp. 388–411.

———. 1984. *Bulgakov: Life and Work.* Ann Arbor, Mich.: Ardis.

Propp, Vladimir. 1946. *Istoricheskie korni volshebnoi skazki.* Leningrad: LGU.

———. 1971 [1928]. *Morphology of the Folktale.* Austin: Texas University Press.

———. 1976. "Edip v svete fol'klora." In his *Fol'klor i deistvitel'nost'. Izbrannye stat'i,* pp. 258–99. Moscow: Nauka.

Pushkin, A. S. 1937–49. *Polnoe sobranie sochinenii.* 16 vols. Moscow: AN SSSR.

———. 1964. *Eugene Onegin. A Novel in Verse.* Trans. (and commentary) Vladimir Nabokov. 4 vols. New York: Pantheon (Bollingen Series 72).

———. 1983. *Complete Prose Fiction.* Trans., intro., and notes Paul Debreczeny. Stanford, Calif.: Stanford University Press.

[Raevsky-]Hughes, Olga. 1974. *The Poetic World of Pasternak.* Princeton, N.J.: Princeton University Press.

———. 1989. "O samoubiistve Maiakovskogo v 'Okhrannoi gramote' Pasternaka." In Lazar Fleishman, ed., *Boris Pasternak and His Times,* pp. 141–52. Berkeley, Calif.: Berkeley Slavic Specialties.

[Rancour-]Laferrière, Daniel. 1978a. *Five Russian Poems: Exercises in a Theory of Poetry.* Englewood, N.J.: Transworld.

———. 1978b. *Sign and Subject: Semiotic and Psychoanalytic Investigations into Poetry.* Lisse: Peter de Ridder Press.

———. 1982. *Out from under Gogol's "Overcoat."* Ann Arbor, Mich.: Ardis.

———, ed. 1989. *Russian Literature and Psychoanalysis.* Amsterdam: John Benjamins.

Remizov, A. 1977. *Ogon' veshchei. Sny i predson'e.* Paris: YMCA Press.

Reyfman, Irina. 1992. "Shestaia povest' Belkina: Mikhail Zoshchenko v roli Proteia." In Boris Gasparov, Robert P. Hughes, and Irina Paperno, eds., *Cultural Mythologies of Russian Modernism: From the Golden Age to the Silver Age,* pp. 393–414. Berkeley: University of California Press.

Richards, David, ed. 1981. *The Penguin Book of Russian Short Stories.* Harmondsworth, Eng.: Penguin.

Riffaterre, Michael. 1978. *Semiotics of Poetry.* Bloomington: Indiana University Press.

Ronen, Omry. 1973. "Leksicheskii povtor, podtekst i smysl v poetike Osipa Mandel'shtama." In Roman Jakobson, ed., *Slavic Poetics: In Honor of Kiril Taranovsky,* pp. 367–87. The Hague: Mouton.

———. 1983. *An Approach to Mandelstam.* Jerusalem: Hebrew University Magnes Press.

Rozanov, V. V. 1970 [1906]. *O Gogole.* Letchworth-Herts, Eng.: Prideaux Press.

Saputelli, L. 1988. "The Long-Drawn Sunset of Fialta." In Julian W. Connolly and Sonia I. Ketchian, eds., *Studies in Russian Literature in Honor of Vsevolod Setchkarev*, pp. 233–41. Columbus, Ohio: Slavica.

Seifrid, Thomas. 1987. "Writing Against Matter: On the Language of Andrei Platonov's *Kotlovan*." *SEEJ* 31, no. 3: 370–87.

———. 1992. *Andrei Platonov: Uncertainties of Spirit*. Cambridge, Eng.: Cambridge University Press.

Semenova, S. 1988. "Mytarstva ideala. K vykhodu v svet *Chevengura* Andreia Platonova." *Novyi mir*, no. 5: 218–23.

Semmler-Vakareliyska, Cynthia. 1985. "Mandelstam's 'Solominka.' " *SEEJ* 29, no. 4: 405–21.

Setchkarev, Vsevolod. 1965. *Gogol: His Life and Works*. New York: New York University Press.

Shcheglov, Yury. 1970. " 'Matrona iz Efesa.' " In A. J. Greimas et al., eds., *Sign, Language, Culture*, pp. 591–600. The Hague: Mouton.

———. 1986a. "Molodoi chelovek v driakhleiushchem mire." In Zholkovsky and Shcheglov, 1986, pp. 21–52.

———. 1986b. "Entsiklopediia nekul'turnosti. Zoshchenko: rasskazy 20-kh godov i *Golubaia kniga*." In Zholkovsky and Shcheglov, 1986, pp. 53–84.

———. 1986c. "Tri fragmenta poetiki Il'fa i Petrova." In Zholkovsky and Shcheglov, 1986, pp. 85–117.

———. 1986d. "Poetika obezbolivaniia (stikhotvorenie Akhmatovoi 'Serdtse b'etsia rovno, merno . . .')." In Zholkovsky and Shcheglov, 1986, pp. 175–203.

———. 1990–91. *Romany I. Il'fa i E. Petrova. Sputnik chitatelia*. 2 vols. Vienna: WSA, Sonderband 26.

Shcheglov, Yury, and A. Zholkovsky. 1976. "Poetics as a Theory of Expressiveness." *Poetics* 5: 207–46.

———. 1987. *Poetics of Expressiveness: A Theory and Applications*. Amsterdam: John Benjamins.

Shemiakin, M., ed. 1977. *Apollon-77*. Paris: Les Arts Graphiques.

Shklovsky, Victor. 1965a [1917]. "Art as Technique." In Lemon and Reis, 1965, pp. 5–24.

———. 1965b [1921]. "Sterne's *Tristram Shandy*: Stylistic Commentary." In Lemon and Reis 1965, 25–57.

———. 1972 [1919]. "The Connection between Devices of *Siuzhet* Construction and General Stylistic Devices." *Twentieth Century Studies* 7–8: 48–72.

———. 1976 [1928]. "On Zoshchenko and Major Literature." *Russian Literature Triquarterly* 14: 407–14.

———. 1978. *Lev Tolstoy*. Moscow: Progress.

Shukman, A. 1983. "Taboos, Splits, and Signifiers: Limonov's *Eto ia—Edichka*." *Essays in Poetics* 8, no. 2: 1–18.

Shveitser, V. 1989. "Mandel'shtam posle Voronezha," *Sintaksis* 25: 69–91.

[Siniavsky]-Tertz, A. 1975a. *Progulki s Pushkinym*. London: Collins and Overseas Publications Interchange.

———. 1975b. *V teni Gogolia*. London: Collins and Overseas Publications Interchange.

———. 1978 [1965]. "Pasternak's Poetry." In Erlich 1978, 9–62.

———. 1982 [1959]. "On Socialist Realism." In his *The Trial Begins and On Socialist Realism*, pp. 127–219. Berkeley: University of California Press.

Skaftymov, A. 1972. *Nravstvennye iskaniia russkikh pisatelei*. Moscow: Khudozhestvennaia literatura.

Slavin, Lev. 1975 [1964–74]. ["Remembering Olesha"]. In Suok-Olesha and Pel'son, 1975, pp. 3–21.

Slonim, Marc. 1977. *Soviet Russian Literature: Writers and Problems, 1917–1977*. 2d ed. New York: Oxford University Press.

Smirnov, I. P. 1978. "Mesto 'mifopoeticheskogo' podkhoda k literaturnomu proizvedeniiu sredi drugikh tolkovanii teksta (o stikhotvorenii Maiakovskogo 'Vot tak ia sdelalsia sobakoi')." In V. G. Bazanov, A. M. Panchenko, and I. P. Smirnov, eds., *Mif—fol'klor—literatura*, pp. 186–203. Leningrad: Nauka.

———. 1983. "O nartsisticheskom tekste (diakhroniia i psikhoanaliz)." *WSA* 12: 21–45.

———. 1985. *Porozhdenie interteksta. Opyt intertekstual'nogo analiza s primerami iz tvorchestva B. L. Pasternaka*. Vienna: WSA, Sonderband 17.

Smolian, A., and N. Iurgeneva, comps. 1981. *Mikhail Zoshchenko v vospominaniiakh sovremennikov*. Moscow: Sovetskii pisatel'.

Sobel, Ruth. 1981. *Gogol's Forgotten Book: Selected Passages and Its Contemporary Readers*. Washington, D.C.: University Press of America.

Sokolov, Sasha. 1985. *Palisandriia*. Ann Arbor, Mich.: Ardis.

———. 1989. *Astrophobia*. Trans. Michael Henry Heim. New York: Grove Weidenfeld.

Sontag, Susan. 1961. "Notes on 'Camp.' " In her *Against Interpretation and Other Essays*, pp. 275–92. New York: Farrar, Straus and Giroux.

Spain, M. L. 1978. *Ivan Bunin's Prose: The Function of the Narrative Consciousness*. Ann Arbor, Mich.: University Microfilms.

Spitzer, Leo. 1962. "American Advertising Explained as Popular Art." In his *Essays on English and American Literature*, pp. 248–77. Princeton, N.J.: Princeton University Press.

Steiner, Peter. 1984. *Russian Formalism: A Metapoetics*. Ithaca, N.Y.: Cornell University Press.

Stillman, Leon. 1966. "Nikolai Gogol and Ostap Hohol." In Dietrich Gerhardt, ed., *Orbis Scriptus: Dmitrii Tschizewskii zum 70 Geburtstag*, pp. 811–25. Munich: Wilhelm Fink.

Suok-Olesha, O., and E. Pel'son, comps. 1975. *Vospominaniia o Iurii Oleshe*. Moscow: Sovetskii pisatel'.

Taranovsky, Kiril. 1963. "O vsaimootnoshenii stikhotvornogo ritma i tematiki." In *American Contributions to the Fifth International Congress of Slavists*, pp. 287–322. The Hague: Mouton.

———. 1976. *Essays on Mandel'stam*. Cambridge, Mass.: Harvard University Press.

Tarlinskaja, Marina. 1989. "Meter and Meaning: Semantic Associations of the English 'Dolnik' Verse Form." *Style* 23, no. 2: 238–60.

Tarlinskaja, Marina, and Naira Oganesova. 1985. "Meter and Meaning: The Semiotic Function of Verse Form." In Gilbert Youmans and Donald M. Lance, eds., *In Memory of Roman Jakobson: Papers from the 1984 Mid-American Linguistic Conference*, pp. 75–93. Columbia: University of Missouri-Columbia.

Teskey, Ayleen. 1982. *Platonov and Fedorov: The Influence of Christian Philosophy on a Soviet Writer*. Amersham, Eng.: Avebury.

Thompson, Stith. 1977. *The Folktale*. Berkeley: University of California Press.

Titunik. I. 1984. "Vasilii Trediakovsky and Eduard Limonov: Erotic Reverberations in the History of Russian Literature." In K. Brostrom, ed., *Russian Literature and American Critics*, pp. 393–404. Ann Arbor: University of Michigan Slavic Publications.

Todd, William Mills III. 1986. *Fiction and Society in the Age of Pushkin: Ideology, Institutions, and Narrative*. Cambridge, Mass.: Harvard University Press.

Tolstaia-Segal, E. 1977. "O sviazi nizshikh urovnei teksta s vysshimi (Proza Andreia Platonova)." *SH* 2: 169–212.

———. 1979. "Naturfilosofskie temy v tvorchestve Platonova 20-kh–30-kh godov." *SH* 4: 223–54.

———. 1981. "Ideologicheskie konteksty Platonova." *RL* 9: 231–80.

Tolstoi, N. I. 1982. "Iz 'grammatiki' slavianskikh obriadov." *TZS* 15: 57–71.

Tolstoy, Leo (ed.). 1906. *Krug chteniia*. 2 vols. Moscow: Posrednik.

———. 1928–58. *Polnoe sobranie sochinenii v 90 tomax*. Moscow: GIKhL.

———. 1935. *Ivan Ilych and Hadji Murad*. London: Oxford University Press.

———. 1964. *Short Stories*. Selected and intro. Ernest J. Simmons. New York: Modern Library.

———. 1966. *War and Peace: The Maude Translation, Backgrounds and Sources, Essays in Criticism*. Ed. George Gibian. New York: W. W. Norton.

———. 1968a. *Anna Karenina*. Trans. L. Maude and A. Maude. New York: W. W. Norton.

———. 1968b. *The Kreutzer Sonata, The Devil, and Other Tales*. Trans. A. Maude and J. D. Duff. London: Oxford University Press.

———.1975. *Biblioteka L. N. Tolstogo v Iasnoi Poliane*. Moscow: Kniga.

———. 1985. *The Kreutzer Sonata and Other Stories*. Trans. and intro. David McDuff. Harmondsworth, Eng.: Penguin Books.

Trostnikov, V. 1965. " 'Posle bala.' " In V. Trostnikov, ed., *L. N. Tolstoi v shkole*, pp. 244–62. Moscow: Prosveshchenie.

Troyat, Henri. 1975. *Divided Soul: The Life of Gogol*. New York: Minerva Press.

Tsivian, Yuri. N.d. *Unreliable Reality: Perception of Cinema in Russian Culture, 1896–1919*. Forthcoming.

Turgenev, Ivan. 1950. *The Borzoi Turgenev*. Trans. Harry Stevens. New York: Knopf.

Tynianov, Iu. N. 1977a [1921]. "Dostoevskii i Gogol' (k teorii parodii)." In Tynianov; 1977c, pp. 198–226.

———. 1977b [1924]. "Promezhutok." In Tynianov, 1977c, pp. 168–95.

———. 1977c. *Poetika. Istoriia literatury. Kino*. Moscow: Nauka.

Uspenskii, B. 1973. "K poetike Khlebnikova: problemy kompozitsii." In Iu. M. Lotman, ed., *Semiotiké. Sbornik statei po vtorichnym modeliruiushchim sistemam*, pp. 122–27. Tartu: TGU.

Vasil'ev, V. 1982. *Andrei Platonov. Ocherk zhizni i tvorchestva*. Moscow: Sovremennik.

Veresaev, V. V. 1933. *Gogol' v zhizni*. Moscow: Academia.

Vickery, Walter. 1972. " 'Ia vas liubil . . .': A literary source." *IJSLP* 15: 160–67.

Vinogradov, V. V. 1976. *Poetika russkoi literatury. Izbrannye trudy*. Moscow: Nauka.

Vygotsky, Lev. 1971 [1965]. *The Psychology of Art*. Cambridge, Mass.: MIT Press.

Wachtel, Andrew. 1990. *The Battle for Childhood: Creation of a Russian Myth*. Stanford, Calif.: Stanford University Press.

Weststeijn, Willem. 1986. "The Role of the 'I' in Chlebnikov's Poetry (On the Typology of the Lyrical Subject)." In Willem Weststeijn ed., *Velimir Chlebnikov: Myth and Reality, 1885–1985*; pp. 217–42. Amsterdam: Rodopi.

Whalen, Michael. 1986. "A Genettian Analysis of 'Legkoe dykhanie.' " Term paper, Department of Slavic Languages and Literatures, University of Southern California (MS).

Winner, Thomas. 1963. "Myth as a Device in the Works of Chekhov." In Bernice Slote, ed., *Myth and Symbol: Critical Approaches and Applications*, pp. 71–78. Lincoln: University of Nebraska Press.

Woodward, J. B. 1980. *Ivan Bunin: A Study of His Fiction*. Chapel Hill: University of North Carolina Press.

Zalygin, Sergei. 1971. "Skazki realista i realizm skazochnika." *VL* 7: 120–42.

Zamiatin, Eugene. 1959 [1924]. *We*. Trans. Gregory Zilborg. New York: Dutton.

Zhdanov, A. 1978. *The Central Committee Resolution and Zhdanov's Speech on the Journals "Zvezda" and "Leningrad."* Bilingual ed.; trans. Felicity Ashbee and Irina Tidmarsh. Royal Oak, Mich.: Strathcona.

Zhdanov, V. A. 1971. *Poslednie knigi L. N. Tolstogo. Zamysly i sversheniia*. Moscow: Kniga.

Zholkovsky, Alexander. 1976. "Zametki o tekste, podtekste i tsitatsii u Pasternaka." In N. A. Nilsson, ed., *Boris Pasternak: Essays*, pp. 67–84. Stockholm: Almqvist and Wicksell.

———. 1980a. " 'Prevoskhoditel'nyi pokoi': ob odnom invariantnom motive Pushkina." In Zholkovsky and Shcheglov, 1980, pp. 87–113.

———. 1980b. "Invarianty i struktura poeticheskogo teksta. Pasternak." In Zholkovsky and Shcheglov, 1980, pp. 205–44.

———. 1980c. "Tema i variatsii. Pasternak i Okudhava: opyt sopostavitel'nogo opisaniia." In Zholkovsky and Shcheglov, 1980, pp. 61–85.

———. 1983a. "Poeziia i grammatika pasternakovskogo vetra." RL 14, no. 3: 241–85.

———. 1983b. "19 oktiabria 1982 g.; or, The Semiotics of a Soviet Cookie Wrapper." WSA 11: 341–54.

———. 1984a. Themes and Texts: Towards a Poetics of Expressiveness. Ithaca, N.Y.: Cornell University Press.

———. 1984b. "The Sinister in the Poetic World of Pasternak." IJSLP 29: 109–31.

———. 1985a. "Mekhanizmy vtorogo rozhdeniia." Sintaksis 14: 77–97 (repr. LO 1990, no. 2: 35–41).

———. 1985b. "Iz Zapisok po Poezii Grammatiki: On Pasternak's Figurative Voices." Russian Linguistics 9: 375–86.

———. 1985c. "Iskusstvo prisposobleniia." Grani 50 (138): 78–98.

———. 1986a [1979]. " 'Ia p'iu za voennye astry . . .'—poeticheskii avtoportret Mandel'shtama." In Zholkovsky and Shcheglov, 1986, pp. 204–27.

———. 1986b. "Liubovnaia lodka, upriazh' dlia Pegasa i pokhoronnaia koly-bel'naia (Tri stikhotvoreniia i tri perioda Pasternaka)." In Zholkovsky and Shcheglov, 1986, pp. 228-54.

———. 1986c. "O genii i zlodeistve, o babe i vserossiiskom masshtabe (Pro-gulki po Maiakovskomu)." In Zholkovsky and Shcheglov, 1986, pp. 255–78.

———. 1986d. "Writing in the Wilderness: On Brodsky and a Sonnet." SEEJ 30, no. 3: 404–19.

———. 1986e. " 'Ia vas liubil . . .' Brodskogo: interteksty, invarianty, tematika i struktura." In Lev Loseff, ed., Poetika Brodskogo, pp. 38–62. Tenafly, N.J.: Hermitage.

———. 1986f. "Grafomanstvo kak priem: Lebiadkin, Khlebnikov, Limonov i drugie." In Willem Weststeijn ed., Velimir Chlebnikov: Myth and Reality, 1885–1985, pp. 573–93. Amsterdam: Rodopi.

———. 1986g. "Zamiatin, Orvell i Khvorob'ev." Grani 140: 178–212.

———. 1987a. "Vliublenno-blednye nartsissy o vremeni i o sebe." Beseda (Paris) 6: 149–55.

———. 1987b. "Aristokastratka," Sintaksis 23: 69–81 (repr. 1991d, pp. 40–50).

———. 1987c. "The Stylistic Roots of Palisandriia." Canadian-American Slavic Studies 21, nos. 3–4: 369–400.

———. 1987d. "Poetu nastoiashchemu spasibo." Strana i mir 4 (40): 133–39.

———. 1987e. "Dialog Bulgakova i Oleshi o kolbase, parade chuvstv i Golgofe," Sintaksis 20: 90–117.

————. 1987f. Review of Ronen, 1983. *SEEJ* 31, no. 1: 115–17.

————. 1988. "Intertextuality, Its Content and Discontents," *SR* 47, no. 4: 726–29.

————. 1989a. "Fro: piat' prochtenii." *VL* 12: 23–48.

————. 1989b. "The Beauty Mark and the 'I's of the Beholder." In Rancour-Laferrière, 1989, pp. 329–52.

————. 1989c. "Three on Courtship, Corpses, and Culture: Tolstoy, 'Posle bala,'—Zoshchenko, 'Dama s tsvetami,'—E. Ginzburg, 'Rai pod mikroskopom.'" *WSA* 22: 7–24.

————. 1990. "La poétique de Boris Pasternak." In E. Etkind, G. Nivat, I. Serman, and V. Strada, eds., *Histoire de la literature russe: Le XXe siècle: Gels et dégels*, pp. 488–504. Paris: Fayard.

————. 1991a. "Ekstaticheskie motivy Pasternaka v svete ego lichnoi mifologii (kompleks Iakova/Akteona/Gerakla)." In Lev Loseff, ed., *Boris Pasternak: 1890–1990*, pp. 52–74. Northfield, Vt.: Russian School, Norwich University.

————. 1991b. "Philosophy of Composition (K nekotorym aspektam struktury odnogo literaturnogo teksta)." In John Malmstad and Ronald Vroon, eds., *Readings in Russian Modernism: To Honor Vladimir Markov*. UCLA Slavic Studies, n.s., vol. 1, pp. 390–99. Moscow: Nauka. Oriental Literature Publishers, 1993.

————. 1991c. "'Mne khochetsia domoi, v ogromnost' . . .' B. Pasternaka: 'Sotsial'nyi zakaz,' tematika, struktura." *SLIa* 50, no. 1: 20–34.

————. 1991d. *NRZB. Rasskazy*. Moscow: Vesy.

————. 1992a. "Bessmertie na vremia: Pasternak's Poetry of Tense and Time." Paper presented at the International Conference on Pasternak at Oxford University, July 1990. Forthcoming in *Elementa*.

————. 1992b. "'Slaughterhouse' Motifs in Mandelstam's *The Egyptian Stamp* and Environs." In H. Birnbaum and M. Flier, eds., *The Language and Verse in Russia*. Los Angeles: UCLA Slavic Studies.

————. 1992c. "On the Intertextual Progeny of 'Ia vas liubil . . .'" Paper presented at the IV Pushkin Symposium at the New York University, Nov. 1985 (rev. MS).

————. 1992d. "Semiotika 'Tamani.'" In A. Mal'ts, ed., *Sbornik statei k semidesiatiletiiu Prof. Iu. M. Lotmana*, pp. 248–56. Tartu: TGU.

————. 1992e. "zh/z: Notes of an Ex-Pre-Post-Structuralist." *WSA*, Sonderband 33: 283–91 (Russian version: *LO*, 1991, no. 10: 31–35).

————. 1992f. "On the Use of Taste." In André Clas, ed., *Words, Words, Witty Words*; pp. 51–60. Montréal: Les Presses de l'Université de Montréal.

————. 1992g. "The Terrible Armor-Clad General Line: A New Profile of Eisenstein's Poetics." *WSA*, Sonderband 31: 481–502.

————. 1992h. *Bluzhdaiushchie sny. Iz istorii russkogo modernisma*. Moscow: Sovetskii pisatel'.

Zholkovsky, A., and Yu. Shcheglov. 1980. *Poetika vyrazitel'nosti. Sbornik statei.* Vienna: *WSA*, Sonderband 2.

———. 1986. *Mir avtora i struktura teksta. Stat'i o russkoi literature.* Tenafly, N.J.: Hermitage.

Ziolkowski, Theodore. 1983. "Talking Dogs: The Caninization of Literature." In his *Varieties of Literary Thematics*, pp. 86–122. Princeton: Princeton University Press.

Zoshchenko, Mikhail. 1928. "O sebe, o kritikakh i o svoei rabote." In Kazanskii and Tynianov, 1928, pp. 7–11.

———. 1940. "O iazyke." In his *1935–1937*, pp. 334–36. Leningrad: GIKhL.

———. 1946. *Izbrannye proizvedeniia: 1923–1945.* Leningrad: GIKhL.

———. 1961. *Scenes from the Bathhouse and Other Stories of Communist Russia.* Trans. and intro. Sidney Monas. Ann Arbor, Mich.: University of Michigan Press.

———. 1963. *Nervous People and Other Satires.* Ed. and intro. Hugh McLean, trans. Maria Gordon and Hugh McLean. New York: Pantheon.

———. 1974. *Before Sunrise: A Novella.* Trans. Gary Kern. Ann Arbor, Mich.: Ardis.

———. 1987. *Sobranie sochinenii.* 3 vols. Leningrad: GIKhL.

Zoshchenko, Mikhail, and Vera Zoshchenko. N.d. *Neizdannyi Zoshchenko.* Ed. Vera von Wiren. Ann Arbor, Mich.: Ardis.

Zoshchenko, Vera. 1981. "Tak nachinal Zoshchenko." In Smolian and Iurgeneva, 1981, pp. 67–90.

Index

In this index an "f" after a number indicates a separate reference on the next page, and an "ff" indicates separate references on the next two pages. A continuous discussion over two or more pages is indicated by a span of page numbers, e.g., "57–59." *Passim* is used for a cluster of references in close but not consecutive sequence.

Library of Congress Cataloging-in-Publication Data
Zholkovskiĭ, A. K. (Aleksandr Konstantinovich)
    p. cm.
    Text counter text : rereadings in Russian literary
history / Alexander Zholkovsky.
    Includes bibliographical references and index.
    ISBN 0-8047-2316-8
    1. Russian literature—19th century—History and criticism.
2. Russian literature—20th century—History and criticism.
I. Title.
PG3011.Z444   1994
891.709—dc20   93-36232   CIP

⊗ This book is printed on acid-free paper.

Text design: Kathleen Szawiola